NATIVE BUT FOREIGN

Connecting the Greater West

NATIVE BUT FOREIGN

Indigenous Immigrants and Refugees in the North American Borderlands

Brenden W. Rensink

Foreword by Sterling Evans

Texas A&M University Press
College Station

First edition

This paper meets the requirements of ANSI/NISO Z39.48–1992 (Permanence of Paper).
Binding materials have been chosen for durability.
Manufactured in the United States of America

Library of Congress Cataloging-in-Publication Data

Names: Rensink, Brenden W., author.
Title: Native but foreign: indigenous immigrants and refugees in the North American borderlands / Brenden W. Rensink.
Description: First edition. | College Station: Texas A&M University Press, [2018] | Series: Connecting the greater west | Includes bibliographical references and index. |
Identifiers: LCCN 2018006306 (print) | LCCN 2018011284 (ebook) | ISBN 9781623496562 (ebook) | ISBN 9781623496555 | ISBN 9781623496555 (cloth : alk. paper)
Subjects: LCSH: Indians of North America—Migration. | Indians of North America—Canadian-American Border Region—Government relations. | Indians of North America—Mexican-American Border Region—Government relations. | Transnationalism. | Indians of North America—Legal status, laws, etc.
Classification: LCC E91 (ebook) | LCC E91 .R46 2018 (print) | DDC 323.1197—dc23
LC record available at https://lccn.loc.gov/2018006306

To those still crossing borders,
seeking refuge, searching for a home

Contents

Illustrations

Figures

Tables

Foreword

Brenden Rensink's *Native but Foreign* is proudly number nine in the Connecting the Greater West Series, and readers will see instantly how it is a perfect fit. This book connects and compares both the US-Mexican and US-Canadian borders and their histories of indigenous peoples negotiating the boundaries, creating new borderlands spaces in a changing American West. There is a growing historical literature that deals with *both* of these North American borderlands (including several other books that appear in this series), and *Native but Foreign* will be one of the important works in that particular category.

Meeting here are the Cree and Chippewa peoples from Alberta who move south into Montana, and the Yaqui Indians from Sonora who migrate north and form a new homeland in Arizona. Rensink explores, analyzes, and compares their distinctive backgrounds, histories, journeys, and efforts to seek federal tribal recognition from the United States government. There is no similar comparative study of Native peoples in the West who migrated from neighboring nation states, which makes this book a much needed contribution to the literature on North American borderlands, Native American/First Nations history, and comparative and transnational history.

To accomplish this feat, Rensink implemented a multi-archival attack to track the stories of these transboundary Indians who became native but foreign in a new country for them. He relied on national archives in Canada and the United States along with a variety of state and provincial archives as well as private collections to provide the sources and voices he needed to weave these comparative stories together. And Rensink tells them here in a compelling way that will be useful and essential for both classrooms and seminars as well as for a public readership interested in anything Native in the greater North American West.

And in these ways then, we welcome this new book to the series. Connecting the Greater West is an ongoing series of scholarly works (monographs and edited volumes) that explores the changing and growing ways that historians and other scholars are coming to view the North American West. This greater region includes a large region stretching from western Canada and the North American side of the Pacific Rim to the American West and northern Mexico, with all the borderlands and connections between them. Subjects of these books range from borderlands and transnational histories, environmental and agricultural histories, gender and social histories, immigration and indigenous negotiations of bordered regions. It is to these last two areas that *Native but Foreign* especially applies, recounting the multidimensional stories of Cree, Chippewa, and Yaqui peoples and their quest for a better life across political boundaries into the western United States. Their histories are yet another way in which we can come to a better understanding of the history of a greater, very transnational, and transcultural West.

Sterling Evans
Series Editor

Acknowledgments

This book began a decade ago as my doctoral thesis, and many people aided its production. With such a passage of time, I will surely fail to thank everyone who has been involved, and I apologize to those I have overlooked.

At the University of Nebraska–Lincoln (UNL), where this project began, I owe the professors I worked with—especially James Garza, Andrew Graybill, Victoria Smith, Douglas Seefeldt, Alan Steinweis, David Wishart, and John Wunder. As my MA and PhD adviser, Wunder modeled the scholar and educator I hope to become. A dedicated scholar and advocate, master editor, and devoted mentor to students like me, Wunder provides an example I will strive to match for the remainder of my career. The support and friendship I received from fellow UNL graduate students like Rob Voss, Shayla Swift, Dave Nesheim, Sam Herley, and Brent Rogers also merit special mention. Thank you, dear friends. Scholars and friends from other institutions have given continual support and expert counsel over the past decade as well. I thank my recent research assistants Drew Rupard and Addison Blair, and I am indebted to James Brooks, Elaine Carey, Mark Ellis, Sterling Evans, Michel Hogue, Benjamin Johnson, Andrae Marak, Sheila McManus, Eric Meeks, and Jeffrey Shepherd for helping me craft, refine, and publish my scholarship. Countless others were kind enough to respond to e-mail inquiries and provide other support, including Larry Burt, Claudia Haake, Sally Hatfield, Matt Herman, Evelyn Hu-DeHart, Leah Glaser, David McCrady, David Miller, Celeste Rivers, Blair Stonechild, Sam Truett, Paul Vanderwood, David Weber, and John Well-off-Man.

Friendly individuals at numerous institutions aided my research. In Montana the enthusiastic support of Ed Stamper and Gerard Vanderberg at Stone Child College on the Rocky Boy Reservation gave me a much-needed boost in confidence. Likewise, Nate and Voyd St. Pierre and the staff at Rocky Boy School have my gratitude for helping me locate a somewhat forgotten archival repository. In Arizona, Yaqui historian Ernesto Quiroga provided similar support and encouragement and shared early drafts of my writing with interested individuals in Yaqui communities. While archival staff at all the repositories I visited aided my efforts, special thanks go to Michael Lotstein and Marilyn Wirzburger at Arizona State University Special Collections, Alan Ferg at the Arizona State Museum, Eric Bittner at the Rocky Mountain branch of the National Archives and Records Administration in Denver, and Jim Bowman at the Glenbow Archives in Calgary.

This project was financially supported by the College of Education and Human Sciences, College of Graduate Studies, Department of History, Bureau of Sociological Research, and Center for Digital Research in the Humanities at the University of Nebraska–Lincoln, as well as the Center for Great Plains Studies, the Western History Association, the Department of History at the University of Nebraska at Kearney, the Joseph Smith Papers at the LDS Church History Library, and the Charles Redd Center for Western Studies and the Department of History at Brigham Young University. With archives spread across the continent, my research would not have been possible without funding support from these institutions. These institutions have also supported my broader scholarly activities, development, and growth.

Finally, I owe thanks to Texas A&M University Press. Connecting the Greater West series editor Sterling Evans and former editor in chief Mary Lenn Dixon went out on a limb to offer me a preliminary book contract. That early vote of confidence carried me through many challenging times. Fortunately, Jay Dew, current editor in chief, was patient with my delayed manuscript submission. I am grateful for his constant encouragement and aid in shepherding the manuscript through to publication. Through Jay I also benefited from two anonymous reviewers who dedicated extraordinary effort to critiquing my work. You know who you are. Thank you. I offer additional thanks for the expert and careful copyediting by Chris Dodge.

Alongside the countless individuals who helped me from the professional side of my life, many have supported me personally. My parents, Peter and Linda, raised me better than I deserved, and their love and support shaped the person I have become. I am also blessed with a supportive and loving sister, Lorinda, in-laws, cousins, and extended families. Close friends like Ken Snider and Jonathan Olsen; the Barrera, Hulse, Johnson, and Newman families in Lincoln, the Pobanz, Snider, and Will in Kearney, and the Clark, Coleman, Rogers, and Van Horn families in Utah have helped keep my family and me happy, safe, and sane through good times and bad. Being continually surrounded by such wonderful people continues as one of the greatest blessings in my life.

I owe the most profound gratitude to my wife, Julianne. I doubt she knew what she was getting into when she agreed to marry me—and two weeks later to move across the country for graduate school. This period, during which she worked to support our family (including two wonderful children, Emilia and Peter), surely tried her patience with my scholarly endeavors. Without her in my life, I doubt I would have finished graduate school, let alone this book. Thank you, Julianne, for sticking with me. Thank you for your love and friendship. I will spend the rest of my life repaying the debt I owe to you.

Finally, Emilia and Peter, you two are a source of joy (if occasional frustration), and I hope that the current amazement you express with my "writing a whole book" continues once you are able to read it.

To the many others who have encouraged me and aided my professional and personal growth, I thank you too. Vă mulţumesc.

NATIVE BUT FOREIGN

Prologue

The most compelling histories are grounded in the personal and the intimate. Much of this book will examine human stories through a macroscopic lens, but I begin with two brief biographies of Indigenous people who inhabited the US-Canadian and US-Mexican borderlands. Their narratives provide not only humanity but also a framework upon which to build everything that will follow.

Grant Chief Stick, O-ki-mahw-mis-tik in Cree, was born in 1895 in Butte, Montana. His family boasted a rich heritage, deeply rooted in the northern Great Plains—by then cast as US-Canadian borderlands. Although his grandmother was Blackfoot, the specter of a coyote haunted her childhood dreams and prophesied that her children and grandchildren would be Cree. Thus, when Crees captured and adopted her into their band, she did not seek to escape. Rather, she intermarried, quickly acculturated, learned the Cree language, and resolved to remain with her adopted tribe.[1] In the years preceding Chief Stick's birth, his Cree and Blackfoot forbears inhabited a broad region between what was becoming Montana, Alberta, and Saskatchewan.[2] They regularly traversed the line that Euro-Americans had drawn across their homelands after the Treaty of 1818 between Great Britain and the United States. Chief Stick's family negotiated a dynamic cultural and political geography that transcended boundaries, both tribal and international. While Canadians and Americans may have viewed their presence as transnational, they did not. "British," "Canadian," or "American" did not define their self-identity: they were Crees.

By the time Chief Stick was born, borderland Crees in Montana traversed precarious grounds. A decade earlier, Crees under the leadership of Big Bear (Mistahimaskwa), Poundmaker, and others had participated in Louis Riel's failed 1885 North-West Rebellion in the District of Saskatchewan, drawing the ire of non-Natives on both sides of the Forty-Ninth Parallel.[3] In the following decade, many under the leadership of Chief Stick's stepfather, Little Bear or Imasees (Ayimâsis)—the son of Big Bear—fled southward into Montana as refugees from the conflict. There in Montana, which became a state in 1889, they struggled to secure permanent legal residence, but in 1896 US officials rounded up Crees across Montana and deported them to Canada. Although born south of the Forty-Ninth Parallel, the infant Chief Stick may have been part of this forced exodus since many US officials failed to recognize distinctions among what they considered transient bands. In the eyes of army officers, Crees were *foreign* Indians, with no place among "domestic" reservation tribes, let alone Montana's burgeoning cities such as Chief Stick's birthplace, Butte. From the 1870s onward, US officials failed to maintain a consistent policy concerning Native labor, immigration, and refugees, and many Montanans then hoped to expel them permanently. With Canadian officials promising amnesty for the North-West Rebellion, many Crees left Montana without resistance. One US official told Crees that they could "do as [they] pleased" once escorted to the border. "So they did," recalled Chief Stick. When Canadian officials promptly arrested Little Bear and other leaders in spite of the promised amnesty, many quickly returned to Montana. Furthermore, "they liked the United States better than Canada," Chief Stick explained.[4] Where the infant Chief Stick was taken during these turbulent seasons is unclear, but by the turn of the century his family was firmly ensconced south of the Forty-Ninth Parallel.

Cree chief Little Bear played a prominent role in Chief Stick's formative years in Montana, as his stepfather. Along with two of Chief Stick's uncles, Little Bear cared closely for the growing child. Chief Stick's early experiences alongside them in northern Montana illustrate how Crees on both sides of the line negotiated the transnational landscape. One summer, Chief Stick crossed north to winter near Medicine Hat, Alberta. However, partway through the season, Little Bear arrived by train to bring Chief Stick back to his parents near Havre, Montana. They crossed south, only to return back north of the border in the spring. Throughout these months, individuals and families from Montana came and went, as Crees congregated in the Cypress Hills in Saskatchewan and Alberta. When they received notice of a Sun Dance in Havre, Chief Stick's family and various families in the region promptly packed their belongings and crossed the border into the United States en masse and without concern. "In those days," Chief Stick recalled much later, "there were no customs officers where you had to report." "The boundary could be crossed at any time or any place," he recollected. "The move was slow and leisurely."[5] Maintaining a strong transnational presence in these years, Crees like Chief Stick crossed the line with apparent ease.

Mobility by Crees in Montana drew from long migratory traditions, moving where they could best secure food, shelter, and safety. The international boundary failed to restrict these traditions, and the need for such movement was great among Chief Stick's people in the first two decades of the twentieth century. Landless in Montana, circumstances demanded mobility. During this period, Crees under Little Bear joined a group of Chippewas led by Chief Rocky Boy (Stone Child) in their efforts to secure lands for settlement. Rocky Boy's Chippewas were a combination of Canadian-born and US-born people who had left the North Dakota–Manitoba borderlands in search of more favorable conditions to the west.

Although camps were independent of one another, they joined in legal efforts. The written historical record in the early twentieth century often blurs distinctions between "Cree," "Chippewa," and "Chippewa-Cree." The tribes held long-standing linguistic, cultural, and familial ties from their centuries-old cohabitation of the Canadian prairies and eastern woodlands. Their cooperation in Montana followed a familiar pattern. Furthermore, Little Bear's Crees and Rocky Boy's Chippewas shared the immediate historical experience of borderlands residence and failure to secure stable residence in Montana. Unwelcomed in Montanan cities and largely unwelcomed on American Indian reservations, their bands subsisted on the peripheries of population centers, finding what work they could and moving frequently. Chief Stick recalled years of constant roving. The winter of 1910–11, he remembered, was "very, very hard." Living in tents outside Havre, Crees and their livestock struggled to survive. "It was very hard on the horses, for they didn't have any feed. There was no hay. The horses were always shaking because of hunger."[6]

In 1911 they hunted coyotes in the Sweet Grass Hills of north-central Montana in the spring, sold pelts for $2.50 in Chester, Montana, summered in Great Falls, paused in Browning for a Sun Dance in the fall, and then established camps on the edge of Great Falls for the coming winter. During 1912, they circulated to similar sites, eventually gathering at the Bear Paw Mountains, where the US Army was providing rations for Crees. "Food was hard to come by [and] it was very, very cold in the tents," Chief Stick recalled. "In spite of being cold and hungry, we were fortunate enough to have a place to dance. All winter we danced there. We had real good dancers. There wasn't much sickness. People were strong. We had good dances."[7] Resilient, they persisted, built some cabins, planted crops, and hoped for permanent settlement. The maintenance of these sites in 1913–14 is a momentous marker in their history. Over the course of the next two years, they secured federal tribal recognition and established a reservation. A home was finally found amid the Bear Paw Mountains in 1916.

Chief Stick spent most of his remaining life on Rocky Boy's Reservation, where he married Bad Looking Big Wind; both were enrolled members. By the time he was interviewed in the mid-1970s, Chief Stick had welcomed grandchildren into his family, but he had mourned the passing of his first wife in 1945. They had been married for nearly thirty years.[8] Chief Stick died on August 8, 1995, at the age of one hundred.[9] His life, like those of so many Native peoples who lived through these years, was one of transition, beginning with nomadism and ending with reservation settlement. As a "foreign" Indian in the United States, however, his story proves unique.

Thirteen hundred miles south from Chief Stick's birthplace in Butte is the Yaqui River Valley in Sonora, Mexico. In 1871, a Yaqui Indian named Lucas Chavez was born there in Tórim. Though far removed from the white-Native conflicts that Grant Chief Stick's Crees experienced along the Forty-Ninth Parallel to the north, Chavez's life in the US-Mexican borderlands bears a remarkable resemblance to his northern plains counterpart. Living in Tórim for his first fifteen years, Lucas Chavez was eyewitness to some of the worst moments in a long history of Spanish and Mexican warfare against the Yaquis.[10] At the time of Chavez's birth, Yaquis stood as one of the last independent, unconquered Indigenous peoples in Mexico. In the Yaqui River Valley and adjoining Bacatete Mountains, Yaquis had resisted and repelled Spanish and Mexican government campaigns against them for centuries. Although they had incorporated Christianity, they had forged a fiercely unique sense of self and religiosity.[11]

Near the turn of the century, Porfirio Díaz's regime instituted policies to rid the region of Yaquis—extermination in Sonora or deportation and enslavement on henequen and sisal plantations in the Yucatán and other points south. It was against these terrible circumstances that the Yaqui leader Cajeme and Lucas Chavez's family fought in the 1880s. Chavez later remembered it as a time of "continual disturbance."[12] Chavez saw his three older brothers and more than one uncle killed. While besieged with Cajeme at the Battle of Buatachive in the spring of 1886, Chavez's parents were killed. Though he escaped with an uncle, he was captured in Tórim and sent by ship on a horrifying and crowded twenty-mile voyage up the coast to Guaymas. Chavez had witnessed the loss of much of his family and defeat that signaled change for his Yaquis as a whole. In the years that followed, Chavez joined other Yaquis as agricultural and industrial laborers in Sonora, coming into their first close and consistent contact with Spanish-speaking Mexicans, learning Spanish, and exploring the broader cultural landscape against which they had long resisted.

In this time of transition, Chavez made a decision that drastically altered the course of his life: he crossed the US-Mexican border to work in the United States. Yaquis had maintained a presence in the Salt, Gila, and Santa Cruz River valleys of southern Arizona for over 150 years. Entering the United States in 1891, Chavez helped forge a path for subsequent Yaqui refugees to follow. The number of Yaquis fleeing Sonora swelled at the turn of the century, and by 1910 some one thousand lived in permanent and semi-permanent settlements across southern Arizona. Many of these, like Chavez, continued agricultural and industrial labor as they had in Sonora. From 1891 to 1910, he worked in Nogales, Yuma, Sasco, and Patagonia, enjoying cordial relations with fellow Yaquis and white American employers. Belying Chavez's relative success, insecurity and fear of deportation haunted the lives of many Arizona Yaquis.[13]

In 1910, Lucas Chavez, by then married to a fellow Sonoran Yaqui named Dolores, settled in the Tucson area. However, like many others, he did not hold legal title to the land on which he lived in Barrio Anita. Fluent in Spanish, Chavez and other Yaquis interacted regularly with other Mexican immigrants and laborers in Arizona. For this and other reasons, many white Arizonans viewed all those from Mexico as one, despite the historic antagonism between Yaquis and the Mexican government. Chavez became Yaqui leader Juan Pistola's primary secretary, having a hand in political and religious leadership, but by the 1940s Chavez's wife had passed away as had many of his friends in the Tucson area, and he was lamenting the general decline of his Yaqui community. Chavez told anthropologist Edward Spicer, who interviewed him then, that he felt his people were "going the wrong way, forgetting the good things, and wishing to become like Mexicans."[14] The Yaqui community was on precarious economic footings. Although they had established squatter communities near Tucson, Tempe, Scottsdale, and Yuma—boasting populations of at least five hundred in each—they seldom held legal claim to the land on which they lived.

The experiences Chavez related to Spicer spanned the first and second of three discernable phases in Arizona Yaqui history: exodus from Sonora and establishment of distinct Yaqui communities and cultural traditions in the state. The third phase, securing legal landholdings and eventual federal tribal recognition and reservation lands, was yet to come. Chavez's experience was born in tragedy but propelled by adaptability and tenacity. Chavez personified Yaqui resilience. His people fled to the United States as fiercely independent, though pragmatic, transnational Natives. Their resistance to Mexican rule had prompted their flight, but this did not preclude them from operating within Mexican and US economic systems. Quite to the contrary, they flourished in their chosen professions while establishing Yaqui communities in Arizona, sustaining and expanding religious and other cultural traditions, and negotiating the precarious borderlands between "American," "Mexican," and Indigenous identity and legal status.

The lives of Grant Chief Stick and Lucas Chavez emblematize the experiences of countless other "foreign" Crees, Chippewas, and Yaquis in the United States. The circumstances of their struggles and triumphs, while unique, can be extrapolated to many of their compatriots. Their words recounting their harrowing experiences should stay in mind as we more broadly explore the borderlands they negotiated. The intimate nature of lived experience, the burden of persistent fear, sorrow, and uncertainty, the relief of stability and refuge—these, sadly, are often absent from the historical record. Too easily we view histories in the abstract, forgetting the real people who lived them, people with joys and struggles. By examining the lives of Chief Stick, Chavez, and others who will follow in this book, we can imbue history with empathy. This empathy in turn can enlighten the complex and all too often cruel past in which our own lives are based.

Introduction

Comparing the US-Canadian and US-Mexican Borderlands and the Transnational Natives Who Crossed Them

In 1975, Yaquis in Arizona, after a decade of political and community organizing, petitioned Congress for federal recognition as an American Indian tribe. There was no doubt about their indigeneity. Yaquis had fought centuries of wars against Spain and Mexico and, as noted in the prologue, by the late nineteenth century were one of the last unconquered Native peoples in North America. In the late nineteenth and early twentieth centuries, they fought wars with Mexico, which resulted in successive waves of Yaquis crossing the international border into the United States. By the 1970s, their descendants in Arizona self-identified as "Indian" and were regularly labeled as such by the whites and Mexican Americans among whom they lived and worked. Why then would their efforts to be recognized as American Indians consistently be rejected by the United States government and neighboring Arizonans, including some Arizona Indian tribes? Arizona's Yaqui peoples were considered Indian, but "Mexican"—Native, yes, but foreign.

It was true that the Arizona Yaquis all had roots in Mexico. However, the "Mexican" label was perverse since they had fled Mexico due to genocidal campaigns against them. They were of course not the only Indigenous people lacking federal recognition, but they were some of the very few labeled as "foreign."[1]

In their organizing for recognition, Arizona's Yaqui community leaders and their allies found significant historical precedent to bolster their case: "the comparable situation of a group of Chippewa and Cree Indians living in the State of Montana . . . born in Canada and [who] entered the United States as refugee Canadian Indians."[2] Montana's Cree and Chippewa group had gained tribal recognition and reservation lands in 1916 after suffering under jurisdictional vagaries created by categorization as "foreign" Indians—and after a struggle of roughly thirty years. While perhaps encouraging to Yaquis, the precedent did not translate to immediate recognition by the US government. In the preceding decades, from the mid-forties to the mid-sixties, federal policy had turned strongly to termination of tribal recognition and sovereignty in the name of assimilation and reform. This "termination era" had shown the federal government most interested in *decreasing* the number of its "Indian wards."[3]

What did (and does) this linkage between Chippewas and Crees in the 1910s and Yaquis in the 1970s mean? Can these two histories—separated by almost fifteen hundred miles and multiple decades and spanning two different international borders—be in conversation one with another? Is there more overlap than this singular moment in the *Congressional Record*? There was no Chippewa-Cree-Yaqui cabal working to forward their parallel goals or collaborating in any way. Read in tandem, however, the two histories present compelling similarities in reasons for which people crossed borders into the United States, struggles they faced, and triumphs they attained.

At the same time, dissimilarities in their stories raise important questions. If they shared so much in their transnational contexts, why did their day-to-day experiences and overarching chronologies diverge so sharply? Their border-crossing sojourns commenced at roughly the same time, but their federal recognition was separated by sixty-two years. Analyzing their histories together, and bringing them into dialogue one with another, reveals a number of important truths that might otherwise go unnoticed. Federal policy concerning transnational Indians was strikingly inconsistent and at times even nonexistent. The US-Mexican and US-Canadian borderlands differed (and still differ) significantly. Non-Indians perceived "Canadian Indians" as different from "Mexican Indians," with the latter being conflated with the general Mexican population. And Native and non-Native labor markets differed, affecting the migrants' ability to attain social, political, and cultural integration in their new Montana and Arizona homes.

The preceding prologue introduced Grant Chief Stick and Lucas Chavez, whose lives shared contexts in broad themes across the North American West, Native American, and borderlands histories. Their lives were both affected by imposed Euro-American boundaries that proved incongruous with Indigenous practice. With static, regulated, and policed boundaries, conflict was inevitable. There was tension between misunderstandings of the environment, competitive sovereignties, and incompatible views of national geographic integrity. In the eyes of Canadian, US, and Mexican officials, the boundaries clearly assigned national identity, citizenship, and jurisdiction of residents on each side of the line.[4] But this classification failed to consider preexisting Indigenous identities in these regions. Crees, Yaquis, countless other Indigenous peoples, and non-Native Americans, Canadians, and Mexicans had conflicting views of Indigenous, national, and international space. Historian Eric Meeks describes transnational populations such as the Crees and Yaquis as "border citizens—people whose rights of belonging were in question, leaving them on the margins of the national territory and of American society and culture."[5] This is foundational to North American Native and borderlands history.

The lives of Arizona Yaquis and Montana Crees (or Chippewas) like Lucas Chavez and Grant Chief Stick provide a useful lens through which to view these conflicts and resulting historic outcomes. Many Natives were not deterred by the arbitrary bifurcation of their homelands or convinced of the immovable nature of the new boundaries and new national identities thereby assigned to them. Yet traditional Indigenous migration that crossed international lines assumed new meanings. To government officials in Canada, the United States, and Mexico, these transnational Natives violated the integrity of their borders. Thus Indigenous peoples could be viewed as refugees or illegal immigrants. This recognition is not absent from existing scholarship, but Cree, Chippewa, and Yaqui examples provide some new insights.

Native borderlands narratives have benefited from a recent surge in scholarly attention.[6] Prominent examples include the stories of Sitting Bull and Hunkpapa and Lakota Sioux exiles seeking asylum in Canada, the attempted flight of Chief Joseph's Nez Perce toward the Canadian border, and Kickapoos, Seminoles, Cherokees, Delawares, and others who crossed southward into Mexico and back north. Others, including Dakota Sioux, Métis, Blackfeet, and Apaches, actively negotiated on both sides of the border, often shaping and even dictating the respective Canadian, American, and Mexican activities in the regions.[7] Natives ignored borders in some cases and leveraged them as a means to escape pursuit at other times. The border held real power, and Indigenous mobility co-opted it. Regardless of their initial acceptance or rejection of the legality of Euro-American boundaries, many Natives quickly adapted to their new geopolitical implications.

Unlike other Indigenous Americans, the Yaquis, Crees, and Chippewas crossed international borders into the United States and thereafter sought permanent residence. The predominant flow was in the other direction: aforementioned groups sought asylum and residence in Canada or Mexico. Involving long and tortuous sagas, the Cree-Chippewa group and the Yaquis stand as unique examples of so-called foreign Indians securing federal tribal recognition and reservation lands in the United States.[8] Their unique narratives not only complicate predominant historiography, they also provide much-needed context for contemporary political debates concerning North American borders and migration and the settling of foreign refugees in the United States.[9]

Comparing Native Peoples and Borderlands

Beyond simply airing stories that have largely gone unnoticed, what avenues will the juxtaposition of Yaqui and Cree-Chippewa experiences open? First, this pairing presents discrete Native histories in broad transnational contexts. It transgresses the constricting bounds of nationally defined historiography, archives, and narratives. "Transnational" Indigenous histories appear within the context of Euro-American and Native empire-building, as Euro-Americans imposed policed international boundaries and Natives challenged them. For Indigenous peoples of the American Southwest and the northern plains, the imposition of Euro-American empires across the continent introduced new and powerful complexity with which they had to deal. Unfortunately, the imposing frame of the nation-state has meant that much transnational history has fallen through the cracks.[10] After examination of how Yaquis, Chippewas, and Crees negotiated their respective borderlands, a new narrative can bridge disjointed national histories.

Second, this dual approach builds bridges between the histories of the North American borderlands themselves. There are three primary Euro-American-nation states involved in this history: Canada, the United States, and Mexico. Clearly, the contributing contexts for the Canadian and Mexican lines in these narratives come from widely differing cultural and geopolitical histories. The differences in how the Canadian and Mexican states governed their boundaries drew from previous Spanish, English, and French legacies. The interplay between these nations and adjacent US federal, state, and territorial powers likewise differed. These are well-established histories, but US policies, a supposed constant in the borderlands, must not be viewed as a constant at all. Close examination reveals tremendous variance in how the United States dealt with its northern and southern borderlands. Historian Sheila McManus states of the two borders, "They are not identical twins, but [neither] are they merely distant cousins."[11] By viewing the borders through the lenses of transnational Yaquis, Chippewas, and Crees, the non-Native borderlands communities in which they settled and the federal policies concerning them their differences become clearer. Likewise we can better delineate when and how the experiences of so-called Canadian Indians and Mexican Indians inhabiting the borderlands aligned and diverged.

Third, comparative analysis complicates the relationships between borders and the peoples inhabiting the borderlands, providing new insights. Most obvious are the ways in which borders have directly affected peoples. For Natives, the arbitrary but often very real bisection of the continent by international boundaries introduced an unfamiliar construct. Their traditional views were of land shared and generally unbounded, with boundaries—if any—flexible and quite porous. As lines on maps became carefully policed barriers to their movements, Native peoples faced new challenges. Borders did not end Native movement but dramatically directed it down new paths. Proximity to international boundaries also affected non-Native Canadian, US, and Mexican residents. At the periphery, they were alternately ignored by federal oversight and allowed great latitude in their dealing, and scrutinized with high intensity when border crises drew the concerned attention of nation state officials. In either case, borderlanders negotiated landscapes with unique geopolitical properties that set them apart from citizens residing closer to their nations' centers.

The influence of Native and non-Native peoples upon the borders is a more subtle, though no less significant, point to consider. The continental US-Canadian border was largely finalized by 1846 with the Oregon Treaty, and the US-Mexican border assumed its final demarcation with the 1853 Gadsden Purchase, but their practical interpretation by federal governments and local residents underwent significant evolution.[12] Increased settlement in adjacent borderlands forced federal powers to consider border regulation more carefully. The "violation" of the border by Natives and non-Natives alike accelerated its tightening. When white settlement extended toward the peripheries of national control, as was the case in Alberta, Saskatchewan, Montana, Arizona, and Sonora, settler fear of Native hostilities added further import to reexamining border enforcement. As these regions shifted from being frontiers dominated by the fur trade and mining to more expansive settler-colonial development, settler reception of Native peoples changed.

Early acceptance of Indigenous border-crossings shifted to near-universal outcry by non-Native borderlands residents and demands that their proximal (and supposedly protective) boundaries be enforced. Few factors transformed the nature of North American borderlands and international boundaries more rapidly than Native disregard for "the line."

This is complex history. Comparative analysis seeks to clarify it.

The following narratives are not intended to serve as comprehensive histories of the Montana Chippewa and Cree community or the Arizona Yaqui communities. They represent narrow treatments of these groups. Their focus on the transnational Native experience of peoples coming *into* the United States offers a counterpoint to the predominant narrative of Indigenous exodus. As large numbers of Crees, Chippewas, and Yaquis remained in Canada and Mexico, these stories help provide nuance to broader ethnographic understandings of widely dispersed peoples. Although they left Canada and Mexico, their stories add to the history of those they left behind, especially as both groups maintain ties with distant relatives across the border to the present day. Their narratives offer new wrinkles to the broader quilt of Native experience in the United States as well. Finally, nineteenth-century and early-twentieth century Yaquis, Crees, and Chippewas offer a comparative point for the study of broader transnational migrant communities contemporary to their crossings and through to the present. As Natives, their experience has been unique, and the differences in their reception and treatment can offer valuable insight. While these narrow bounds eliminate from this study enormous portions of the Cree, Chippewa, and Yaqui experience in the United States, I hope it will still be of value to these communities.

The transnational Chippewa-Cree history does not end in 1916 with the establishment of Rocky Boy's Reservation. Likewise, transnational Yaqui history does not end in 1978 with the creation of the Pascua Yaqui Tribe and reservation. Both groups persist today and are transnational despite fixed residence. Residents of Rocky Boy's Reservation boast complex genealogies, many of which incorporate Cree, Chippewa, Métis, Assiniboine, Blackfeet, French, and English ancestry, and all of which stem from north of the Forty-Ninth Parallel. Many still maintain communication with relations in Alberta and Saskatchewan. Likewise, Arizona Yaquis maintain relationships south of the border and are rebuilding relationships once severed violently. Those whose families have incorporated Mexican heritage and self-identity persist in transnational communities too. After more than a century in the United States, both groups display a unique blend of Native, American, and "foreign" identity. Transnational Yaquis, Chippewas, and Crees have negotiated a volatile multinational landscape with great adaptability, tenacity, and strength. Operating across different borders, Yaquis and Crees saw their struggle through to the end and forged strong senses of identity and community in the process. It was in the milieu of these complex geopolitical landscapes that individuals such as Grant Chief Stick and Lucas Chavez lived their lives. Their actions in transnational landscapes are of a sort shared by only a select few in Native North America.

Methodologies, Terminologies, and Organization

A discussion here of terminology and definitions used in this study will alleviate the need to make clarifications repeatedly throughout. How Yaquis, Chippewas, Crees, and others will be collectively labeled is complicated. There are differing views from competing academic disciplines, differing from person to person within academia and in tribal communities. Some prefer "American Indians" and others "Native Americans." In Canada "First Nations" and "aboriginal" dominate the literature. For others, the broader adjective "Indigenous" is favored. Here specific names such as "Yaquis," "Chippewas," "Crees," and "Chippewa-Crees" will be used when such specificity is appropriate. When speaking more broadly, this study will freely interchange "Indigenous" and "Native." "Native American," "First Nations," "American Indian," and "Indian" will also appear. Variance will be determined less by context than by grammatical structure, cadence, clarity, and simplicity.

Individual tribal names are not always simple to distinguish. Yaquis have historically been known by a variety of names. The official name used by the people themselves in Arizona is Yaqui, though some variance is present depending on community, family, and individual.[13] Current historical, anthropological, and ethnographic scholarship has favored "Yoeme" and "Yaqui." Most legislation and primary documents concerning the people uses "Yaqui," and I will follow this precedent. Crees, Chippewas and Chippewa-Crees are distinct groups, and their labels will be clearly distinguishable. There is a great deal of variance between various Cree and Chippewa subgroups across the northern plains (in the United

States, "Ojibwe" or "Anishinaabe are often used as self-descriptors), but as this study deals little with the differing groups within broader continental Cree or Chippewa histories, simple "Cree" and "Chippewa" labels will be used to identify clearly defined groups as they enter the narrative.[14] When describing Crees and Chippewas eventually combined into a single tribe in Montana, the nomenclature will shift to the present-day Rocky Boy's Reservation style—"Chippewa Cree."

This study also warrants clarifications over the usage of geopolitical terminology. A number of the territory and state names in this study changed over time, but rather than reference the "District of Assiniboia," which few are familiar with—it was the name of a historical district of the North-West Territories—I will use "Saskatchewan" throughout. Time-specific designations will be made clear, and the designation "present-day" will be noted for general purposes.

Terms such as "border," "international boundary," "the line," and "borderlands" will all be used to denote related geopolitical constructs. The first three all clearly refer to the lines on maps or their physical correlates where the United States fronts Canada or Mexico. The concept of borderlands is more elusive. In this book, "borderlands" refers to regions where competing spheres of national and international influence abut and overlap. The terms is used by the likes of Herbert E. Bolton, John Francis Bannon, David Weber, and others who wrote of buffer zones in the American Southwest between Euro-American empires: regions where neither Spanish, French, English, Mexican, American, or Native empires and peoples held absolute control.[15] Writing of the Great Lakes region in the seventeenth through nineteenth centuries, Richard White spoke of a "middle ground": a "place in between cultures, peoples, and in between empires and the non-state world of villages."[16] With hints of Turnerian frontiers, where civilization mixes with wilderness and savagery, the predominant historiographic conceptualization of borderlands history is one of simultaneous contest, accommodation, and negotiation.

Some have suggested that a meaningful shift in geopolitical terminology and actual on-the-ground impact occurred when enforced international boundaries (duly agreed upon by competing countries, drawn on maps, and policed) separated contested borderlands or frontier regions into clearly defined national spaces.[17] This suggested transformation from nebulous and entirely porous borderlands into fixed and impermeable "bordered-lands" is intriguing but potentially too formulaic.[18] Interpreting broad regions and diverse peoples by such singular theoretical models may be useful at times but does not offer a comprehensive perspective. This book will selectively use these distinctions in terminology and definition. The Turnerian and New Western History debate over the frontier and borderlands as place or process is relevant but not central to the task at hand. When the evolving nature of these regions is important, I will comment on that as necessary. For example, porous sections of the US-Canadian border for a time allowed Crees to cross it easily, so more rigid policing of those sections had a swift impact on the Crees involved. As noted of other groups along the border, this meant that "native peoples had lost the freedom to pursue their own objectives by using the boundary as a tool. The Canadian borderlands had become bordered lands."[19] In this case, a substantive transformation had taken place and relevant conclusions could be made. Generally, however, "borderlands" will refer broadly to the geographic, cultural, and economic regions that overlap and abut international boundaries.

Broad conceptualization of transnationality and Native peoples as transnational migrants, refugees, or illegal immigrants deserves comment as well. Transnational actors and forces can transgress both the physical boundaries of the nation-state and national narratives and historiography. This helps complicate traditional narratives about Native peoples and their relations with nation-states. However, most of these concepts build on Eurocentric frameworks and infer that the geopolitical constructs of Canada, the United States, and Mexico held superior authority. Thus, transnational Natives violated Euro-American geographies that were considered more primal, inherent, or natural than their own. Moreover, using "US-Canadian" or "US-Mexican" to label borderlands in writing about a time before those nations held firm control over them may imply that the people living there were destined to assume respective national identities. Such reverse teleology strips history of important contingencies. Weighing the short tenure of Euro-Americans on the continent with that of Native peoples, it is clear that these geopolitical constructs were not inevitable. Blindly accepting this model overlooks Native resistance, historical and contemporary, against the imposition of a nation-state's identity upon them. Maps matter. Comparing them over time we can discover empire-building, identity formation, and identity imposition. We must interrogate, or at least acknowledge, suppositions about national identity and borders.[20] An alternative would be to rewrite the present received narrative in converse terms: a story of transnational Euro-Americans transgressing Indigenous lands and spheres of influence.

Both frameworks are biased. The latter approach, however, would insert a subtle presupposition that Native geopolitical landscapes were likewise an inherent and static part of the geography. This could be equally fallacious. Precontact Native America was as dynamic in its contested geopolitical landscape as North America in the post-contact era. The centuries preceding European contact featured not only Native migration, but also vigorous economic, military, and cultural conflict and negotiation.[21] Post-contact Native migrations, as Cree and Chippewa histories will illustrate, and even Native empire-building further underscore the reality of dynamic Native geographies.[22] This increases the difficulty of using Native political geographies as the reference point of a comparative borderlands study.

The selection of Euro-American geopolitical foundations for casting terms of transnationality and borderlands migration is not an assertion that these geographies were any less dynamic than Native ones—they were often in flux, and border regimes evolved over long durations. Yet these are the political geographies I will use as the landscape over which transnational Natives moved. Furthermore, active Native co-option of Euro-American borders to further their own needs illustrates their cognizant willingness to operate within Euro-American constructs. Regrettably the word "transnational" belies the true self-perceived nationalities and identities of Yaquis, Crees, and Chippewas, who viewed themselves far less in terms of "Mexican," "American" or "Canadian" than simply as Yaquis, Crees, and Chippewas. Thus the nationality suggested by the "transnational" label is equally biased and Eurocentric as the acceptance of Euro-American boundaries as a basic framework. The Eurocentric bias, however, is an angle from which I will study and analyze, giving significant attention to the experience of Yaquis, Chippewas, and Crees as influenced by the Euro-American perceptions of them as transnational—or, in the case of US perceptions, "foreign"—Indians.

Undertaking a comparative analysis of these histories also presents methodological and practical problems that merit discussion. Foremost is the question of organization. The case study model, in which each case is studied discretely, helps develop narrative. The histories of Chippewas, Crees, and Yaquis could be drawn out and expounded for narrative themes that emerge naturally from the uninterrupted long durée of their stories. An opposing model would be to select content—vignettes, data, documents, histories—from those existing narrative case studies and weave them together into thematically and chronologically organized chapters.

There are, however, significant drawbacks with this latter organizational scheme. The back-and-forth comparative analysis breaks narrative flow, can be disorienting, distracts from individual and group stories, and fractures history to the point where context is lost and the stories are no longer compelling. For these reasons, this book will take a middle-ground approach. Divided into four parts, it will feature comparative and narrative approaches.

Part 1, "Homelands, Transnational Worlds, and Border Encounters," contains two thematically organized comparative chapters. Chapter 1, "Crees, Chippewas, and Yaquis in Early Transnational Contexts," considers all three groups, tracing their patterns of mobility and expansion. This chapter seeks to provide some deep context for the primary narratives that begin in the late nineteenth century, demonstrating how later border-crossing movements grew from centuries of territorial movement and drew upon long traditions of geopolitical and economic negotiation. Chapter 2, "Transnational Encounters and Evolving Prejudice in Montana and Arizona, 1800–1900," again features all three groups and fully immerses the reader in the primary time frame of this study. Attention is given to Cree and Chippewa traders as well as Yaqui miners and laborers who worked in the United States. Economic forces are highlighted, as are the demands of settler-colonial expansion and their effect on how non-Natives welcomed or rejected transnational Native peoples. In these years, white borderlands residents formed profound prejudices against both groups, north and south. Together the two chapters of part 1, dealing with multiple Native peoples, nation-states, boundaries, and border regimes, provide foundation and context for the histories that follow in the remainder of the book.

Part 2, "Native Peoples as 'Foreign' Refugees and Immigrants," also contains two chapters. Starting here, the Montana and Arizona stories are divided into discrete chapters to foster continuity and internal narrative flow. Chapter 3, "Yaqui Refugees and American Response, 1880s–1910s," begins with the first discernable wave of Yaqui refugees who fled to Arizona to escape violence in Sonora. These represent a different group than the laborers who traveled similar paths before them and concurrent with their migration. Their reception in the United States was complicated by the opposing forces of sympathy for their plight and suspicion regarding their violent resistance and persistent warfare with Mexico. Chapter 4, "Cree Refugees and American Response, 1885–1888," follows the story of Crees who fled to Montana as refugees after the failed 1885 North-West Rebellion. This story entails their troubled reception in the United States: Montanans had already formed a strong prejudice against these bands, whose past actions in Montana made them largely unwelcome. Together these chapters build on part 1's historical context and follow Yaqui and Cree populations as they worked to firmly establish a permanent presence in the United States.

Part 3, "Native Struggles to Make American Homelands," features four chapters that follow the aftermath of the initial refugee migration and efforts to remain in the United States and secure legal, unambiguous, and permanent settlement. Chapter 5, "Crees in Limbo and Deportation, 1889–1900," examines the events of the 1890s when Montana and US Army officials undertook a campaign to deport Crees to Canada. This chapter also introduces the Chippewas under the leadership of Chief Rocky Boy as their Montanan narrative begins at this same time. Chapter 6, "Arizona Yaquimi and Integration in the United States, 1900s–1950s," details the various settlement patterns and economic, political, and cultural strategies used by Yaquis to secure stable homes in Arizona. Chapter 7, "Yaqui Legality and Belonging in Arizona, 1900–1950s," overlaps slightly with the preceding chapter but explores a series of legal crises Yaquis faced. In the context of broader immigration reforms and deportations, Yaquis faced varied threats depending on when individuals arrived in the United States and under what circumstances. Chapter 8, "Cree and Chippewa Attempts at Permanent Montana Settlement, 1900–1908," traces the repeated and failed early-twentieth-century efforts by Little Bear and Rocky Boy to secure permanent settlement for their respective peoples.

Part 4, "New Allies, New Efforts, and Ultimate Resolutions," contains the final two chapters of the main text and features successful collaborations between Crees, Chippewas, and Yaquis and prominent Americans in devising new plans for their peoples' futures. In both cases a series of efforts were undertaken, with varied results and constant resistance from local interests, until final strategies led to federal recognition as American Indians and the successful securing of reservation lands. Chapter 9, "Cree and Chippewa Legislative Battles and Victories, 1908–1916," follows the efforts of Rocky Boy, Little Bear, and American allies such as Frank Linderman. The eventual 1916 establishment of Rocky Boy's Chippewa Cree Reservation was hard-won, and the constant setbacks and disappointments along the way testify to the tenacity and dedication of all involved. Chapter 10, "Yaqui Struggle for Land and Federal Tribal Recognition, 1962–1980," follows a series of collaborations between Yaqui leaders, congressional allies such as Morris K. Udall, and academics like Muriel Thayer Painter and Edward Spicer to help resolve problems faced by Yaqui communities. First, lands were secured via a nonprofit organization for the creation of the New Pascua Yaqui settlement, and later, after a concerted push, federal recognition was attained. As their Montana counterparts had decades earlier, Yaquis and their allies met staunch and continual resistance. Their triumph was miraculous.

The book ends with a brief epilogue meant to tease out a few revelations about the US-Canadian and US-Mexican borders in comparison. In addition to the notes and bibliography, the book is augmented by a companion website, www.nativebutforeign.org, where additional sources and analysis are available. There readers can also ask questions and participate in ongoing discussion.

To the Indigenous communities this book investigates, I want to be transparent in not claiming to present a comprehensive, definitive history of the Cree, Chippewa, Chippewa-Cree, or Yaqui tribes in the United States. While such definitive histories merit pursuit, they would need to be based on how your communities tell their own history. This book comes from a different place and with different purposes. It is first and foremost a work of comparative borderlands history. Indigenous peoples are the primary actors, but the points of analysis are often the borders themselves, the borderlands cultures and societies, the legal and political frameworks that existed in these regions, and the economics and labor markets of Arizona and Montana. These could all be points of discussion in more traditional ethnohistorical and definitive tribal histories, but they would certainly not be as strongly pursued as in this book. That said, this book has benefited immensely from the encouragement that your tribal communities have offered, and I hope you will find it of value as you continue to strengthen, grow, and evolve your communities in their transnational worlds.

For other readers, ones not members of the Chippewa-Cree or Yaqui communities, these transnational histories can clarify contemporary issues—the likes of immigration, refugee crises, border crossing, and Indigenous sovereignty—and offer helpful perspectives. Legacies of Euro-American settler colonialism, often tragic and troublesome, burden our present, and they demand our joint striving for understanding through compassion and open discussion.

Part 1

Homelands, Transnational Worlds, Labor, and Border Encounters

Before Crees, Chippewas, and Yaquis established their transnational presence in the US-Canadian and US-Mexican borderlands, they had long histories of contact, exchange, and expansion. It is worth spending some time with these earlier years to illustrate a number of important commonalities and distinctions between the three groups. Post-contact, all three demonstrated ability and willingness to engage with Euro-American markets and trade, undertake expansion and move when needed, and incorporate distant locales into their identities. The expansive geography of Cree and Chippewa narratives is much larger than that of Yaquis—ranging nearly across the entirety of the Canadian interior and south into what would become the United States—but Yaqui expansion beyond their traditional homeland (Yaquimi) northward is no less noteworthy. Part 1 will examine these expansions and trace some early transnational exchanges in the United States.

In their earliest transnational endeavors, along and across the edges of European empires from the moments of first contact onward, Crees, Chippewas, and Yaquis crossed Euro-American boundaries pushed by Euro-American encroachment in their territories and pulled economic opportunity across the line. In the case of Crees and Chippewas, the growing French and British influence in the Hudson Bay region propelled them south toward the continental interior over the course of centuries. This entailed being pushed by aggressive encroachment and intentionally moving to engage in fur trade networks. Exhibiting a dynamic ability to adapt to new landscapes, methods of survival and subsistence, and negotiations with new Native and non-Native neighbors, Crees and Chippewas prospered during much of this process—becoming a trade power across the northern

Great Plains. As Canadian expansion shifted from resource extraction (the fur trade) to settler colonialism, the state sought to restrict Native mobility and control of land and resources on the northern plains. This hindered Natives' ability to exploit the full range of their sphere of influence and pushed them across the border. For example, displeased with Treaty 6, proposed and signed by many other plains and woods Crees in 1876, Big Bear crossed south of the line, following well-established bison-hunting routes into Montana's Milk River Valley and surrounding environs. Big Bear and others undertook the transnational passage not only as part of a hunting tradition but also in reaction to friction with the Canadian government. Chippewa migrations followed different routes to Montana but were compelled by similar forces and contexts.

Yaquis in Sonora were also pushed and pulled into the US Southwest. Although centuries of resistance to Spain and Mexico testify to their attachment to their land, they were not a static people. Yaquis in the mid-nineteenth century took advantage of new economic opportunities to the north in mining and trade. The demand for labor in the north, coupled with pressures on their Sonoran homelands, led many to establish new Yaqui communities in the United States. Unlike Crees and Chippewas, Yaquis were not pressed by unfavorable treaty negotiations in Mexico or enticed by open rangelands in the Southwest. Yaquis did not cross to persist in a seminomadic life—they were not seminomadic. Their goals were to work and possibly settle.

As various geopolitical and economic forces caused Crees, Chippewas, and Yaquis to traverse lands, the growing Euro-American empires increasingly sought to control their peripheries. At times, increased policing of boundaries conflicted with economic market forces that encouraged open movement of Native peoples. Euro-American perceptions of mobile, now transnational Natives thus evolved unevenly. By many accounts, the early envoys were welcomed as positive contributors to the American economies into which they ventured. Indigenous allies helped Euro-American empire-building projects gain footholds in contested territories. These early encounters offer a unique comparative scene: Indigenous economic actors traversing transnational divides (as defined by the imposed Euro-American boundaries) and being welcomed into evolving labor markets and economies. But the warm welcome would not last. As markets oscillated along the boom-and-bust cycles prevalent in the nineteenth-century US West, initial similarities between the experiences of Crees and Yaquis in the United States diverged. Moreover, as Montana and Arizona Territories sought statehood, they focused on growing their white population and promoting white settlement, industry, and investment. Now the economies to which Crees and Yaquis contributed took on very different trajectories. On the one hand, Crees found themselves on the outside of Montana's project of territorial growth, while Yaquis became prized as skilled laborers in the industries Arizona sought to develop. These differences led to diverging experiences for Crees and Yaquis in the United States.

The background of these early expansions into and exchanges along the US-Canadian and US-Mexican borderlands reveal remarkable overlap, however, with peoples pushed by Euro-American encroachment and pulled by economic opportunities. Establishing some of this commonality leads to one of the primary problems this book seeks to resolve. Why did such shared context lead to such different historical chronologies and outcomes?

Chapter 1

Crees, Chippewas, and Yaquis in Early Transnational Contexts

The Cree Indian came first to Montana with the Assiniboines away long ago; my father was a Cree that lived on the Snake River with Moose and Two Horns, and they came here—in Butte—long ago when we hunt buffalo and deer here on this hill, where now these big mines send black smoke to kill the game and the birds.

—CHIEF LITTLE BEAR, March 30, 1913

Although they are more numerous than other [Indian nations], they are here missing two-thirds, as they are dispersed . . . in Soyapa . . . Sracache . . . Vizcaya . . . Chihuahua . . . Parral, Santa Bárbara and El Oro.

—PEDRO TAMARÓN Y ROMERAL,
margin notes in 1765 census of Yaqui territory[1]

Prior to the late nineteenth-century Montana sojourns of Crees and Chippewas, the two groups participated in parallel eighteenth-century and early nineteenth-century migrations to what is now Montana from the northeast. Examination of these early southward forays in the northern plains helps contextualize tensions that would arise later. It is a complex story that can only be briefly explored here, a story of migrations and expansions, multiple economic markets, intertribal and intra-tribal blending and division, and environmental history.[2] Both groups have historic roots extending eastward to the woodlands between the Great Lakes and Hudson Bay. This was a highly trafficked region during the sixteenth and seventeenth centuries, and Crees and Chippewas living there came into increasingly intimate contact with French, English, and later Canadian and American fur traders, settlers, and government officials. In response, Chippewa and Cree territory expanded farther and farther from those eastern homelands along Hudson Bay. Thus, the regular appearance of Chippewas and Crees south of the US-Canadian border in the 1880s was anything but unnatural, as Americans oft viewed their incursions. Rather, their presence represented the most recent in a long succession of movements that had brought the two groups across the northern plains and into the foothills of the Rocky Mountains both north and south of the Forty-Ninth Parallel. Although an alarming development in the eyes of white Montanans, only recent arrivals themselves, it stood as the logical outcome for peoples who, for centuries, had migrated and adapted to new socio-economic and military realities, often maintaining traditional homelands and expanding to incorporate new ones.

The name "Cree" originates from the 1640s, when Jesuits labeled the people as Kristineaux, Kiristinous, or Kilistinous. With other Algonquians they dominated portions of Hudson Bay and were a significant partner in the growing regional European fur trade. Chippewas (Ojibwe) traditionally lived south of these Cree lands and were related linguistically and otherwise culturally. They played similarly dominant roles according to early accounts of the fur trade in their regions. Both had traditional ranges along the western and southern coasts of Hudson Bay and extended outward into present-day Nunavut, Manitoba, and Ontario. Multiple centuries of expansion to their 1880s locations along the US-Canadian border first involved moves westward and then southward, totaling well over two thousand miles for many groups.

The impetus for these migrations is the subject of debate. Alexander Mackenzie's early nineteenth-century accounts of Crees and Chippewas in the Canadian interior have traditionally been interpreted to mean that their push westward was exclusively within the context of their burgeoning fur trade participation. While the fur trade likely played a factor, Mackenzie's account also suggests that these westward movements followed well-established lines of trading and raiding—including locales that may have long been part of seasonal territories.[3] Whatever the initial catalyst for Chippewa and Cree westward migration, by the mid-eighteenth century their territory extended southwest to Lake Manitoba, Lake Winnipeg and even the Mandan villages on the Missouri River—well south of the Forty-Ninth Parallel in present-day North Dakota.[4]

The extent of their expansion across the continent, however, proves much broader. With long-established camps along the western banks of Lake Winnipeg, Cree hunters and traders regularly traveled as far as the Eagle Hills in western Saskatchewan, north of the Saskatchewan River.

According to the account of Saukamappee, an elderly Cree man encountered by Canadian explorer David Thompson during his travels in the late 1700s and early 1800s, Crees' domain had extended this far as far back as the 1730s. At the time of Thompson's travels he placed the Crees largely south of the Fifty-Sixth Parallel.[5] To the south, Chippewas likewise moved into the continent's interior, moving closer to the Forty-Ninth Parallel, out of the woodlands and onto the plains. Distinct from their eastern woodland origins, this establishes a far-reaching, western band of plains Cree and Chippewa territory by the mid-1700s.

When Alexander Mackenzie attempted to follow the Slave River to the Pacific Ocean in 1789, he reported that Cree raiding parties had reached the western banks of the Great Slave Lake some years previous. Mackenzie further observed evidence of Cree encampments over two hundred miles farther northwest, near the confluence of the Mackenzie and Liard Rivers. During his subsequent 1793 voyage along the Peace River westward, Mackenzie again noted Cree encampments well into present-day British Columbia near the headwaters of the Peace River. He even heard stories of Cree raiding parties venturing over the Rocky Mountains into the Fraser River Valley.[6] Whether motivated by military expansion or involvement in the fur trade, the Crees, according to Mackenzie's and others' accounts, engaged in activities that nearly spanned the continent.[7]

While these accounts affirm expansive Cree and Chippewa territories in the plains, the majority of their eighteenth-century activities centered on regions surrounding Lake Manitoba and Lake Winnipeg, extending southeast toward Lake Superior and southwest towards the Souris River in western Manitoba. At these latitudes, trading activities focused around the confluence of the Pembina and Red Rivers near the present-day border town of Pembina, North Dakota.[8] Their role as intermediaries between European fur traders and Natives on the northern plains and into the northwestern reaches of the interior drove much of their western movement.[9] Together with Assiniboine traders, Crees dominated the region, exchanging European goods to interior tribes at increased prices and establishing themselves in the region well before European settlers ventured into the continental interior in large numbers. Athabascan Chipewyan traders made similar moves to the north, serving as intermediaries supplying Europeans with fur and interior Natives with European goods.[10]

While historians have read Cree and Chippewa western expansion through an economic lens, the Chippewas and Crees who together secured reservation lands in twentieth-century Montana saw things differently.

Both held that lands south of the Forty-Ninth Parallel had long been part of Cree or Chippewa homelands. One shared Chippewa-Cree tradition told of two young men who traveled southwest from their northeastern homelands. Upon their return, they described geographies that match the Rocky Mountains, Pacific Ocean, and deserts of the Southwest. They had seen "Great Rocks" that were so high as to have snow on them during the summer and a "Great Water" that lay west from those high peaks—perhaps the Rocky Mountains and Pacific Ocean. Farther south, they related, "a long long ways, there is a land where there are trees with sharp branches. A person cannot touch the trees. Also the large plants have sharp needles. They are in a warm country and it is a long ways from here." Of greater import than cactus, the young men also told of herds of "buffalo as far as they could see."[11]

Another tradition introduced Montana itself into ancestral Chippewa-Cree landscapes. Before Crees or Chippewas began their westward trek from what would become the eastern provinces of Canada, an elder saw the Bear Paw Mountains of Montana in a dream. In the vision, he was told that the Bear Paws would become a "rich place" and a homeland for his grandchildren. Upon sharing his dream with other tribal elders, they rejoiced "because this place [the Bear Paw Mountains] was marked for [their] people." This elder joined his family when they started their movement west, stopping at Red Lake (Minnesota), Mandan villages (North Dakota), and Glasgow (Montana) during the early to mid-nineteenth century.[12] Little Bear, the chief who led Crees back to Montana in 1885 had a similar experience. A figure in a dream instructed him that the Bear Paw Mountains were the place for his people.[13] According to these Chippewa-Cree traditions, Montana and the Bear Paw Mountains where Rocky Boy's Reservation was eventually established were long present in the minds of their ancestors. Their homeland was broadly conceived as stretching from Hudson Bay to the east, the Rocky Mountains to the west, and dipping south into the United States.

Establishing a Cree and Chippewa Presence along the US-Canadian Border

At the beginning of the nineteenth century, Cree and Chippewa traders regularly traveled south of the Forty-Ninth Parallel. Hudson's Bay Company reported Cree traders in present-day southwestern Alberta in 1793.

Dispatched to explore the region and forge trading alliances, Peter Fidler met with Crees encamped with Piegans on the Highwood (Spitcheyee) River—a tributary to the Bow River.[14] Much to his consternation, Fidler observed Cree traders buying furs from Piegan hunters to sell in northern Saskatchewan to the Hudson's Bay Company at considerable profit.[15] This placed Crees almost within what would later become Montana Territory. Fidler then traveled southward to Chief Mountain—located just south of the Forty-Ninth Parallel in the Lewis Range of the Rocky Mountains—to visit Snake and Kootenay traders. Fidler made no specific mention of Crees likewise venturing farther south in the 1790s, but their immediate proximity to the not-yet-established Forty-Ninth Parallel boundary and economic ties with Piegan traders make the occasional presence of Crees in central and western Montana during the late eighteenth century and early nineteenth century a distinct possibility.

Less than a decade later, Lewis and Clark's Corps of Discovery noted potential Cree presence in present-day eastern Montana. In their explorations of the Missouri River drainage, they identified the headwaters of the Saskatchewan River as the center of Cree activities but posited that Crees might be drawn into American trade as far south and west as the confluence of the Yellowstone and Missouri Rivers due to their propensity for "wandering" and "rov[ing]." This would place Crees well south of the Forty-Ninth Parallel in the northern reaches of the present-day Montana–North Dakota border.[16] Lewis and Clark also placed Chippewas south of the Forty-Ninth Parallel at Sand, Leach, and Red Lakes (in present day-Minnesota) and Pembina.[17] One prominent Chippewa leader, Little Shell, made regular appearances south of the Forty-Ninth Parallel at Pembina in the early 1800s. Alexander Henry Jr. reported regular Cree trading and long-established settlements throughout his stay at Pembina from 1801 to 1808. He placed Crees and Chippewas farther west, trading regularly down the Red River and south to the Mandan villages along the Missouri River. He stated that they would have moved farther south and west but were under the constant threat of Sioux attack if they did so.

Taken together, these accounts map an enormous Cree trading sphere by 1810, throughout Saskatchewan, northwest to Fort Vermillion in northern Alberta, throughout the lands directly northwest of Lake Superior, pockmarked with small lakes, down into the Pembina region along the Forty-Ninth Parallel, and farther southwest to the Missouri River in present-day north-central North Dakota.[18] Chippewas traded in many of these same areas and operated extensively farther east along the Red River and Pembina Mountains.[19] By the 1830s, Chippewa and Cree traders were active all along the Forty-Ninth Parallel in the fur trade with the Hudson's Bay Company and later North West and American Fur Companies.

Other Transnational Peoples

Crees and Chippewas were not the only Indigenous peoples whose traditional and evolving homelands were cast in transnational contexts by the formation of the US-Canadian border. The Montana-Canada border divided Blackfoot Confederacy (Niitsitapi) bands of Blackfeet, Piegans, Bloods, and Siksikas. Many persisted there and exerted a transnational presence between the Blackfeet Reservation in northwestern Montana and reserves in Canada. Various Métis groups whose immediate ancestries came from Alberta, Saskatchewan, and the Red River drainage of Manitoba, North Dakota, and Minnesota had a well-established presence in Montana.[20] Michel Hogue has successfully argued that northern plains borderlands cannot be understood without using Métis history as a focal point, and Métis histories overlap considerably with Cree and Chippewa narratives most everywhere on the northern plains, interconnected by marriage, economics, geography, et cetera.[21] In Montana, Métis were focused largely in the Judith Basin and Spring Creek region between Lewistown (originally a Métis settlement), Havre, and Glasgow, and along the eastern slopes of the Rocky Mountains.[22] As early as the 1860s, Métis from the Red River region had moved through the borderlands of North Dakota, Montana, Manitoba, Saskatchewan and Alberta, eventually settling along the divide. During the 1873–74 US-Canadian boundary survey, Métis were noted in large numbers encamped at Wood Mountain (Saskatchewan), the Cypress Hills (Alberta and Saskatchewan), and along the Milk (Montana and Alberta) and White Mud (Manitoba) Rivers, and at many trading posts along the Missouri River.[23]

White Montanan settlers often viewed Métis as a suspect foreign presence. The cooperation of Métis and Crees in the 1885 North-West Rebellion reinforced this view, even though many Métis from the state had remained in Montana, opting not to participate in the rebellion. With extensive historical connections via intermarriage and trade, Métis were often discriminated against as "Canadian Crees," but ultimately they forged an ethnic identity and legal presence in Montana divergent from the Crees.[24] The tendency of US Army officials and white Montanans to differentiate inaccurately between Canadian Natives, Métis, and other mixed-blood Natives caused considerable problems. Native peoples' interaction, cohabitation, intermarriage, cooperation, and occasional shared heritage provides context for such errors.[25] Newspapers regularly interchanged "Cree," "Chippewa," "Mixed-Blood," "Half-Breed," and "Breed" with little explanation if any as to the distinctions.[26]

Strengthening ties, Crees and Chippewas had long frequented Métis homelands in the borderlands along the Red River in North Dakota and Manitoba (see figure 1.1). Indeed, in many ways, Cree and Chippewa migrants to Montana followed paths established by Métis traders and settlers much earlier.[27] As evidence, consider the 1900 census, which lists most Métis as claiming Chippewa and Cree ancestries as their primary Native bloodlines. Métis, Crees, Chippewas, and others shared cultural and familial lines. This was why Chippewas were improperly included in the 1896 Montana-ordered deportation of Canadian Crees from the state. During that process, US officials inappropriately deported a number of American-born Chippewas and Métis, as well as Assiniboines and Gros Ventres from the Belknap Reservation. A Montana newspaper report at the time described these Chippewas as having been "camp followers and

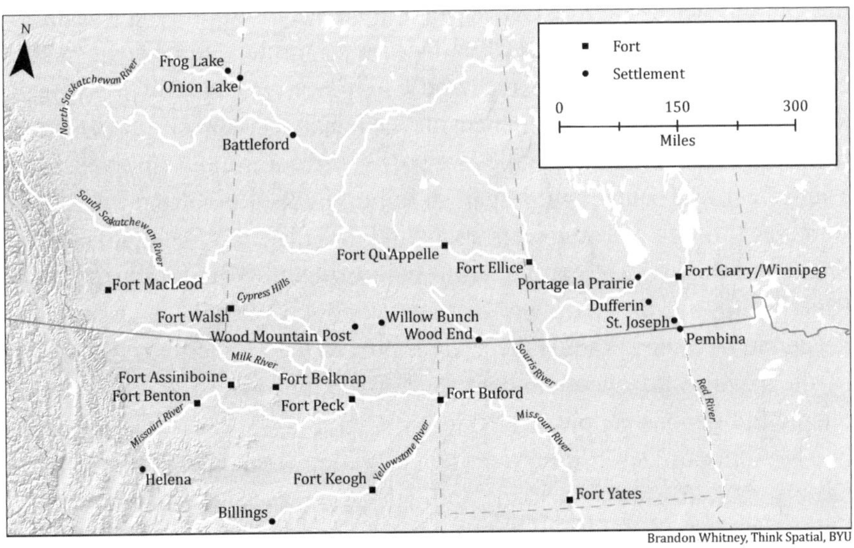

Figure 1.1. Key locations in nineteenth-century Cree and Chippewa borderlands. Brandon Whitney, Brigham Young University, Think Spatial.

hangers on about the Assiniboine and Gros Ventres camps since the memory of man runneth not to the contrary."[28] While this report neither offers precise dates nor specifically identifies these Chippewas, the mention of their association with other Natives in Montana since time immemorial suggests a well-established presence and familiarity between them.

These reports indicating Indigenous movement in the evolving US-Canadian borderlands provide some background to the subsequent histories of "foreign" Indians south of the Forty-Ninth Parallel. Yaquis shared similar mobility but had a much different strategy for integrating into economies. While Crees and Chippewas would suffer from a collapse of the fur trade markets in which they operated, Yaquis experienced continued demand for their labor in mining and other industries. Where Cree and Chippewa economies required access to open land and game, Yaqui labor skills fit better with American settler colonialism, state-building projects, and urban growth.

The Yaquimi on the Edge of Spanish and Mexican Empires

The homelands of Sonora's Yaquis were more violently contested than the lands of their northern Cree and Chippewa counterparts. From the sixteenth century onward, their lands were variously claimed by Spain, Mexico, and the United States, all challenging traditional Yaqui mobility and territoriality. Moreover, Yaquis were often faced with military force and threat of conquest in ways that the Crees and Chippewas engaged in western fur trading were not. The Yaquimi became the locus of colonizing efforts, multinational conflicts, and struggles for power and control of resources. From Yaquis' earliest contact with Spanish military expeditions and Jesuit missionaries through repeated wars stretching into the early twentieth century, Spain and then Mexico struggled to control them.[29] They saw the Yaqui River Valley on the periphery of their empires as a wild landscape that needed to be tamed. Yaquis themselves proved determinedly resistant, and by the dawn of the twentieth-century they remained Mexico's sole unconquered Indigenous people.

The Sonoran Desert and Yaqui River Valley are home to a number of closely related Cáhita-speaking Indigenous peoples, including Suaquis, Mayos, Ocoronis, Ahomes, Tehuecos, Cinaloas, Conicaris, Macoyahuis, Tepahues, and Yaquis—with Mayos being the most closely related to the Yaquis.[30] Yaquis controlled valuable fertile lands along the Yaqui River and extended their sphere of influence well into the surrounding plains, deserts, and Bacatete Mountains. The first contact with colonial Spain, Captain Diego de Guzmán's 1533 expedition into the region, ended violently and set the tone for subsequent exchanges. Guzmán's forces retreated, reportedly in awe of Yaquis' military prowess. Contact with Cabeza de Vaca in 1536 (on the last leg of his journey back to New Spain) and Francisco de Ibarra in the 1560s ended more amicably and fueled Spanish intentions to return.

In 1617, Jesuits arrived in the Yaqui River Valley and reported being well received. Padre Andrés Pérez de Ribas wrote of his early-seventeenth-century missionary activities with the Yaqui in somewhat contradictory yet ultimately positive terms. While calling them "the most barbarous people" of the Americas, he also emphasized their trustworthiness, interest in Christianity, impressive work ethic, general friendliness, and hospitality.[31] Rather than relying on Spaniards, Jesuits such as de Ribas laid considerable trust in local Yaqui leadership and within the first few years after contact baptized some forty-nine hundred children and three thousand adults.[32] In 1684, silver was discovered in the Yaqui River Valley, bringing more aggressive Spanish colonization to the region. In 1740, Yaquis and Mayos joined in rebellion, driving out the new Spanish intruders, killing as many as one thousand Spanish but losing up to five thousand of their own.[33]

Expulsion of the Jesuits in the 1760s, entrance of the Franciscans, and slow decline of Spanish control over the region strengthened Yaqui independence and resistance. As the Spanish intruded on their lands, stressed resources, and attempted to impose taxes on Yaqui lands in the late eighteenth century, Yaqui resistance grew, and the resistance persisted into the early nineteenth century. In the 1820s, Juan Banderas led a Yaqui revolt and succeeded in wresting control of the region from the new Republic of Mexico until his execution in 1833. Friction between Yaquis and the growing Mexican populations waxed and waned in the following decades. Yaqui commitment to homeland and resistance to subjugation is one of the most enduring legacies of Spanish-Native relations in the region. In one twentieth-century author's estimation, Yaquis exhibited "shrewd intelligence, deep-seated feeling for freedom, extraordinary love [of] their land, strong attachment to traditions, clear concept of the racial unity, and above all, an unyielding commitment to defend their homeland (their own lands and lands of their ancestors), race and rights."[34] Throughout, however, despite fiercely holding on to their identity, Yaquis' excelled in navigating colonial Spanish and Mexican legal, political, and economic worlds.[35]

Early Yaqui Activities in the Future United States

In a fashion similar to Crees and Chippewas to the north, Yaquis dynamically negotiated geographic and economic landscapes in the face of European pressures and markets. While Crees and Chippewas expanded across the Great Plains engaged in the fur trade, Yaquis exhibited an ability and willingness to migrate in response to Spanish and Mexican settlement, mining development, and even Jesuit and Franciscan missions, as many had converted and incorporated Christianity into existing religious and cultural practice. As with their northern counterparts, this brought them into lands that would later fall within the United States border. As an unpoliced Spanish frontier evolved into contested US-Mexican borderlands and then a policed US-Mexican border, Yaqui mobility took on new transnational contexts.

Mexican Yaqui presence in what would later become Arizona stretches back as far as 1732.[36] In that year, Yaquis were brought to Pimería Alta, as the Spanish referred to northern Sonora and southern Arizona, to help with missionizing Pima people, and they were later employed by Austrian Jesuit Johann Grazhoffer at his Opata Guevavi mission.[37] In the 1760s, Franciscan friars regularly used Yaquis in Pimería Alta missions.[38] This practice was still going on when the 1796 Jesuit census of the Tumacácori mission (Mission San José de Tumacácori) enumerated half a dozen Yaqui families in the immediate vicinity. By that time, they served the predominantly Pima and Papago (O'odham) mission as the craftsmen supervisors, helping other Native groups learn "civilized" trades.[39] Though only some fifteen miles north of the future US-Mexico border, this northern Yaqui presence is a full three hundred miles north of the traditional eight Yaqui pueblos in the Yaqui River Valley in southern Sonora.

Straying from the mission system, Yaquis followed labor demands elsewhere. In October 1736, it was a Yaqui who discovered immense silver deposits near the present site of Nogales, Arizona, with the ore actually lying about in *planchas* and *bolas* (chunks and slabs). The discovery led directly to the earliest Spanish settlement and development in southern Arizona outside of the mission system. The naming of the future state of Yaqui exile, Arizona, is said to have come from a nearby Spanish mine,

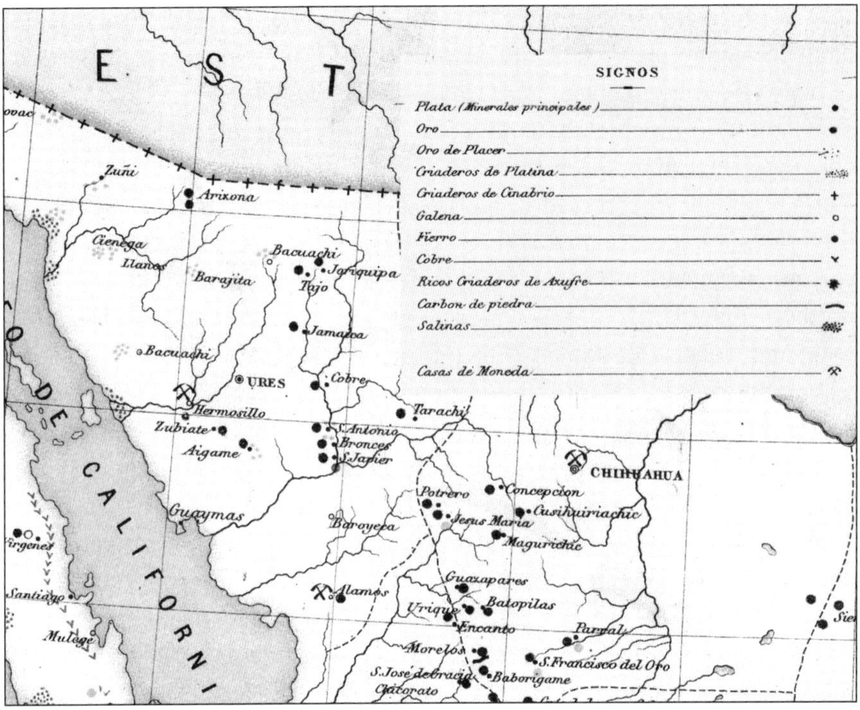

Figure 1.2. Northwestern Mexico mining sites. From Antonio Garcia Cubas, *Carta Minera* (Debray Sucesores, 1885). Courtesy of David Rumsey Map Collection, www.davidrumsey.com.

Real de Arizonac.[40] Whether Yaquis first came to the region as part of the mission system is unclear, but this presence hints at broad Yaqui activities in the far northern reaches of Sonora. From their traditional pueblos in the Yaqui River Valley, these outlying activities demonstrate an expansive Yaqui landscape.

By 1810, the first groups of Yaqui refugees fleeing violence trekked northward from the Yaqui River Valley to the Tumacácori region, where other Yaquis had been present for almost a century. There was no border for them to cross as proper political refugees, but the flight set precedent for future generations to follow. They were welcomed as the primary labor force for the newly reopened Guevavi mine near Tubac. Records of the "Yaquis de Guevavi" during the following years indicate a steady population of dozens of families.[41] Though few in number, these Yaquis represent a permanent historical settlement in the future United States—a full century before that land was purchased from Mexico in 1848 and 1853. They set the precedent for subsequent mobile Yaquis to leave their traditional lands for economic opportunities and permanent settlement, sometimes as refugees fleeing violence.

By the mid-nineteenth century, the Yaqui presence in what would become Arizona diversified in character and became more varied in how Euro-Americans perceived it. During the first half of the nineteenth century, Tucson records show an intermittent fear of a Yaqui presence in the region. During Juan Banderas's late 1820s Yaqui rebellion, citizens of the northern outpost of Tucson feared joint attacks by Yaquis, Apaches, Yumas, and Tohono O'odham (Papago) people, with 1740 Yaqui agitation of neighboring tribes a troubling precedent. On March 4, 1827, Apache scouts sent warning to Mexican officials in Tucson that Yaquis had attacked Cananea (twenty miles south of the future US border and roughly midway between the border towns of Agua Prieta and Nogales) and were maneuvering to attack Tucson. Though no attack materialized, Yaqui ties with other Native peoples proved worrisome for Mexicans in Tucson.

The Yaqui relationship with Tohono O'odhams also vexed Franciscans attempting to "civilize" Tohono O'odhams. They blamed Yaqui influences for increasing violence among their ostensible devotees. Though Spanish missionaries had previously trusted Yaquis as a civilizing influence on northern Native converts, mid-nineteenth-century Mexican officials saw Yaquis in a strikingly more menacing light. The Tohono O'odham–Yaqui connection again raised concern during the 1842 Gándara revolt in Sonora, in which Yaquis participated. Yaquis mining in the Altar Valley, 150 miles southwest of Tucson (less than fifty miles southwest of Nogales), threatened to join Tohono O'odhams in attacking Mexican settlements. These relations between Native peoples provided more links between Yaquimi and Yaquis' future Arizona homeland.[42]

Crees, Chippewas, and Yaquis as Transnational Natives

In time the United States, Canada, and Mexico would assign transnational identity to Crees, Chippewas, and Yaquis, and some from these groups would view themselves as transnational. All "foreign" Natives would increasingly have to understand how others saw them, but it is doubtful that many experienced major shifts in their self-identity as they crossed evolving boundaries. Crees were Crees, Chippewas were Chippewas, and Yaquis were Yaquis, even as the United States, Canada, and Mexico forged their own national identities and attempted to impose them on Native peoples. Herein lies an intrinsic function or effect that boundaries impose upon the people who cross them. Arbitrary lines drawn across ancient Native landscapes ascribed new realities that all had to negotiate. The negotiation of these transnational landscapes—complex sets of geopolitical, cultural, ethnic, and economic borderlands—is the framework upon which the following narratives of Crees, Chippewas, and Yaquis in Montana and Arizona build.

Chapter 2

Transnational Encounters and Evolving Prejudice in Montana and Arizona, 1800–1900

I never was tired of a Tribe as I am of this one.

—FIRST LIEUTENANT GUSTAVUS DOANE,
Fort Assiniboine, Montana Territory, March 26, 1882

Even in this vicinity [Nogales, Arizona], 300 miles distant from the scene of hostilities, the Yaquis employed in various kinds of work are in a state of disquiet. . . . Some fears are expressed of a descent up on a town similar to that of August 1896. . . . It is from the motives of revenge that the Yaquis now on the war path have killed Americans. . . . In the former wars they have always respected Americans, never molesting them.

—SPECIAL REPORT FROM NOGALES,
Arizona, August 11, 1899[1]

As noted in the preceding chapter, Cree and Chippewa fur traders expanded aggressively from regions between Hudson Bay and the Great Lakes throughout the seventeenth and eighteenth centuries. Some fifty years after Lewis and Clark opined on trade potential with Crees, Crees were regularly traveling south of the Forty-Ninth Parallel. In 1850, Cree traders were noted as far south as the American Fur Company post of Fort Sarpy, located on the Yellowstone River just west of its confluence with the Bighorn River. Unorganized territory at that point, this was well south of the Forty-Ninth Parallel and almost in reach of the future Montana-Wyoming border.[2] A few years later, Edwin A. C. Hatch, a soldier stationed at Fort Benton in the newly organized Nebraska Territory (future Montana Territory) made a number of nonchalant mentions of Crees and Chippewas near the post. His notes suggested a familiarity with them and describes them as traders and couriers of intertribal and international geopolitical information.[3] Together with Blackfeet, Gros Ventres, Piegans, Bloods, Flatheads (Salish), and Chippewas, Hatch included Crees as part of a large network of transnational Natives whose presence was noteworthy, if not welcomed. By diverting trade away from Hudson's Bay Company posts to the north, they played well into competing international markets and American economic designs for the region.[4]

To the south, Yaquis were likewise making inroads in the American economy, specifically its labor markets. Mining was the primary draw in the nineteenth century and a major factor in the development of the American Southwest and Mexican Northwest. A number of other economic opportunities, such as US Army service, irrigation or canal-building labor, and railroad labor also played a role in drawing Yaquis to the United States. After the Treaty of Guadalupe Hidalgo gave northern Mexico to the United States in 1848, land that would be known as the Mexican Cession, Yaquis continued mining north of the newly established international border. Various accounts even attest to a noticeable Yaqui presence during the mid-century California gold rush—including future Yaqui leader José María Leyva Cajeme.[5] The US-Mexican War culminated by the Treaty of Guadalupe Hidalgo had stymied some mining in Arizona, but Yaqui labor in Arizona Territory resumed soon thereafter. One account, related in 1912 by an elderly Mexican resident of Arizona, placed Yaqui miners deep in Cochise's Apache country by the late 1850s. It was said that long before Euro-American miners struck it rich at Bisbee, Tombstone, or elsewhere in Arizona's rugged southern ranges, one plucky American prospector had employed Yaqui and Mexican miners in Arizona's Little Dragoon Mountains, at the later site of the Johnson Camp mine between Benson and Wilcox, Arizona. This report has Yaquis straying from the Tumacácori region and pushing some seventy miles north of the border.[6]

Within years of the Treaty of Guadalupe Hidalgo and subsequent 1853 Gadsden Purchase, Yaqui labor was a regular part of Arizona economies. Yaquis were present in the so-called 1859 Sonoita Massacre, in which one Yaqui was killed (and four Mexicans).[7] In mines such as Santa Rita and Hentzelman in 1860 and Mowry in 1864, Yaquis joined Opatas, Tohono O'odhams, and mestizos from Mexico in comprising 80–94 percent of the labor force.[8] In 1865, teamster and merchant Nathan Appel brought a number of Yaquis with him from Sonora to prospect for gold on lands he had acquired southwest of Prescott, Arizona. They "were good gold hunters," recalled Appel, testifying to Yaquis' growing reputation as valuable and hardworking laborers in the Arizona-Sonora borderlands. This reputation was echoed in 1878 in Clifton, Arizona. When local miners were considering hiring Chinese labor, Tucson paper *Las Dos Repúblicas* commented that Yaqui labor was far superior and could be attained for the same cheap price.[9] Mining would be the first of many industries in which Yaqui refugees and immigrants would find their place in Arizona. No wonder that many of these sites of Yaqui mining became sites of later permanent Yaqui settlements.

Growing Yaqui labor in Arizona extended beyond mining. In early 1864, when Arizona governor John Noble Goodwin authorized the muster of four companies of Arizona Indians to fight in the Apache Wars, Yaquis were included with Pimas, Maricopas, and Mexicans of mixed heritage.[10] General George Crook similarly enlisted Yaquis in the 1870s during resumed Apache campaigns.[11] As Indian scouts and enlistees were of greatest value to Crook for their knowledge of the land, Yaqui inclusion speaks to their perceived or actual familiarity with the borderlands region. Showing willingness to venture from Sonora, Yaqui Indian dance troupes traveled as far as Oakland and San Francisco in 1876, performing in much-celebrated shows.[12] A precursor to the Semana Santa and public dances that later brought considerable public attention to Arizona Yaqui refugee communities in the early to mid-twentieth century, these cultural expositions highlight Yaqui mobility and economic flexibility.

In the early 1880s, amid mounting violence in Sonora, Yaqui migration was typified by individual laborers moving largely along rail lines and without kin.[13] They made up as much as 40 percent of some north–south railroad labor forces, so the corridors were naturally established.[14] Whereas later violence and pressure uprooted full families, most Yaqui families opted at this time to weather the storm and remain in their homelands. Individual Yaquis who did wander north often did so in stages. One example offered by anthropologist Edward Spicer tells of Yaquis originally working on the railroad between Guaymas and the Arizona border at Nogales but subsequently continuing northward until reaching the established Yaqui settlements in Arizona.[15] Aside from Tumacácori, the settlements of Nogalitos and Patagonia (at the southwestern end of the Sonoita Valley) both had Yaqui populations with longtime residents and recent immigrations. These Yaqui enclaves increasingly attracted itinerant Yaqui laborers during the 1880s as a base for their migrant labor. Soon mining areas in the Santa Rita Mountains northeast of Nogales and Tumacácori attracted Yaqui laborers as well.[16] The Arizona Yaqui population was of sufficient significance by the late 1880s to be specifically mentioned as a unique group. In a report on pearl fisheries in Baja California, the *Salt Lake Herald* refers to Yaqui divers "from the state of Arizona" as the primary workforce.[17] Having a history of working in the pearl fisheries, some Yaquis had moved to Arizona, stayed long enough to establish a discernible Arizona identity, and then moved back south and west for other labor opportunities.[18] This picture suggests people who were highly mobile and adaptable, characteristics to be displayed too in the years to follow. Together with records of the establishment of permanent Yaqui enclaves north of the border, these accounts reveal extensive Yaqui labor in the United States, valued by multiple industries in the region.[19]

For Crees too, American borderland residents' initial positive reception of their transnational presence was predicated on the economies to which they contributed. As early frontier development in Montana transitioned away from the fur trade and toward settler-colonial projects like city-building, ranching, mining, and agriculture, settlers' view of these transnational Natives changed as well. As white Montanans' attention shifted toward encouraging white settlement, importing eastern economies, and attaining statehood, these territorial citizens' perception of international boundaries changed. Arizona settlers were moving in the same direction as those in Montana, but Yaqui contributions to mining and infrastructure development there proved more valuable than Crees' activities in the north. Both Yaquis and Crees, however, began to be increasingly perceived as "foreign"—as illegal aliens, political refugees, and burdens upon public welfare—and they were targets of violent threats. This made life in the United States unstable and unpredictable. Both groups faced these reactions to their transnationality, but their subsequent experiences in US labor markets quickly diverged.

Evolving Prejudice in the North

Even while Crees and Chippewas were welcomed south of the Forty-Ninth Parallel on the Great Plains, unrelated geopolitical developments conspired to complicate their transnational movements. In 1842, the Aroostook War and Webster-Ashburton Treaty concerning the Maine–New Brunswick border drew both American and Canadian attention to their shared border. Casting a long gaze beyond the plains to the Pacific Coast, James L. Polk's fiery "Fifty-Four Forty or Fight!" rhetoric during his 1844 presidential campaign amplified growing tensions ("Fifty-Four Forty" referred to what was then the northern border of Oregon Territory). With conflict focusing attention on the far eastern and western ends of the US-Canadian border, the interior plains boundaries were overlooked for a time, but federal concern soon grew over border security coast to coast, and border-violating Natives became seen as a problem.[20]

By the middle of the nineteenth century, Canadians and Americans began looking more to their countries' interiors for settler-colonial expansion and agriculture. At the same time, decreasing demand for beaver and other pelts led to collapse of the fur trade market in which Crees and Chippewas had participated. This hastened the shift toward agrarian development of the region. In the United States, the rhetoric of Indian policy shifted toward increased regulation, confinement, and control of Indian "wards" as "domestic dependent nations," and the previous focus on Crees or Chippewas as trading partners diminished.[21] The labeling of Native peoples as "domestic" or "foreign" was intrinsic in new policies. Quickly the labels "Canadian Indian" and "American Indian" were applied to Natives navigating the borderlands. "Canadian Indians" were to remain in Canada, "American Indians" fell under the jurisdiction of the US government, and the presence of "foreign" Indians was no longer acceptable under any circumstance. And while accounts a decade earlier had varied in tone, Overland Trail migrants by the 1860s spoke menacingly of Crees.[22]

The full collapse of the fur trade in the 1870s dramatically devalued Cree contributions to Montana's economic development. This marked a pivotal moment. By 1880, federal attitudes toward Crees had clearly shifted. Simultaneously, Sitting Bull's successful flight to Canada and Chief Joseph's attempted flight north across the border heightened US concerns about nontreaty Indians from Canada and the United States disrupting white settlement. White Montanans feared collaboration between Sitting Bull and Crees, especially with reports of Big Bear asking Sioux to "help him fight British soldiers."[23] Confirmed Cree relations with Louis Riel, the leader of the failed 1869 Red River Rebellion in Manitoba who had lived in exile in Montana since 1878, were similarly worrying.[24] In short order, transnational Crees went from welcomed economic actors to suspicious border-crossers and then military threats who needed to be expelled. A policy of tracking, numbering, and deporting "foreign Indians" quickly emerged.[25]

In the summer of 1881, the US Army translated these policies into action, and the language with which they described Crees reveals important truths in how the US government was beginning to define and view them. Fort Assiniboine received the following instructions: "Send out as strong a force as possible under a careful officer to notify the foreign Indians to return to their own country, and so prevent them from driving the game away from the hunting grounds of our own Indians."[26] There are two significant phrases within this order. First, the Indians were to return to "their own country." This could be interpreted to mean either Canada or more broadly to the Indians' traditional territories north of the line. If the former was meant, this proves somewhat problematic, as the Indians in question surely held little sense, if any, of Canadian national identity. If "their own country" meant traditional territory, this was equally problematic, since many Crees' sense of territorial homelands entailed land south of the Forty-Ninth Parallel. In either case, "Canadian Indians" was likely incongruous with how Crees viewed themselves.

The 1881 communiqué to Fort Assiniboine also illuminates how the US government viewed reservation Indians in Montana Territory. Fort Assiniboine forces were to prevent foreign Indians "from driving game away from the hunting grounds of our own Indians." "Canadian" Indians' claims to territory or hunting grounds south of the border do not seem to have been seriously considered, if at all. "Our own Indians" rhetorically interposed an immutable divide and shows how the US government viewed its relationship with domestic and foreign Indians. Just as the border itself was immovable in its geography, the classification of Indians and the paternalistic responsibility for (or deportation of) those Indians was firm, immutable, and divisive. To further enforce these definitions, instructions were given to remove "all foreign Half Breeds and Indians from the [Gros Ventre, Piegan Blood, Blackfeet, and River Crow Indian] Reservation" and to make note of their names to facilitate prosecution should they again violate the US border.[27] Having labeled peoples as either domestic or foreign Indians and physically separating them and otherwise treating them as such, the US government sought to prevent the two groups from any future contact and to eliminate the policy crisis of having to deal with foreign Indians.

The determination of American borderlands residents to shore up any porous sections of the border stemmed from the looming uncertainty created by Native mobility. South of the line, troops stationed at regional forts could deal with troublesome "American" Indians with well-established protocol. In principle, the perceived threat presented by wandering non-treaty Indians, whether domestic or foreign, was the same. In practice, however, the presence of foreign Indians south of the line posed a much greater problem. With no basis for negotiation, no treaty or reservation, US officials had no established policy in these cases. Moreover, if they pursued deportation, the continued looming presence of those groups a few miles north of the line persistently undermined the perceived stability of the region. More importantly, it eroded the confidence of settlers, ranchers, and US Army officials in their ability to impose order over their surroundings. Their proximity to the border—and its jurisdictional bisection of Native groups into foreign and domestic—left these parties unable to assure their own sense of security. For this reason, strict border policing was a top priority.

Underlying these tensions was a fundamental incompatibility between Indigenous and Euro-American views of the nature of the international boundary. If Natives were unconcerned about the border's sanctity or defied it, the United States was increasingly wary of any Native crossings. In an 1880 interview, speaking of Hunkpapa chief Sitting Bull's flight to Canada, General Nelson A. Miles revealed frustration with the failure of Canadian authorities to prevent Native crossings.[28] Likewise the crossing of so-called "Canadian" Indians southward from Canada, regardless of any previous or traditional presence in the United States, was interpreted as lack of border enforcement by Canadian officials.

As Americans chafed at Canada's inability to prevent Natives from crossing the "Medicine Line" and using it to their advantage, some Natives vocalized disregard for the border.[29] On July 27, 1882, Chief Little Shell led Chippewas south from Manitoba into the Pembina region of North Dakota—an area long frequented by his people. Charged customs fees for the first time, he refused to pay: "We recognize no boundaries, and shall pass as we please."[30] This pronouncement may be emblematic of broadly held Native views. US and Canadian officials regarded the international border as sacrosanct, but their Native counterparts did not. Natives had long negotiated boundaries but likely viewed them as shared buffer zones rather than sharply defined lines on a map or blockades. Little Shell's Chippewas and others like them viewed the Medicine Line in terms that were incongruous with US and Canadian conceptions. The notion of strictly bisected geopolitical landscapes simply did not coincide with Native views. When Natives did recognize the border, it was more often in terms of the Medicine Line, acknowledging the fact that US and Canadian officials policed the line but not that they themselves should not freely cross it.

The US response to Little Shell in 1882 was emblematic of the disconnect between Native and non-Native understandings of the border. Officials at Pembina reported that military intervention would be necessary. Not only were the "pugnacious" Canadian Indians (also then considered "British Indians") refusing to pay customs and recognize the international border, they were also ordering white settlers off their land.[31] This is not the first example of Natives moving southward across the US-Canadian border, but the brief confrontation typifies the broader philosophical conflict. Two irreconcilable views of the US-Canadian border were pitted against one another. Indigenous inhabitants of the newly delimited borderlands region refused to recognize the authority of Euro-American boundaries, while Eu-

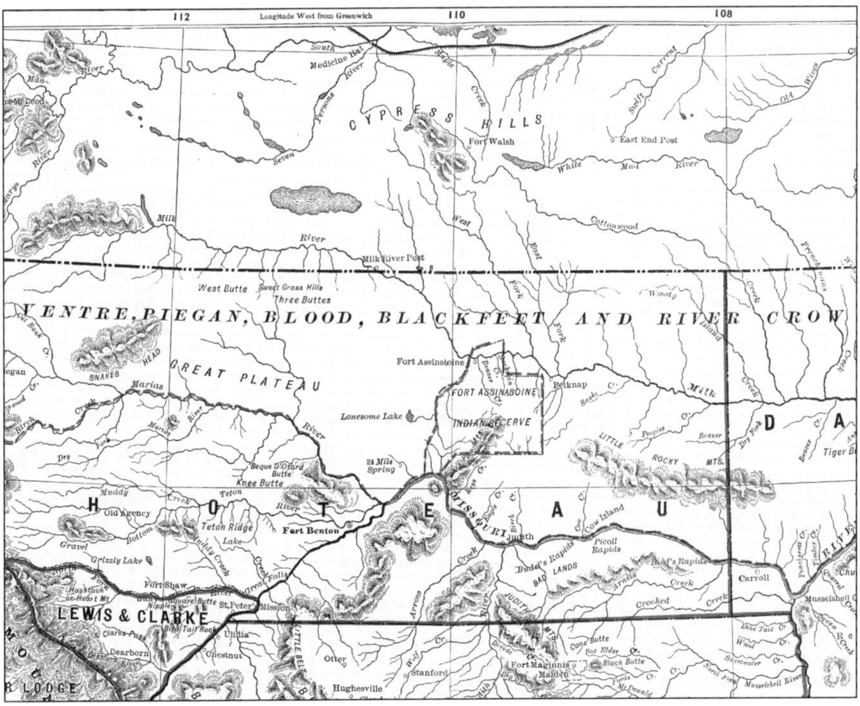

Figure 2.1. Waterways across the Montana-Alberta border. Excerpt and adaptation of George Franklin Cram, *Montana* (Chicago: A. C. Shewey, 1883). Courtesy of David Rumsey Map Collection, www.davidrumsey.com.

ro-Americans insisted that the sanctity of their borders be respected by all. Perhaps the latter ought to have seen how rivers, mountains, and wildlife —the environment itself—traversed and violated border sanctity (see figure 2.1). This conflict of worldviews is foundational in understanding the turbulent history of Native-white conflict in North American borderlands.

Each spring, summer, and fall, Crees ranged across the border, following natural corridors along the South Saskatchewan and Milk Rivers and various other valleys and ranges. They would cross, hunt, possibly rustle livestock, and dispassionately return north—enraging Montanans and US military officials. But American efforts to bring order to its territories involved first defining Native populations and then removing them or containing them in reservations. If Native groups could be defined as "foreign," this obviated the responsibility for the United States to proceed in the costly, complicated, and potentially violent steps of removal or containment. Crees' foreign origins allowed the United States to solve the "Indian problem" by disclaiming responsibility.

Montanans' anger over Cree "depredations" meanwhile grew, and the anger focused on the Cree chief Big Bear. His people were struggling to survive, but Montanans were intolerant of their chosen transnational subsistence. Military actions pushing them north over the line were followed by immediate southern crossings. "I never was tired of a Tribe as I am of this one," wrote one cavalryman from Fort Assiniboine in 1882.[32] The perceived injustice of this inversion of the usual power differential was echoed in the press. Commenting on Big Bear's repeated crossings and evasion of US forces, the *Daily Helena Independent* related that "the hostiles from the Queen's dominions declare their intention of running the Milk river region to suit themselves." The paper quipped: "Wonder what Uncle Sam is going to do about it? Perhaps the Secretary of the Interior will recommend the removal of the troops from Montana *for fear they may degrade the morals of the reds*. As he has recommended the removal of troops from the Indian agencies in Dakota, it would be no surprise if he next recommended the removal of the troops from all the Indian countries."[33]

In 1883, word arrived in Montana that Big Bear had accepted treaty terms in Canada. The *Benton Weekly Record* explained the significance that this event had for residents of northern Montana: "There is much importance attached to Big Bear's accepting the treaty, in as much as to him can be ascribed the major part of the depredations committed by North Cree Indians. He has disturbed the people of this Territory by his raids upon stock, and his war parties have more than once within the past few years alarmed the settlers north of Benton . . . and while it may be a somewhat embarrassing confession, it is none the less true that Montana settlers have only the Montana Indians to fear since Big Bear's yielding to the treaty.[34]

The following spring, however, in 1883, resumed Cree raiding rivaled that of previous years and included members of Big Bear's own band, led by his son Little Bear (Imasees). Looking ahead to the presumed spring 1884 outbreak of border raiding, a Fort Maginnis soldier opined, "One thing is certain; if the boys get a chance they will show them no mercy."[35] Montana had no interest in affording transnational Crees any place in the region.[36]

The first half of the 1880s witnessed a dramatic shift in public opinion regarding transnational Crees. The fur trade had ended, Montanans moved toward statehood, and military eviction of the Crees was seen as the sole solution. The border that had previously been ignored by whites and Indians alike was now ascribed significance by both. Montanans looked to the Forty-Ninth Parallel as a protection, however ineffectual, from "foreign" Indians and argued for its strengthening. Indians from Canada looked to the line as something to cross to escape pressures from the Canadian government and military, and they also used the border as a means to raid American settlers and flee unmolested with their spoils. As the next wave of Crees crossed into Montana under very different circumstances in 1885—under duress and as political refugees—the prejudice that had built up against them in the preceding years would trouble their settlement efforts. By 1885, Montana had fully soured on transnational Indians, be they Cree, Chippewa, or other.

Complicated Prejudice in the South

As changing economics and border developments placed Crees in disfavor among Montanans, Yaquis fared differently in the south. Yaqui labor emerged as a boon for the Arizona economy. Growing mining, railroad, and agricultural industries clamored for Yaqui labor. This afforded transnational Yaquis a number of advantages denied to their northern Cree counterparts. The multiple labor markets offered Yaquis greater ability to develop permanent settlements in Arizona. Crees enjoyed no such sense of permanence. Furthermore, the employed Yaqui population was better able to weather negative press and growing prejudice against them.

From initial Spanish and Jesuit contact in the sixteenth century to the rise of President Porfirio Díaz in 1876, Yaquis had mustered large-scale uprisings and wars in 1825, 1834, 1857–62 and 1899 (and they would do so again in the 1910s and 1920s), and remained the last unconquered Indigenous population in Mexico.[37] Their reputation for bravery and recalcitrance was widespread, and the resumed Yaqui Wars of the Porfiriato created new concerns in the United States. Yaqui resistance threatened the Díaz regime's plans to develop the Yaqui River Valley and entice foreign (including US) investment in the region. American borderland residents had long viewed infamous Yaquis in their midst with some suspicion, but direct Yaqui threats to American investment south of the border quickly turned press coverage to outright condemnation. This left Yaquis in Arizona in an uneasy position.

As Sonora was engulfed in warfare and some Americans were killed (usually while prospecting in Sonora), Arizona newspapers relayed gruesome details of alleged Yaqui brutality and barbarity. For many Arizonans, the regular reports of Yaqui trouble south of the line (and even violence or criminal activities crossing north of the line) left lasting imprints on perceptions and prejudices they bore in future encounters with Yaqui immigrants and refugees.[38] Increasing Yaqui arms dealing across the international line further deteriorated Arizonans' opinions. Finding it difficult to secure arms and supplies in Sonora, some Yaquis crossed north into Arizona to work and then, with their earnings, purchased arms, ammunition, and supplies to take back to their troops in the Sierra de Bacatete. Although ordered to prevent the return of Yaqui rebels, Mexican border officials found this difficult to enforce.[39] Such border violations cast Yaquis in dim light among many Americans and Mexicans.

Herein emerges another sharp divide between how Americans in Montana and Arizona negatively viewed Crees and Yaquis, respectively. In both cases, the previous acceptance (or willingness to ignore) "foreign" Natives in the United States was tied to commerce and labor markets, and as those changed, so did Cree and Yaqui experiences in the United States. Borderlands US citizens identified both as unique Indigenous peoples, but implicit distinctions were made by economic actors (and politicians by extension) to mark which Natives' foreign presence would be rejected, allowed, tolerated, or ignored. By the 1880s, white Montanans did not see any positive contribution to Montanan development and statehood from fur-trading, bison-hunting, and later livestock-thieving Crees. Thus, their presence was rejected. In contrast, Yaquis' labor was highly sought by the very industries on which Arizonans based their development. Thus, however negative and bellicose the Yaquis' reputation, they enjoyed less resistance to their activities in the United States. The American Indian reservation system created its own labor market systems of agriculture and other pursuits for Indigenous peoples, separate from the broader Arizona and Montana economies, but Crees and Yaquis were denied participation in that system. This explains why and how non-Native economics had such profound impact on Cree and Yaqui experiences in the United States.

Prejudice, Economics, and Perceived Ethnicity

American perceptions of ethnicity also affected divergent Cree and Yaqui experiences. Americans regularly failed to differentiate between Indigenous peoples, but when viewed in the context of groups crossing borders from Canada and Mexico, a sharp contrast emerges in American perception of Cree and Yaqui ethnicity and indigeneity. This merits explanation. When Crees crossed into Montana during the late nineteenth and early twentieth centuries, their Indigenous identity linked them to economic systems incompatible with the new goals of Euro-American development in Montana. Non-Native Canadian immigrants were readily integrated into Montana's various economic systems, but Native Canadian immigrants were not. Crees were defined as Indigenous and thus denied entrance into various settler-colonial labor markets that non-Native Canadians could readily enter. If denied full participation in non-Native labor markets due to prejudice or lack of necessary skills, would not Crees' Indigenous identity funnel them into reservation-based Native-specific labor markets that were designed to specifically cater to Native skills and abilities? US Indian policy assumed incongruence between Native and non-Native "American" societies, and by the 1880s the government had an established program of reservation settlement and de facto quarantine. As the United States defined its relations with American Indians, reservation-based Native labor systems stood as the sole avenue for Cree acceptance and economic integration in Montana. Crees, however, were not "American" Indians, and thus integration via reservation settlement was denied. Crees were left in limbo. They were Native but foreign.

Conversely, Arizonans often failed to differentiate between Spanish-speaking Mexicans, mestizos, and Mexican Indians. The ignorance of white

Americans in distinguishing allowed many Yaquis to blend in with general Mexican immigrant-labor networks. This allowed some of them enough latitude to carve out permanent settlements, neighborhoods, and communities, however tenuous and threatened. The perceived overlap between Mexican and Yaqui ethnicity allowed Yaquis to use their economic expertise and enter non-Native labor markets. Herein emerges an important revelation. Labor markets allowed or disallowed Yaqui and Cree or Chippewa participation depending on the perceived levels of their indigeneity. The perceived ethnic differential permitted Yaqui participation in non-Native labor markets but relegated Crees to Native-specific reservation labor markets—from which they were promptly denied entrance.

Conclusion

The paired experiences of early Cree and Yaqui transnational economic dealings and labor networks, with the Yaquis being more valued by American industries and employers, bear a striking resemblance superficially. Both were pushed and pulled across US borders by similar forces—non-Native encroachment in their lands, mounting conflict, and potentially lucrative ventures. Reacting to these forces, they moved across international borders into lands that were historically familiar to them but peripheral to their core homelands. For both, their early reception in the United States was warm and often solicited. Under the surface, however, fundamental differences would project each group toward contrasting experiences.

At the most basic level, the economies in which Crees and Yaquis were participating were on opposite ends of the familiar boom-and-bust cycle that pervades so much of Western history. The fur trade, which had pulled Crees and Chippewas south to the plains and then across the border, was waning by the 1870s. Its demise quickly transformed the transnational Cree presence from one of economic contribution to one of suspicion and potential threat. On the other hand, Yaquis drew from their extensive mining experience to establish their transnational presence in an industry that was at the early stages of a series of booms across southern Arizona. With every discovery of gold, silver, and later copper, their favorable reception in US labor markets was reinforced. Economic integration stood at the base of Yaqui, Cree, and Chippewa transnational experience as "foreign" Indians in the United States, but only for Yaquis was the timing just right.

Part 2

Native Peoples as "Foreign" Refugees and Immigrants

Crees and Yaquis, often with economic motivation, ventured across international boundaries and found varied levels of reception in the United States. As time went on, however, more of them began to be a different category of migrant—the refugee. Violence underlies European and American settler-colonial projects in North America, Natives crossed borders to escape this violence and seek safety or protection. Familiar narratives, like those of Sitting Bull in Canada or Geronimo in Mexico, feature Natives who fled from the United States, whereas Yaquis, Crees, and Chippewas crossed borders to seek protection in the United States. From the north, Little Bear led Crees across the border into Montana, fleeing prosecution for their involvement in the 1885 North-West Rebellion and associated Frog Lake Massacre. If apprehended in Canada they faced trial and potentially execution. From the south, Yaquis fled warfare, a campaign of extermination against them, and a Mexican program of deportation and slave labor in the Yucatán.

These transnationals represented a new class of Natives: political refugees, seeking asylum, protection, and permanent settlement in the United States. Viewed from the perspective of Canada and Mexico, they were fugitives. Their immigrant identity was multifold: Indigenous, foreign, fugitive, and refugee. This last new distinction likewise marked an abrupt shift in the kinds of Native border-crossings and associated reception. Moreover, their physical context and their experience of their border-crossing was evolving.

Individuals and groups from Canada and Mexico fled across the border under duress and were granted often-vague degrees of amnesty. American observers celebrated the bravery and even nobility of Cree and Yaqui leaders, albeit begrudgingly at times and in opposition to Cree and Yaqui aims for independence. Yaquis' extermination and enslavement in Mexico was different than Crees fleeing prosecution for massacring whites, but Yaquis had a much longer and recent history warfare with Mexico, and American citizens had sometimes been caught in the crossfire. Why then were Yaquis allowed to integrate marginally into Arizonan society but not receive tribal recognition and reservation lands until 1978, whereas Crees were forcefully marginalized by Anglo and Native Montanan society but received a reservation in 1916, some thirty years after crossing south?

Chapter 3

Yaqui Refugees and American Response, 1880s–1910s

Taken all in all, the tragedy of the Yaquis is perhaps without a parallel in American history.

—HERBERT WHITAKER, 1909

Over there don't matter neither. Yaqui. He don't matter to Uncle Sam.

—ANTONIO VALDEZ to Janette Woodruff, 1915[1]

For Yaquis, late-nineteenth-century flight as refugees into the United States was a long time in development. It unfolded unevenly, concurrent with transnational labor movements, over decades. Looking back to the 1880s, overlapping and interrelated phases of Yaqui exodus to the United States are apparent. Juan Flores, who fled persecution in Mexico at the age of seventeen in 1888, provides a good example of hybrid motives. Fleeing under duress, Flores feared throughout his passage north to Nogales, Tucson, and San Xavier that he would be "tied to the tail of a horse and made to run back home" by his pursuers. At the same time, however, he chose Arizona as the terminus of his flight due to economic considerations. In Arizona, he earned fifty cents a day plus room and board. In Mexico, his fifty centavos per day was worth roughly half that, and no food was provided.[2] Lucas Chavez, whose story was featured in the preface, labored in the 1890s in Nogales, Yuma, Sasco, and Patagonia, Arizona. Other late-nineteenth-century Yaqui immigrant laborers like him lived in a precarious balance between gainful employment and capture and deportation. Following long established trails, both literal and figurative, Yaquis entering Arizona could find employment and in many regions could find fellow exiles with whom to form budding Yaqui communities.

Starting as a trickle, these northward migrations may at first have seemed aberrant to Arizonan onlookers, only hinting at what was to follow, during which the hybridity of refugee and economic immigrant would persist. As Yaqui conflicts with Mexico continued and evolved from the 1880s through the early twentieth century, the few became many, and a veritable exodus of Yaquis fled violence, persecution, deportation to Yucatán, enslavement, and even execution in their native Sonora. Often including entire families, these waves increasingly represented people seeking a peaceful place to live, with economic opportunity decreasing as a prime motivator. In the eyes of anthropologist Kenneth M. Stewart, the mid-1880s turbulence marked the beginning of the primary Yaqui exodus across the US-Mexican border into Arizona.[3] The final overlapping wave in the late 1890s and early twentieth century represented Yaquis fleeing violence—crossing the line expressly as political refugees. At this stage they represent the most compelling similarity to the Crees in the North.

Tension in the Yaqui River Valley

Centered in the traditional eight pueblos of Cócorit, Bácum, Tórim, Vícam, Pótam, Ráun, Huirivis, and Belén, and extending to the surrounding Yaqui River drainage and Bacatete Mountains, Yaquis had forged an identity independent from Spain and Mexico while also adeptly navigating Euro-American worlds. The Yaqui River Valley was not on the border, but it had long been on the perimeter of imperial or state control. The creation of a US-Mexican border shifted the dynamics of the region's position in relation to Mexico City. The political geographies that had bolstered the maintenance of an independent Yaquimi were eroding, but Yaquis remained determined to assert their independence and protect their lands. Explaining their relationship to their lands, Mexican army surgeon Manuel Balbás wrote in the 1920s, "[Yaquis] wish to maintain a homeland within this region isolated from the rest of the world, absolutely free, independent and sovereign."[4]

In the preceding decades, settlers, many of whom were former or current Mexican soldiers, encroached on Yaqui lands, and Yaquis' refusal to yield or to participate in mainstream Mexican socio-economic practices increasingly frustrated non-indigenous Sonorans.[5] American settlement schemes were among those attempting to develop the Yaqui River Valley (see figure 3.1). Opatas, Mayos, and others also resisted development by outsiders, but the Yaquis were the most successful. In the words of Czech anthropologist Aleš Hrdlička, who traveled in the region at the turn of the century, "This is the only tribe on the continent that, surrounded by whites from the beginning of their history, have never been fully subdued, for they still intermittently carry on a fight for their lands and independence, as they conceive it,—a conflict which commenced with Guzman's invasion in 1533."[6] As Hrdlička wrote in 1904, a series of "pacification campaigns" by Sonoran state troops had resulted in stalemate, and it appeared that Yaquis would again succeed in resisting control. The administration of Porfirio Díaz would break the stalemate, however.

Having seized control of the presidency in an 1876 coup, Porfirio Díaz rapidly forwarded Auguste Comte–inspired programs of social evolution and positivist modernization throughout the country. Porfirians' attendant scientific thinking from growing fields of sociology, history, and political philosophy sought to advance and develop the Mexican state by identi-

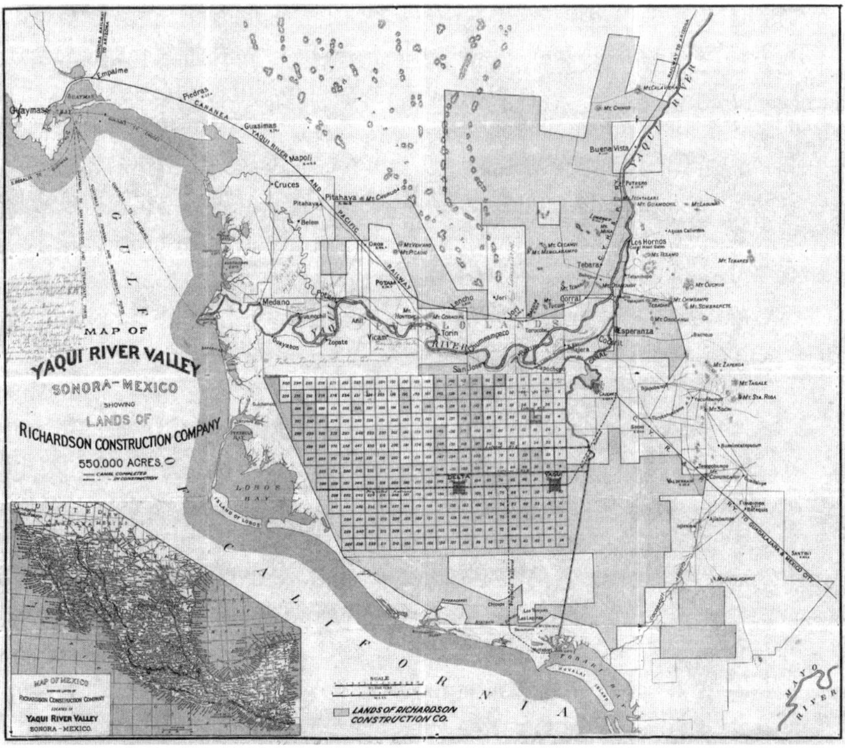

Figure 3.1. Yaqui River Valley and encroaching development, Sonora, Mexico, 1910. Richardson Construction Company. Courtesy of David Rumsey Map Collection, www.davidrumsey.com.

fying perceived problems and applying correctives. Spanish and Mexican officials had long viewed the Sonoran Desert as a region devoid of value.[7] As a veritable oasis, however, the highly productive Yaqui River Valley quickly caught the eye of Porfirians bent on development. The Porfirian regime viewed the fertile valley as a region in dire need of where they could showcase "progress." The independent, resistant, and otherwise "antiprogressive" Yaquis and Mayos in the region were simply incompatible with Porfirian plans. Numbering some thirty thousand, Yaquis defied state control, refused to pay taxes and had enjoyed de facto autonomy since Mexican national independence from Spain. For the Díaz regime, Yaquis were the sole obstacle blocking regional development.[8]

Positivist *científicos*—"scientists," or technical advisors—felt that Yaquis and their lands required transformation. Justo Sierra suggested that they needed to be converted into "*valores sociales*"—social assets—as the principle colonists of an "intensively cultivated land."[9] Porfirians justified new military campaigns. Budding Mexican scholar Fortunato Hernández wrote that "without [Yaquis'] black treachery, without their false protests of surrender and without their ingratitude for the Supreme Government's benevolence and indulgence," Mexican armed "pacification" would not have occurred.[10] Manuel Balbás put it more succinctly: "They must be civilized." Civilization of the "semi-savage" Yaquis, he wrote, was an obligation Porfirians bore with great reluctance. It was to be a campaign offering progress and prosperity. A "diferencia inmensa" stood at the crux of Porfirian justification for the subsequent warfare, persecution, and enslavement of Yaquis in Sonora.[11]

In the face of this new affront to their independence, divided Yaqui factions coalesced under the leadership of José María Leyva Cajeme. His military experience extended back to the 1867 defeat of Ferdinand Maximillian's Second Empire in the French intervention and continued in resistance to General Ignacio Pesqueira's anti-Yaqui campaigns. Initially Pesqueira, the governor of Sonora, appointed Cajeme as the alcalde mayor of the eight Yaqui pueblos and Mayo villages in 1874, hoping to control Yaquis through him. However, it quickly became apparent that Cajeme's allegiance to the governor was tenuous at best. Rather, the "urge for independence [which] was dear to *every* Yaqui heart" led him to reorganize the Yaqui people to continue in "active territorial defense and communal autonomy."[12] Upon the eve of the first military engagement of renewed Yaqui resistance in 1875, Cajeme was offered a chance to negotiate but rebuffed a government emissary, telling him to tell Governor Pesqueira that he would not surrender—"espero para combater." He wanted to fight. Once again, Yaquis rose in full rebellion with a charismatic, experienced military commander at their head—an indomitable warrior, with valor "that nobody dare[d] to deny."[13]

Much to the consternation of Sonoran officials, Cajeme's Yaquis continued to operate autonomously into the 1880s.[14] To rationalize their campaigns, Porfirians cast them as the antithesis to reform and progress, occupying the most fertile lands but squandering their value. All the while, the officials amassed arms and war materiel and complained about federal inaction. Already moving forward with irrigation projects on the Yaqui River, Sonoran officials and landowners were frustrated by the lack of federal support. Border officials even welcomed Mormon missionaries across the border in hopes that their proselytizing might pacify the Yaquis.[15] Concurrently, in 1885, Sonora finally settled enough of its internal political divisions and intrigues to secure federal troops sufficient to mount attacks against Cajeme.[16]

Across the border, Arizona onlookers mused over the possible motives for the new campaign. Although some saw Yaquis as aggressors, many suspected Mexicans to be chiefly at fault for the violence. Views differed as to whether war was a conspiracy by government contractors aimed at profiting from selling military supplies, a plot by Mexican officials as pretense for driving Yaquis out of Sonora altogether, or a scheme by corrupt Sonoran politicians who stood to inherit Yaqui lands. Americans saw Mexican refugees fleeing the draft, read constant reports of high mortality rates among Mexican and Yaqui troops, and occasionally even suffered casualties in borderlands skirmishes. It was enough to sour them on Yaquis and Mexico alike.[17]

In May 1885, Mexican forces marched into Yaqui territory but failed to defeat Cajeme's well-entrenched forces. Yaquis agreed to end their rebellion but demanded that Mexican troops fully abandon their valley. The negotiating official, Colonel Lorenzo Torres, refused. Conversely, general amnesty terms offered to the Yaquis were "accepted by few."[18] Bolstered by reinforcements, the Sonoran National Guard and Mexican army jointly mounted new campaigns the following spring, gaining ground against Cajeme's increasingly indigent forces. The Yaquis were fully defeated by late 1886, with some six thousand Yaquis and Mayos surrendering. Cajeme escaped capture for a time but was apprehended and executed before his people on April 25, 1887, at Cócorit.[19] Mexican officials hoped that they had quelled the Yaqui rebellion for good.[20] General Angel Martínez believed the Yaqui problem was solved and ordered troops to leave Cócorit in the beginning of June. Within two days of their departure, a new Yaqui rebellion kindled, and Yaquis killed Mexican officials and looted the town.[21] This prompt resumption of armed resistance was led by Juan Maldonado, or Tetabiate. Under Tetabiate, many of the political structures established by Cajeme dwindled, but the vision of an independent Yaquimi—cultural, social, and political sovereignty—persisted and would underlie community building by Yaqui exiles in Arizona.

Tetabiate's Yaquis faced the looming reality of resumed warfare with an increasingly strong, better-organized, and well-funded Mexican military presence in the Yaqui River Valley and surrounding mountain regions. For their part, Mexican officials downplayed the resumed violence, insisting that the "Yaquis were utterly subdued and broken down."[22] Clearly exacerbated by such claims, the *Arizona Champion* editorialized, "Notwithstanding the grandiloquent report from the Mexican side of the question, the Yaqui Indians are not by any means subjugated. On the contrary they have about six thousand well-armed men and are still actively defiant. Orders have been issued on both side to give no quarter, and the war of extermination is still going on."[23]

Over the following years, relations between Tetabiate, his Yaqui troops, and Mexican officials alternated between periods of tenuous peace and outbursts of violence. As Mexican officials controlled the valley, Yaqui insurgents fortified redoubts in the Sierra de Bacatete, some *rancherias*, and defensive trenches left over from Cajeme's campaigns. By 1890, the Comisión Científica de Sonora attempted to entice Yaquis to accede through settlement, irrigation, and development projects, but "not a single individual rose to the offered inducements."[24] "They tried to make slaves out of the Yaquis," recalled Balthazar Guadalupe, "Each of us received a card saying that we couldn't move from one hacienda to another."[25] Persecution divided settled "pacíficos" and the defiant "broncos" in Bacatete strongholds. Though the latter were anxious to return to their settlements in the fertile lowlands, they insisted upon settlement on Yaqui terms, not those created by Mexican officials.

The 1890s were thus a decade of continual violence—of "guerrilla warfare," as historian Evelyn Hu-DeHart terms it.[26] At various points Mexico declared victory, but their proclamations were little more than bluster and propaganda. On April 15, 1897, Tetabiate, his second-in-command José Loreto Villa, interpreter Julián Espinoza, and four thousand troops surrendered a large cache of munitions and signed a tentative peace with Mexican officials. "!Viva la Paz del Yaqui!" exclaimed the inscription on a Yaqui flag at the signing.[27] This, recalled one Yaqui decades later, was considered the "holy peace."[28] But despite the enthusiasm and pageantry, the peace only lasted two years. By 1899, settled Yaquis began to "revive their love of country against the usurpers of their land and take up arms."[29] The fight for an independent Yaquimi recommenced. With new campaigns underway, Mexican persecution, enslavement, and "campaigns of extermination" prompted another exodus of Yaquis across the US-Mexican border. Border proximity and traditional migration routes again served refugee Yaquis.

Most US press coverage of these conflicts initially painted Yaquis in a dim light. What little sympathetic press Yaquis received in Arizona highlighted the admirable tenacity of Yaqui spirit or despicable cases of excessive Mexican brutality. After Yaquis suffered a major loss in 1894, one Arizona report asserted that "the Mexican government may someday learn that [Yaquis] have some rights that the government is bound to respect."[30] "I suppose [Mexican military campaigns] must result in [Yaqui] extermination and the turning over of their lands to the greedy speculators who have hungered for them so long," lamented John A. Gowan in the *San Francisco Call*.[31] Another report saw a great Native nation on the verge of collapse and extolled Yaqui character: "No nation or tribe of aborigines on the American continent has showed so sublime a love of liberty, greater bravery or as much wisdom."[32]

Porfirian Extermination, Deportation, and Enslavement of Yaquis

The Porfirian campaign to eliminate Yaquis from northern Mexico by extermination, deportation, or enslavement hastened Yaqui exodus to the United States. In his 1911 book *Barbarous Mexico*, John Kenneth Turner wrote: "The extermination of the Yaquis began in war; its finish is being accomplished in deportation and slavery."[33] According to Evelyn Hu-DeHart, this "final solution . . . could have amounted to genocide [had it not been] abruptly curtailed."[34] Turner's use of the word "extermination" would have considerable contemporary and lasting influence.[35]

Yaqui exodus to Arizona can only be properly framed by more fully showing the brutality suffered south of the border, and this includes the Porfirian deportation of Yaquis to Yucatán, for which precedent existed. In colonial times, Spain deported Apaches and other Native peoples to the Caribbean, among other places. During the Yaqui revolt under Juan Banderas in 1827, Yaqui prisoners were deported from Sonora to Mexico City and later drafted into the marines of Veracruz. During Yaqui rebellions in the 1850s and 1860s, Mexican officials captured Yaqui women and children, deporting them to northern borderland settlements to work as domestic servants.[36] As the Díaz regime tightened its grip on the Cajeme-led rebellion, General Martínez may have considered these precedents when he suggested to Díaz that they deport Yaquis from their homeland. Díaz, however, initially rejected the idea, stating that "the Indian prefers death to exile" and would fight to the death rather than face deportation. Under such circumstances, Díaz reasoned, the effort would turn the war of "pacification" into a war of extermination: a transition he was apparently unwilling to shoulder at that juncture.[37] A decade later, such reticence waned.

The first instance of Yaqui removal came as early as 1887. The *Chicago Daily Tribune* reported in January 1888 that for some time, the Mexican gunboat *Democrata* had been removing captured Yaquis and Mayos to the southern state of Colima. Numbering some fifteen hundred in total, relocated Indians were "dying of fever and other diseases."[38] According to Turner's *Barbarous Mexico* exposé, this same *Democrata* would be used four years later in the murder of two hundred Yaqui men, women, and children. All prisoners from Navajoa, the group was purportedly taken to sea and then dropped into the ocean somewhere between the mouth of the Yaqui River and the Guaymas seaport in southwestern Sonora.[39] Some years later, Lorenzo Torres, by this time promoted to general, denied this, explaining: "Nothing of the kind ever happened or could have happened, for we are not barbarians but a civilized nation, with tender hearts and sympathetic natures. No Mexican is capable of such inhumanity. The incident upon which this brutal story is founded was the removal of a number of rebellious Yaquis from the scene of their depredations to a tract of unoccupied land near the fort at Manzanillo, where they could be more effectually prevented from committing further atrocious crimes."[40]

Yaquis would later recall the era with horror. Mexico's "Campaña sin Igual [Unparalleled Campaign]" against Cajeme's forces paled in comparison to what those remained in Yaquimi suffered: "deportations, murders of women and children . . . the horrific butchery of adults and children, the persecution . . . torture, theft and abuse."[41] The majority of Yaqui deportees were placed on trains, transported south to Guaymas, loaded onto ships bound for ports at San Blas, San Marcos, or the Isthmus of Tehuantepec, taken by rail to Veracruz or Mexico City, and finally loaded back into ships for transport along the Bay of Campeche coast to be offloaded on the Yucatán Peninsula, often at Progreso.[42] Over the course of the journey, deportees suffered immensely. Of the trip from Sonora to Guaymas, one eyewitness related: "I saw one bunch of Indians brought from the interior to Guaymas . . . and was informed that they had been hauled 484 kilometers [three hundred miles] in stock cars, which had not even been cleaned out after being used for transporting cattle. There were 1,500 of these poor devils—men, women and children, huddled together in the cars like so many hogs. It was one of the most pitiful scenes I ever witnessed."[43]

"The excessive summer heat, and the closely packed Indians turned the box cars into coffins," wrote a reporter years later of one such trip, "Every Yaqui had died before the port was reached."[44] Others, forced to walk from Hermosillo to Guaymas, a distance of over 130 kilometers, saw compatriots die along the way "like starving cattle."[45] At Guaymas, many were detained for months. Chepa Moreno, a Yaqui woman deported from Sonora, recalled being "crushed into a small cell . . . with a number of other Yaquis." "There was not room for everyone in the cell to lie down at the same time," she continued. "Everyone had to eat and perform the necessities in this cell, which was cleaned out infrequently."[46] Also at Guaymas, children were separated from their families and integrated into the city's domestic servant workforce, of which they comprised a large percentage by 1907.[47]

Whether arriving by overcrowded and unsanitary rail car or forced to make the trek by foot, many Yaquis arrived in Guaymas in dire condition. The subsequent journey by ship was equally difficult, if not worse. Chepa Moreno's group was forced belowdecks and not allowed to exit until the port was reached.[48] Many who boarded would never again touch dry land. Of the voyage from Guaymas to southern ports, a 1905 US newspaper grieved, "The indiscriminate deportation of innocent men, women and children continues. They are sent to the coast loaded in rotten vessels, a large portion of which never reach Yucatán. Many dead bodies of Indians are found along the coast, and it is asserted that the poor devils are dumped overboard out at sea before having time to make the trip to their pretended destination."[49]

This claim echoed the aforementioned 1888 accusations of death at sea, and the implied pattern horrified many American observers. In February 1908, word of suicide en route furthered American outrage. The *New-York Tribune* reported, "Those rescued declared they preferred death to serving on plantations or in the army in the 'hot country' of Mexico."[50] As he had when questioned about the *Demócrata* in 1888, General Torres denied that Yaqui suicides had occurred during deportation on the Sea of Cortez.[51]

Citing the affidavits of American onlookers and Mexican sources, others asserted that Yaquis, as in 1888, were actually being murdered—pushed overboard once at sea. "Whole shiploads disappear on voyage to Yucatan," declared the *Washington Herald.* Ships that should take a full week or more to complete the round trip from Guaymas to the Isthmus of Tehuantepec were returning empty within three days. Mexican officials, many concluded, were engaged in the "wholesale slaughter" of Yaquis, and President Díaz's "capital scheme to rid the country of the Yaquis by deporting them to the Yucatan, [is] made to serve for the slaying of the Indians by the hundreds."[52] Whether suicide or murder, many men, women, and children who were forced from their Sonoran lands died on the Sea of Cortez. John Turner's interview with an unnamed Mexican colonel revealed that the officer had taken some three thousand Yaquis south to San Blas in six months and had orders to hurry another fifteen hundred south.[53] It is uncertain how many Yaquis made this voyage and how many of those failed to reach their destination port, but the traffic was clearly extensive.[54]

Once at port at the Isthmus of Tehuantepec, San Blas, Tepic, Guadalajara, or elsewhere, Yaquis had to travel overland to Veracruz. Those at San Blas were marched to San Marcos via Tepic, a fifteen-to-twenty-day march, along which "'Bull Pens,' or concentration camps," were erected to contain the Yaquis, Turner wrote.[55] Among Chepa Moreno's group, men and women were separated before the march to Tepic, where her son Carlos died. From San Marcos, they were placed on trains to Guadalajara and then to Mexico City.[56] At Mexico City, Yaquis were "sold like so many goats," as Yucatecan *patrones* chose groups to have transported to their plantations.[57] Most were entrained for the penultimate step to Veracruz and then taken by boat to Progreso via Mérida. Turner accompanied a group of 104 Sonorans from Veracruz to Progreso, "shoved into the unclean hole astern of the freight steamer *Sinaloa*." It was revealed that most of the group were actually Pimas and Opatas, but in the words of one, they were "all Yaquis to General Torres." "It makes no difference to [Torres]," they explained, "You are dark. You dress in my clothes and you will be a Yaqui—to him. He makes no investigation, asks no questions—only takes you."[58]

One Mexican officer admitted that as many as 10–20 percent of the fifteen hundred he had been ordered to transport had died, due to lack of funds to feed them. The Yaquis sold, he explained, for sixty-five dollars apiece in the Yucatán, of which he kept ten dollars. Throughout the deportation process, and in the Yucatán, families were separated. "Children were sold to the rich men. Young girls were sold to the Chinamen," recalled Guadalupe Balthazar.[59] Older Yaqui women were also sold as wives to Chinese laborers in the region, and, according to Turner, children born of these forced unions could be sold for as much as one thousand dollars apiece.[60] Contemporary and later Yaquis generations viewed their treatment as enslavement.[61] Many Americans agreed.

In the Yucatán, Yaqui labor was used in agriculture, often on henequen or sisal plantations. With high demand for binder twine made from henequen fibers coming from the plains of the United States and Canada, plantation owners welcomed the ready source of cheap Yaqui labor.[62] Other Yaquis were put to work in mines in the region and others still sent to sugarcane, tobacco, and other plantations in the Valle Nacional of Oaxaca.[63] Some, according to one report, were even conscripted to fight against local Maya insurgents in the region.[64] Very little documentation has survived concerning the government-sanctioned enslavement—or employment of Yaqui "prisoners of war"—but all tangential reports suggest federal, Sonoran, and Yucatecan state involvement.[65]

Many surviving reports and accounts from the ensuing years of Yaqui exile in the Yucatán tell of fevers and tropical diseases, hard labor, and widespread death. If they had not died en route, as the *Deseret Evening News* claimed most did, many died within less than a month in the "New World Siberia of Yucatan."[66] Repeatedly referred to as the "hot country" by Yaquis, "El Infierno de Yucatán" tried Yaqui stamina and health with an unrelenting and unfamiliar combination of heat and humidity.[67] The home life of Yaqui laborers, as recalled by some surviving women, was horrific. They were often separated from their husbands, beaten for disobedience, and tasked with hard labor—all while suffering disease, the death of children, and constant oppression by hacienda overseers.[68] Those who survived would remain in exile at least until the revolution began in 1910. Even then, many hesitated to return to former Sonoran battlefields and opted to remain as exiled laborers elsewhere in the country. For those able to do so, a return to their homelands took considerable time.[69]

In the early 1900s, the extermination and deportation campaigns accelerated, and some Americans were horrified. As recent scholars describe it, "In the Sonora of Governor Izábal and the Mexico of Porfirio Díaz, being Yaqui meant peonage or death."[70] In a single defeat at Mazocoba on January 18, 1900, more than four hundred Yaquis were killed, and eight hundred were taken prisoner.[71] Tetabiate was killed the next year, in 1901. While deportation policy had been pursued previously, Izábel's 1902 proclamations officially stated a new dual policy: "War of total extermination" and "massive deportation."[72] By 1904, surviving correspondence suggests, 822 had already been deported, and by 1908 over 1,000 had been forced to leave. In 1907, Izábel stated that 2,000 had been deported, with an additional 4,000 to soon join them.[73] As the deportation peaked in 1908, it can be safely assumed that the final number was somewhat greater.[74] During this decade, Yaqui refugees crossed into Arizona by the hundreds and eventually by the thousands. Their transnational passage was fraught with difficulty, but possible capture at the border was far less daunting than the "genocide and deportation" in Sonora.[75] Indeed, border arrests were not unheard of, and those suspected of direct involvement with southern rebellions faced particular hazard in these cases. Yaquis crossing into Arizona to stay, rather than traffic in arms, generally followed established economic networks. "The majority entered as contract laborers, drifting here to work in the mines or work as laborers on the ditches and irrigation projects or worked as farm hands," explained one concerned onlooker. Many of these refugees were among the "peaceful Yaquis . . . who had tired of hopeless war." "The Indians say," wrote the *Graham (AZ) Guardian*, "they prefer to seek honest labor in a faraway country" instead of attempting to weather available conditions offered by General Torres in Sonora.[76]

Following familiar routes, many Yaquis headed north to Arizona, where many had relations and had heard of "alluring tales of the life of peaceful industry led by the 'pale faces north of the border.'"[77] The combination of warfare, eventual threat of deportation and extermination, and economic opportunity across the border pushed and pulled the Yaquis, and their transnational exodus built on decades of precedence. The turn-of-the century appearance in Arizona of work-seeking Yaqui immigrants and peace-seeking Yaqui refugees is best cast in borderlands contexts. Their centuries-long habitation in the hinterlands of the Spanish empire and then Mexico offered Yaquis latitude, on an individual and national basis, in negotiations with Mexicans. The historical reality was one of easy Yaqui mobility and frustrated, overextended Spanish and Mexican officials at a disadvantage in the hinterlands.

The Treaty of Guadalupe Hidalgo in 1848 imposed a new northern sphere of influence upon Yaquis and drew an international border through the complex Native landscapes they had so adeptly traversed. Yet, with the border at first poorly policed, Yaquis adapted to new realities, seizing economic opportunities offered by American development in the Southwest and exploiting their ability to leave Mexican problems behind. Yaqui mobility took on new meaning as their border crossing redefined them as immigrants and refugees. These new definitions would steer much of their subsequent experience in the United States. The border crossing itself and establishment of permanent settlement in Arizona initiated a new phase in Yaqui history, still firmly ensconced in the borderlands paradigm but more constant and less transnational in character.

The United States and Yaqui Removal

Arizonan and broader American responses to the shifting context of Yaqui flight across the US-Mexican border were mixed. Some newspapers, generally hostile, tended to focus on stories of Yaqui borderlands violence and arms trafficking, while sympathetic press ran stories on the Porfirian extermination, deportation, and enslavement campaigns. Yaqui migrants and refugees had to navigate public opinion carefully. At times being able to blend in with all non-Yaqui Mexican migrants—including, perhaps, some of the very men who had soldiered in the front lines of the very troops the Yaquis were fleeing—afforded them opportunities to enter the United States and establish somewhat stable lives in Arizona. Before the waves of refugee Yaquis fled across the border to escape Porfirian persecution, southern Arizonans were likely already accustomed to Yaqui settlements and activities in their state. Arizona newspapers in 1890s reported on Yaqui crime, comical superstitions, questionable marriage practices, public dances, and settlement, with growing awareness of Salt River Valley (Phoenix) and Scottsdale Yaquis. So the Yaquis were known, or at least their presence was known, though they were not warmly welcomed.[78] By decade's (and century's) end, these Yaqui immigrants and settlers had established a steady, if small, presence north of the line.

How then did Arizonans and the US government deal with Yaquis' growing presence? The reactions were mixed. Influenced by the press coverage focusing on Yaqui rebellion and violence, many Arizonans held broad suspicions. Arizonans were somewhat familiar with rhetoric justifying wars of extermination against resistant Natives, so many may have viewed Yaqui suffering as lamentable but military efforts against them as justifiable. To criticize Mexican policy against Native peoples would be, in effect, criticism of recently concluded US military campaigns against Indians. Arizonans had only recently, in 1886, seen the surrender of Apache leader Geronimo and his band. US investors interested in Porfirian Yaqui River development certainly added weight to sway publicity against the Yaqui cause and limit sympathy.

Americans were much more sympathetic when viewing the Yaqui refugees in contexts detached from prolonged warfare. In the light of Porfirian extermination, deportation, and enslavement, some Americans expressed outrage, but this sort of reaction may have served multiple purposes. Such criticism elevated the United States to a moral high ground, looking down upon the ostensibly more savage Mexican state, and allowed Americans to assuage their own collective guilt regarding their nation's recent Indian atrocities. Prominent American publications, including the *Los Angeles Times* and *Harper's Weekly*, decried Mexican brutality and lynching of Yaquis. There is irony in this. As one historian notes, "The United States chastises Mexico even as African Americans were still being lynched in the country in record numbers."[79] Some Americans drew from collective memory of Indian wars to justify or overlook Mexican extermination campaigns, but others seem to have overlooked US slavery entirely when decrying the early-twentieth-century Porfirian deportation campaigns.

One of the most prominent US voices on Mexico was that of John Kenneth Turner, whose 1909 exposés for the likes of *American Magazine* and the *New-York Tribune* led to the 1911 book *Barbarous Mexico*. Turner's accounts were echoed by others detailing Mexican perfidy, the selling of Yaqui women and children to the highest bidder, massacres of innocents, and the like.[80] While some Arizona papers continued to deride Yaquis and their plight, it is evident that their enslavement struck a sympathetic chord elsewhere in the United States. Turner's book eased the entrance of Yaquis into the United States up to the mid-1920s, as many were able to petition for political asylum during ongoing violence in Sonora.[81] Working against them, however, were the never-ending warfare and threats to Americans' economic interests in Sonora.[82]

For Americans viewing the deportation saga through exposés such as Turner's, there were as many sources refuting the reported atrocities. A year before printing a sympathetic treatment of Yaquis in 1909, *Harpers Weekly* in May 1908 featured a three-page article detailing alleged Yaqui atrocities and threats to Sonoran (and US economic interests') stability. "If the government expects to subjugate the Yaquis," writer Marc Reynolds concluded, "soldiers must be sent into the hills, and an active campaign of extermination be rigidly carried out."[83] While various others mentioned Yaqui deportation indifferently, some "vehemently refute[d]" reports of Yaqui enslavement.[84] Elisha Talbot in *Moody's Magazine* aggressively and systematically deconstructed the claims made by Turner and others. While not denying deportation of Yaqui rebels, Talbot painted benevolent pictures of Yaqui treatment in the Yucatán, replete with photographs of spacious houses, happy Yaqui families, well-groomed Yaqui children reading at plantation schools, and even commodious open-air seaborne transport of Yaquis to Yucatán plantations.[85] American readers had two diametrically opposed portrayals of the Yaqui situation in Sonora and the Yucatán, and, for many, interest waned. Though initially showing potential to catalyze broad reform, like Harriet Beecher Stowe's *Uncle Tom's Cabin* or Helen Hunt Jackson's *Century of Dishonor* and *Ramona*, Turner's *Barbarous Mexico* and similar reports sparked only temporary outrage.

US officials were aware of the deportation policy, even in its earliest stages. In 1905, the US ambassador to Mexico, Powell Clayton, wrote to Secretary of State John Hay, informing him that Sonoran officials had taken "drastic measures against the apparently peaceful Yaquis" employed by American-owned businesses in mining regions of the state, and that already "the great bulk of Yaqui Indians had been deported from Sonora to Yucatán."[86] Later that year, US diplomat Fenton McCreery sent Secretary Hay news clippings from the *Daily Record* and *Mexican Herald*, both Mexico City newspapers, detailing the Yaqui deportation and forced labor, as well as the veritable death sentence that life in the Yucatán meant for most Yaquis.[87]

Ambassador Clayton's remarks, couched in a discussion of US mining interests in Sonora, reveal not only US awareness of deportations but also the notion that not all Sonorans (or US businesses in Sonora) approved of the policy. Indeed, many heads of industry greatly lamented the prospective loss of valuable Yaqui labor. This view crept into various reports of Mexico's new war against the Yaquis. "The extermination of the Yaqui Indians simply means the destruction of the manual labor in Sonora. The Yaquis are not only the best and most trusted workers in Sonora, but they constitute the largest number of able workingmen in that state," wrote Californian intellectual Gustav Eisen.[88] A Sonoran mine foreman told John Kenneth Turner that "one Yaqui laborer [was] worth two ordinary Americans and three ordinary Mexicans."[89] Deportation, it was said, would "deprive the industries of [Sonora] of their most reliable laborers."[90] For the Porfirian regime, however, the concern of recurrent Yaqui revolt overshadowed these economic interests.

Though American reports and muckraking exposés widely disagreed as to the motives for, details of, or even the reality of Yaqui deportation, their coverage is revelatory. It is important to keep in mind that, at the time, these reports informed local opinions, those of residents of Arizona's borderlands. In the earliest accounts of the new deportation policy, there was a deep rift between the coverage by borderlands newspapers and those elsewhere in the country. In January 1901, the *Graham Guardian*, published in the Gila River Valley town of Safford, Arizona, informed its readers that certain Yaquis were being removed from Sonora to regions where they could be controlled with greater ease.[91] The paper sympathized with the Yaqui impulse to protect their homeland but chided them for doing so at the expense of their families' suffering. Mexican deportation policy was not put on trial but mentioned only as a passing fact. Many of the early mentions of Yaqui deportation showed no inclination to do otherwise and engage in a debate to justify or renounce the policy.[92]

In following years, however, the *Guardian*'s accounts of Yaqui deportation increasingly strayed to justify the policy and dismiss accounts of Mexican injustice and persecution. In response to rumors that innocent Yaqui miners had been brutally executed by Mexican troops, the *Guardian* quipped that most everything in the report was true except for the part about the Mexicans shooting fourteen Yaquis.[93] Showing even greater contempt for the Yaqui plight, the *Guardian* later used them as fodder for jokes as in one correspondent's travelogue of a train trip to Nacozari, Sonora: "During the trip I discovered that a Yaqui was a human being after all. There was an infant specimen aboard and he squawled just like an American baby."[94]

If the *Guardian* is an indication of regional prejudice against Yaquis, the contrasting consensus presented by newspapers across the country was one of considerable concern for the Yaqui plight. Many praised Yaquis' innate strength and extolled their superiority over nearly all the continent's Indigenous peoples. Simultaneously they lamented the murder and execution of Yaquis and condemned Mexico's spilling of innocent blood. The *Washington Post* offered a chilling description of Mexican plans to kill *all* adult Yaquis and deport children to southern Mexico to be incorporated into Native tribes already laboring there. In Sonora, "peaceful" Yaquis, it was reported, were being hanged, and violence was widespread. The violence against women and children had particular resonance throughout the United States.[95]

An affidavit of all known deportation atrocities, printed in 1909 by *Harpers Weekly*, offers a damning conclusion to the expository nature of many US reports, describing

> the Yaqui who after centuries of struggle and for no other crime than patriotism, has been sold into perpetual slavery to the planters of Chiapas and Yucatán; sold to a servitude of so vile a reputation that fifteen men and women jumped overboard in transit to Campeachy from Vera Cruz last year, choosing death before its torrid rigors. In the last four years five thousand Yaquis—farmers, laborers, miners—have been expatriated under conditions that were rendered unnecessarily cruel by the spite of brutal Mexican soldiers. Rounded up in scores, while their men were off at the mines, women have been taken away on the trains. In the general round-ups wives were separated from husbands, sisters from brothers, children from mothers—infant babes were torn from the breast and left behind on the ground, while their mothers were driven away. The deportation was carried out with absolute brutality, and in accordance with a policy that aimed at the scattering of tribes and families. Taken all in all, the tragedy of the Yaquis is perhaps without a parallel in American history.[96]

Conclusion

By the early twentieth century, Yaqui experiences in Sonora, across the US-Mexican border, and in Arizona were overshadowed by violence and threat from every side. If ever there was a humanitarian cause for Americans to support—especially one where blame could be rested upon the shoulders of a foreign state, Mexico—the Yaqui plight should have garnered universal interest in the United States. Sympathy abounded, but the continual specter of Yaqui violence and feared cross-border criminality haunted their steps and stymied any American movement to address their needs. Apparently unwilling to turn a completely blind eye, however, American officials and eager Arizona employers allowed Yaquis to establish a permanent presence north of the border. This led to Yaquis occupying an ambiguous legal landscape, though one markedly less threatening than the homelands they had left in Sonora. The clear context of their transnational past would collide with the legal ambiguity of their Arizonan present in coming years.

Chapter 4

Cree Refugees and American Response, 1885–1888

It has been said many times that Cree knew no boundaries. When the white man came and drew the Medicine Line that divided the continent that had always been their home it meant nothing to them except a nuisance.

—"THE CREE," undated manuscript[1]

As the flow of Yaqui economic immigrants to Arizona was augmented by refugees escaping extermination and enslavement, a similar shift occurred in the history of Crees in Montana. By 1885, plains Crees in the Assiniboia (present-day southern Saskatchewan) and Alberta-Montana borderlands stood at the end of tumultuous years. For many who settled on various Canadian reserves, there were new complications, and the settlement process and attendant assimilation programs were disastrous for some. As James Daschuk devastatingly illustrates, many government programs exhibited ill will and intentional mistreatment, using starvation to control Native peoples.[2] Yet settlement and reserve lands could mean stability that those who refused treaty agreements or those who fled the country did not enjoy. For the remnants of Cree chief Big Bear's bands, the borderlands offered potential escape from their troubles in Canada following the 1885 North-West Rebellion.

In 1885, Crees long associated with Montana participated in the 1885 North-West Rebellion, led by Louis Riel. During the rebellion, Crees were party to a massacre of whites and later faced prosecution and potential execution if they remained north of the line. In this context, a number of groups fled back to Montana where their families had gone in the preceding years. Unlike their predecessors, who came as traders or hunters, these Crees came as refugees—seeking asylum and protection from Canada.

However, their reputation haunted them. Their preceding activities as transnational Natives, perceived and actual participation in livestock theft, and the deep-seated Montanan prejudice built upon this transformed familiar borderlands into places increasingly intolerant of Cree settlement. Montana borderlands became dangerous for Cree bands. To understand how they were received in Montana, the 1885 North-West Rebellion and Frog Lake Massacre must be examined.

Crees and the 1885 North-West Rebellion

In the spring of 1885, Métis under the leadership of Louis Riel and others revolted against Canadian authorities. When word reached Montana papers that Crees had joined Riel's North-West Rebellion, this dovetailed neatly with the prejudices Montanans had built against Crees during the preceding years.[3] Reports of Big Bear's involvement confirmed their worst suspicions. In the years to come, this would play an exacting role in how Crees were treated in Montana. Big Bear's negative reputation—from Cree border-crossings in the early 1880s to his involvement in the bloody North-West Rebellion—would dominate the minds of Montanans when Big Bear's son, Little Bear (Imasees), crossed into Montana and made a decades-long attempt to establish permanent residence.[4] With layers of prejudice stacked against them, Cree efforts to settle in Montana were troubled from the start.[5]

By early 1884, the efforts of Big Bear to secure agreeable treaty rights for his people had been failing. After initially refusing to sign Treaty 6, starvation had forced his hand, and he had complied on December 8, 1882, at Fort Walsh.[6] Poor conditions for his people persisted, however. In the cold 1883–84 winter, Big Bear and lodges associated with him were camped near Frog Lake in east-central Saskatchewan, near the present-day border with Manitoba. As winter gave way to spring, Native leaders were frustrated by Canadian failure to uphold treaty agreements. Big Bear joined Poundmaker and other plains Crees in mass negotiations to secure more favorable annuity agreements that summer of 1884 but to little effect.[7] Their justified discontent contextualizes their subsequent participation in the 1885 North-West Rebellion. Riel's fiery rhetoric spoke to their experience.

Riel recruited Métis and Crees on both sides of the border. In Montana he told Crees, according to Chippewa-Cree tribal elder George Denny over half a century later, that "there was a large band of Plains Indians involved and that if the uprising was successful, the Crees could have choice lands along the International Boundary with a promise of livestock and equipment so that they could live like white men."[8] Such prospects stood in stark contrast to the string of broken promises their counterparts suffered under British authorities. Americans in Montana subsequently viewed the Crees in their midst—whether they went north during rebellion, remained in Montana, or came later—as willful participants to a bloody uprising, with hands collectively stained by the blood of massacred whites. Herein lies cruel irony, as subsequent generations of Montana Crees viewed their nonparticipation as central to their identity south of the line. "It must be understood that not all of the Cree went north to help in the uprising," Denny noted.[9]

The Frog Lake Massacre

In the midst of the 1885 North-West Rebellion, Crees encamped at Frog Lake participated in the slaughter of nine whites and kidnapping of many others. In the broader narrative of the North-West Rebellion, the violence of April 2, 1885, was a pivotal moment for refugee Crees in Montana since American observers immediately linked familiar Crees, such as Big Bear, with the massacre.[10] While recent historiography successively carves out a middle ground between the polarized historic accounts of the event, Cree guilt was the standard understanding at the time, which made it difficult for Crees who fled to Montana in the massacre's dark aftermath. What were the motives behind the Frog Lake Massacre? What were the role of Big Bear, Little Bear and other individual Crees, and what connections can be drawn between Riel's broader rebellion and the events at Frog Lake? A selection of contemporary and later historical accounts will help answer these questions and contextualize the forces pushing Cree refugees across the border. In the following chapter, these will also provide background for how Montanans viewed the links between the massacre and Crees in Montana.

Individual Crees and the Frog Lake Massacre: Big Bear

The Canadian distrust of Big Bear is perhaps best illustrated in a highly melodramatic book published within the year of the North-West Rebellion. According to its author, Joseph Edmund Collins, Big Bear "reign[ed] supreme in the district" and was "a noisy, meddlesome, savage, who is never in his glory save when he is the centre of some disturbance." Big Bear, according to Collins's dubious account, had said, "There will soon be bloody work. Government break em treaty with Injuns. Lots of Injuns now ready to go out and scalp servants of Government and white men." Collins wrote, as in the style of the novels he concocted at the time, "When, therefore, tidings reached the land of the Stoney Indians that the half-breeds, with Louis Riel at their head, had broken into revolt, Big Bear pulled off his feathered cap and threw it several times into the air. He went to his wives, a goodly number of which he is in the habit of keeping, and informed them that he would soon bring them home some scalps."[11]

Collins's book suggests eager and wanton violence that was generally premeditated by Big Bear. He was, in the eyes of many Canadians, not a Native who could be trusted or pacified. After attempts to evangelize Big Bear, one Indian agent morbidly opined in June 1885 that he would only be converted "with a hempen collar."[12] Collins concurred, writing, "There must be a pretty wholesome hanging in the North-West." Big Bear, of course, was featured on the list to meet the gallows.[13] A Canadian inspector writing from the Frog Lake region in April 1885 had postulated, "I believe it is their [Big Bear's Indians] intention to exterminate the Whites in this Section."[14] While this correspondent wrote about the band as a whole, he still singled out Big Bear as their leader. In the eyes of Anglo officials, with leadership came direct responsibility. Canadians viewed the Frog Lake Massacre as a direct outgrowth of Big Bear's recalcitrance and inherent aggression. This habit of singling out specific individuals upon whom to focus mass blame runs through many subsequent Canadian accounts, not just that of Collins. Recent analysis by Jill St. Germain contends, however, that among Big Bear's band in particular there were few social structures "to inhibit such outbursts."[15] The Anglo conceptualization of top-down, hierarchical military leadership and structure does not always fit Native contexts.[16] There is no debate that Indians associated with Big Bear's band committed the atrocities at Frog Lake. However, the role of Big Bear himself, as an individual Cree and as a Native leader who allegedly ordered the actions, is questionable and needs nuanced analysis.

There is considerable evidence that Big Bear made serious efforts to discourage the violence that broke out at Frog Lake. In the weeks previous he had encouraged restless members of his band to wait and be patient, explaining that "someday things would be better," according to Big Bear's granddaughter Isabelle many years later.[17] On the morning before the massacre, Big Bear attended Mass at the small Catholic church at Frog Lake and warned some whites there that his younger braves were leaning toward violent actions. William Cameron, survivor of the massacre, claimed that Big Bear later told him that he had come to Mass to "prevent bloodshed." Given that Cameron's account is regarded as one of the more negative toward Crees, this view is striking. Concluded Cameron, "I am convinced Big Bear would have flung himself upon the first of his savage followers to point a gun and fought for our lives."[18] According to Isabelle Big Bear, that same day Big Bear met with an Indian agent, Thomas Quinn, and discussed the growing unrest, warning that there was little to be done to quell the unrest this late in its development.[19] According to these accounts, while aware of the looming threat of an uprising, Big Bear in no way endorsed or encouraged it.

When the shooting started the next morning, Cameron related that Big Bear tried to stave off further bloodshed. At the crack of gunshot, Cameron observed Big Bear storming out of a building and bellowing, "Tesqua! Tesqua! (Stop! Stop!)" Having left the scene of the original shooting, Isabelle Little Bear, a young girl at the time, later recalled observing the settlement from a small knoll. "We heard my grandfather Big Bear yelling at the top of his voice, 'Brothers, at least spare the cloth,'" she recounted. Astride his horse, his attempts to prevent the murder of the village priests and restore order were in vain. "But he might as well have appeared to a pack of wolves," recounted another Métis eyewitness.[20] Coupled with the fact that senior warriors had ample chances to kill others, such as Cameron himself, the general confusion described at the scene suggests that the attack was not premeditated. While tensions had been rising and bellicose words had been rife, Chief Big Bear had not ordered the attack. When later brought to trial, Big Bear testified, "I never approved."[21]

If Big Bear did not approve of the bloodshed, then why did he later admit that he had led his people to Frog Lake, where he knew violence was likely to occur? Part of the confusion over the leadership role of Big Bear comes from the chief himself. According to his granddaughter, Big Bear felt that as his band's leader, he was entirely responsible for their actions, regardless of whether he condoned them. As Mary PeeMee (See-as-cum-ka-poo), Big Bear's daughter-in-law, explained in 1975, "The warriors heard of the half-breed uprising at Batoche. The men held council. They wanted to fight. Big Bear talked in the council against the fighting. He talked until he could talk no more. The warriors said they would fight. Big Bear had to lead his people to war for he was chief and he was responsible for what his people did. Big Bear could not stop the fighting at Frog Lake."[22] An early twentieth-century Cree storyteller concluded, "I believe that he was no more responsible than any of his headmen, and much less responsible than some who only incited the killing. That he was Chief gave him no power to command without question."[23] Leading one's people in actions that one disapproves of runs somewhat counter to Anglo notions of leadership, but Big Bear was adamant. Even when his warriors later urged him to escape capture, he refused. In the recollection of Mary PeeMee: "His warrior told him to go but he said, 'No, I am your chief.' Because I chose to lead you in war. I am responsible for what happens to you." In the end, Big Bear was charged with treason and sentenced to two years in Stony Mountain Prison. Upon release he went to the Little Pine Reservation and died soon after of illness. In the words of one of Little Bear's sons, Four Souls, "The shame killed him."[24]

Individual Crees and the Frog Lake Massacre: Wandering Spirit

While Big Bear was often guilty in the public's eyes for his leadership role, many contemporary sources held him apart from the "bloody wolves who perpetrated the butcheries at Frog Lake," as Joseph Collins's sensationalized account phrased it.[25] One individual in particular stands as a constant across all the telling of the April 2, 1885, events: Wandering Spirit. Wandering Spirit stood at the forefront of the younger, frustrated faction of Big Bear's band.[26] Big Bear had warned Agent Quinn to this effect, relating, as Mary Dion later recalled, "You know that I have always tried to keep my people contented and at peace. You know also that times have changed. My word as chief does not carry the weight it had of old." As Big Bear's son Little Bear was rising to lead the group, he was swayed by the rhetoric of Wandering Spirit. As poverty began to take its toll on Big Bear's people, the views of Wandering Spirit, Little Bear, and other "young hot headed" people prevailed.[27]

The night of April 1, 1885, many gathered to the tents of Wandering Spirit and Little Bear and held a war dance. In the words of Jimmy Chief, grandson of Little Bear, at one point, Wandering Spirit arose and called out, "Tomorrow I am going to eat two-legged meat [i.e., kill someone]. So what do you think? . . . If you don't want to join me, then go home and put on your wives' dresses!"[28] And this bluster was put into action the following day. All accounts agree that it was Wandering Spirit who spilled the first blood that morning as he shot down Agent Quinn. Even the 1887 account of Wilbur Bryant, which placed heavy blame on the shoulders of Big Bear, singled out Wandering Spirit, stating, "That stalwart savage appears to have been the real leader of the movement."[29] Sam Pritchard, a white survivor, likewise singled out Wandering Spirit, as did William Cameron, who called Wandering Spirit a "war chief" among Big Bear's band. Four Souls, however, refuted this, stating, "He wasn't a chief at all, he was just a brave man, a mad man." His actual position in the band is inconsequential, however, as enough braves were clearly willing to follow his violent example in killing at Frog Lake.[30] In the massacre's aftermath, Canadian military efforts to apprehend the perpetrators likewise suggest a broad acceptance of Wandering Spirit as the most culpable person.[31] Telegrams from Major General Fred Middleton detail the evolving military perspective concerning individual Crees and the massacre. When interviewed prior to his execution, Wandering Spirit expressed regret and said that he deserved the death sentence placed upon him.[32]

Individual Crees and the Frog Lake Massacre: Little Bear

The role of Big Bear's son Little Bear was never scrutinized to the degree attendant with Big Bear and Wandering Spirit.[33] The US press of the time focused on Big Bear, and the Canadian press and military officials were most concerned with Big Bear and Wandering Spirit. This is not to say that Little Bear escaped their gaze. His name was known and included in the list of convicted murderers (coupled with Iron Body for the murder of trader George Dill).[34] Regardless of Little Bear's flight to the United States after his conviction, it is perplexing that there was not more consistent consternation among Canadian and American officials regarding his involvement in the Frog Lake Massacre. Although Big Bear stepped forward and took primary responsibility, Little Bear's rise in prominence should have placed him directly in the center of the post-massacre scrutiny.

Little Bear's daughter Isabelle would later recount the transfer of power from Big Bear to Little Bear as being linked to her grandfather's earlier failure to secure permanent settlement in Montana. Little Bear's complaint on this matter, she remarked, "would cause my grandfather to feel very humble because it reflected on his inability to lead his people. It was at this juncture that my father [Little Bear] quite unofficially became our leader, although Big Bear was still our chief."[35] Faced with subsequent frustrations in negotiating agreeable terms with Canadian officials, Big Bear's power deteriorated further. Little Bear, already troubled by his father's failings and the band's homelessness and indigence, was influenced by the more bellicose rhetoric of Wandering Spirit, Little Poplar, and others.[36] Big Bear's continuous attempts for reconciliation distanced his position from that of Little Bear, and the increasingly divided band faced increasingly destitute conditions. Big Bear's grandnephew Joe Dion concluded much later, "It may truthfully be said that Big Bear's chieftainship had more or less ended. He was getting old and wanted nothing better than to be left alone while he tried to adapt to the new mode of making a living."[37]

Cree Reckonings of Frog Lake

Cree accounts of Frog Lake assert that the massacre must be contextualized, seen in conjunction with the broad Cree discontent with conditions on their reserves and relations with Canada. Big Bear's grandson Four Souls later explained that Big Bear was upset because he understood that the negotiated terms were tantamount to the Crees being cheated out of innumerable valuable resources. "Big Bear knew and realized that [Treaty 6] was far from being adequate for what he valued for the northwest. Which is true . . . the farms, ranches, cities, industries, that derived from this land [once] belonged to Chief Big Bear. . . . to Cree people."[38] With prophetic foresight, Four Souls argued, Big Bear knew that the land they had ceded held great future value. This aggravated the chief.

Exacerbating this underlying frustration was the fact that Canada was not living up to the promises it had made to Big Bear. Mary PeeMee explained the condition of Big Bear's people: "They were hungry. The agencies had taken away the horses and guns for they were afraid the men would fight. The game was scarce. There were only a few rabbits and little animals. The people were dying from the sicknesses of the white man. Without buffalo skins or hides, we didn't have warm clothes for the long hard winters. We couldn't afford to buy the white man's clothes."[39] Cree elder Grant Chief Stick echoed this description in 1974, explaining that the band "was very hungry and in need of food, and everywhere [they] went to ask for food [they] were turned down. Everyone was hungry; the children, the old people. They started to get discouraged. That was when the trouble started. All kinds of food was available at the post, but the people couldn't get any. Finally they took up arms and killed the superintendent, because he was the one in charge of distributing food.[40]

Francis Harper, grandson-in-law of Big Bear (and nephew of scouts that pursued Big Bear after the massacre), stated plainly, "This is the reason the

Indians revolted at Frog Lake as they weren't given food as promised.[41] The reported singing of "Sioux Speaker [Agent Quinn], will you again shake your head when I plead, a piece of bacon?" by Crees after the massacre reinforce this explanation.[42] It was not violent tendencies that caused the Frog Lake Massacre, it was hunger and betrayal.

Isabelle Little Bear later recalled:

> Around the campfires the conversation centered around the present poor supply of food, and each family would elaborate on how meager rations were and how dark the future was. Many times, it was resolved that a delegation from the Indian Main Camp would go and see Mr. Quinn and try to obtain provisions on credit. Every such attempt failed. Mr. Quinn would always shake his head in a negative way and repeat the same words over and over again. "My orders from the government are such that I cannot let any provisions out of the agency unless I receive money or trade for them." He would then say, "Go back home and work." . . . To be told by Mr. Quinn to go back home and work was like saying, "Go back home and starve."[43]

With the promise of "you will never again suffer for want of food" still ringing in their ears, the painful reality of starvation was made starker.[44] Auguste Henri de Tremaudan's 1929 Métis history claims that Quinn purposefully "exploited Big Bear and his band to the utmost" to further his own economic interests.[45] After having denied Big Bear's requests for food in the days preceding the massacre, Quinn likewise rebuffed Little Bear's pleas: "Ayimasees, Ayimasees, I cannot give anything to your father, I *will* not give him anything. Why should I give him anything? *I* am the one who gives food to the people." The apparent arrogance concerned Big Bear and outraged Wandering Spirit, who replied to Quinn, "Well brother, there are going to be difficult times here now."[46] As Big Bear biographer Hugh Dempsey concludes, "On the surface all seemed calm . . . but, in fact, the camp was like a hungry, sleeping grizzly, needing only a small provocation to send it raging through the countryside."[47] Sympathetic views, such as these were not prevalent in the years immediately after the massacre. Thus, while the massacre at Frog Lake may now be understood in proper historical context, this was not the case for Montanans in the late nineteenth century. Rather, their personal experience with Crees in years preceding 1885 was coupled with negative accounts that portrayed Crees in the most savage terms.

The Legacy of Frog Lake

The exposition of Cree leaders' real and imagined connections with the Frog Lake Massacre and broader North-West Rebellion is important to the subsequent story of Crees returning to Montana. In the immediate aftermath of the rebellion and in the decades following, Montanans and federal officials alike would point back to these individuals and their involvement in the violence. Discussion of these past events would become a large part of the debate over whether to settle Crees in Montana or return them north of the line. As this debate oscillated between various foreseen outcomes, the direct link between Crees and the massacre remained constant. They were forever labeled not only refugees from the North-West Rebellion but also Natives fleeing persecution for their involvement in the massacre of white settlers. This disturbing history and subsequent stigma marked the wandering Crees in Montana for decades. Individual blame had been debated and punishment meted out to various individuals—Big Bear imprisoned and Wandering Spirit and others hanged (as was Louis Riel)—but Crees in Montana would bear the weight of April 2, 1885, and suffer collectively. Chief Thunderchild's 1923 lament resounds: "The scars of that day are with us still. . . . That fatal day at Frog Lake is like a curse upon us all and upon our relationship with the white man."[48]

The Return of Little Bear

As Riel's rebellion collapsed, Little Bear looked southward for his people's future. He had long regretted and resented his father's inability to secure permanent settlement for his people among the Long Knives, or Americans, and had wished to remain south of the line in the Milk River region.[49] As recounted by Four Souls, one night, in a dream, a figure told Little Bear that the "land of the Big Knife" was the place for his people. Pointing south, the figure told Little Bear to look, and before his gaze stood the Bear Paw Mountains.[50] Hence, when Big Bear's band was being pursued, it was decided that Little Bear, Little Poplar, and others who knew the traditional but secret Cree trails into Montana would flee south of the Medicine Line to the "traditional refuge of the oppressed."[51] While a small group fled, Big Bear, Wandering Spirit, and others were to remain and give themselves up to Canadian officials and hope to be dealt with mercifully. Little Bear was unconvinced that leniency would be granted or that promised food-for-arms exchange would be upheld. "Now they have tricked you," Little Bear told his compatriots (according to Grant Chief Stick), "I am running to the United States Government to seek help from them."[52] This he did, leaving sometime during late June to early July 1885, while others in the band surrendered at Fort Carlton on July 2. Leaving with as few as sixteen initially, Little Bear was joined by Little Poplar and Lucky Man and their families, and they were immediately pursued by Canadian troops—and suspected of a number of crimes along the way.[53]

The trek southward was long and arduous, some four hundred miles, with thousands of troops in hot pursuit. Their escape is a wonder. After slipping past Battleford, they succeeded in trekking across the South Branch of the Saskatchewan River and the Forty-Ninth Parallel practically without detection.[54] Somewhere along the journey, it is possible that the group split to avoid capture. One account asserted that as many as four hundred Crees had fled but that the band split into two parties, 150 traveling southeast to Minot, Dakota Territory, and the remaining 250 continuing south toward Fort Assiniboine.[55]

Although ultimately successful, the journey was harrowing. Cree stories about it speak of the fear of capture, and early-twentieth-century Cree elders said that Manito, the Great Spirit, protected and shielded them in their flight. "Imasees was a great man and Manito was good to him and the Crees," they would say.[56] Traveling at night and hiding, the group, eventually including women and children, suffered sore feet, forcing them to stop at one point to make new moccasins for all. "The people starved," tells another account. "Hundreds of them with the few possessions they had been able to salvage onto their hand-made two-wheeled carts and headed across a friendly border, penniless refugees."[57]

The Crees' arrival in Montana did not go unnoticed by local residents, but this did not provoke the acrimonious outcry that might have been predicted. By late July, at least one Montana newspaper had reported that some of Big Bear's band was possibly on its way.[58] The Crees were likely already south of the line by this date. Given the precedent—Montanans determined to expel Crees from the state—one would think that the report of participants in the Riel rebellion seeking refuge in their state would have been met by severe resistance. Montana papers had run stories on the North-West Rebellion and had included details about Crees going "on the warpath."[59] Attention had even been paid to the supposed involvement of "American" Indians in the uprising, so cross-border connections were not going unnoticed. Crees from Fort Pitt, where Big Bear's band resided, had been directly involved in the Frog Lake Massacre, it was reported.[60]

Furthermore, attention had been paid to the likelihood of Crees fleeing south into Montana if things got "too warm" north of the line. Hence, it was not with surprise that the *River Press* in Fort Benton made note of their arrival and concluded on October 7, 1885, that they "had come to stay."[61] Nor was it unreasonable for Crees to expect that they might be given permanent residence in the region, since much of northern Montana Territory was still Indian land.[62] It was labeled on maps as a broad "Gros Ventre, Piegan Blood, Blackfeet, and River Crow Indian Reservation." Why not add "Crees"? The precise number of refugees that arrived in the first wave is uncertain, but it was somewhere between one hundred and two hundred. In late August, Canadian officials reported that an additional seventy Cree families had fled.[63] Crees who had remained in Montana during the previous years may have also joined the group. By summer's end, hundreds gathered in refugee encampments.

The initial reception by regional military commanders was cool. At Fort Assiniboine, Little Bear was invited into Colonel C. S. Otis's office. Little Bear entered and extended his hand to shake, but Otis refused. Clearly aware of the connection between these inbound refugees and the North-West Rebellion, as recollected by Four Souls, Otis said, "Your hands are still bloody. I can't shake hands with you."[64] Perhaps unsure of his jurisdictional authority concerning "foreign" Indians—fugitives from Canada, no less—the commanding officer appeared to hold some personal grudge against the Crees as well. This is a consideration that may well be laid at the foundation of much of the subsequent US-Cree relations. Officially their presence was recognized on a legal, diplomatic plane—concerned with the international implications of border crossing and US Indian policy. But personal prejudice surely informed the decisions of individual Montanans and military officers interacting with the Crees. This is evident in the refusal of a handshake.

A different account of this meeting adds details. In 1974 Chief Stick concurred that after crossing the border Little Bear went straight to Fort Assiniboine to ask the commander for help. After stating his request, the officer, presumably Otis, wired Washington, DC, for instructions. Two days later, Otis was given the following proposal for Little Bear: Fort Assiniboine would assist the Cree refugees if they would remain near the fort and serve as scouts in the event of a battle. Chief Stick said, "Little

Bear called a meeting with the people to talk over the proposal. Most were against adopting it because they didn't want their children to have to suffer any more wars and battles."[65] So they turned down the offer, and their immediate future was a matter of debate between post commanders and Washington. The exact date of this initial meeting at Fort Assiniboine is unknown, but it likely occurred sometime in August between reports of their flight southward in late July and their arrival at Fort Belknap in mid-September. No extant records of Fort Assiniboine, the Departments of the Interior and War, or the State Department note this first exchange between Otis and Little Bear, a fact that remains a mystery.

The first official military recognition of the Cree presence in Montana dates from September 1885.[66] At that point, a number of officers sent correspondence regarding the refugees. On September 16, the commanding officer and Indian agent at Fort Belknap, Major William L. Lincoln, noted the presence of Crees near his agency. Two days later he reported that Little Bear, Lucky Man, and others—"all notoriously bad Indians"—were present and that they were selling items that directly linked them back to the Riel rebellion. At this same time, Sergeant D. Paterson of the North-West Mounted Police (NWMP) arrived, and Lincoln informed him that they were present with their associated familiar bands. Apparently eager to "capture the renegades and take them back over the line," Paterson was disappointed at Lincoln's reluctance regarding this, due to unclear jurisdictional authority. Lincoln wished to comply with Paterson's request, to ensure that the Crees be "driven North again across the line," but had yet to hear back from the Department of the Interior concerning the matter. Perhaps seeking to assuage Paterson's frustration, Lincoln stated that he planned to "write another [request] and make it stronger."[67] Lincoln informed Paterson further that there were about seventy-five Crees in the camp who had been sent from Fort Assiniboine to Fort Belknap by Colonel Otis. While camped near Fort Assiniboine, they had befriended local Assiniboines and were helped by them.

The Department of the Interior forwarded Lincoln's initial requests to the Department of State with the recommendation that arrangements be made to deport the fugitives. The secretary of state, however, replied that without "specific demand from the Dominion authorities . . . being good under the extradition treaty and followed by a warrant of surrender, the Indians in question cannot not be returned by us to Canada, nor can the United States authorities, military or civil, properly connive at their being kidnapped and sent over the line."[68] On October 17, Lincoln's subsequent request made its way to the secretary of the interior by way of a report by Inspector M. A. Thomas, who had arrived in the region on August 13. Thomas reported that on October 15 he had found "about 100 Cree Indians (men, women and children) refugees from the British possessions." Thomas described Little Poplar's presence and expressed conviction that these Crees were the same as had committed the "rape, murder and theft" of recent date, though Little Poplar had told Thomas through an interpreter that he knew "nothing about the outrages committed and begged *not* to be sent back into the British possessions."[69]

In conclusion, Thomas offered two options for consideration. First, simply put them back across the line (not that it would have been simple). Second, instruct Major Lincoln to issue them rations. Thomas added, apparently with a sense of foreboding, "otherwise they will give trouble through this country."[70] Little Poplar had not shown signs of planning to cause trouble, but his intention to stay south of the line was clear. Perhaps confused by Sergeant Paterson's presence in Montana, Little Poplar asked if the "Boundary Line was done away with." As it was not, he professed his intention to stay at Belknap until spring and then leave for the Crow Reservation.[71] In a way, the conclusions of Little Poplar and Inspector Thomas align. If the Crees were to remain in Montana, they needed to be officially supported with rations. The alternative, clearly understood by both parties, would be disastrous for the Crees and, in the mind of Thomas and surely Montanans, troublesome for surrounding white settlement.

That same month, Lincoln at Fort Belknap began correspondence with NWMP superintendent John Henry McIllree. As the NWMP was attempting to keep the more worrisome Cree bands away from the boundary to the south, McIllree was sent to intercept a reported group of Crees, led by Grizzly Bear's Head and Little Pine, that was heading in that very direction. He ascertained that the band of about sixty was already across the border and had recently been ejected from a reservation in Montana. Seeking more information, McIllree contacted Lincoln. Having received word back from Washington concerning the legal requirements for extraditing Crees, Lincoln's reply characterizes the bureaucratic chaos and legal perplexity that their presence created:

> I have to inform you that I, upon [the Crees'] arrival, notified the head of the Indian Department of the situation, and received orders

> to remove them from the reservation; but a few days before receiving said instructions they had all moved to the neighborhood of Fort Assiniboine, out of our jurisdiction. Had they remained, I should certainly have placed them on the British side of the line. We desire to be rid of them, but unless they come back within my jurisdiction, it is not probabl[e] that anything will be done with them unless you make application under the Extradition Treaty.[72]

Lincoln's reply indicates the general uncertainty among US and Canadian officials on the relationship between Canada, the United States, and Crees and regarding Cree citizenship in either country and the rights to which they were thereby entitled.

After this initial flurry of communiqués, little was done concerning the Crees. Officials in Washington said they needed a formal request from Canada for extradition, Canada provided no such request, and in Montana military officers and Indian agents were left with their hands tied, having neither the authority to deport nor supplies to support the Crees. There was the option for Major Lincoln to detain the Crees until Canada officially requested extradition, but this was predicated on firm evidence that such action from Canada was eminent.[73] After Paterson's stated desire to capture fugitive Crees, nothing more was heard from Canadian officials. Furthermore, the Crees who had been encamped near Major Lincoln moved out of the Fort Belknap jurisdiction before he was able to undertake any action. For the time being, the combined bands of Little Bear, Little Poplar, and Lucky Man were in limbo.

Without promised annuities from the government, without bison herds upon which to subsist, and unwelcomed by local settlers and ranchers, Little Bear's Crees faced a potentially tragic winter. A group of one hundred or so made their way toward Fort Benton seeking refuge among their traditional enemies, the Blackfeet. So hungry that they were forced to eat some of their horses, their children dying, the Crees threw themselves at the mercy of the Blackfeet, who welcomed them with tremendous mercy. Unfortunately, they were turned away by the Indian agent at Fort Benton and not allowed to remain.[74] Eventually understanding that they would be on their own for the winter, the group sought out a suitable camp. In this search, they laid significant groundwork for their future efforts in gaining permanent residence in Montana. For one thing, members of the Cree band made their acquaintance with Frank B. Linderman during the 1885–86 winter. Then a greenhorn teenage trapper in the Flathead Valley, Linderman would grow to be a prominent writer and politician in Montana and a decisive force in the eventual establishment of the Rocky Boy's Reservation.

It is possible that Crees chose to winter in the Flathead Lake region for the same reasons Linderman had chosen it for his first attempts at trapping: abundant game and far removed from civilization. Linderman recalled: "I had to have unspoiled wilderness. . . . I remember that I felt glad when the Flathead Lake country in northwestern Montana Territory seemed yet to be farthest removed from contaminating civilization. I'd go as straight as I could to Flathead Lake." Perhaps sensing the immediate futility of trying to gain support from surrounding Montana reservations, forts, or cities, some fled to the remote wilderness near Linderman. The latter would recall in his memoirs, "Some of them were wounded, and all had seemed to me to be upstanding men. Since our first meeting we had been warm friends."[75] "This friendship has lasted unbroken since 1885," Linderman later explained to a friend.[76] The wintering Crees near Flathead Lake numbered some thirty lodges (teepees) in total. Others found their way to the eastern slope of the Rockies (the Lewis Range) along the Sun River and ranging from Great Falls northwest to Dupuyer Creek and Heart Butte.[77]

The main camp, however, chose a more populated region for winter. In early December, their choice of the Judith Basin, southeast of Great Falls, caused immediate concern for the Department of War. Knowing of the Crees' destitute condition, they feared that the Crees would commit depredations against settlers out of sheer desperation. With this in mind, the secretary of the interior suggested that funds previously indented for "prisoners of war, including Indians," be made available for the refugee Crees.[78] By the end of the year, nothing had come of this, and fears of what the starving band might do in the region spurred military action in late December. Operating out of Fort Assiniboine, Lieutenant Robinson of the First Cavalry rounded up and arrested 137 Crees, about twenty-four lodges, at Rocky Point on the Missouri River. Seventeen lodges from near Fort Belknap were also taken in.[79] Deportation requests were made to the State Department but denied. Instead, word was received from Washington that the Crees had been granted amnesty.[80] By the new year, refugee Crees were spread in disparate camps across northern Montana. Allowed to remain but not warmly welcomed by locals, Crees' quest for permanent residence commenced. They boasted traditional ties to the land that extended farther back than most Americans in Montana, but it would take decades

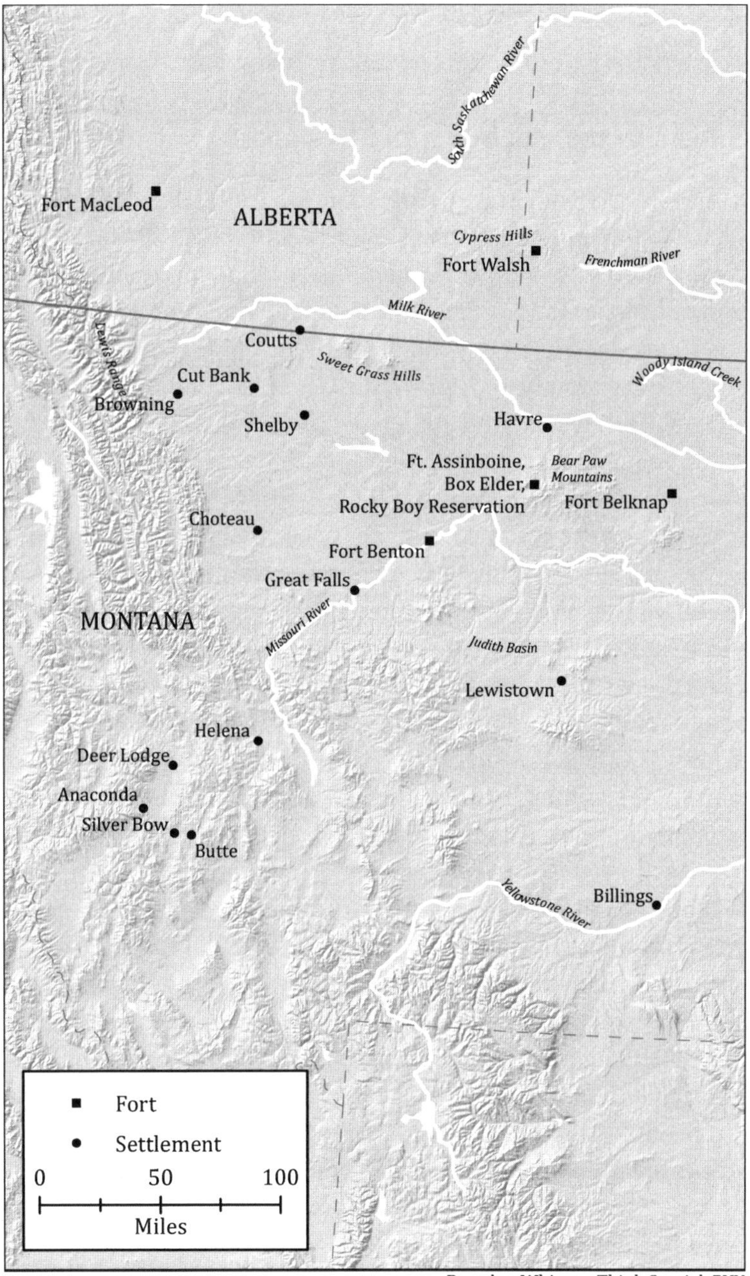

Brandon Whitney, Think Spatial, BYU

Figure 4.1. Important locations in Montana Cree and Chippewa history, 1880–1916. Brandon Whitney, Brigham Young University, Think Spatial.

of tribulation, patience, and perseverance to secure permanent residence in the United States.

Little Bear's Quest to Settle in Montana

The winter of 1885–86 was a dark time for Little Bear's Crees. "They didn't have anything to eat," it was later widely recalled. Concerned over his people's ability to survive through the cold months, Little Bear again approached Colonel Otis at Fort Assiniboine. Asking for assistance, Little Bear also declared that his people would be willing to work for their provisions.[81] Apparently moved by the destitute condition of the Crees, Otis offered an amenable, though temporary solution. Provided with tools from Fort Assiniboine, the group was told to move up into the Bear Paw Mountains to cut and provide wood for the post.[82] Mutually beneficial for both sides, an agreement was made. By February 23, 1886, Special Agent Charles H. Dickson from the Office of Indian Affairs visited with Colonel Otis at Fort Assiniboine and was informed of the agreement that had been made with Little Bear's group. Perhaps under his own prerogative, Otis had also fed the Crees through the depths of winter, using military stores. Dickon put an end to the agreement and distributed four days of rations on February 23. Without further support, Little Bear's band crossed the Missouri River southward but was turned back by officials at Fort Maginnis. Returning to Fort Assiniboine, they remained until April 1. From there they were instructed to move to the Fort Belknap Agency.[83]

About one hundred Crees trekked to Fort Belknap and once again faced the somewhat difficult Major Lincoln. No less cantankerous than he had been previously, Lincoln informed the Crees that he "could not and would not feed them unless specially directed to do so." Requesting instructions regarding them, Lincoln wrote to the secretary of the interior on April 13, stating that they were still camped near the agency and were "terribly poor." Lincoln was not oblivious to their plight but chaffed at government support as a solution. Instead he tried to convince the band to return to Canada, "where they belong[ed]," but the group resolutely refused. Lincoln concluded his report:

> There is no place to remove them to, and having gotten here there is no way that I can see but to let them remain. I do not for a moment

> suppose that this Government, although having these Indians on its hands, by wish or act is ready to say that they may starve, for that is the practical result unless assisted, for they are on the verge of starvation, so that I can see no other way than to recommend that they be taken up and rations issued to them the same as to our own Indians. For my own part I would much rather have nothing to do with them, but in the interests of mercy I have to make the above recommendation.[84]

With Lincoln's recommendation, the acting secretary of the treasury put forth a proposal to appropriate $5,000 "to enable the Secretary of the Interior to furnish such relief to certain renegade British Cree Indians, now on the Blackfeet Indian Reservation in Montana, as will prevent starvation among them."[85] Though only a temporary solution, it would prevent immediate starvation for some Crees in the territory.

The increased mobility offered by spring and summer brought forage and hunting opportunities for Cree bands across northern Montana. The resumption of friendly relations with Métis in Montana also helped Crees support themselves. This decreased their reliance on local forts. US officials shifted focus that summer to Gros Ventres horse-thieving raids against Blood Indians in Canada and Blood Indian retaliation south across the line.[86] The following winter, 1886–87, promised to return Crees to the spotlight as their dependence on settlements and military posts for subsistence would grow. In early November, one hundred or more Crees arrived at Fort Benton, and the *River Press* there raised a voice of concern and demanded that they not be allowed to visit white settlements and that they be confined to the reservations. While the Crees had "behaved themselves" since arriving a year earlier, they simply could not be allowed to "go where they will." Repeating the concerns from the previous winter, the paper continued, "The propensity to steal is so strong in them that when hunger causes them to draw their belts tighter they will look for beef to satisfy their craving. There is no work for them here and how they are to subsist is one of the questions which cannot be answered except as we have stated."[87] During this time, Little Bear established a camp at Breed Creek, southwest of Augusta, near existing Métis camps. Crees would winter there, along neighboring Willow Creek, at Fort Benton, and along the south fork of the Sun River.[88]

The winter of 1886–87 was among the coldest on record. With temperatures ranging down to thirty-five to forty degrees below zero and fifteen inches of snow on the ground, Crees were reported "in destitute condition."[89] Visiting the region at the time, the commissioner of Indian Affairs was snowed in at Choteau and Draper for over two weeks as the region suffered severe coal shortages and cattle died off by the hundreds. Crees later remembered that the snow was so deep that one could simply club coyotes after having spotting them on cattle trails. Deeply depressed by his people's plight, Little Bear worried that many would perish. In ages past, Crees had relied upon bison herds and open plains to subsist and had weathered the harsh winters. Now Little Bear feared what the disappearance of plains buffalo would mean. As a 1942 WPA manuscript on the Crees would put it, he feared that there would be no buffalo in the "Happy Hunting Grounds" of the life to come.[90] That winter some traveled to Fort Shaw west of Augusta in search of provisions, but most remained at Little Bear's camp, receiving occasional assistance from local benefactor Samuel Ford. Regarding the group that traveled to Fort Shaw, a dispatch was sent to the *Helena Independent* telling of their plight: "They are said to be entirely destitute of food and clothing. . . . These Indians subsist almost entirely by hunting and fishing and the low temperature and heavy snow fall has rendered it impossible for them to secure enough to subsist on."[91] Having numbered as many as four hundred a year earlier, their number had since been reduced by death. It was the *Independent*'s conclusion that the government appropriations bill, then pending, needed to be passed, and soon.

Touched by the desperate scene described by the *Independent*, some settlers in the region assisted.[92] Some provided employment when circumstances permitted, but charity could only suffice for so long. Many reacted by proffering the solution of returning Crees to Canada, but the *Independent* explained that this would be impossible: the camp only had ten emaciated ponies left, insufficient clothing, dilapidated teepees, no food, and no weapons, and there were two feet of snow along the trail northward.[93] Citizens from nearby Augusta sent a petition to territorial governor Samuel Hauser asking for aid, which he requested from the legislature. Offering more immediate relief, Helena citizens John R. Watson and Blizur Beach sent a total of $100 to Augusta for the alleviation of Cree suffering. The *Independent* suggested that others join in supplementing their generous act of mercy. The paper also ran this notice under the heading "To the People of Montana":

> Forty-seven Cree Indians—twenty men and twenty-seven women and children—are starving to death on the south fork of the Sun River. The people have petitioned his Excellency, the governor, and the Indians have applied to Gen. Crooke, at Fort Shaw, and can get no relief, as the government will do nothing. Any subscriptions left with John R. Watson Jno., N. Sweeny, T. H. Carter or I. Greenhood, will be properly furnished in food at once.
>
> [Signed] Samuel Ford, Phil A. Manix, A. C. Fleming, M.D.[94]

Hauser pleaded before the territorial legislature, attesting to the upstanding character of those making the private petitions, and a joint resolution approved an appropriation of $500. These acts of kindness were sorely needed and surely welcomed by Little Bear's struggling band. Friendship between Cree leaders and individual Montana citizens, and the advocacy they would provide on the Crees' behalf, would prove important in the years to come.

Having survived the abnormally harsh winter, a group of mixed-blood Crees sought to find a more secure residence for the upcoming years. Traversing west of the Lewis Range, they descended into the Flathead Valley and established camps on the Flathead (Salish) Reservation. They remained there from early spring until the end of the following autumn. Their stay was tenuous. From the onset, Flatheads were not entirely welcoming.[95] Throughout the summer, tensions grew until in mid-August a council was held between leaders of the confederated Pend d'Oreilles and Kootenais on the reservation and Métis Cree representative Pierre Busha. Busha related the recent Cree history following the North-West Rebellion and pleaded for the sixty-odd Cree families in his camp. Though listening with apparent sincerity, the Flathead Reservation residents were unmoved. Pend d'Oreille Chief Micial replied that "however deplored the misfortunes of the Crees," they simply could not offer them homes on the reservation.[96] The Flatheads had firm reasoning, and though the parties left on friendly terms, Busha's return to the Cree and Métis camp was surely sour.[97]

In the face of another winter without a proper home, about two hundred Crees returned to the vicinity of the Blackfeet Agency and set up camp along Dupuyer Creek. They had received aid the previous winter along the eastern slope of the Lewis Range and surely hoped to reconnect with previous regional benefactors. The commissioner of Indian affairs echoed the charitable sentiment of some locals in his report to the Department of the Interior:

> While it is true that these Indians have no rights on this side of the international line, and are not under the care of any agent of the Indian department, still I regard it as the special province and duty of this office, not only to notice their presence and be watchful of their doings on this side of the line, but to pay suitable regard to the pitiable stories told of their poverty and suffering, especially as they are to some extent related by blood to our Indians, and hold constant communication with them in their wanderings through the country, and I think a generous public sentiment would sustain any efforts that might be made by this Department tending to relieve their sufferings even though they are not natives of our soil; and I think it is fitting that this office should take the initiative in providing some way for their very pressing needs, or at least in proposing such relief.[98]

Toward this end, a further $3,000 was requested and paid by the War Department.[99] This appropriation, it was hoped, would obviate the difficulty of their preceding winter in the region, far removed from the assistance of Fort Assiniboine. Reports of their condition varied. One man, John W. Collins, was charitable enough to give them forty snowbound cattle for food but was later disappointed to find that Crees had subsequently raided his ranch during his absence. Making matters worse, some locals may have actively tried to hinder the Crees by poisoning coyotes that the people later ate.[100] Such incidents heightened non-Native concerns. At the same time, some 160 Crees were encamped outside of Fort Assiniboine. During the preceding summer Otis, the commanding officer had been feeding the Crees and furnishing supplies for the camp in exchange for their hunting and working for the fort, but he had needed additional funds to do this. On February 4, 1888, he requested that a similar disbursement in order to manage and support the Cree camp.[101]

With the winter waning, the Indian agent at nearby Fort Belknap offered to accept the Fort Assiniboine Crees and train them in agricultural pursuits. Although they would not gain land rights where they farmed, it was preferable to the secretary of war's alternative option of deportation. In the eyes of War Department leaders, the only options were deportation or managed settlement near an agency. The Indian Office commissioner concluded that even if "forcibly driven across the border . . . [the Crees would] probably return."[102] This recommendation was placed before the Senate on June 4, 1888.

The proposed move from Fort Assiniboine to Fort Belknap proved impossible for some who had been forced to sell much of their provisions and horses to procure food. Effectively, the result was some forty lodges under Thunder Chief unable to leave Fort Assiniboine—demoralized, hungry, and sick.[103] Many Crees had survived for three years in Montana, but they were on precarious grounds. In 1889, US military escorting of Crees to the border foreshadowed the full-scale deportation that would follow.[104]

Conclusion

The North-West Rebellion, Frog Lake Massacre, and early years of Little Bear's return to Montana establish important contexts for the years that would follow. With Crees already suffering from poor reputations in Montana, the violent events of 1885 only worsened their position in Montana. Although they did not expel Crees from the United States, US officials did not provide a lasting solution to their predicament. This moment was crucial. If, at any point in Crees first years back in Montana, an official had decided to push hard for Cree settlement, that might have been quickly achieved. Instead, their precarious situation persisted without resolution, and Montanans began viewing them as a nuisance and threat. If settlement had immediately followed amnesty, Little Bear's Crees might have been saved from thirty years of suffering, wandering, and struggle.

Part 3

Native Struggles to Make American Homelands

After Crees and Yaquis established their presence as refugees in the United States, their experiences diverged in significant ways. Crees in Montana gravitated to regions they had frequented in previous years—around Fort Assiniboine and Fort Belknap, on the Sun River and creeks along the eastern slope of the Lewis Range, and near Havre, Great Falls, Butte, and other towns. They had crossed the line into Montana in hopes of continuing their traditional activities in the region. However, with bison herds eliminated and white settlement hindering their seminomadic subsistence, the traditional life was no longer possible. They were in familiar lands but forced to live in unfamiliar ways, and prosperity and security eluded them. As the economic and political landscape in Montana evolved during their first decade as refugees, their tenuous life in the United States came under constant threat, and most serious of all was the call for their deportation. Conversely, in Arizona, Yaqui refugees were able to integrate themselves into the labor markets and settlement patterns their forbearers had established. Whereas Cree subsistence labor was incompatible with Americans' settler-colonial project of settling Montana, Yaqui labor skills in mining, railroads, and other industries were in high demand. This allowed Yaquis to secure a more settled life, blending in with the wider population of Mexican immigrants when needed, asserting their identity when "Yaqui labor" was specifically desired.

Government response to "foreign" Indians in the United States was uneven, largely because there was no set policy for dealing with such groups. If the US federal government had established provisions for the surely inevitable border crossing of Native peoples from Mexico and Canada and their desire to remain in the United States, many of the subsequent struggles and sorrows of Crees, Chippewas, and Yaquis might have been avoided. US Indian policy was well established, but "foreign" Natives were not covered by it. Similarly, evolving US immigration policy was not clear. Despite all of its complex divisions of racial categories, nationalities, and quotas, it did not have any classification for Natives from Mexico or Canada. They were not accepted as "regular" Mexican or Canadian immigrants, and they could not be defined as "American Indians." They were "foreign" Indians, and the United States did not have any mechanism with which to deal with them.

As borderlands inhabitants, Crees, Chippewas, and Yaquis faced one possible US policy that other Natives in the United States did not: deportation. Unwilling to incorporate them into US immigration or Indian policy, US officials sought to remove Crees and Yaquis physically. Early irregular efforts to gather and deport Crees in the late 1880s evolved into a full, comprehensive deportation in 1896. This required coordination with Canadian federal officials and North-West Mounted Police. No such coordination ever developed across the US-Mexican border. During the 1920s and 1930s, reconfigurations of immigration policy and later Mexican repatriation programs called attention to the Yaquis' ambiguous status as "political refugees." Most escaped repatriation, but the fear of forced removal deeply affected Arizona Yaqui communities—breeding distrust and anxiety and deepening poverty. Ambiguities, legal loopholes, and gaps in jurisdiction spelled years of uncertainty and struggle for Crees, Chippewas, and Yaquis seeking stable settlement and prosperity in the United States.

Yet Crees and Chippewas in the North and Yaquis in the Southwest asserted their Indigenous identity and presence. Religious ceremonies and dances that Crees and Yaquis alike performed comprise the clearest parallel in cultural terms. The contexts for these were distinct, however. Crees in Montana had long performed Sun Dances in Montana, and an executive order from the Montana governor John Rickards had banned the dances for a time. When Crees and other Natives resumed the dances around the turn of the century, they charged non-Natives admission—to earn money and forge ties with the surrounding white communities. The fees they charged were low, but they desperately needed any income. The decision to make the dances public was shrewd: it not only meant income but also led to some positive reports in the Montana press.

Like the Crees, early Yaqui refugees for a time (ca. 1900–early 1910s) performed their traditional religious ceremonies privately, even secretively, as they sought to maintain a low public profile and avoid potential negative repercussions of being identified as Yaquis from Sonora. Unlike the Crees' public dances, however, Yaqui dances, Passion Plays and Easter ceremonies, were community- and church-based. Due to the stable community and church location and regularity of ceremonial events, Arizonans and others became more aware of these and interested in them, and Yaquis would eventually use the events to increase public awareness of their condition and forge new relationships with concerned outsiders.

In terms of a public Indigenous economic presence, the two narratives could not be more divergent. Yaquis integrated fully into Arizona labor markets, often identifying publically as Yaqui—they comprised a strong niche in the regional economy. In some industries, they were indispensable. Their public image was favorable: based on respect for their work ethic and value to the market. Crees and Chippewas, on the other hand, found no such niche. They found occasional, intermittent, contract labor with ranchers, the US Forest Service, and the US military, but these were often odd jobs, offered out of pity. Some enterprising Crees made their own market by collecting, polishing, and selling bison horns and bones, but this market was limited and by no means an essential portion of the broader Montana economy. Hence, their public economic image, as portrayed in the press, usually went hand-in-hand with tales of their indigent existence and desperate scavenging in city dumps.

These differing circumstances deeply affected the lives and livelihoods of refugee Crees and Yaquis. It is difficult to comprehend the cumulative stress and trauma of Crees who for decades lived tenuous homeless lives in Montana, constantly worried by the threat of deportation and the possibility of starvation. Desperation can be read in the persistent efforts of Cree (and Chippewa) leaders in the early twentieth century to secure legal resolution and settlement. Yaquis faced tenuous circumstances too—even the threat of deportation—but the stabilizing effect of their permanent settlements marks a significant difference from their northern counterparts. Still, Yaquis also struggled with poverty and sometimes tense relations with surrounding white populations. Unique to their experience was the continued prejudice built by ongoing Yaqui warfare in Mexico. Fortunately for Crees or Chippewas attempting to carve out a homeland in Montana, the treaty and reserve-settled First Nations in Canada did not perpetuate or create new prejudice for them south of the line.

Chapter 5

Crees in Limbo and Deportation, 1889–1900

[Cree] presence here is very offensive to all settlers who are unfortunate enough to live in the vicinity of their camps. It is the habit of these renegade Indians to wantonly destroy all game, without regard to local laws or regulations, to steal stock of the settlers, and, general subsist by larceny and plunder. They have no business whatever here, and should be immediately removed to the British Possessions, where they belong.

—US ATTORNEY ELBERT WEED, December 2, 1892[1]

The Road to Deportation

On November 8, 1889, Montana was admitted as the forty-first state of the Union, freeing it from the federal oversight associated with territorial status. This allowed Montana greater latitude in managing its own affairs. The Department of the Interior still held oversight for Indian affairs, but the ambiguity over the "foreign" Crees created jurisdictional overlap with state authority. Almost immediately, Governor Joseph K. Toole's office began receiving complaints that "British Crees" were flocking into the state.[2] Ranchers and settlers in the northern reaches of the state were increasingly fixated on the perceived Cree nuisance. Whereas many regional press reports in the years after their 1885 arrival had focused on their destitute condition and poverty, the tide of public opinion was shifting. Growing more accustomed to their surroundings and driven by necessity, Crees were turning to livestock rustling for survival. This could not have come as a surprise to white Montanans. Regardless, the shift from public pity to outcry marked a new hurdle impeding Crees' efforts to establish themselves in Montana.

This shift is best displayed in newspaper reports. "Their presence this side of the line should not be tolerated by the government," decried a Choteau paper after Crees passed through.[3] In June 1890, the *River Press* of Fort Benton wrote: "Cree Indians are permitted to run over the country at their own sweet will, killing the stock of cattlemen; stealing and running horses across the line; terrorizing isolated families, and annoying the people of every town with their disgusting presence, importunate begging and petty thefts. . . . Their presence is offensive, and their immediate proximity is always accompanied by more or less danger to the life and property of residents."[4]

The *River Press* asserted that the Crees did "not belong to the United States," were "essentially Canadian Indians," and should "be compelled to remain there [in Canada]." Speaking directly to their newly empowered state legislature, the *River Press* called for action. The country was no longer "a wilderness." It had moved beyond its territorial beginnings, and settlement, industry, and immigration needed to be encouraged. The foreign, disruptive Cree presence stood in the way of the state moving forward. Even if unintentional in their frightening of white residents, impeding progress, or simply causing trouble, the Crees were seen as incompatible with the establishment of more "civilized" society in the state.[5] However, as Cree historian Raymond Gray wrote, "The Cree Indians did not read the papers and if they did, they would have probably asked,—who is the foreigners in this Indian country? Where did the editor of the *River Press* live before he came to Fort Benton?"[6]

Crees were not oblivious to the outcry against them. In January 1891, the *River Press* and *Calgary Herald* engaged in a debate over which country should take responsibility for the Crees. Understanding the instability of their situation, the Crees left the Choteau and Dupuyer region, where the tide of public opinion was turning against them. They wisely removed themselves from immediate confrontation, but opinions continued to turn against them elsewhere more broadly in the region. The call for deportation grew louder. "They should not be permitted to wander over the country, armed to the teeth, a menace and a terror to outlying settlements," berated the *River Press*.[7] The paper called upon the governor to ensure that "the state [be] well rid of these Indians for once and all." "If they are British or Canadian Indians," wrote a resident of Silver Bow County to Governor Toole, "they should be compelled to go there."[8] By January 1892, the State Department informed US Attorney Elbert D. Weed in

Montana that it was considering the adoption of a measure to remove the Crees from the state.[9]

Over the following months, nearly constant rancor came from papers such as the *River Press*, and Toole's office faced an influx of letters, complaints, and proposed solutions from concerned citizens. Crees circulated around north-central Montana, from the Sweet Grass Hills north of Cut Bank and southward to Great Falls and even Butte. Locals' concern over their presence filled each report of their movements sent to Toole's office.[10] New communication with Canadian officials in the spring of 1892 made some progress toward deportation. Having requested Canadian co-operation, Secretary of State James G. Blaine received official word from Julian Pauncefote and the Canadian Privy Council on April 6, 1892.[11] An approved report from the Canadian Privy Council claimed no knowledge of Cree refugees having crossed into Montana and suggested that perhaps Montanans had confused them with "French Half-breeds." Nevertheless, the council asserted that the North-West Mounted Police would be able to receive at the boundary line any Canadian Indians who had been found guilty of "marauding in the United States territory."[12]

Toole and concerned private citizens welcomed the co-operation of Canadian officials, but the task of apprehending, processing, and deporting the disparate bands of wandering Crees presented serious logistical problems. First, it was nearly impossible to ascertain which of the Crees were among the group received as political refugees in 1885 and which had been here prior to that date or had crossed the boundary subsequently.[13] The acting secretary of war, L. A. Grant, pointed out these challenges to Governor Toole. Further complicating matters, Grant reported that he'd had overwhelmingly positive reports about Crees from post commanders and citizens. Rather than being a menace and a terror, Crees were employed chopping wood, doing laundry, and engaging in other work. Grant said he had been told that "they are very useful, are well conducted and would be greatly missed in the industries of the country were they now removed."[14]

Undeterred, US Attorney Weed and various individuals continued to demand Crees' deportation, using every angle of complaint possible.[15] In late November, Thomas Miles wrote an editorial in Butte's *Daily Inter-Mountain* lamenting, "Why is it that we cannot get rid of those Cree Indians? . . . It would seem strange that after a full and amicable agreement between the United States and Canadian authorities that those pests are still permitted to go where they please. . . . There is a lack of duty somewhere and who is to blame?"[16] In response to this complaint, the equally frustrated Weed commiserated with Miles. "They have no rights here whatever," he wrote directly to Miles. "I am altogether unable to understand why the Government does not insist upon their speedy removal."[17] Writing concurrently to the secretary of war, Weed concluded, "These Indians are renegades . . . they belong across the border, and should be under the charge of the officials of the Canadian government."[18] Much to their consternation, no deportation developed from the agreement with Canadian officials.

The determined efforts to expel them caused understandable frustration among the Crees. When able, Crees had always attempted to work for their keep, offering what services they could in exchange for food and supplies. It had only been under the most extreme circumstances that they had been forced to request assistance. In the face of this considerable campaign against them, some Crees again tried to obtain a more secure and lasting residence on the Flathead Reservation. They found employment with the Flatheads and Métis who could afford to hire them. The leading Flathead councils, however, proved no more welcoming than the white settlers the Crees were attempting to avoid. The Flathead agent, Peter Ronan, expressed his concern over expelling the Crees during the winter months. They were "good men and women with families, who are industrious and law-abiding," Ronan explained, "seeking to better their condition by working . . . [for those] who can afford pay them for their labor."[19] Whether attempting gainful employment or not, whether among whites or Natives, Crees struggled to find welcoming neighbors.

With options for obtaining a secure future in Montana dwindling, Crees began to consider a new path—citizenship. In Great Falls in 1893, Little Bear, Buffalo Coat, and other Cree leaders approached John Hoffman, an attorney in Great Falls, and drafted a letter to new governor John Rickards requesting citizenship papers. After Rickards sent requests to the federal government, the *River Press* scoffed, "It is doubtful if anything will be done at Washington."[20] Uncertain how to proceed, a court clerk in Great Falls inquired of US Attorney Weed and was told that there was no law prohibiting Indians from becoming citizens. Soon thereafter, Crees near Great Falls filed sixty more applications for citizenship, and then Weed told the clerk to stop accepting applications.[21] In a striking scene, Crees "swore to renounce all allegiance to any foreign power, prince or potentate, more especially Queen Victoria and to support the constitution of the United States," the *Great Falls Leader* reported.[22] Little Bear and Governor Rickards both wrote letters in the following months to the federal government. Echoing his previous overtures to the State of Montana, Little Bear wrote to President Grover Cleveland and expressed his people's desire to "adopt the habits and customs of the whites" and abjure allegiance to Queen Victoria. At the crux of Little Bear's appeal was the jurisdictional limbo in which Crees toiled and the persistent poverty to which it subjected them.[23] Having a dim view of Rickards's request to the secretary of the interior, Montanans opposing the idea were vindicated a month later when the Department of the Interior declared its impotence in granting a reservation to Little Bear's Crees.[24] The power to do so, they reasoned, lay solely with Congress.

Raymond Gray would decades later write: "This was not an idle experiment on the part of the Cree Indians at Great Falls. If they were granted the right to become citizens of the United States they undoubtedly [would] have settled in one place on land which they would eventually own. The Cree Camps under Little Bear were becoming better organized."[25] Little Bear wrote to Governor Rickards himself, declaring, "Our object in coming to the United States was to procure for ourselves homes and better treatment than that to which we had been subjected under Canadian laws." He continued to explain that some had come before and others after the Rebellion, but that they had all come with the idea that they "could become naturalized citizens" of the United States and apply for homesteads. To this end, they had attempted to conduct themselves well and felt they were well-qualified to be granted citizenship.[26] Understanding that they were unlikely to be treated as white immigrants, Little Bear requested that they be treated as other tribes and "become wards of the government and be placed upon a reservation." Little Bear's expressed 1893 desire of "becoming American Indians" signaled a new approach for Crees in Montana and a turning point for their efforts.[27]

Little Bear's Crees' increased public profile stirred considerable indignation in the following year. Their new legal tactic drew them toward urban Montana in both physical and cultural terms. Perhaps emboldened by their citizenship efforts and clearly hoping to create and strengthen ties with the Great Falls community, Little Bear's Crees announced plans to stage races, a "sham" reenacted battle with two hundred Indians and horses, and a large Sun Dance at the Great Falls fairgrounds in June. Little Bear enjoyed the support of some local lawyers, and the addition of interested lay citizenry figured to aid Little Bear's cause, but the announcement was received with more negative than positive views from citizens of Great Falls. At the heart of the ensuing controversy was the fact that Little Bear's Crees were non-reservation Indians without land. Their ambiguous legal standing in the state and country unsettled Great Falls opinion. Citizens wanted Montana's Native population carefully monitored and consigned to reservations.

The public and state government responses to Little Bear's Sun Dance reveal the continued problem that Crees' quasi-legal status impressed upon the band. On the one hand, in late May 1894 the *Great Falls Weekly Tribune* reported favorably on the public announcement of the event and suggested enthusiastic pubic approval.[28] Christian ministers in Great Falls however, presented a solid front against the event. Their case, laid out in the *Daily Tribune* a week later, entailed five points:

> The Sun Dance was "contrary to good morals."
>
> It would tarnish the community's reputation as "enlightened, orderly, and progressive."
>
> The thus-damaged reputation would hinder settlement of the city and surrounding region.
>
> The presence of so many Crees in Great Falls would hurt commerce.
>
> The claims that the event should be permitted as a religious performance were "humbug"; the "cruel, indecent and revolting" spectacle was incongruent with their notions of religion and culture.[29]

In cultural, moral, and economic terms, the ministers objected to Crees establishing any presence in Great Falls—be it physical, cultural, or social. In response to these allegations, Little Bear invited Great Falls citizens to his camp to observe firsthand how Crees conducted their religious ceremonies. Instructing his band to guard their actions and do nothing that would give credence to the negative press targeting them, Little Bear attempted to sway public opinion.[30] His overtures, however, were received with outrage.

In response to Little Bear's persistence, the matter was brought before Governor Rickards. Shocked by the Sun Dance practice that sometimes entailed skin piercing, Attorney General Haskell summarized that the "suppression of such ceremonies and barbaric rites would [not] interfere with even the smallest prerogative granted by the bill of rights." Recalling the Crees' questionable legal residence in the state, Haskell demanded that

Rickards not only outlaw the Sun Dance but also deport the "wards of Canada" from the state.[31] Apparently swayed, Governor Rickards issued a proclamation on June 5, 1894. Citing the ceremony's purportedly shocking nature, Rickards prohibited the festival to be conducted anywhere within the state.[32] The fact that Crees were not federally recognized as Indian wards, Rickards explained, meant that the state had full jurisdiction to make such decrees. He further authorized local officials, in Great Falls and elsewhere, to enforce the decree as needed.

Much to Rickards's consternation, the planned races and dance were largely held as planned. Speaking at the event, Little Bear's response to the controversy was poignant:

> We are here today to worship the Great Spirit. He brought us into the world and has taken care of us. My people take this method of expressing our gratitude. God put us here to love each other. Every day I and my people ask mercy of God and thank him for feeding us and keeping us healthy. For two days and two nights I do not eat. Ever since I was born I have worshipped my God at this season of the year. I do not think it right for the white people to stop me from hold[ing] the Sun Dance. It is my method of devotion and my people want it. We mean no harm to anyone, but want to save our souls. My people cut their skin in the shoulders. Christ was put on the Cross and had nails driven through his feet and hands the same as my people do. But if the white men object we will not do this. We do not want trouble with the white race.[33]

Subsequent public response to the controversy expressed empathy for Little Bear's Crees and questioned the governor's right to prohibit the Sun Dance or his wisdom in doing so.[34] In the end, the Sun Dance went on as planned. Despite Little Bear's stating that they would refrain, the objectionable self-piercing were carried out as well, "with all the torture attachments," as one report observed.[35] The controversy reignited debate over the Cree presence. As concluded by one observing reporter, the only future solutions for the limbo in which the Crees existed were for them to "be deported, put on a reservation or gotten rid of in some way."[36] The following year, the Montana house of representatives echoed these options. "We most respectfully represent that it is in the power and it is the duty of the general government," explained state representative Wyllys A. Hedges, "to remove them or support them in some way consistent with the peace, safety, and rights of our own people."[37] These concepts came to fruition soon thereafter.

Deportation of 1896

Outraged by the Cree defiance of his proclamation outlawing the Sun Dance in 1894, Governor Rickards moved against Little Bear's band in earnest in 1896. "Now the Cree were to pay," recalled a Cree account of Rickards's vindictiveness.[38] In January he wrote to Secretary of State Richard Olney, complaining, "In default of a reservation and the restrictions of the Federal government they become an intolerable nuisance constantly violating our [game] laws, foraging upon our herds, and not infrequently looting isolated cabins." "The patience of our people has been sorely tried," he continued, "and I have at times feared that bloodshed would result." Unable to solve the problem, Rickards noted that new Crees were arriving from Canada and that action had to be taken to "not only get rid of these annoying us, but prevent others from coming."[39] Rickards's goal was a wholesale elimination of the Cree presence in the state. Whether refugees from 1885, more recent immigrants, or Crees who had remained in Montana during the Riel Rebellion, Rickards sought to expel all persons of Cree ancestry. This would satisfy the occasional public outcry over the "roaming menace to health" and "constant and aggravated nuisance" that the Crees represented.[40] Whether seeking to alleviate his own annoyance at receiving a steady stream of complaints, to garner votes from disaffected regions, or truly to save the state from bloodshed, as he claimed, Rickards hoped to be the man to finally solve the Cree quandary.

Rickards's lack of differentiation between the different groups of Crees presents a series of legal problems. First, Crees who had left Montana before and during the 1885 North-West Rebellion and subsequently returned never renounced their traditional hunting rights south of the Forty-Ninth Parallel. With "vested *right* in the United States as a hunting ground and home," their ill treatment has puzzled some.[41] This, however, assumes that the United States recognized their traditional hunting grounds south of the line as the basis for rights as citizens. There is strong evidence that some adults actually were born south of the line, as were many of the children born over the previous ten years. Little Bear himself once told Frank Linderman that he had a "perfect right" to remain in the United States because he was born to a Chippewa mother in Wisconsin.[42] Thus, Rickards's efforts to deport all Crees from the state failed to recognize the possibility that some adults may have been born in the United States and that many children certainly had. Richard Burton Deane, part of the Canadian forces processing deportees at the line, reported multiple US-born Crees being forced north.[43]

Even if Little Bear's Crees were not US-born, Rickards's broad deportation effort was problematic. The Crees of Big Bear's band had official legal connection with the Canadian government. After Big Bear acquiesced to signing Treaty 6 in late 1882, he and his band officially became "Canadian" Indians with rights under the British crown.[44] In the eyes of Canada and the United States, however, this was clearly not the same as full citizenship. As one Cree history queried, "If [Governor Rickards] were correct that the Cree were not citizens—why were they then different from European immigrants who had chosen Montana over life in the native countries?"[45] Natives within the United States who had signed treaties and accepted reservations held a clear set of rights and obligations in relation to the federal government. Likewise, citizens of other nations, Canada included, were accorded the possibility to immigrate and establish full residence in the United States. Treaty Indians from Canada, however, were not given the same opportunity. There was no specific immigration policy or law restricting their immigration because they held no citizenship in any country. Apparently Natives were not simply to be wards of the state but wards of a specific state—as if the transfer of supposed ownership or stewardship was impossible. Little Bear's Crees found themselves in the middle of this legal quandary.

Rather than grapple further with the complexities of the situation, Rickards opted for wholesale deportation. In response to Rickards's request, Secretary of State Olney stated that the British embassy had been contacted and that Montana should ready itself to deliver the Crees northward.[46] Unsatisfied, Rickards shot back, demanding that the federal government, not the State of Montana, oversee the deportation and that it be undertaken regardless of Canada's response. By early April, Rickards received word from the commissioner of Indian affairs for the Northwest Territories, A. E. Forget, that Canada was ready to accept charge of the Crees and wished to do so at the earliest possible date.[47] Rickards eagerly forwarded this communication to Secretary Olney with the request that the US government accept the Canadian proposition and rid the state of what one paper claimed were "thousands" of Crees. A survey conducted by Canadian officials made a more conservative estimate of seven hundred Crees in Montana, detailing just how spread out the various Cree bands had become over the preceding decade: 18 lodges at Great Falls, 40 lodges at Silver Bow (near Butte), 40 lodges on Horse Plains Prairie in Flathead country, 5 lodges in Missoula, 2 lodges on the Blackfeet Reservation, 35 lodges at the Crow Reservation, 20 lodges at Glasgow, and 20 lodges at Bull Hook Creek near Havre.[48]

Much to the elation of anti-Cree Montanans, the proposed legislation moved quickly through Congress. "Our friends, the Crees," would certainly be expelled soon, Choteau's *Montanian* noted sardonically.[49] Just over a month after full negotiations were made between Canadian and US officials, on May 13, 1896, the Senate and House of Representatives unanimously passed HR 8820, "an Act making provision for the deportation of refugee Canadian Cree Indians from the State of Montana and their delivery to the Canadian authorities." The amount appropriated for the campaign to deliver "*all* refugee Canadian Cree Indians in [Montana]" was $5,000.[50] The legislation made no mention of how the army would proceed should Crees offer resistance.

Hoping to continue the momentum swinging in their favor, the *Montanian* reported that the Crees near Missoula were ready and willing to march to the Canadian frontier with no resistance. "There will probably be a few who will try to conceal their identity and remain here," the paper's editors reasoned, "but the majority of them will start at once if they are not already on their way to Her Majesty's domain."[51] A council of Crees also hinted that they might be willing to leave, the *Anaconda Standard* reported.[52] The *Great Falls Tribune* was less optimistic. "Buffalo Coat Will Resist—Chief of the Crees, Encamped on the West Side, Likes Montana Very Well," read a headline a week after the passage of HR 8820. Buffalo Coat and other Cree leaders were optimistic that Crees would be granted amnesty in Canada but feared that former leaders of the North-West Rebellion would be punished. "I put my foot in a trap once," Buffalo Coat explained to a *Tribune* reporter, "and it got caught; now I am going to kick, and Buffalo Coat will not put his foot in it." In actuality, Canada had granted amnesty in 1887, but word had not reached them in Montana.[53] Dismayed by this report, the *Montanian* added its belief that Crees might make "armed resistance" to deportation efforts unless they were granted full amnesty. The *Montanian* supposed that, fearing the death sentence if they returned, many might take the alternative of "fleeing to the mountain and becoming 'bad Indians.'"[54] As the reality became clearer of what deporting up to one thousand Crees who had been in Montana for ten years would entail, the dreams of a quick and easy affair dissolved into fear and anxiety.

Officials on both sides of the line shared frustration. Canadian officials had initially expressed their desire to have Crees delivered via rail as soon as possible. Rickards's first communication with Commissioner Forget promised that 500 to 750 Crees would be delivered no later than May 20.[55] That date came and went. A later agreement stated that 500 to 600 Crees would be delivered at the Sweetgrass-Coutts border crossing north of Shelby, Montana, on June 2, 1896. The US Army, however, failed to deliver, and Forget traveled to Montana to learn why the United States had failed to "comply with its promise."[56] He was disgusted with the bureaucratic red tape on the Montana side of the line. Disagreement over which Crees were to be deported caused some stalling. Governor Rickards demanded that all Crees be deported, whereas provisions had earlier been requested for individuals holding official Canadian documents certifying that they were no longer "treaty" Indians.[57] Governor Rickards had no desire to wait any further to sort through which Crees held such certificates and which did not. His simpler solution was to deport all. By shipping them via rail fifty to sixty at a time, Rickards reasoned that an efficient process could be worked out.

Crees were not without voice or opinion in the matter. Some, as already evidenced, threatened to resist any efforts to remove them from the state. Some turned to their lawyer friends to attain a writ of habeas corpus, but the deportation was to begin before it would be returnable on June 23.[58] As officials made considerable efforts to allay Cree fears that their leaders would be incarcerated upon crossing the border, many accepted the idea that general amnesty had been declared. One who counseled with the Crees near Great Falls assured the public that "the Crees would prefer to voluntarily leave the United States, rather than be hauled out in cars." "However," the man continued, "Crees would be unlikely [to leave] unless they were absolutely certain that the alternative threat of forced deportation was imminent."[59] Little Bear's response to the threat is unclear. Having previously been out of state with Don Davenport and C. L. Beveridge's "Montana's Wildest West Show," billed as one of "the only people in the United States without a country," Little Bear may have been absent during the early stages of the deportation affair. The are conflicting reports. One Cree elder later recalled, "As soon as [Little Bear] got into Montana, the governor was ready to send them back to Canada."[60] Whether there all along or having just returned, Little Bear and other Crees were not given much time to decide—and arrests began the following week.

At 1:30 p.m. on June 18, 1896, then-unknown John J. Pershing, first lieutenant of the Tenth Cavalry Regiment at Fort Assiniboine, crossed the bridge west of Great Falls that led into the Cree camp of Little Bear, Buffalo Coat, and others.[61] Accompanied by thirteen of his African American troops, sometimes termed Buffalo Soldiers, Pershing found that Little Bear was absent but subchief Buffalo Coat was present. Buffalo Coat's tent was surrounded, and a council was held. Pershing told Buffalo Coat that Canada had granted a full pardon and that no punishment awaited the Crees. Having placed guards around the camp, Pershing gave further instructions on how they would be transported to the border. Commenting on the cordial nature of the exchange, the *Great Falls Tribune* reported, "It was very nicely done, but they were arrested just the same."[62] Thus began the wholesale forced removal of Crees from Montana.

Immediate complications arose.[63] Following their arrest, efforts were made with lawyers to make an appeal to the district court, contending that the Crees had violated no law and had not been arrested under due process. District Court Judge Charles H. Benton ruled the next week that the state court had no authority to act on the matter since the US Congress had approved the campaign and appropriated funds. In reply, the Cree representative, John Hoffman, contended that the appropriation law called for the deportation of "Canadian Crees" but that at least sixty American-born Crees had been deported unconstitutionally.[64] Judge Benton was still unwilling to act. The *Tribune*'s June 19 report had already noted that many of the children in the camp were likely US-born. Within the first week, a number of Crees took the tactic of claiming to be Gros Ventres, Assiniboines, or Chippewas, and up to seventy were released on such grounds. Others, according to observers in Choteau, made "their way to the mountains where we suppose they feel secure."[65] As others readied to leave for North Dakota or Idaho, Governor Rickards and army officials persuaded Little Bear to convince his Crees to comply. Promised that none would be prosecuted on the Canadian side, Little Bear traveled to the dispersed Cree camps, encouraging all to conform and obey the deportation proceedings. Taking a tragic turn, one Cree who had been present at the Frog Lake Massacre and feared punishment in Canada, Raining Bird or Day Bow, opted for suicide rather than face deportation. His reported last words: "I am a brave man and am glad to die."[66]

Complications aside, the first train holding 110 Crees, 176 horses, thirty vehicles, and a quantity of worldly possessions left Havre, crossed the border at Sweetgrass-Coutts, and arrived at Lethbridge on June 20, 1896.[67] One observer described the scene as utter chaos, plagued with the innumerable problems of loading, unloading, and reloading Crees, livestock, and belongings at the border. A couple days later, a train from Great Falls containing 96 Crees, 177 horses, and many possessions joined them. Anticipating the issuance of a writ of habeas corpus, the Great Falls group apparently offered some resistance and had to be forced by the Fort Assiniboine cavalry troops to break camp and entrain. Over the following days three other groups, consisting of 98, 77, and 71 Crees, were delivered to the border, the last of which arrived on June 25. Of the last group, many were sick, and four died. "They had received very hard treatment for several days previously while in the trains," reported NWMP superintendent Richard Deane.[68] Surviving, however, were Cree chiefs Little Bear and Lucky Man.

Although general amnesty had been granted to all for the 1885 North-West Rebellion, Deane immediately took both Little Bear and Lucky Man into custody upon their arrival in Lethbridge.[69] Little Bear and Lucky Man apparently fell under the amnesty proclamation's exemption clause that excluded "persons who may have committed homicide otherwise than actual warlike conduct."[70] As their actions at Frog Lake had not taken place during an actual battle, they were not protected. Calling upon a local Catholic priest for advice, Little Bear expressed his confusion. "We have led good lives. . . . Why have they taken me prisoner?" he queried. Both were sent to Regina for trial. The oft-sympathetic *Great Falls Tribune* expressed outrage at the "outrageous breach of faith." "As it now stands," the *Tribune* concluded, "Indians have a right to say that the word of the US Army officer was used to induce them to walk into a trap which had been treacherously laid for them." Superintendent Deane offered some consolation, stating that Crees had been deceived into believing that the deportation had been initiated by request of the Canadian government. This belief has persisted among Crees in Montana, that "the Queen of England sent a request that she wanted her Indians back."[71] While Canada had agreed to accept the Crees, the impetus of the deportation came from south of the line.

By late July 1896, the deportation was largely complete. Pershing's Buffalo Soldiers had gathered Crees from camps near Great Falls, Havre,

Malta, Custer, Missoula, on the Flathead Reservation, and elsewhere. As appropriation funds had run dry, some had even been forced to walk with their possessions to the border, sick with bronchitis, colds, and measles. The *Helena Weekly Herald* reported at the end of the month that 532 Crees had been sent north and that 100 others had crossed of their own volition.[72] Upon arrival, most were divided into camps of those wishing to travel to reserves to the east (Battleford) or west (Edmonton). All would be relocated to reserves far north from the border, removed from railway lines, and Deane warned that they would not be allowed to "run about the country." Many went to a group of reserves west of Edmonton, where one called the Montana Reserve existed. Except for those arrested and sent to Regina, they would be afforded the same rights and protections as other Natives living on Canadian reserves. Pleased with the outcome, President Grover Cleveland concluded in his eighth State of the Union Address that Cree deportation had been "compulsory but peaceful."[73]

As for Little Bear and Lucky Man, the outlook was grim. The *Great Falls Leader* predicted that they would "probably go the same route their infamous leader took after the sentence of death had been passed upon him. . . . That Canadian authorities have done as Little Bear feared and broken faith is apparent. . . . Little Bear and Lucky Man were lured to Canada by false promises and now probably will pay the full penalty." As word spread of Canadian treachery, many Crees remaining in Montana quickly dispersed to evade deportation. To the surprise of many, however, both Little Bear and Lucky Man were eventually found innocent due to lack of evidence.[74] The Cree wife of Indian agent Thomas Quinn, who was at the center of the Frog Lake Massacre, was subpoenaed to identify Lucky Man and Little Bear as among the murderers, but she failed to do so. An eyewitness gave the following account:

> Mrs. Quinn . . . walked up to the two prisoners and gave them careful scrutiny. It was a tense moment. There is no doubt that both men knew that what the woman said meant their freedom or shameful death, but neither gave the slightest sign. Aimiceese [Little Bear] continued to boldly stare about the room, sometimes focusing his eye upon something of the white man's furnishings with which he was unfamiliar. Lucky Man paid no attention. There was silence a moment, broken only by the metallic clink of the handcuffs on Lucky Man's wrists. Then the woman came to a pause and spoke in Cree to the Interpreter. "What does she say, Pritchard?" said Forget. "She says, Sir," said

> Johnny, "she has never seen either of these two men before." "By Gad!" said Mr. Forget, "I might have known. These are her own people and it was only her husband that they murdered."[75]

Both men were subsequently released. The disdain they must have felt towards the Canadian treachery, however, surely dampened the joy of their release. Little Bear temporarily settled at the Onion Lake Reserve and in February 1897 traveled to Ottawa to secure amnesty and treaty lands for his people in Canada. While initial reports suggested that he had succeeded on all accounts, a later report explained that they would be allowed to settle on an existing reservation but not receive their own. One source claims that Little Bear, subchiefs, and others received farming implements and other materials from Canada for their settlement but only stayed in Canada long enough to sell them and return to Montana.[76]

The great distrust that the arrest of Lucky Man and Little Bear spread among fellow Crees was quickly made evident. It is estimated that as many as 75 percent of those deported quickly returned to Montana.[77] The popular Cree story states that most of the deported Crees were back in Montana before Pershing's troops made back it to Fort Assiniboine. "These Indians remember the broken promises of the Canadian government, when Little Bear was arrested," Raymond Gray, wrote. "Then they entertained no idea that they were ever going to live in the Dominion of Canada."[78] Due to legal technicalities concerning the North-West Mounted Police ability to restrict Cree movements off of their reserves, Canada was largely powerless to prevent Crees from leaving. One group stayed for a winter in Alberta on a reserve with other Crees and then "started to wander away again." A Cree elder whose parents stayed in Canada later recollected, "Their excuse was that they were going berry picking, but they left for good." Frustrated, Governor Rickards appealed again to the federal government for aid in early 1897, complaining that the Crees were "again on the rampage in Montana." Throughout the spring and summer of 1897, northern Montanans complained of the returning Cree, and Great Falls reported that Little Bear was among them by October 1897. He had returned to Montana aiming "to make a legal battle" for his people to live in Montana, going straight to new governor Robert B. Smith upon arrival.[79]

No further military actions were taken against Crees in Montana during the nineteenth century. As the new century approached, Crees again spread out into various bands across their now accustomed ranges of more than thirty years. Some occasionally made efforts to attain citizenship, but little was accomplished. In the spring of 1898, Buffalo Coat requested state aid, land, and citizenship for his band near Great Falls. When asked why he had returned to Montana, he explained that they were ill treated in Canada.[80] Governor Smith, however, and the federal government claimed no jurisdiction to settle the group on a reservation. The *Great Falls Tribune* speculated that it would likely be cheaper to give them a reservation than to continue the cycle of offering emergency aid or deporting them. Buffalo Coat's Crees were not going to return to Canada, so the question before them was how to sustain existence in the state.

Previously encamped near Butte, Little Bear returned by April 1898 to Great Falls to consult with other Cree leaders. Little Bear expressed his desire to purchase public land from the state for his people. "If the state will donate an equal number of acres to [the Cree] purchase," it was reported, "[Little Bear says that] his people will become self-supporting and never again ask aught from the government." An alternative proposal for them to join an already existing reservation was also put forward.[81] These and other efforts were for naught.[82] The State of Montana often seemed most content to ignore their presence. When the public noted their presence, at least as noted in the press, it was as a perceived nuisance or threat or as a cultural peculiarity. In the summer of 1899, Havre city officials raised an alarm when word was received that smallpox-infected Crees were heading to their town. Quarantines and a statement urging that the public "have no dealings with the Indians and to by all means keep away from the camp" were readied but dismissed after investigation proved the allegations to be untrue.[83] Weeks later, Havre's *Milk River Eagle* reported on a Sun Dance by Crees and Assiniboines and offered an exoticized description of the ceremony.[84] In both of these examples, public rhetoric concerning Crees failed to address the central issue to their landless predicament. They were a presence to be noted but not dealt with.

Rocky Boy's Band of Chippewas in Montana

While Crees under the leadership of Little Bear and others struggled to secure permanent and stable settlement in Montana, a much broader landscape of transnational Natives existed along the Forty-Ninth Parallel. Northern plains Indigenous peoples, in large groups, small family bands, and individuals, carved out lives on both sides of the border. One group eventually joined the Cree narrative in a significant way—Rocky Boy's band of Chippewas.[85] This transnational Chippewa story blended with that of Little Bear's Crees near the turn of the century when they joined efforts to secure lands for settlement. Their joint story entails the 1916 establishment of Rocky Boy's Reservation south of Havre, Montana, and federal recognition of the Chippewa Cree Tribe. From early intermittent interaction in the late 1890s to consistent combined efforts, Crees' and Chippewas' histories under Little Bear and Rocky Boy slowly merged. The resultant mix of ethnic, linguistic, and other cultural backgrounds of the Chippewa Cree Tribe was—and continues to be—complex.

To provide context for their eventual joint history, some background on Rocky Boy (Ahsiniiwin or Asiniweyin) and his band is necessary. Frank Linderman explained that the more direct translations of his name would be Rocky Man, Stone Child, or Stone Native—"Rocky Boy" being affixed by white men attempting to belittle the chief.[86] A Chippewa named Wap-ah-noo or Wabuno (translated as "Coming Morning"), reported as Rocky Boy's father, had been a visionary man and leader when his people were still living in the eastern woodlands south and west of Hudson Bay. The well-liked Coming Morning gathered a group of one hundred Chippewas and told them of a vision: to the West, he explained, there was "a promised home" in the mountains. In the vision, as the story would be passed down, he had been visited by a young man who showed him the Bear Paw Mountains of Montana and designated them as a "good place to raise his grandchildren and their children . . . a rich place."[87] Tribal tradition relates that Coming Morning's followers placed their faith in him, not questioning the daunting nature of the trek he proposed. One account reads as follows:

> They did not ponder how they, a forest and stream people, who lived off rice and fish and corn, would fare in the mountains. They knew Manitou or Creator would look out for them. It was good that the vision had come. Now they knew what they would do. They would follow Wabuno to a land they had not been in all their travels in the lake country of the North American continent. They prepared to follow the vision. The women made a supply of moccasins and packed food. They made new mossbags in which to carry the babies. They set out with travois pulled by horses. . . . Their journey eventually led them to what was the Montana Territory, to the land of mountains seen in the vision of Wabuno.[88]

Their journey to Montana took them past Red Lake (Ontario), the Red River Valley, and eventually westward to Glasgow, Montana. During the journey, they made stops with Mandan people in present-day North Dakota and sojourned north of the border in Canada for a time.[89] Their party numbered around one hundred men, women, and children.

The exact year of their arrival in Montana is uncertain, but it may have been as early as 1889.[90] One prominent Chippewa elder, Malcolm Mitchell, or Yellow Bird, was born in 1889 at Birch Creek, near Browning, Montana. He echoed stories told by his grandfather Day Child (and grandmother Yellow Sky) of thirteen Chippewa families leaving the East, traveling through the Turtle Mountain area (where two families remained with the Turtle Mountain Reservation, established in 1882), before making their way into northern Montana.[91] It is unclear whether this group was the same as Rocky Boy's father's encampment of one hundred people, but it follows a similar trajectory. Whether the same or two different groups of Chippewas, these stories both place Chippewa immigrants in Montana by the 1890s. Explaining his history to US officials some years later, Rocky Boy himself placed his people's arrival in Montana around 1890.[92] By 1896, when Crees were being deported, Rocky Boy and his father were encamped with other Chippewas just west of Butte, Montana, at Silver Bow. When some Chippewas moved to Canada along with Crees, Rocky Boy remained, soon assuming leadership of the Chippewa band at Silver Bow.[93]

Chief Rocky Boy's personal history is as elusive as it is controversial. On one hand, the aforementioned narratives of Chippewa westward migration suggest that Rocky Boy and his family arrived in Montana in the late nineteenth century. Contradicting this, Rocky Boy told officials in 1908 that he was born in Silver Bow County, Montana. As he was reported to be fifty-six years old during a 1909 enumeration, this would place his birth in 1853, and no other sources place his band of Chippewas in Montana that early.[94] To others, Rocky Boy stated that he could not say exactly where he came from, but assured "it was from the American side of the Canadian line." John C. Ewers's reading of sources led him to conclude that Wisconsin was the most likely locale for Rocky Boy's birth.[95] In later years, when the question of Canadian or US birthplaces became an important talking point, many who were known to have been born in Canada asserted of US birth locations. Especially in light of the 1896 Cree deportation and the extreme prejudice Crees faced in being from Canada, Rocky Boy and his people had ample incentive to assert US roots. This adds some qualification to sources regarding Rocky Boy's birthplace, but it is reasonable to assume it was indeed in the United States—whether in Montana, Wisconsin, or elsewhere.

Some sources suggest that Rocky Boy came to Montana in 1885 after participating in the North-West Rebellion. Linking him directly with Little Bear's band in its flight to Montana is a significant proposition. Frank Linderman, close friend and ally of Rocky Boy and Little Bear, stated that Rocky Boy led defeated Chippewas and Little Bear's Crees to Montana.[96] Offering a different angle on the 1885 Rocky Boy–Little Bear relationship, Montana state senator William T. Cowan later explained that Rocky Boy did not accompany Little Bear's refugee group from Canada. To the contrary, he stated that Rocky Boy was already established in Montana, and that Little Bear directly sought him out upon crossing the border.[97]

Senator Cowan's explanation as to why the young Cree leader, Little Bear, would seek out Rocky Boy, a Chippewa, is significant: they were related. Cowan states that Rocky Boy's first wife was a sister to Little Bear's father, Big Bear. This would make Rocky Boy Little Bear's uncle by marriage. Four Souls, son of Little Bear, stated that Little Bear often referred to Rocky Boy as his "older brother."[98] Four Souls explained further that Rocky Boy's wife and Big Bear's wife were distant cousins.[99] As Little Bear regularly claimed that his mother was a Chippewa born in Wisconsin, this is a definite possibility.[100] It appears that Rocky Boy and Little Bear were indeed related, although sources differ on exactly how. It thus makes sense that the refugee Little Bear would seek out his older relation, Rocky Boy, upon arriving in Montana. The question of when or how Rocky Boy arrived in Montana is difficult to answer with certainty. His origins remain a mystery and even a controversial subject to descendants and associated tribal members to the present. One thing is certain, however. By 1890 Rocky Boy was in Montana, and by 1900 he had assumed leadership of his band of Chippewas and was intent on securing lands upon which they could settle. Rocky Boy was determined to make Montana his home.

Conclusion

Through the many years following the North-West Rebellion, transnational Crees under the leadership of Little Bear and others demonstrated their persistent desire to take up permanent residence in Montana. Suffering greatly from poverty, prejudice, and their vague legal standing in the United

States, even congressionally ordered deportation failed to dissuade them from their goals in Montana. Despite their best efforts, however, they continually suffered from the negative prejudices that followed them from the North-West Rebellion and Frog Lake Massacre. In the following years, external forces previously unavailable to them—other Natives and prominent white Montanans—would bolster their tenacity. The new century would bring new opportunities for success in making Montana their homeland. A long, arduous road, however, lay ahead. They had escaped persecution in Canada and returned after the deportation campaign, but escaping the label of "foreign" Indians would prove more difficult.

Chapter 6

Arizona Yaquimi and Integration in the United States, 1900s–1950s

America proved a Paradise to my People who are without a home. . . . May they remain in peace in this Powerful Land of the fearless and the free.

—PRIVATE JOE D. ROMERO, 1942[1]

While Little Bear's and Rocky Boy's Crees and Chippewas struggled to make stable homes in Montana, Yaquis in Arizona fared somewhat better. The push of persecution in Sonora and the draw of peace, stability, and prosperity hoped for in the United States had caused thousands of Yaquis to cross the international border to establish new homelands as political refugee exiles in Arizona. The subsequent unfolding of a full Arizona Yaqui narrative is rooted in the physical and quasi-legal establishment of Yaqui communities in the state. Over the first three decades of the twentieth century, Yaquis braved the passage across the US-Mexican border and established temporary and permanent Yaqui camps, villages, and towns in Arizona. These physical sites of home, family, and community are the bedrock upon which Yaqui successes in Arizona were built. Exploring the historical geography of these settlements and their connections with Yaqui labor can provide a base for further analysis and contrast to the landless and itinerant Crees and Chippewas in Montana.

The passage of Yaquis across the border during the last decade of the nineteenth and first decade of the twentieth century remains a dark past for Arizona families whose ancestors fled to the United States as transnational refugees. A pall too hangs over the perils those ancestors left behind. Before crossing, many had already fled their traditional Yaqui villages and lived covert lives as hacienda laborers or as workers in cities such as Guaymas. Attempting to obscure their Yaqui identity, they were under constant threat of discovery and deportation. The risks associated with flight across Sonoran desert to the border were no less dangerous than the perils of remaining in Sonora. Anthropologist Edward Spicer relates: "The insecurity led to nighttime escapes, desperate journeys on foot carrying children through the deserts northward to the United States. Yaquis in Arizona in the 1930s told frequently of these forced journeys. . . . Often little groups managed to cross only a few hours ahead of Rural Police who were on their trail . . . the trickle of escaped peons . . . continued to move across the international boundary; the United States, insofar as notice was taken at all of the phenomenon, admitted them as political refugees."[2] Compounded by informers within their own Yaqui communities, life in Sonora was an increasingly difficult and anxiety-ridden experience for Yaquis. Spicer concludes rightly, "The only safe course was to escape into the United States."[3]

In 1975, sixty-year-old Ferminia provided Spicer a telling example, an account of her family's harrowing exodus from Sonora. After Mexican troops captured, deported to Mexico City, and then killed Ferminia's grandmother, Ferminia's great-grandmother took her three grandchildren (five, four, and three years old), with a donkey or two for transport, and walked the entire route from the Yaqui River Valley in Sonora to southern Arizona. Ferminia's parents were living and working near Sasco, Arizona, when she was born in 1915, one of four children who survived out of fourteen born. In 1918 they moved to Tucson, and later they moved to Marana, where an existing Yaqui enclave was growing.[4] Ferminia's multigenerational story demonstrates how the violence in Sonora and subsequent migrations divided Yaqui families and also how waves of immigrants and refugees followed one after another across the border and gathered in settlements.

Certainly terrified upon arrival, Yaqui refugees must have crossed the border with great relief. Although the immediate risk of enslavement and dissolution of family units via deportation to southern Mexico faded, the new threat of forced repatriation loomed. Rosalio Moisés, who crossed with his grandmother in 1906, offered a detailed description of the passage in *A Yaqui Life*, published in 1971. When asked by border guards for letters of recommendation, which they did not have, Rosalio's grandmother dishonestly stated that they were going to Tucson to visit her son, Miguel Valenzuela. In reality, Rosalio's father was working as a miner and not living in Tucson. She offered fake names for all in her party, which the inspector recorded. Then, in a stroke of luck, a passing Mexican carriage driver vouched for them, bluffing that he personally knew the fictitious

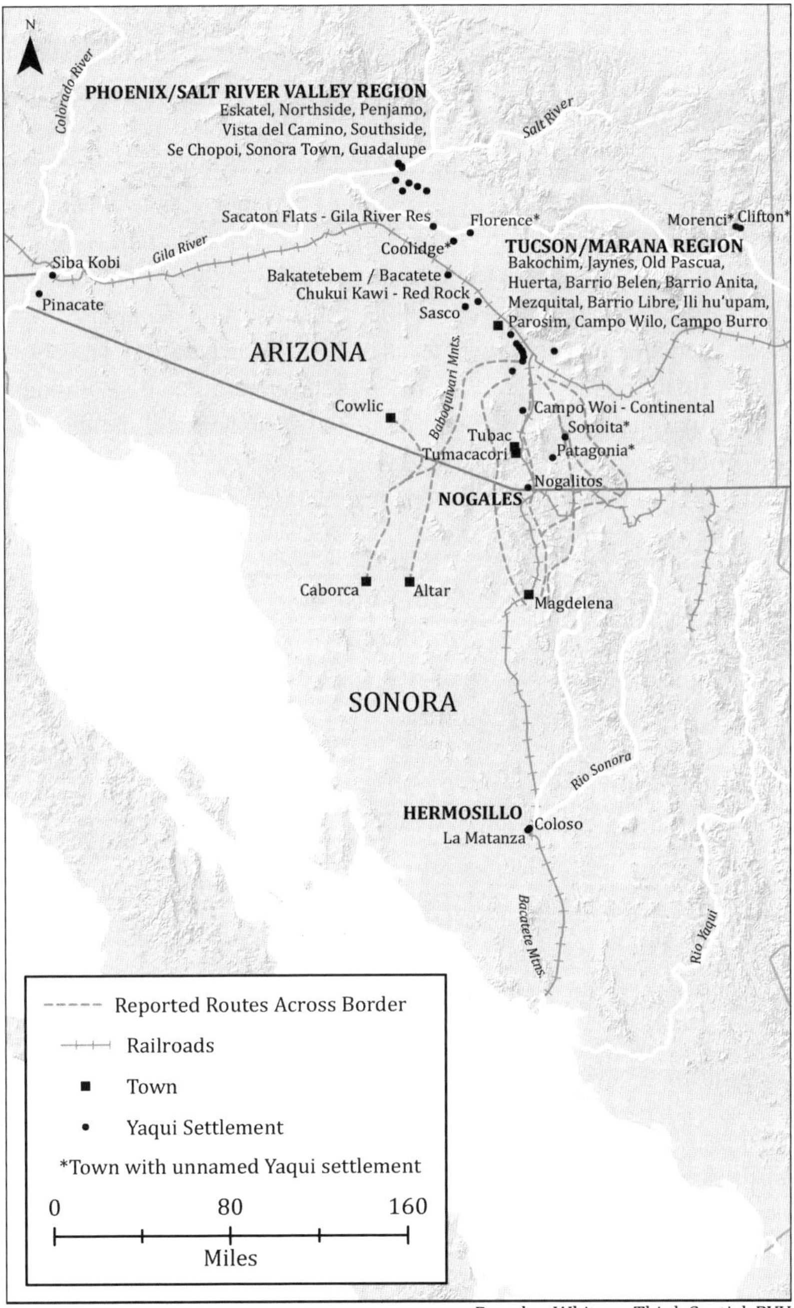

Brandon Whitney, Think Spatial, BYU

Figure 6.1. Yaqui passage routes and Arizona settlements. Brandon Whitney, Brigham Young University, Think Spatial.

Miguel, and took them to a Yaqui village three miles east of Nogales. Border security and scrutiny of Yaqui refugees was nothing as minimal as this for early immigrants.[5] Most Yaquis followed this route through Nogales, but others took a more westerly course, travelling north through the Altar Valley and crossing the border into the Baboquivari Mountains (see figure 6.1). Often resting there among Tohono-O'odhams at Cowlic and other villages before continuing on, some Yaquis even intermarried with southern Arizona Indians and this left a lasting impression on the region.[6]

Upon arrival, Yaquis followed well-established Yaqui geographic routes, economic ventures, and settlement locations. Newly arrived Yaqui men joined other Yaqui laborers in migrant work on the Southern Pacific Railroad and in various mining operations (see figure 6.2). Women and children often stayed sedentary in burgeoning Yaqui villages, often maintaining traditional gendered divisions of labor in a more strict fashion than surrounding Mex-

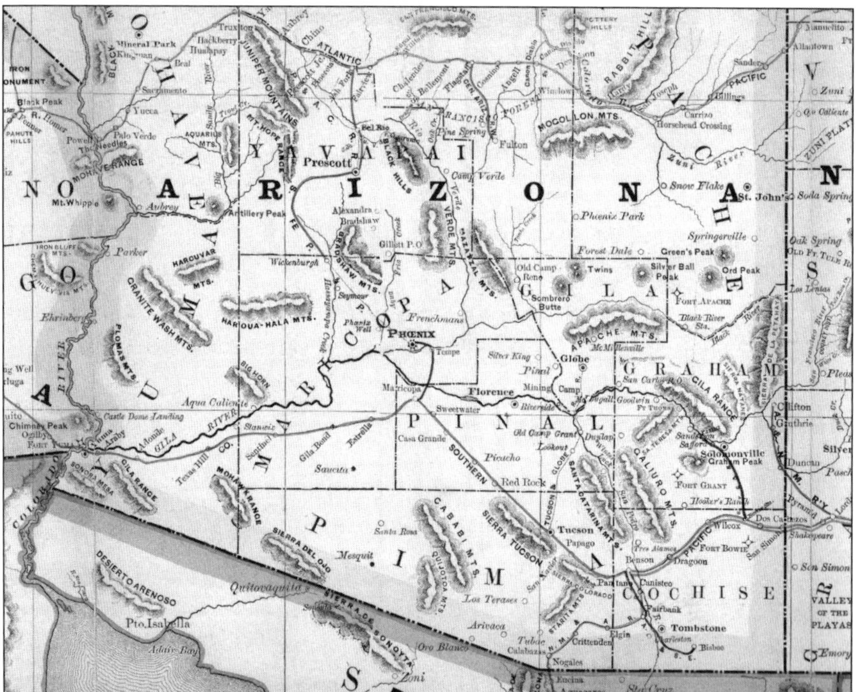

Figure 6.2. Southern Arizona railroads and major mountain ranges in 1877. Excerpt from *US Southwest, Mexico Railroad Map of the United States* (Rand McNally & Co., 1891). Courtesy of David Rumsey Map Collection, www.davidrumsey.com.

ican immigrant populations.[7] For example, an early 1902 group of Yaqui families was reported as having stopped at mining camps south of Tucson, where women remained as camp laborers, while the men continued to Prescott and Clifton to secure employment in the mines.[8] In the case of Rosalio Moisés, adult males in his group immediately left for Patagonia to work in the mines while his grandmother began networking with relatives and other Yaquis in Nogalitos. Soon thereafter, Moisés received word that his father was working in the Silver Bell Mine west of Tucson. He remained in the Nogales region for two months, working for a white Arizonan who hired him for thirty-five cents a day plus board. When his father arrived, he escorted the family to Barrio Libre, a growing Yaqui village on the south side of Tucson. From there they continued to Barrio Anita, a Yaqui settlement on the northwest side of Tucson. Others told of similar carefully planned, multistage itineraries. These Yaqui migrations were anything but haphazard. Migrants followed predetermined routes, congregated with other Yaquis, and re-created sociocultural worlds and communities they left behind in Sonora.[9]

By the time the 1910 Mexican Revolution toppled the regime of Porfirio Díaz and the Yucatán deportation and enslavement ceased, Yaquis were spread from southern Mexico to southern Arizona and even Texas.[10] Some slowly made their way back to Sonora, and the exodus to Arizona slowed considerably. In Arizona, the Yaqui population increasingly centered in permanent Yaqui villages. Yaqui laborers traveled extensively in southern Arizona, and small settlements were scattered along rail lines, near mining centers and agricultural regions, but they increasingly settled in communities near Tempe-Phoenix and Tucson. From 1910 onward, these settlements grew steadily in number until eventually numbering in the thousands. Early-to-mid-twentieth-century settlements spread broadly across southern Arizona (see figure 6.3).

Many of these early settlements were close to the Southern Pacific Railroad corridors in the state. With Nogalitos as the southernmost, the next grouping around Tucson included Huerta and Mezquital just east of the city, and Barrio Libre and Old Pascua respectively on the south and north sides of Tucson. Moving northwest from Tucson along the Southern Pacific corridor, other Yaqui settlements were in a close succession: Bakochim near Cortar; the Marana settlements of Ili hu'upam, Parosim, Campo Wilo, and Campo Burro (Camp Buru); Chukui Kawi near Red Rock; and Bakatetebem near Eloy. Farther west were the Siba Kobi and Pinacate settlements near Yuma and Somerton. The other Yaqui settlements were grouped to the north in the Tempe-Scottsdale-Phoenix region and during early years was centered on Guadalupe, just west of Tempe.[11]

Table 1. Arizona Yaqui settlements, 1900–present

Settlement	Region
Nogalitom (Nogalitos)	Nogales
Pinacate	Yuma-Somerton
Siba Kobi (Cliff Corner)	Yuma-Somerton
Los Tres Mesquites	Yuma-Somerton
Tubac	Tubac-Tumacácori
Campo Woi (Camp Two)	Continental
Barrio Libre	Tucson
Mezquital	Tucson
Old Pascua	Tucson
Tierra Floja	Tucson
Barrio Anita	Tucson
Huerta (Orchard)	Tanque Verde
Bakochim (Snakes)	Cortaro
Jaynes	Cortaro
Ili hu'upam (Little Mesquites)	Marana
Parosim (Rabbits)	Marana
Campo Wilo (Skinny Camp)	Marana
Campo Burro (Yoem Pueblo)	Marana
Rillito	Marana
Chukui Kawi (Black Mountain)	Red Rock
Sasco	Sasco
Bakatetebem (Tall Bamboos) / Bacatete	Eloy
Sacaton Flats	Gila River Reservation
Se Chopoi (Hightown)	Chandler
Southside	Mesa
Sonora Town	Gilbert
Guadalupe	Tempe
Turicate / Eskatel / Northside	Scottsdale
Pénjamo / Vista del Camino	Scottsdale

Along with less-established sites of Yaqui labor in southern Arizonan mines or in agriculture, these comprised the primary early settlements. Later discussion of Yaqui labor and Yaqui land will include the development and addition of other settlements. Two primary regions deserve specific attention for their early history: Pima County settlements in and near Tucson and Salt River Valley settlements in and near Tempe, Scottsdale, and Mesa. In the decades following the establishment of these first communities, these two regional clusters eventually boasted the majority of Arizona's Yaqui population and were the loci for Yaqui political activities. Their establishment as uniquely Yaqui spaces had physical, cultural, and psychological ramifications for individuals and families.

Tucson Yaquis and Pascua Village

While Yaquis had been residents of Tucson for quite some time, distinct Yaqui enclaves took form during the 1904 exodus from Sonora.[12] The first members of the new diaspora settled on strips of unused land where they established themselves as squatters. In the irrigated farmlands of Tierra Floja north of Tucson, agricultural companies recruited Yaqui laborers as early as 1906 (see figure 6.3). A few miles southwest of Tucson's city center and on the east bank of the Santa Cruz River, Yaquis working on farms and for the railroad established the community they called Mezquital. By 1907, eight Yaqui houses stood at the center of a growing settlement. With increased Mexican immigration during the 1910 Revolution, Yaquis also moved into a burgeoning Spanish-speaking community on the northwestern edge of Tucson, Barrio Anita. In these and other surrounding locations, Yaquis did not own land.[13] For Yaquis and concerned US officials, such uncertain grounds led to discussion of forming a legal permanent settlement for Yaqui residents and immigrants to come.

By the late 1910s, a self-appointed Yaqui leader, Juan Pistola, had begun to serve as a public voice for the Yaquis and along with concerned white Arizonans began a campaign to secure a permanent legal site for Yaqui settlement. Pistola was instrumental in negotiating employment opportunities for early Yaqui arrivals and by 1912 established a relationship with US Attorney Kirke T. Moore.[14] The two developed a plan to establish a location where all inbound Yaqui immigrants would be required to report and receive documentation. By 1918, Pistola was already reporting inbound refugees to US officials with assurance from Arizona governor George

W. P. Hunt of their acceptance as political refugees.[15] A central location for the enumeration and settlement of Yaquis was still needed, however. A single concentrated Yaqui community, Moore and others believed, could help Yaquis prosper in the state while simultaneously providing a base for controlling arms smuggling along the border.[16] From 1918 to 1921, Moore, Pistola, and others worked to consolidate Yaqui and Tucsonan support for the plan. Just northwest of Barrio Anita and Tucson proper, many Yaquis had been squatting on land owned by A. M. Franklin. Through the influence of Moore, an agreement was struck with Franklin and Tucson banker John Metz for legal Yaqui settlement, and Pascua Village was born.

The 1921 deal with Franklin, as originally planned, was for his land to be divided into individual family plots and sold to Yaquis on the installment plan.[17] Encompassing nearly forty acres, the land was presented to Tucson's Yaquis as a site for settlement and gaining legal title to land. Franklin and Metz stressed that a separate Yaqui settlement such as this would be in their best interests, as their current settlement with "Chinese, Negroes, and Mexicans who had different customs from the Yaquis" was already troubled by animosity from the other parties. In their own village, explained Franklin and Metz, they could engage in their cultural and religious observances without harassment.[18] Settlement, however, was contingent upon Yaquis procuring a permit from Metz.

Yaqui reaction to the plans was mixed at first. Some were immediately enthused by the prospect of owning land and quickly entered into the agreement. The initial group at Pascua Village consisted of twenty Yaqui families, most coming from the closer Yaqui communities at Barrio Anita and Tierra Floja. According to Spicer, however, many (if not most) of Tucson's Yaquis rejected the idea of being forced to report their whereabouts. Fearing "constant surveillance" by US officials, they made no plans to

Figure 6.3. Tuscon area Yaqui settlements, 1900–present. Compiled from Felipe Molina, "Arizona Yaqui Communities," Spicer Papers, Arizona State Museum, Tucson, series 8, box 5, folder 278; William Simpson, "An Ethnographic Account of Yaqui Guadalupe Compared with the Culture of Poverty" (master's thesis, Arizona State University, 1969); Edward Spicer, "Yaqui Villages Past and Present," *Kiva* 13 (November, 1947): 2–12; Edward Spicer, People of Pascua (Tucson: University of Arizona Press, 1988), 6, 78; and Edward Spicer, fields notes from Yuma, June 7, 1940, Spicer Papers, Arizona State Museum, series 8, box 7, folder 438.

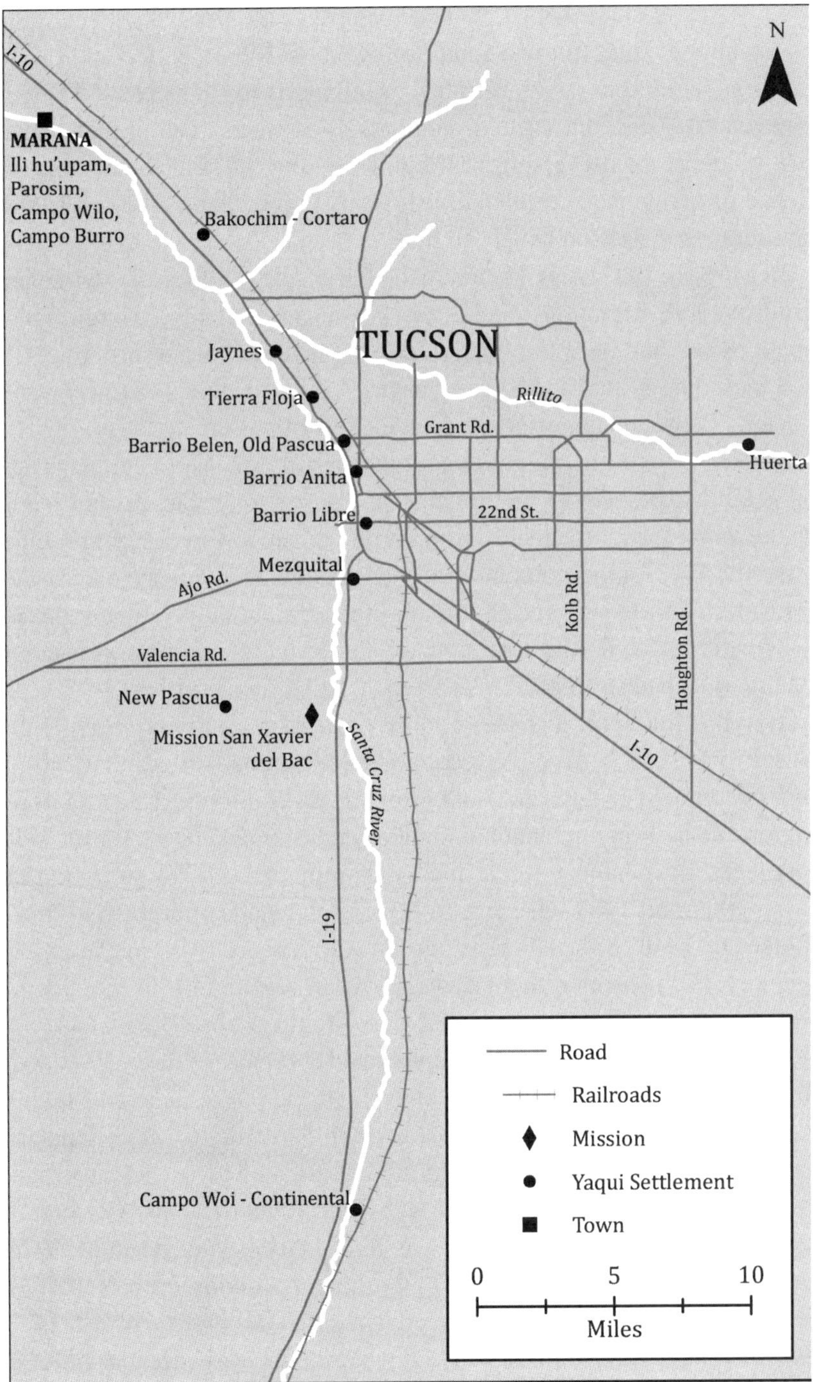

Brandon Whitney, Think Spatial, BYU

move.[19] Actual surveillance of the village was minimal, however, and as this became evident, more Yaquis followed. In Moore's recollection, few Yaquis succeeded in paying the full installments for their plots. They did, however, "treasure the written contracts very much, feeling that it [was] good evidence of ownership."[20] Yaquis' valuing of land, ownership, and a sense of permanence in the United States was evident. Above all, Yaqui communities in Tucson sought to make a home.

On May 16, 1922, Juan Pistola died after a year of illness. He had named Francisco José Matus his successor. Pistola's leadership, though not accepted by all, had been publically declared by a number of prominent Yaquis, including Matus and Lucas Chavez.[21] After Pistola's death, however, divisions between supporters of Chavez and Matus created lasting rifts in the community. Matus sought to continue Pistola's quest to purchase lands and establish permanent settlements in Tucson.[22] At the Pascua Village site, he and others attracted Tucson corporate support in securing building materials. The Southern Pacific Railroad provided ties for the construction of a church and fences, the Mountain States Telegraph Company donated wire for fences, and others gave materials for building a central plaza. By 1923, Yaquis had succeeded in erecting a school in the village.[23]

Over the following decade, Yaquis from many outlying communities moved to Pascua Village. As economic conditions shifted, demands for labor evaporated or relocated, and growing generations of US-born Yaquis outgrew the earliest migrant communities and congregated at Pascua. While there were movements to other locations, influx of new Yaqui immigrants during 1927 and 1929 uprisings in Sonora also added numbers to Pascua Village. In 1940, Spicer estimated that 400 Yaquis lived in Pascua Village, and 450 presented themselves for alien registration in that year. Of those 450, Spicer found that only 82 were Mexican-born.[24] By 1946, when the Tucson public school district conducted a census of Pascua Village, it counted 347 Yaquis living there, along with 438 Mexican, 18 Mexican-Yaquis, 10 Mayos, 8 Chinese, 8 Mexican-Navajos, 6 Mayo-Opatas, 6 Opata-Pima-Mexicans, 4 Pima-Mayos, 4 Mexican-Mayos, 3 Mayo-Opata-Mexicans, 2 Navajos, 1 Opata, 1 Mayo-French, and 1 Mayo-German. Altogether, the population in 1946 was 858. During later decades, Yaquis purchased land in the Adelanto neighborhood bordering Pascua Village to the south, and their population totaled some 850 individuals by 1972.[25]

As the Yaqui population steadily grew during the early decades of Pascua Village's settlement, so did Tucson infrastructure. A small Yaqui church, having existed in northwest Tucson since 1911, was enlarged, moved to Pascua Village, and dedicated in 1925 as San Ignacio Church.[26] With aid from the Catholic Daughters of America, its members purchased a bell for San Ignacio and later built Santa Rosa de Lima on the edge of Pascua Village in 1930.[27] Throughout the 1920s, 1930s, and 1940s, public Easter celebrations and dances and increased facilities at the central plaza established and reinforced the unique Yaqui cultural spaces in Tucson's wider public consciousness. Yaqui students, whose population quickly outgrew the small facilities at Pascua, crowded surrounding schools, further bolstering their physical presence in the city.[28] Although modest, the other structures in Pascua grew in number and permanence. By 1940, when the Works Projects Administration published its Arizona guide, Pascua was described as consisting of "sixty-five Indian huts constructed of mud-chinked cactus sticks, rusty sheet iron, and other materials salvaged from junk heaps."[29]

The growth of the village, however, belied its unstable foundation. Few of those who originally signed contracts with Metz and Franklin succeeded in fully paying off what they owed on their installment plans. As early as 1932, Franklin personally petitioned the Tucson Board of Equalization to lower the property taxes in Pascua Village. Only a decade into the plan for Yaqui purchase of the lands, Franklin explained that he and Moore had attempted to foster the growth of a strong and vibrant Yaqui city, "a little replica of the famous empire of Cuzco in Peru where the Incas reigned." To this end he had helped in the drilling of a well and the building of a church and school. During this time, he lamented, "Not one cent rent do I receive from the Indians." The Yaquis were failing in their commitments, Franklin was paying the real estate taxes that Yaquis were supposed to be paying, and, while he still supported their continued settlement, he also called for a lowering of taxes that he was paying on their behalf.[30] Even among those who fully gained title to land, many struggled to pay taxes and often lost it due to delinquent payments. Of seventy families that moved to Pascua Village after 1921, by 1970 only twelve had managed to pay for their lots.[31] Those who never fully paid, those who paid in full but then lost title to their plots due to failure to pay taxes, and the descendants of both eventually became squatters there. The passage of the ownership of land in Pascua Village through various hands during the decades made much of Yaqui settlement permanent in façade only.

While much of Tucson's attention concerning Yaqui settlement focused on Pascua, other communities in the area flourished. Barrio Libre, located on the south edge of Tucson about halfway between the city center and Mezquital, became a permanent Yaqui community as well. Though they did not have the same sort of deal as those in Pascua Village, many Barrio Libre Yaquis succeeded in purchasing the lands they lived on. If not for the building of a freeway almost directly through the settlement in the late 1950s, Barrio Libre might have emerged as a more dominant Yaqui enclave in future decades.[32]

Marana, a town along the Southern Pacific Railroad corridor, just fifteen miles northwest of Pascua Village, boasted a strong Yaqui presence through much of the mid-twentieth century. There the Yaqui enclaves of Campo Burro and the smaller neighboring settlements of Ili hu'upam, Parosim, Campo Wilo, and Rillito comprised a Yaqui population of as many as 150 near Marana. These Yaquis lived on land owned by large corporate farms and worked for the same.[33]

Together with scattered Yaqui families and individuals elsewhere nearby and in Tucson itself, Pascua, Barrio Libre and Marana made up a persistent Yaqui presence in the region's physical and cultural landscape. Tucson-based settlements attracted and protected successive waves of Yaqui refugees from Sonora and, as years passed, were home to their growing progeny. Other regions of southern Arizona, most notably around Nogales and Yuma, also had persistent Yaqui populations, but Tucson received most immigrants. It is little surprise, therefore, that Tucson became the home for predominant Arizona Yaqui political institutions and an eventual reservation. Whether Yaquis truly "found peace" at their "little village," as was claimed in a 1931 *Arizona Daily Star* report, their attainment of more of a permanent home must certainly have added to a sense of security.[34]

Salt River Valley (Phoenix) Yaquis

A little over one hundred miles north and west of Tucson and past the outlying Yaqui settlements in Cortaro, Marana, Sasco, Red Rock, and Eloy, thousands of Yaquis settled around the greater Salt River Valley and the Phoenix-area cities of Tempe, Scottsdale, Chandler, Mesa, and Gilbert during the early to mid-twentieth century (see figure 6.4). Though later Yaqui generations living there would collaborate with their Tucson-based counterparts, for decades these Yaquis operated independently. In contrast to the mining or railroad labor markets that molded southern settlement patterns, agriculture and irrigation projects in Phoenix's East Valley shaped northern settlements. The rapidly growing cities on whose borders Phoenix Yaquis established themselves required Yaqui mobility, as expanding suburban sprawl engulfed their once peripheral and ignored squatter settlements. Phoenix Yaqui settlement evolved under circumstances and developments different from southern compatriots, but it served a similar role in accepting, integrating, and establishing exiled Yaquis in new Arizona homelands.

Yaquis may have passed through the Phoenix Salt River Valley for centuries, but a certain presence stretches back as far as 1845—three years before the region would become a US possession.[35] Proper "founders" of the Phoenix Yaqui community came in the 1880s, when Franciscan friars brought a group of thirty Yaquis to Phoenix. The friars later purchased five acres of land from Tempe homesteader Sylvester Roche on February 1, 1898, for a church site and Yaqui settlement. With a small Catholic church, wattle-daub houses, and a cemetery, Yaquis named their village Guadalupe. These were likely the Yaquis reported in 1902 encamped near the crossroads at Priest and Baseline Avenues southwest of Tempe.[36] Concurrently, hundreds flocked to the Phoenix area due to its high labor demand. In 1906, the Salt River Valley Water Users' Association encouraged Yaqui settlement near Phoenix to ensure a ready, cheap, hardworking labor supply for its many irrigation projects. Many settled at Guadalupe. In 1917, the

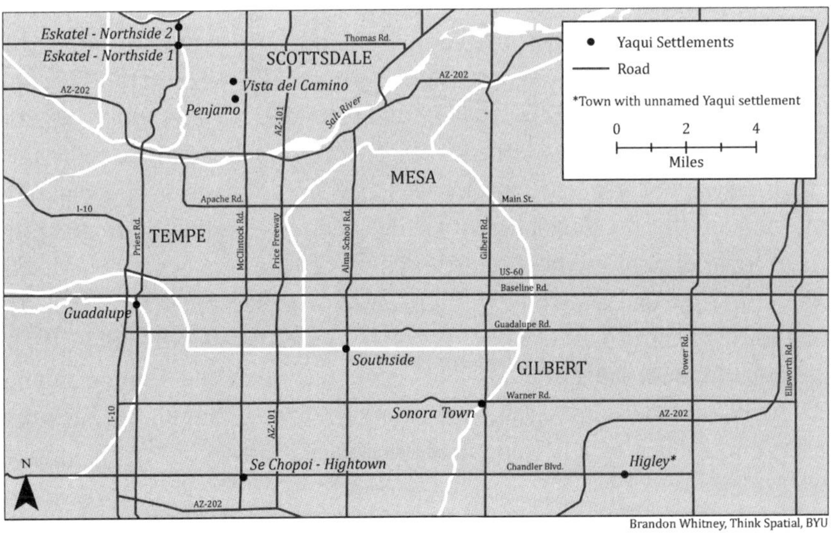

Figure 6.4. Salt River Valley Yaqui settlements, 1900–1970. Brandon Whitney, Brigham Young University, Think Spatial.

Goodyear Tire and Rubber Company encouraged Yaqui settlement near its cotton fields in Chandler, where the Se Chopoi Yaqui settlement grew.[37] The pattern of industry and labor shaping settlement patterns is clear.

By 1908, one reporter took note of this "Yaquitown," Pueblo de Guadalupe, and told the story of humble Yaquis giving what little they had to build a church.[38] Led by Juan María, volunteer Yaquis built Iglesia de Guadalupe themselves, an act that impressed the Anglo onlooker.[39] Soon, however, Yaquis at the original town site outgrew their four-acre plot. Furthermore, they and other Yaquis squatting on private lands abutting South Tempe canals faced problems with irrigation rights, flooding, and contention with neighboring farmers and developers. Resident friar Lucius Zittier spearheaded efforts in 1909 and 1910 to secure legal title to lands for Guadalupe Yaquis but was frustrated as the US Reclamation Service deemed the chosen lands adjoining the Western Canal too valuable. Eventually Marian Higgins, a local widow, donated a nearby (and non-irrigable) forty-acre tract of land for their use along the high ground west of the Highline Canal.[40] Although aided by Senator Carl Hayden, this involved considerable wrangling and politicking, as some local farmers and boosters did not want Yaqui neighbors.[41] On September 19, 1912, the United States deeded title of the northeast quarter of the southeast quarter of Section 5, Township 1 North, Range 4 East to the Superior Court of Maricopa County, Arizona, to be held in trust for refugee Yaqui settlers.[42]

Plotting of the town site took some time, but finally on November 14, 1914, President Woodrow Wilson signed patent 442696 over to Maricopa County judge John C. Phillips "to have and to hold . . . in trust for the several use and benefits of the occupants of the Townsite of Guadalupe, according to their respective interests, and to his successors in trust, as aforesaid."[43] Unfortunately for the Guadalupe residents and those in the future, the process of individual property allotment and ownership was never completed. Town law stipulated that Judge Phillips, who later became governor of Arizona for over thirty years, turn over title to Guadalupe town authorities to execute individual sales of lands. This never occurred, and Yaqui residents essentially squatted on the land. As future groups of Anglo and Mexican settlers encroached on adjoining land, this placed Yaquis on legally ambiguous ground.

In 1924, Jennie Biehn, an enthusiastic Presbyterian missionary widow, purchased and donated about one hundred acres of land directly east of Guadalupe, and in 1930 she gave another forty acres southwest of the town for Yaqui settlement. As previously, this land was held in trust (this time by the Presbyterian Church) and not deeded to individual Yaqui residents.[44] It was eventually transferred from the Charles H. Cook Bible School to the Board of National Missions of the Presbyterian Church and then to the Presbytery of Phoenix in 1948.[45] As with other lands held in trust, title was never transferred to Yaqui residents. In the recollection of Guadalupe educator Ruby Wood, the forty acres were "supposed to have been deeded out to the people. [The church] had a plan but they never told [the Yaquis] how to do it. Everybody just put their house where they wanted. . . . They made little twenty-five feet lots, which, you know, isn't big enough for a house with a big family like most of those people are."[46] Again Yaquis had little if any legal claims to the land upon which they lived.

In the estimates of a 1919 observer, Guadalupe could be viewed then as the new "capital of a once great Yaqui nation." For the perhaps two thousand Yaquis in the Salt River Valley in 1919 and beyond who were picking cotton, working as other farm labor, or building and maintaining the Salt River Project canal system, Guadalupe served as a physical and cultural focal point.[47] Though it provided an important gathering place for Yaquis in the region, the settlement was largely overlooked by white Arizonans. If regarded at all, it was seen as an oddity of poverty, thoroughly foreign in character, and backward in culture or civilization. "Clouds of dust blow in from east, south and west," noted one observer, "Guadalupe is a place generally unnoticed by the passing traveler."[48] Supporting this conclusion, the Works Project Administration's 1940 Arizona guide offered only a brief entry for the village. After directions down 6.9 miles of dirt roads from Tempe, the travel guide listed "GUADALUPE INDIAN VILLAGE . . . the home of the expatriated Yaqui who fled from Mexico" and brief mention of ceremonies and dances performed during Lent.[49]

In the following years, the number of Yaquis living in Guadalupe grew in number, and numbers also grew in several other settlements in Phoenix's East Valley. Most growth was due to heavy recruitment in Tucson and Mexico by the Salt River Valley Water Users' Association (SRVWUA), whose members were said to consider Yaqui laborers "the finest labor force attainable."[50] The largest of these settlements were clustered in southern Scottsdale. According to Felipe Molina, a Yaqui leader from Marana who collaborated with Spicer often, a large number of Yaquis abandoned Guadalupe in 1924 (even burning or demolishing their homes there) and settled in southern Scottsdale.[51] Their new settlement stood at the southeast corner of the intersection of Thomas Road and Sixty-Fourth Street, on the west side of the Crosscut Canal. In December 1927, the SRVWUA officially established and funded a residence camp at the site for its laborers and provided tents that rudimentary Yaqui-built homes augmented in the years to follow.[52] The SRVWUA referred to this settlement as Northside and locals called it Yaqui Town, but to Yaqui residents it was Eskatel or Campo Viejo.[53] When Spicer visited in the summer of 1940, all Eskatel residents were SRVWUA employees.[54]

In the following decades, the SRVWUA invested in building better housing for Eskatel Yaquis, but water and electricity were shared and limited commodities. The SRVWUA's lease on the Eskatel site was set to expire on May 15, 1943, and the company opted to relocate the Yaqui settlement about a half-mile north to the intersection of Sixty-Fourth Street and Osborn Road in the fall of 1942. By 1946, the SRVWUA had constructed fifty-one one-room and two-room concrete block homes for Yaquis at the new site also called Eskatel by the Yaquis and Northside by the SRVWUA.[55] The new site offered electricity to all homes, a health clinic, and a SRVWUA-run grocery store. The new location filled quickly and non-SRVWUA Yaquis barred from living in company housing soon settled across Crosscut Canal from the original Eskatel site. This settlement was called Turicate Village. In 1956, the SRVWUA discontinued support of Northside. Concurrently, some Yaquis with improved finances were purchasing cheap lands along the Indian Bend Wash flood plain at McDowell Road in a subdivision called Vista del Camino. The closing of Northside accelerated Yaqui congregation at the new location. Yaquis called the new settlement Pénjamo. Severe flooding in 1966 and 1971 forced Yaquis to relocate south to Seventy-Seventh Street and Roosevelt. The land overlooked the Indian Bend Wash to the west and was donated by Scottsdale. At New Pénjamo, a small neighborhood of Yaquis persists today.[56]

Yaquis established other distinct settlements during these first decades of employment with the SRVWUA in the East Valley. As a southern counterpart to the Northside community, the SRVWUA established Southside on the banks of the Western Canal at Alma School Road in the late 1920s, improving it from a tent camp to forty permanent houses in the mid-1940s.[57] Although the settlement is now gone, the Salt River Project office and storage facility at the site still bears its name: Southside Water Service Center. Two other settlements of note were home to steady Yaqui populations throughout the early to mid-twentieth century: Se Chopoi (or

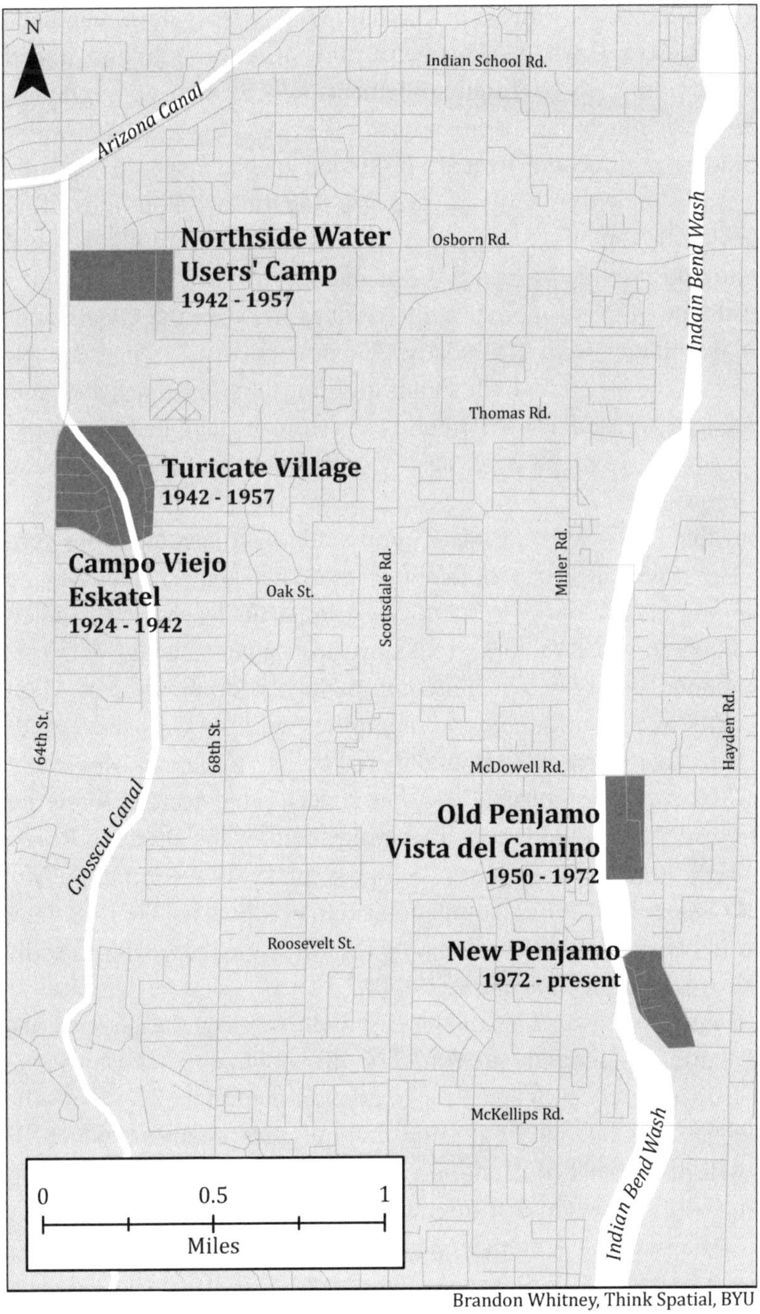

Figure 6.5. Scottsdale Yaqui settlements, 1898–present. Brandon Whitney, Brigham Young University, Think Spatial.

Hightown), located southeast of Guadalupe in present-day Chandler, and Gilbert's Sonora Town.[58] Along with other more mobile and transitory SRVWUA camps, these Yaqui settlements spread their demographic influence across much of Phoenix's East Valley.

Estimates of number of Yaquis who settled in Guadalupe, Scottsdale, and elsewhere in Phoenix's East Valley vary. Regardless, thousands of Yaqui refugees in the region extended the Tucson-based Yaqui influence well to the north and provided a steady labor market. In 1937, immigration officials estimated three hundred Yaqui families between the Guadalupe and Scottsdale villages, with 225 mostly US-born children.[59] Spicer and others estimated some five hundred Yaquis residing at Guadalupe and another four hundred at Eskatel.[60] Whether these estimates included Southside, Se Chopoi, Sonora Town, or other nearby settlements is unclear, but the number is significant.

From the 1960s to the 1980s, Yaqui settlement became more complicated. By 1963, the *Arizona Republic* estimated that Guadalupe and its surrounding neighborhoods, Sende Vista in particular, hosted as many as fifteen hundred "pure Yaqui[s], speaking their native language at home and at ceremonial times."[61] The *Republic* noted the dominance of Mexican immigrants in the surrounding communities, and by 1969 the 125 Yaqui families in Guadalupe were outnumbered by an "intolerant Mexican population" of over four thousand and thus concentrated near the western border of Guadalupe, roughly a quarter-mile south of the Baseline Road and Fifty-Sixth Street intersection in Tempe.[62] In 1980, when Felipe Molina wrote to Spicer concerning population estimates, he gave the following totals for Phoenix East Valley: Pénjamo (South Scottsdale), 100; Se Chopoi (Hightown), 80; and Guadalupe, 1,450.[63]

Extending well over half of the twentieth century, the physical establishment and demographic growth of Yaquis in Phoenix's East Valley and the Tucson area reflect exiled Yaquis' commitment to making a new home in Arizona. Smaller outlying Yaqui communities, many of which dissipated with the winds of economic change, hint at a resilient Yaqui population, willing to settle and migrate in Arizona as times demanded. The Siba Kobi–Somerton settlement near Yuma included some hundred Yaqui families in 1936 and 250 Yaqui individuals in 1940 and lasted through the 1970s. The Bacatete settlement near Eloy totaled about one hundred individuals before its dissolution after World War II. Migrant agricultural Yaqui camps at Casa Grande, Coolidge, Morenci, Clifton, Higley, Arizona

Farms, and Florence; Yaqui mining populations at Patagonia, Sasco, and elsewhere; and the oldest Yaqui enclaves in Nogales and Tubac round out the Yaqui presence in Arizona.[64]

Though later swallowed up by the urban and suburban sprawl of Tucson, Phoenix, Scottsdale, Tempe, Chandler, Mesa, Gilbert, and other cities, most of the Yaqui settlements were clearly separated from Anglo districts, which underscored their uniqueness. As the *Arizona Republic* reminded readers in 1964, "When the Yaquis congregated in Pascua around 1920, they were in the desert far from Tucson proper. Today, Pascua sits in the middle of an industrial district, surrounded by a freeway, busy Grant Road, the modern motels and nightclubs of Miracle Mile."[65] This sort of change took place around the Phoenix East Valley Yaqui settlements too. In the case of Se Chopoi—Hightown, however, it would not be until the 1990s and later that the growing Chandler-Tempe suburbs engulfed the farmlands and desert brush surrounding the Yaqui and Mexican enclave. All of these communities illustrate Yaqui independence of spirit, tenacity, and commitment to autonomy. Though far removed from the eight traditional villages of the Yaqui River Valley in Sonora, thousands of twentieth-century Yaquis fashioned a new Yaquimi in Arizona.

Labor Connections in Yaqui Settlement Patterns

With the exception of Guadalupe, whose location was influenced by Anglo missionaries at its founding, most Yaqui settlements were located in relation to employment, and some began as company towns. As noted earlier, Yaquis not only fled the hazards of Sonora but were also pulled to Arizona by economic opportunity, and in Arizona they were recognized as hardworking and adaptable. Working in agriculture, mining, and other industries, they made the most of labor demand when and where it arose.[66]

A 1921 *Los Angeles Times* article noted, "Throughout Arizona, in the mines and on the farms, the Yaqui has been accepted as one of the most dependable of workmen, uniformly sturdy and good-tempered, demanding a vacation only for attendance [of] his tribal and religious celebrations."[67] This reputation in the southern Arizona labor market provided Yaquis with the financial means to establish and develop communities, as noted above, and it also promoted a positive image of all Yaquis in Arizona. This countered negative press and bias lingering from Yaqui strife across the border. Although they did not explicitly sever cultural or economic ties with their kin in Sonora, Yaqui immigrant laborers gained a new transnational identity that was cast as distinctly Arizonan, and this became increasingly set as they and their families participated in state and regional affairs.

As noted, distinct characteristics of Yaqui labor in the United States, from its earliest days, included dynamism, flexibility, and adaptability. The story of Tomás Alvarez provides a telling example. Upon crossing the border in the early 1900s at the age of fifteen, Alvarez proceeded to Benson, Arizona, where he found work at the railroad commissary. He worked there for two years until his employer died in a railroad accident, and then he relocated for a job in a store in Fairbank, south of Benson and just west of Tombstone. The job did not last long, and he moved to Tucson where he got a job for a dollar a day as a water boy for road crews digging Fourth Avenue and other streets. After three months, he found a better job transporting picks for a Mexican contractor and continued this for three years.[68] In following years, Alvarez worked in various locations between Benson and Gila Bend for the Southern Pacific, rising to assistant section foreman for a time. Before settling in Barrio Anita and immersing himself in community politics and religious institutions, Alvarez's travelogue of work experience was emblematic of many Yaquis.

Early Yaqui involvement in railroad work and mining throughout southern Arizona, noted in chapter 1, was characterized by migration of individual laborers rather than entire refugee families. These workers' routes would eventually be followed by Yaquis with families, and perhaps they all traversed existent of irregular Yaqui networks dating back even earlier. Yaqui communities sprang up at mining sites, along railroads, and on migratory routes. With the increased exodus from Sonora to Arizona in the first two decades of the twentieth century, many Yaquis gravitated to these industries, while others made inroads in agricultural work. Subsequently, reliance on railroad and mining gave way to agricultural work.

Yaqui poet Refugio Savala writes in his memoirs, "We hail the Southern Pacific for having provided all these Yaqui refugees shelter, wage work, and food."[69] Still, although invaluable for early Yaqui refugees, railroad work was problematic. The migrant nature of the work went against the Yaqui impulse to establish permanent settlements in Arizona. Savala writes of railroad projects that employed Yaqui work gangs, followed from site to site by their wives and children. Martina Cruz, a Yaqui girl whose father took her and her family with him on railroad jobs during the 1920s and 1930s recalled living in a rail car that accompanied work crews from Arizona to

Los Angeles, New Mexico, and Texas. So, while this was valuable employment, it was difficult on families hoping for a stable community.[70] It carried "individuals or families far away into other states for long periods of time," in the words of Spicer. As it turned out, increased mechanization of manual labor formerly done with pick and shovel diminished the need for railroad labor. Furthermore, mixed housing in railroad camps, where Yaquis were forced to live intimately with non-Yaqui Mexican immigrants, compelled many to seek employment elsewhere as soon as possible.[71]

The initially high ratio of Yaquis employed by railroad companies such as the Southern Pacific Railroad, Arizona Eastern Railway, and El Paso and Southwestern Railroad steadily declined during the twentieth century, as many found steady employment elsewhere. But such Yaqui employment did not cease entirely, and some Yaquis continued to find seasonal work on the Southern Pacific, as track walkers and section hands, through the mid-twentieth century. They were prized employees, perceived as possessing an "uncanny ability" that other workers were thought to lack. By the mid-1970s, however, very few remained employed by the railroads as section hands.[72]

The shift in Yaqui labor away from mining followed a similar trajectory. Though not demanding the same mobility as railroad jobs, the previously high ratio of Yaquis employed by mines steadily dropped during the twentieth century. The most obvious reasons for this shift were the economic downturns in the 1910s and early 1920s and the Great Depression that forced many mines and smelters across southern Arizona to close. Pima, Santa Cruz, and Greenlee Counties, along with Douglas, Globe, and Prescott, all regions heavily dependent on mining, reported widespread unemployment in 1921. Pima County noted two hundred unemployed Yaquis. The hundreds and thousands of unemployed "Mexican" laborers counted in other locales may have included Yaquis. Many Yaquis, had "already gone elsewhere" for work, officials from the Douglas Chamber of Commerce said.[73] Many sources report that the growing cotton industry was picking up some of the slack. Yaquis were already prominent in southern Arizona's agriculture, cotton or otherwise, and many unemployed Yaqui miners found work alongside Yaquis already established in the industry. Later the Great Depression would have a similar effect, compelling Yaqui miners to turn to agricultural labor.[74]

Agriculture provided employment for a large portion of Arizonan Yaquis during the mid-twentieth century. Within years of Yaquis arrival from

Sonora, it became "common knowledge" among Arizonans that large numbers of Yaqui refugees were sneaking into the state to work in "citrus and cotton ranches" as well as mines.[75] In 1919, the *Christian Science Monitor* claimed that up to two thousand Yaquis were employed in cotton growing or other farm work in the Salt River Valley alone.[76] The arrival of Yaqui laborers was fortuitous for all involved, as demand and prices for cotton skyrocketed with World War I.[77] Capitalizing on the demand, large farming corporations opened their own labor camps, housing their workers in close proximity to the fields. In the late 1910s, Yaqui agricultural camps were opened at Marana, Eloy, Somerton, and Chandler, as well as other locations. Yaqui labor was cheap, reliable, and well worth the investment in housing. For individual Yaquis, the wages were decent. Savala, just a teenager at the time, recalls picking cotton in Flowing Wells, just northwest of Tucson, for two dollars per hundred pounds. He and his brother together picked enough to earn about a dollar per day.[78] Similar Yaqui labor in the citrus and other agricultural industries would continue through most of the mid-twentieth century.[79]

For Yaquis in the Salt River Valley, the most ubiquitous labor was with the SRVWUA. A large percentage of Phoenix Yaquis who did not live in Guadalupe lived in SRVWUA-owned settlements. Their employment with the SRVWUA began in earnest in the early 1920s, and Yaquis were a prized labor force. Their work on SRVWUA canal project established their permanent presence across the Salt River Valley and Phoenix's East Valley.[80] Coupled with regional agricultural work throughout the following decades, Yaquis such as those in Scottsdale earned enough money to purchase homes outside of the SRVWUA camps and establish a comfortable, if modest, life. For years in the Salt River Valley Yaquis demonstrated both the ability to adapt to new labor opportunities and to excel at their new work.

In the late 1940s and early 1950s, many Yaquis in the Salt River Valley and Tucson area found themselves out of work.[81] Increased mechanization reduced labor demand in many of the industries where they had been the primary labor force. As noted, this led to the SRVWUA closing of Yaqui camps in the Salt River Valley. For decades, Yaquis had succeeded in the Arizona labor market, but now Yaquis in other regions too found themselves out of work—and evicted from company housing.

Conclusion

Establishing a new life in exile was never easy for Arizona Yaquis. Beyond the trauma of leaving their Sonora homelands and making the dangerous and arduous passage across the US-Mexican border, the process of reestablishing prosperity and stable community life required decades of concerted effort. Throughout, Yaquis demonstrated great resolve. Adaptable and hardworking, they succeeded in establishing stable settlements across southern Arizona and securing relatively steady employment. When those sources of stability were threatened or removed in the mid-twentieth century, Yaquis faced new challenges. It is within this context that the subsequent stages of Yaqui history in Arizona are best understood.

In the face of new challenges in the 1950s, a new generation of Arizona Yaquis again adapted and prepared to move ahead. This new generation emerged with a strong voice, its members proclaiming their place in Arizona society and demanding reconfigurations of their relationship with state and federal governments. Established for decades in the United States, Yaquis in the 1950s–1970s pushed for something more. They were ready to stand, to be counted, and to be recognized as American Indians.

Chapter 7

Yaqui Legality and Belonging in Arizona, 1900–1950s

We all believe in the American creed, in the United States of America as a government of the people by the people, and for the people whose just powers are derived from the consent of the governed, established on those principles for which American patriots sacrificed [their] lives and fortunes. We want to stay here in your county.

—CAYETANO LOPEZ to Arizona governor George Hunt, 1931[1]

While Yaqui immigrants established communities in Arizona with relative ease compared to the plight of landless Crees and Chippewas in Montana, this belies the uneasiness that hung over the lives of many. Yaquis' ambiguous legal status in the United States undermined their stability, as did not owning land (as many did not), and extradition to Mexico presented a threat to some.[2] In addition, throughout the early to mid-twentieth-century, Yaqui individuals and communities were scrutinized by neighboring Arizonans suspicious of their "foreign" origins. The common view of others that they were not "American" added to Yaquis' persistent unease and even sense of danger. It was against this background that twentieth-century movements sought to define Yaquis' legal status in the United States, and debates unfolded about political refugee status, immigration restrictions, and possible repatriation. In the face even of the latter threat, Yaquis increasingly wore their identity with pride, in greater and greater public view. They would not be cowed.

Long Shadows of Continued Violence in Sonora

The context for debates about Yaqui legal status must include the final stages of Yaqui border crossing during and after the Mexican Revolution.

Chapter 3 discussed the Yaqui plight in detail, but it bears repeating that American discussions of Yaquis affected their experience in Arizona. As Yaquis continued to flee persecution, Yaqui-Mexican warfare continued south of the border, and this may have stirred fears in Arizona. US press reports were mixed, as with this one from Nebraska in 1911:

> "Exterminating" the Yaqui Indians has been a favorite pastime with the established government of Mexico ever since the time of Cortes, and, though thousands of these people have been shot and thousands more sent to die on the plantations and in the swamps of Tehuantepec and Yucatan, there are still enough ablebodied [*sic*] Yaquis left to cause considerable trouble. Insurging [*sic*] has been the vocation of every Yaqui, man, women or child, since long before the present rebellion broke out in Mexico. Rebellion and warfare seem to be inborn traits of the Yaquis, carefully cultivated from one generation to the next. That it is right to shed the blood of a Mexican official or soldier is a Yaqui tradition, and it is one that has been carefully lived up to.[3]

This report recognizes the persecution of Yaquis in Mexico and even implicitly lauds their defiance, persistence, and fighting abilities. But Arizonans who employed Yaquis or lived close to them might read such reports with trepidation. Seeing Yaquis as naturally insurgent made them potentially dangerous. All Yaqui activities south of the line affected Yaquis north of the line, regardless of whether or not individual Yaquis were directly involved in revolt, arms dealing, or violence.

The onset of the Mexican Revolution ended the Porfirian deportation policy, but this by no means eliminated Yaqui struggles for independence in Sonora.[4] During the first years of the revolution, US newspapers alternately reported on supposed Yaqui peace accords and on resurgent Yaqui violence along the border. The latter fed suspicions and distrust of Yaquis among white Arizonans. Widely publicized Yaqui involvement in the banditry of Pancho Villa along the US-Mexican border during the 1910s particularly tarnished their public image. Any report of Yaqui violence throughout the decade-long Mexican Revolution was bad for Arizona Yaquis by association.[5] Subsequent debates over Yaqui legal status in the United States must be understood with this background in mind.

In reality, few Yaquis remained in Sonora when the Mexican Revolution broke out in 1910. Many of the traditional eight Yaqui towns there had become largely non-Yaqui communities. Those who remained in Sonora were scattered and disorganized after years of persecution. Their history of fierce independence, however, prompted many ascending Sonoran and Mexican leaders to seek their cooperation. Almost immediately after Francisco Madero "captured" Mexico City in June 1911, a Yaqui delegation of eleven chiefs traveled there to confer with him and request "the restoration to the Yaquis [of] their lands along the Yaqui River and . . . the return of Indians who were banished to Yucatan."[6] Madero received the delegation and promised to restore Yaqui lands and exempt them from taxation for a number of decades. Concern for avoiding a new Yaqui revolt clearly loomed on the minds of new democratic Mexican officials.[7] With Madero's assassination in February 1913 and the subsequent rule of Victoriano Huerta, Yaqui allegiance gravitated toward Sonoran revolutionaries like Francisco "Pancho" Villa. This development eventually troubled US relations with Yaquis.

During the revolution, Yaquis joined in anti-Huerta and later anti-Obregón rebellions. Their involvement threatened American lives and businesses in Sonora and often featured cross-border violence. This compromised the safety and stability of refugee Yaqui communities in Arizona. One incident, in particular, illustrates the implied complicity of Arizona Yaquis in Sonoran violence. In May 1915, Sonoran Yaquis attacked Esperanza and a nearby American settlement. Just southeast of Guaymas and neighboring Cocorit, this area had a long history of Yaqui-Mexican warfare. Sixty-five Americans, including women and children, perished, and then an "overwhelming number" of Yaquis besieged the fifty American survivors. After other Yaqui attacks, destruction of American property, and killing of livestock at Tonichl, Pesqueira, Navajoa, Cocorl, La Colorado, San Marcial, Resario, and other interior Sonoran locales, the United States sent the cruiser *Colorado* from San Diego with two companies of marines to save the besieged Americans.[8] Although the United States did not engage Yaqui forces, the bad press cast long shadows over Arizona Yaqui refugee communities.[9] As much as they tried to extricate themselves from the transnational context in which Arizonans viewed them, immigrant Yaquis could not escape their "foreign" roots or associations with Yaquis south of the line.

Pancho Villa's infamous border-crossing campaigns likely affected Arizona Yaquis, as their Sonoran counterparts regularly took part in these. In October 1914 and October 1915, Yaqui clashes with US troops along the border and damage of US property heightened Arizonans' fears.[10] "I can see their camp fires every night," reported an Arizonan regarding the Yaqui rebels just across the line. In November 1915 Villa proclaimed, "If necessary, I will fight the United States army assembled along the border," and then "bullets rained" on the US side of the border, making the Yaqui more tangible.[11] During the US Army's "punitive expedition" against Villa the following summer, some US officials hoped that Yaquis would join the American effort. A group of Sonoran Yaquis had expressed desire to fight with the United Stated against him, but this seems not to have materialized.[12] While such a turn might have improved Arizonans' perception of Yaquis, reports were otherwise: some Yaquis reportedly fled south across the border for fear of being pressed into US Army service.[13] Resumed Yaqui violence across the border in subsequent months and years ensured—or at least perpetuated—the negative portrayal of the Yaqui nation as a whole.

Yaqui arms smuggling during the 1910s also hurt Yaqui reputations north of the line. This was a familiar story and concern, extending back to the late nineteenth century when Yaquis transported arms south to support their revolts in Sonora. Arizona Yaqui cooperation in such activities was apparent during the Mexican Revolution. Yaquis routinely procured arms in the United States, moved them largely through Nogales along Yaqui migratory routes, and siphoned them across the border.[14] The US Tenth Cavalry stationed at Fort Huachuca, which just a few years earlier had operated out of Fort Assiniboine to catch and deport Crees from Montana, reported continued troubles with Yaqui arms traffickers along the US-Mexican border throughout the mid-1910s.[15] US Army detachments along the border and local police forces spent considerable energy in "hunts" for Yaquis purchasing arms in the United States to traffic across the border.[16] In 1918, after Mexican officials expressed concern that Arizona Yaquis might ally with expatriate disaffected Mexicans and cross the border in a joint invasion, US officials found little evidence of any such expedition and instead focused on stemming the arms smuggling.[17]

In the late 1920s, renewed altercations between Sonoran Yaquis and Mexican troops rekindled southern Arizonan opinions against Yaquis. In 1926, Yaquis became convinced of betrayal by President Álvaro Obregón, and Mexican troops fired on Yaqui settlements. A Yaqui uprising against Mexican authorities ensued. A subsequent "pacification" campaign involved twenty thousand Mexican troops, airplane bombings of Yaqui strongholds, deportation of Yaqui insurgents (to Mexico City, Mérida, Veracruz, and

Tlaxcala), and an oppressive Mexican army occupation of Yaqui territory.[18] During this new and last full Yaqui revolt, Yaquis smuggled a large amount of arms and war materiel across the US-Mexican border. In June 1926, Yaquis living in Tucson were found to have illegal arms in their homes, "with the intention of transferring them to Mexican territory for organizing an armed movement" against the government of Mexico. The US State Department tried to assure Mexican officials that the amount of arms being smuggled by Arizonan Yaquis was minimal, that guilty parties were being convicted, and that future violations were being prevented.[19]

Regulation of this transnational traffic was complicated since many Yaquis crossing into Arizona were not arms smugglers. They constituted a new wave of refugee families fleeing violence in Sonora. Pascua and Barrio Libre in Tucson both saw large influxes of Yaqui immigrants during this period.[20] In addition to arms smugglers and peaceful refugee families, many migrants were Yaqui soldiers using the border as a shield from Mexican pursuit. "Whenever things got too hot for them [in Sonora], they simply crossed the line into this country to lick their wounds and bide their time until returning to the wars," explained one Border Patrol officer.[21] This made for tense border relations. Border Patrol officers were said to be "worn to frazzle" by the stress, and Yaquis certainly fared no better. For those tasked with guarding against illegal transnational traffic, even decreased activity was viewed with anxiety, perhaps as a "lull in the storm."[22] For Yaquis trying to flee violence, renewed concern for border security led to increasingly difficult transnational mobility.

All of these perceived and actual transnational Yaqui connections with violence during and after the Mexican Revolution were the backdrop to the 1920s–1940s debates concerning Yaqui status in the United States. Indeed, the ensuing movements to classify them as "illegal," to grant or deny them US citizenship, to treat them the same as other immigrants from Mexico, to repatriate them to Mexico, and to grant them federal recognition as "American Indians" cannot be understood outside of this context. Underneath all discussion of Yaquis in Sonora and Arizona was mistrust bred from publicized Yaqui violence.[23]

Yaqui Legal Status in the United States

The 1910s and 1920s Yaqui-Mexican violence along the US-Mexican border created an atmosphere of fear and danger for many Yaqui refugees in

Arizona. Anxieties lessened somewhat after the United States promised protection from the Díaz regime and after the Porfirian threat of deportation or extermination in Sonora ended. Still, the constant public defamation they faced was unsettling. At least one earlier attempt by Arizona Yaquis to engage with the US federal government to gain official status or protection had not borne fruit.[24] US government interaction with Arizona Yaquis was often tied to the question of warfare in Sonora. In 1919, Yaqui leaders met with a number of government officials, but this was to discuss the problem of arms trafficking.[25]

An event in 1927 further illustrates the link between the Sonoran Yaqui revolt and Arizonan Yaqui legal status and provides a segue for a broader discussion of Yaqui legal status in the United States during the early to mid-twentieth century. On April 29, 1927, fifteen US troops from the Twenty-Fifth Infantry at Nogales happened upon a Yaqui force in possession of large quantities of money and weapons and encamped on the US side of the line in the Bear Valley, twenty-five miles west of Nogales. Three of the US officers were invited into the Yaqui camp, where the Yaquis agreed to accompany the US troops to Tucson upon one condition: amnesty.[26]

Thirty-seven Yaqui soldiers were thus taken into US custody and held under military guard at Camp Stephen D. Little in Nogales. Apparently having numbered as many as ninety when they left the Bacatete Mountains in Sonora, the Yaquis told of a harrowing two-week journey to the border, during which time they had engaged Mexican forces in battle more than once. The latest battle, at Planchas du Pluta, had left over one hundred Mexicans dead and the Yaquis scattered. Their captured comrades, explained the Yaquis, had been summarily tried and hanged "in full view of the railroad line and main highways." This claim was substantiated by reports of a number of Yaqui bodies hung from trees near Nogales, Sonora, with barbed wire.[27] Tucson's *Arizona Daily Star* detailed the quandary US officials then faced:

> What to do with the Indians is the next question. To return them to Mexico means to return them to certain punishment. To let them remain in the United States means to harbor an enemy of a foreign nation. However, it would not be the first time that a military enemy of a friendly nation has sought refuge in this country. Although the Yaquis have waged a persistent fight against the Sonora government . . . during

> the past few months and may be considered technically rebels against their country, we cannot help but look upon them with pity. The lot of the Mexican Indians has never been comfortable; hatred of government has been bred within them from the clay of the conquistadores. Grant that the Indians may have been on the wrong side of every argument that has arisen, they nevertheless have their views of right and wrong, and the fact that they have fought, goes to prove they believe they were justified in making the effort. If they have been used by politically ambitious leaders as pawns in a political war, their measure of guiltlessness is so much larger.

The *Daily Star*'s balanced view is striking. It lauded Yaqui struggle as perhaps justified. Furthermore, the Mexican manipulation of Yaquis in the conflicts of the preceding revolution absolved Yaquis of some guilt. The paper concluded, "Whatever is done with the 37 Indians, let it be done with mercy and in the realization that they have committed no graver offense to the United States than crossing the line without proper legal authority under the stress of necessity. The American army acted well in capturing them; now let the civil authorities act kindly in the treatment of the prisoners."[28]

Days after the internment of the thirty-seven Yaquis in Nogales, an additional seven voluntarily surrendered to Border Patrol officers, raising the total to forty-four. An additional two offered to lead Border Patrol officers to a large cache of munitions northwest of Tubac.[29] Word then came from Washington, DC, that the Yaquis, officially held as "political refugees," should be turned over to the US Immigration Department. At Tucson, officials refused to divulge the specifics of the order from Washington, but they said that "the Indians would not be turned back to the Mexican government." "The only solution," explained the *Daily Star*, "is that of paroling the Yaquis in Tucson, where many of them have friends." Some suspected further that the Yaquis were actually Arizona residents who had gone south to fight and were just now returning. The interned Yaquis refused to comment, and Yaqui chiefs at Pascua replied simply, "Quien sabe [Who knows]?" The Yaquis were released under supervision on May 26, 1927, with a final decision by the Immigration Department pending. Their later fate is unknown. Mexican officials offered to accept the Yaquis back in Mexico, settle them and any others who wished to join them, and give them a full pardon, but none stepped forward to accept.[30] Likely blending with Tucson- and Phoenix-based Yaquis, the refugees disappeared from public view and interest.

How does this 1927 example of Mexican-Yaqui transborder violence fit into the broader Arizonan debates concerning the Yaquis' legal status in the United States? Nineteenth-century industries of southern Arizona, labor-starved, had readily accepted Yaqui immigrants along with countless non-Yaqui Mexican laborers. Few, if any, questions had been raised concerning immigration restrictions. Nevertheless, the early-twentieth-century Yaquis entered the United States with considerable fear of being recognized as such. During well over a decade of Porfirian persecution, many Yaquis had made a careful craft of blending in with other populations and not standing out as a Yaquis. This cautious practice followed them across the border in their new Arizona settlements. It was not until 1909, anthropologist Rosamond Spicer said, that Yaquis slowly began to realize that "they need not be afraid in the United States."[31] Given the threats of extermination or deportation and enslavement driving them across the US-Mexican border, their fear, caution, and hesitance to test their rights in the United States was understandable and prudent.

For the last years of the Porfirian regime and well through the Mexican Revolution, Yaquis entered the United States covertly and only publicly revealed themselves as such once settled north of the line. In 1918, Arizona governor Hunt arranged for Yaqui entrance and settlement in the state provided they register with Yaqui tribal leaders upon arrival. Orchestrated by Pascua leader Juan Pistola, this process of enumerating and providing paperwork for incoming Yaquis was difficult to enforce—and rarely was. In the later recollections of Refugio Savala, if a Yaqui was "caught out on a ranch somewhere without passport, all he would have to do would be to say that he was already reported from Pascua."[32] By the mid-1930s, when Savala spoke with Edward Spicer, the reporting process had long since ceased, and few Yaquis knew anything of Governor Hunt's arrangement. The self-perceived status of pre-1920s Yaqui immigrants is thus somewhat ambiguous. Although some were aware of US legal protection, many may not have been. Moreover, though the fear of deportation may have subsided after the first wave of exodus in the first decade of the century, the lack of official legal documentation, alien registration papers, or citizenship certainly worried Yaqui leaders and individuals.

In 1920, Juan Pistola's Pascua Yaquis made official overtures that they wished to secure US citizenship. Claiming four thousand Yaquis in the state, Pistola stated the Yaqui desire for full "Americanization," education, and title to land.[33] His pronouncement to Governor Hunt was timely, as new immigration restrictions were soon to be passed. In 1921, the United States passed the Emergency Immigration Act, which set an annual quota limiting immigration to 3 percent of any ethnic group's US population as of the 1910 census.[34] This was followed in 1924 by the Johnson-Reed Act, which dropped the quota to 2 percent of the group's US population as of the 1890 census. Promising for Arizona Yaquis, the 1924 act exempted Latin American immigrants, including Mexicans, from these restrictions. However, it increased regulation for registering immigrants. Yaqui status as "Mexicans," a problematic concept, was accepted by default if it was their country of origin, but the complexities of the new regulations left the status of many ambiguous. The act "cleaned up some of the murky racial lines in US society," explains historian Julian Lim, but it was unclear on which side of whiteness Yaquis would fall.[35]

When Edward Spicer interviewed a southern Arizona Border Patrol officer concerning the Yaquis status during the early 1920s, the officer explained what he believed to be very reasonable regulations specifically instituted for Yaquis. However, at nearly every turn, the conditions of Yaqui life in Arizona precluded many from being able to follow the regulations. First, the officer explained, "Aliens in this country before 1921 are not deportable; however, in order not to be deportable they have to prove residence before 1921."[36] They did not have to have taken out citizenship papers, but they had to have registered their presence in the state for proof of residence. While some Yaquis had registered under the agreement established by Governor Hunt and Juan Pistola, most surely had not. Though resident for nearly two decades, some might still have been classified as deportable under the new 1921 regulations.

Up until 1921, Yaquis were welcome to immigrate to Arizona if they could secure employment and pass a mental and physical exam. Many, however, skipped the exam process. From 1921 to 1924, regulations required Yaquis to produce a visa from the consulate in Mexico and then be approved after undergoing examination at the line. For new Yaqui immigrants, the ten-dollar fee associated with the visa may have proved prohibitive. For those already residing in Arizona, this offered no further legality to their status. After 1924, new Yaqui immigrants found without proper visas were to be deported to Mexico. A one-year waiting period was imposed before they could acquire a visa, present themselves at the border again for examination, and be granted entrance into the United States as "desirable aliens."[37] Yaquis who had immigrated before 1921 but had no registering documents in the United States lived with the constant possibility of deportation.

Fortunately, explained the officer, the United States had a strict policy not to deport anyone whose "life would be endangered in another country . . . appl[ying] to political and religious refugees." This, if nothing else, offered Yaquis nominal protection since their original flight had been under duress.[38] There was no official protection for the initial wave of Yaqui immigrants, those arriving during the first two decades of the twentieth century, but their status was significantly more secure than that of those who arrived after 1924. Those from 1926 to 1929, who "had given up their arms to the US Army representatives as they crossed the border, had accepted parole, and had claimed the status of refugees asking for asylum," fell under a different category.[39] Both groups were accepted at the border as political refugees, but under very different eras of immigration law in the United States the latter were targeted more for deportation.

The ambiguities and complications depending on whether one was a new immigrant or not, and immigrants' varying legal status, led to divisions among Yaqui groups. According to one report, immigration officials in the 1920s, attempting to enforce the new restrictive policies, paid older Yaqui immigrants to betray newcomers and reveal their whereabouts. The practice was largely based among Tucson Yaquis, who often informed immigration officials when groups of newer immigrants were moving north to join Yaqui communities in Phoenix's East Valley. Unable to speak English, many legal US residents were deported along with those without legal status. While the extent of such Yaqui collaboration with deportation was surely limited, it demonstrates an internal friction.[40] From 1922 to 1936, at least two hundred Yaquis were forced to return to Mexico.[41] Whereas Yaquis may have temporarily enjoyed a relative sense of security before 1920s immigration reform, the new regime reinstituted a familiar climate of caution, distrust, and fear.

Repatriation and Alien Registration

During the Great Depression, the United States instituted broad Mexican repatriation programs that resulted in the voluntary departure and deportation of hundreds of thousands of Mexicans from the US Southwest.[42] While most left voluntarily, many were forced out, including thousands who were US-born but could not prove citizenship. The question of including Yaqui refugees in repatriation was a point of great debate. Although they had originated from Mexico, Yaquis had not entered the United States in the context of regular immigration. "They are in Arizona as political refugees," reminded the *Casa Grande Dispatch*.[43] In the preceding decade, immigration officials had largely ignored this, as no official proclamation of amnesty had been made. "The Yaqui Indians were allowed to remain in the United States as political refugees," explained a Tucson report, "but have become subject to deportation on following the granting of amnesty by Mexico. The status of alien Yaquis living in colonies [in Tucson] and near Phoenix is the same as that of any other Mexican Citizen and all whose residence violated immigration laws are subject to deportation, according to officials."[44] With amnesty offered, Yaqui refugees could no longer use political refugee status as a means to escape deportation for improper documentation or border crossing.

A full decade earlier, in 1921, the post-Revolution government in Sonora had attempted to encourage Yaqui repatriation but to little effect. A 1921 report explained that Mexican officials offered free transportation for willing Yaqui repatriates and promised that no duties would be enforced on goods and property Yaquis brought with them from their Arizona exile. It was anticipated that the invitation would "practically depopulate Yaqui villages near Tucson, Arivaca, Patagonia and Nogales," but no such exodus occurred.[45] By 1931, Pima County sheriff Walter Bailey claimed that Sonoran "feeling against the Yaquis [had] subsided to a great degree." Guadalupe Flores, a prominent Tucson Yaqui and refugee from the 1926 uprising in Sonora, formed a coalition of Yaquis to attempt a mass exodus back to Sonora.[46] In a secret meeting with local New Deal administrator Edgar Goyette, Flores and his group proposed the mass migration with little knowledge of the Phoenix Yaqui community—or of their own Tucson community, it seems. Subsequent publication of news about the plan in the *Arizona Star*, the *Tucson Citizen*, and *El Tucsonense* deeply divided Yaquis.

In Edward Spicer's composite narrative account of meetings between Cayetano Lopez, who emerged as a strong opponent of the plan, Guadalupe Flores and others concerning repatriation, a complex divide was revealed. One exchange between Flores and Sixto Valencia, Lucas Matus, Nacho Alvarez, and Angel Acuña was related as by Spicer:

> "It is said that you are going to send us all back to Sonora." Sixto's voice was hostile. Guadalupe laughed rather quietly and said, "That is a foolish thing to say. I have no power to send anybody anywhere. If

> that is what is being said, I will tell you what should be said. I will tell you the truth. No one has ever heard me say anything but the truth."
>
> His manner was open and confiding. All who listened, including Sixto and Lucas and Angel, thought, at least momentarily, "Here is a good man who has nothing to hide." Guadalupe's manner was helping people feel comfortable with him.
>
> Guadalupe went on, "I have learned how it is in the Rio Yaqui now. The Yoemen [Yaquis] have their land back. They are raising good crops. Here is a letter from my brother in Tórim. He tells how there are Yoemen all around him beginning to plant for the summer rains. His family has plenty to eat. They are happy. The Lenten ceremony was the finest he has ever seen. Everybody in Tórim was able to fulfill their obligations. It has not been like this in anybody's memory. I think you should all know this and decide to leave this hard life in Arizona. The Rio Yaqui is where we all belong."

Sixto Valencia broke in to disagree, in Spicer's account:

> "To go and live with the Yoris [non-Yaquis]! That is what it is like on the Rio Yaqui now. There are Yoris on all the town lands. I too have letters and I know that between the railroad and Vicam Pueblo there are many Yoris running cattle. I do not want to live among the Yories." It was Sixto, speaking in his firmest manner. It was hard to think as he spoke that there could be any way other than his. Cayetano, standing against the church wall of old railroad ties, felt strongly the force of Sixto's words.[47]

According to Spicer the exchange continued, with Flores insisting that conditions in Sonora were improved and others insisting that non-Yaquis were their enemy and always would be.

Together, Sixto Valencia, Lucas Matus, Nacho Alvarez, and Angel Acuña recruited Francisco Matus and appointed Cayetano Lopez as their spokesman. They outlined a letter to Governor Hunt in protest of Flores's plan:

> Dear Sir. Mr. George W. P. Hunt:
>
> I write you this few lines just to let you know that my Indian Yaqui tribe are afraid to go back to Mexico. The ones that came in May 1927 do not know what they talk about and one of these is Guadalupe Flores. The other Yaquis—who is all of them—told me to make some arrangements with the government of the United States and so I pass it

> to you. The Yaqui Indian people will not go back to Mexico. Because the time that the Yaquis were living on the Yaqui River, the Mexican government started to make trouble and kill the Indians just like a dog and hang them by the neck. They will kill the poor Yaqui womans and the childrens and the Yaqui workers and this is why the Yaqui people [came] to Arizona to save their lives and we thank the American government because he keeps us under the American Flag.

The first part of Cayetano's reasoning stressed the horror that had driven Yaquis from Sonora in the first place, and by extension, their understandable fear in returning. To further strengthen his case, however, Cayetano underscored Yaqui commitment to their new Arizona homelands:

> We all believe in the American creed, in the United States of America as a government of the people by the people, and for the people whose just powers are derived from the consent of the governed, established on those principles for which American patriots sacrificed [their] lives and fortunes.
>
> We want to stay here in your county, because we are afraid of the Mexican government. He will kill us or send us to Yucatan.
>
> Respectfully submitted,
> Cayetano Lopez, Chief of All the Yaquis of Arizona
> Sixto Valencia, Mayor of Pascua Village
> Francisco Matus, Mayor and Captain-General
> of Barrio Libre Yaquis[48]

Hunt replied to Lopez in September 1931, assuring him that the US government did not intend to "force any [Yaquis] to return to Mexico against their will." "I believe you can rest assured that your people can continue to reside undisturbed in Arizona so long as they respect and obey the laws of the land and do not permit themselves to become public charges," Hunt concluded.[49] Hunt's caveat that Yaquis obey US law left broad latitude for immigration officials to determine whether Yaquis lacking proper documents would be deported or not. The plan, explained US officials, was simply to obtain a declaration of amnesty so Yaquis could have the option of voluntary repatriation. Thousands of non-Yaqui Mexican were voluntarily returning to Mexico, and US officials hoped to remove the Yaquis refugee status so they could join in the broader repatriation movement. In the following years, many Yaquis, in fact, were deported from Arizona.

Sometime in 1936, the US embassy in Mexico received word from the Mexican government that it would accept repatriated Yaquis with full amnesty—no punishment for previous rebellions.[50] Then, in late February 1937, General Román Yocupicio, governor of Sonora, publically petitioned President Lázaro Cárdenas that Yaquis exiled in the United States be repatriated. When Yocupicio visited Yaquis in Guadalupe, personally inviting them to return, Arizona papers widely publicized the development.[51] Yocupicio, a full-blooded Mayo, along with General Henríquez Guzman, would soon champion Indigenous rights and rehabilitation in Sonora as Yaquis returned from exile, descending from strongholds in the Bacatete Range to attempt to resume farming in the now-irrigated Yaqui Valley.[52] Yocupicio's decree began considerable negotiations between Yaqui leaders in Sonora and President Cárdenas, and these eventually resulted in significant restitution of Yaqui lands in the valley. This was concurrent with Mexican plans to repatriate "political deportees from Veracruz, Tucatan Tlaxcala, and other locations."[53] The atmosphere of warming Yaqui-Mexican relations spurred US efforts to push Arizona Yaquis to return to Sonora, but Yaqui opinions during the 1937–38 repatriation debates were mixed. In Sonora, a delegation of Yaqui leaders wrote to Mexico City requesting that Arizona Yaquis *not* be allowed to return.[54] While it is uncertain whether this was a widely held view among Yaquis in "los ochos pueblos," it suggests a diversity of opinions south of the line.

In the Tucson and Phoenix Yaqui communities, Yaqui opinion was also sharply divided. From the Cayetano-Flores division in the beginning of the decade, no consensus was ever reached. By 1932, it appears that Flores's plans for mass repatriation may have softened, as a Tucson newspaper report indicated: "In the squalid village of mud huts called Barrio Pascua Guadalupe Flores is chief, a bearded taciturn man who points to the south and mumbles in Spanish that this people are afraid to return. But his wishes are objected to by the younger men who say they want to go to the land of their fathers. They are starving here and have no jobs."[55] In 1937, this same schism emerged in Guadalupe to the north. "Young men of the squalid village," explained the *Tucson Citizen*, "born and educated in the United States, would like to go to Mexico if they could, just for adventure and romance." Interviews with the opposing parties were striking: "*Sure I want to go*," said one Yaqui youth who spoke good English. "*Why?*" he was asked. "*Oh, I haven't anything else to do*." Pablo, an eighty-year-old water carrier, spoke for the older men. "*Mexico?*" he mused. "*No, I don't want to go there*."[56] Another Mexican-born Yaqui, Rosario Escalante, who had suffered Porfirian deportation and jailing, explained his reasoning for opposing a return to Mexico: "In Mexico el gobierno is always molesting you. Here you come and go as you please."[57]

This generational divide is telling. Arizona Yaquis often spoke longingly of their traditional Yaqui Valley lands, and some younger Yaquis may have found these fond reminiscences enticing. What the older generation painted in such idyllic terms, however, was not the Mexican Sonora they had known previously. It was a Yaquimi long since overrun. Personal memories of persecution in Sonora may have helped older generations make this distinction, but some younger Yaquis, only acquainted with the dire poverty of Arizona, were apparently willing to try their luck in Sonora. Alternately, a 1936 survey of Pascua residents indicated that the older generation then favored returning to Mexico. By this point, even Flores, who had previously championed return to Mexico, now expressed distrust of the Mexican government. Flores did not deny the possible sway of opinion among his people or the possibility of a return south, but a disdain for Mexico was evident. Ironically, Flores himself was deported later that year along with his wife and Lucuano Alvarez as part of what had become a "routine program" of forced repatriation.[58]

Correspondence between Arizona's US senator Carl Hayden and various US officials reveals considerable confusion surrounding the entire 1937–38 repatriation debate. Soon after the February 1937 statements by Sonoran governor Yocupicio were published, Senator Hayden inquired of the State Department whether Mexico had forwarded repatriation plans to the United States. A reply in March revealed that no such plans had been received, but the US Department of Labor indicated that it was interested in deporting certain Yaquis. Senator Hayden next contacted Edward Shaughnessy, deputy commissioner of immigration and naturalization, inquiring of his agency's plans for Yaqui refugees.[59] The Immigration Department was aware of the Yaqui refugees, explained Shaughnessy, but he said that those who came in 1926–27 were fully undocumented and thus in the United States illegally. However, granted their political refugee status, deportation had not been pursued in earnest.

With the announcement of amnesty by Mexico in 1936, however, the Department of Immigration began to prepare and made some preliminary deportations. Its plan was to select certain Arizona Yaqui leaders and deport them "in the hope that others would follow them to Mexico in the event of their deportation." It was during this effort that the aforementioned deportation of Pascua leader Guadalupe Flores occurred. During these efforts, immigration officials deported thirty-four Yaqui leaders. Four others voluntarily left, one died in custody, one was released, and by May 1937 eight arrest warrants were still pending. Further efforts may have been made, but the fact that a large percentage of the Tucson, Guadalupe, and Scottsdale Yaquis were by this point US-born discouraged efforts. Of the three hundred or so Yaqui families in Guadalupe and Scottsdale, Shaughnessy explained, almost all of the 225 children were US-born. Deporting parents with dependent, US-born children apparently worried immigration officials. Furthermore, although it was certain that "some of the Yaqui Indians who are not American citizens [had] made various illegal entries into the United States, none of them [would] admit it." Lack of proof likewise stymied deportation proceedings.[60] These qualifying circumstances aside, the eagerness of some US officials to remove Yaquis from Arizona is striking. Even before a full repatriation program was approved, they were carefully laying groundwork upon which it could unfold.

No full Yaqui repatriation program was ever instituted in Arizona. By 1937 the federal government's Mexican repatriation efforts were slowing. A final development in the early-twentieth-century history of Yaquis in Arizona occurred in 1940. Just as the United States had done in 1918, the Immigration Department instituted a full alien registration campaign that forced Yaqui refugees to gather, make themselves known to US officials, and be counted. In Tucson, the registration began on August 29 and was to continue until December 26, 1940. All aliens were required to register, but two groups had no chance for securing actual citizenship: Chinese and Yaquis.[61] In the light of recent deportation and repatriation rhetoric and rumors, this campaign troubled Yaquis. Edward Spicer's 1937 words regarding Yaqui distrust of outsiders and desire to remain aloof still applied: "The fact remains that there is a definite disinclination on the part of Yaquis everywhere in Arizona to give facts about themselves or other Yaquis to whites with whose purposes they are not thoroughly familiar. . . . Yaqui secretiveness here is a result of an ever-present fear of being deported to Mexico."[62] Yaqui desires to secure citizenship would continue to crest publicly on occasion, but the predominant narrative was one of suspicion and evasion.

Spicer personally accompanied some Yaquis through the alien registration process, vouching and swearing for those who spoke only Yaqui.

A few days before the registration began, Spicer organized an event and filled out paperwork for about thirty individuals. Information about jail records was required, and Spicer noted that most had extensive sentences for public drunkenness. Those with clean records were applauded by all and jokingly acclaimed as "muy buen hombre," and "muy buen gente," but it was not a lighthearted event. Yaquis expressed great fear to Spicer over the registration process. They worried about having to read English instructions and about the possible repercussions of failure to answer questions correctly. Yaquis stood to lose a great deal if the process did not go well, so Spicer's aid was certainly appreciated. At the registration itself, Spicer helped additional Yaquis fill out papers and prepare answers regarding birthdates and birthplaces so each could appear as competent as possible when questioned, and he helped them make their way through the different lines and procedures. Although he was not "in charge" of the Yaquis, as the young white man doing fingerprinting assumed, Spicer's aid was significant.[63]

During the registration process, Spicer estimated that there were 450 Yaquis at Pascua, 82 of whom were Mexican-born. The majority of those born in Mexico knew the precise date when they entered the United States. Extrapolating from these numbers, Spicer estimated that approximately 25 percent of Arizona's Yaquis were Mexican-born and that, of those, some 50 percent had entered the United States prior to 1907. Yaquis who entered the United States prior to July 1, 1906, were eligible for citizenship if they paid an eight-dollar registration fee. For those who came to the United States between July 1, 1906, and July 1924 but lacked prior registration papers, citizenship was not an option. They were technically in the country illegally. However, as a Border Patrol officer explained to Spicer, there was no provision to start deportation proceedings against most pre-1924 refugees. Although not in the United States legally, they could remain. For those who entered between 1917 and 1924, deportation proceedings could be initiated if they fell into the "criminal" or "immoral" classifications, the latter essentially referring to prostitution.[64] Immigration officials focused the 1940 alien registration proceedings on identifying immigrants who entered after 1924, when registry upon entry from Mexico became law. If they had not filled out the requisite papers upon entry, they were in the country illegally and eligible for deportation. Failure to present themselves at the alien registry also jeopardized their status, threatening subsequent deportation.[65] Spicer's final calculations suggested that as many as 19 per-

Table 2. Passage dates of Mexican-born Yaquis registered in Arizona in 1940

Date of Immigration	Total
1880–1885	2
1900–1904	21 (most 1903–1904)
1907–1910	17 (most 1907)
1914–1918	21 (most in 1916–1917)
After 1920	1

cent of all Yaquis in Arizona fell into categories that denied them legal residence or citizenship. Of the remaining 81 percent, three-quarters might become citizens by virtue of the fact they were US-born.[66]

One further underlying issue troubled the registration of Yaquis. Mexican "Indians" were apparently not eligible for US citizenship. While the US Constitution had left Native peoples in an ambiguous middle ground, neither "guaranteed opportunities for citizenship" nor recognized as sovereign foreign citizens, the Naturalization Act of 1790 opened citizenship to "white" immigrants, including Mexican immigrants.[67] Whereas foreigners could experience, in the words of scholar I-Mien Tsiang, "a new political birth" as naturalization severed allegiance to a native country, Native Americans were not categorized in the same terms.[68] The 1924 Indian Citizenship Act granted universal citizenship to "American Indians," meaning that they would no longer have to "give up being Indian in exchange for citizenship," as some political scientists explained. However, Yaquis fit in neither category—neither considered white Mexicans nor American Indians.[69] Hence, when Yaquis in earlier years had attempted to fill out citizenship papers and identified themselves as "Yaqui Indians," their applications had been denied.[70] Beyond denying Yaquis the stability and security of citizenship, this also barred them from voting and criminalized their marrying of non-Indians.[71] Spicer discussed the issue with postmaster Harold Collins, who was in charge of the registration procedure in Tucson, and noted, "Collins admitted in response to my question that Yaqui Indians are denied citizenship under any circumstances. I pointed out that they merely have more publicity than other types of Mexican Indians and hence why not let them become citizens like other Mexicans. He said I was right about publicity. . . . He seemed not to have thought about other

Mexicans having Indian blood."[72] "They are here," concluded the Catholic *Indian Sentinel*, "but they are not eligible to become American citizens."[73] Though Yaquis were decades removed from most of the negative US press concerning "Yaqui Indians" and their struggles with Mexican authorities in the late nineteenth and early twentieth centuries, the prejudice and stigma remained.[74] No longer true citizens of Mexico and denied citizenship in the United States, Yaquis were indeed people without a country, as so many reports had described them. Once registered, Yaquis not flagged for deportation returned to their work in Arizona. For the remainder of the 1940s and 1950s, questions of Yaqui legal status lessened with each passing year. As the growing progeny of the original refugee generations tipped the Arizona Yaqui population from mostly Mexican-born to mostly US-born, they solidified their place in the United States.

Evolution of Public Yaqui Culture

As Yaquis built stable and secure communities, they increasingly used public performance of their culture, including religion, to assert their Indigenous identity and place in community. This would be instrumental in their emergent political presence in Arizona in the 1960s and 1970s. Perhaps the Yaquis' most visible presence in Arizona revolved around their Easter festivals, Passion Plays and dances. The earliest reports of these stem from the Guadalupe village south of Tempe, but the practices of Tucson-based Yaquis dominated later press.[75] For centuries in Sonora, Yaquis had blended Indigenous beliefs and traditions with Christian pageantry, and the resulting spectacle became a hallmark by which they were known throughout Mexico. As early as 1906 to 1909, when the Yaqui exodus from Sonora was in full flux, Yaquis in Arizona began to be visible in public through their Easter dances.[76] Throughout the years from the last major Yaqui immigration in the 1920s to the political organizing of the early 1960s, the majority of local and US press concerning Yaquis dealt with these Easter dances, increasingly opened to the public. During subsequent efforts to secure federal funding, lands, and recognition, the cultural value of these Yaqui Easter pageants was always forwarded as a major argument. By 1958, Yaqui leader Anselmo Valencia even announced that photography, long banned, would be allowed at the ceremonies—signaling a new step in Yaqui outreach to neighboring communities.[77]

In Tucson, the chamber of commerce appointed a special committee, led by Muriel Thayer Painter, to aid Yaquis in publicizing and holding the festivities. Previous economic ventures had temporarily flourished in Phoenix that were based on the annual dance held at Guadalupe.[78] In many cases, their dances were the only thing about Yaquis known to the general Arizona and US public.[79] However, Yaqui dances were usually exoticized by the mass media, and the dances' "foreign" origins were referenced. Indeed, most newspaper reports concerning anything Yaqui-related made note of Yaquis' origins outside the United States.[80] This reinforced stereotypes that later generations seeking US integration may have regretted. Still, via dances and other cultural exhibitions for public consumption, Yaquis in the early to mid-twentieth century laid an important foundation upon which something greater would be built.

Conclusion

After their exodus from Sonora during the Porfirian era of deportation and enslavement, thousands of Yaqui refugees established both transitory and permanent settlement in Arizona, but their legal status in the United States was ambiguous. Although Yaquis' physical, geographic, and demographic presence was indisputable, the US government failed, for the first half of the twentieth century, to satisfactorily address their unique situation. Yaquis were alternately allowed to remain and deported, and their exile in Arizona was precarious although preferable to persecution in Sonora. As their public presence through labor, cultural celebrations, and sociopolitical activities evolved, Arizona Yaquis continued to be saddled by settlement difficulties, troublesome effects of Yaqui-Mexican strife, and unanswered questions about their legal status.

Chapter 8

Cree and Chippewa Attempts at Permanent Montana Settlement, 1900–1908

The hot days are passing and we are not making any money. When winter comes we will be without food and wood and clothing and blankets. What are we to do? We must have help. The white man lets foreigners come here and gives them work, but they will not do that for the Indians and we will starve. Will you see that we get it? If we do not, there is nothing left but starvation.

—LITTLE BEAR, July 19, 1913[1]

In late 1899, just as a turbulent century of Anglo-Native relations drew to a close, an immigration inspector from Great Falls made a visit to Havre, Montana. There to investigate the continued presence of "foreign" Cree Indians in the region, he estimated there to be roughly 2,000–2,200 "alien Indians" in the state, and he called for drastic measures. "The Indians have proved such a nuisance to the people of Northern Montana," he concluded, "that an attempt will be made to have the state department make such arrangements for a second deportation."[2] Many white Montanans lamented the failed 1896 deportation under Governor Rickards. Crees had immediately returned. Their leader, Little Bear, had been tried in Canada for the Frog Lake Massacre and released, then traveled to Ottawa and received an offer from the Canadian government to settle his people on an existing reserve. However, by October 1897, Little Bear had returned to Montana, joined those who had already crossed back south, and declared his intentions "to make a legal battle" for his people to settle permanently in Montana.[3] Meanwhile, new officials aimed to learn from previous mistakes and end the long-standing problem Crees represented. Bands, families, and individuals would be apprehended, property would be confiscated if necessary, and Montana would be rid of foreign Crees.

Such was the political atmosphere at the beginning of the new century in northern Montana.

For the groups of Crees from Canada that for as long as twenty years had sought peaceful residence in the United States, this was ominous. It did not ensure definitive exile from the United States, but it dampened the promise of permanent settlement. Although the Rocky Boy's Indian Reservation (upon which Chippewas and Crees settled) would be founded in 1916, the preceding years often lacked any promise. One must block the habit of reading history backward and imposing known outcomes as having been predestined. The years from 1900 to 1916 were tenuous and difficult for foreign Natives striving to secure livelihoods in Montana. Until 1908, Chippewa and Cree efforts at settlement were stymied for a number of reasons, and this chapter will explore many of them. After 1908, a new phase began in which Crees and Chippewas, along with their Montanan allies, succeeded in building relationships with the federal government, resulting in the passage of legislation for their benefit, eventual tribal recognition, and creation of a reservation.

Nuisance, Threat, or Cultural Curiosity

The early-twentieth-century history of local and federal government interaction with Crees and Chippewas in Montana followed roughly parallel trajectories. Though the two groups were dealt with independently at times, they were regularly mistaken for each other in the press, and they were united in a joint quest for securing lands in Montana. During the first years of the new century, three predominant trends emerged in how white Montanans viewed the Natives. Together they provide context for understanding how and why disparate landless Indian groups combined into singular entities.

First, white Montanans viewed the lingering Native presence on the outskirts of cities as a nuisance. This meant constant complaints but no serious action against their camps. Second, the general complaints sometimes escalated into alarmist warnings that Crees and Chippewas were serious threats to public health. Much of this centered on blaming Indians for smallpox outbreaks in Montana. Third, when Cree and Chippewas began exerting their cultural presence publicly by hosting Sun Dances, Montanans viewed them as an exotic oddity, a curiosity. Newspaper reports about Sun Dances, though still laced with cutting quips about Natives, were generally less negative about them. These trends comprised the tenuous foundation upon which federal policy would be constructed concerning these so-called foreign Indians. In this climate Chippewas and Crees began a new phase of efforts for legal settlement.

Public rhetoric that cast Crees and Chippewas as pests—contrary to the common good—was not new in Montana, of course. Indians as pestilent was virtually a stereotype, but what is significant in this case is how the trajectory of rhetoric went from expressions of annoyance to alarms regarding public safety.

By 1900, residents of Butte, Great Falls, Havre, and other towns in Montana were accustomed to a Cree and Chippewa presence nearby and intermittently expressed negative commentary about them. A turn-of-the-century report from the Choteau *Montanian* reveals white settler familiarity with Crees in their midst and even tacit acceptance of them. Telling of Crees making "their annual trip north for annuities" from Canadian officials, the *Montanian* was convinced that Canadian Crees were playing both sides of the line, siphoning resources from Canadian and US borderlands residents alike. Of this supposed regular practice, they quipped, "Montana Crees are always sure to be on time."[4] Belying the palpable animus they held against the presence of "Canadian" Indians in the state, their denotation of the group as "Montana Crees" suggests that some settlers had begun to recognize their permanent presence and unique identity in the state, however reluctantly. General distaste continued to be expressed in public rhetoric, but the previous tones of outrage or confusion were fading. Montanans by this time seem to have become resigned to Cree and Chippewa persistence. "Hell, let 'em stay," joked some old-timers.[5]

It was Montanans' complaints focused on the Natives' hunting and foraging that spurred Crees and Chippewas to action. Unable to secure lands on which to farm and without hunting rights, Indians had been forced to sift a livelihood from the public domain, sometimes driven by starvation. The resultant press coverage was telling: the Crees were said to be "notoriously uncleanly in their habits, veritable swine of the prairies . . . scavenger swine," "slaughtering game that is protected by state law." They subsisted on deer and elk, which provided meat, skins for moccasins, shirts, and beaded belts that they sold or traded for goods.[6] Around the turn of the century, Chippewas operated similarly and under the assumption that they had the right to hunt any place they could find game. This, however, landed many in jail, as whites feared their hunting "would scare all game away before hunting season could be opened."[7] The majority of these problems centered on the winter months, when Natives were less able to obtain food for their families. Hence, tightening Montanan game laws increasingly deprived them of food precisely when it was most needed.

At this juncture, some enterprising Chippewas and Crees discovered that there was a market for bones. "Immediately," explained Frank Linderman, "with Red River Carts, rickety wagons drawn by tiny Cayuse teams, and even with packhorses, the Chippewas and Cree of all ages began gathering the thousands of tons of buffalo bones which were scattered over hundreds of square miles of Montana's plains, hauling them to the railroad stations and here they stacked them in immense piles, ugly monuments to the wantonness of white men." The irony is striking: Cree hunting of elk and deer, of which they used the entire animal for food, clothing, and trade, was meanwhile restricted. To subsist, Crees gathered bison bones and horns and sold them as tourist souvenirs. Linderman concluded, "When they could find no more horns, and the buffalo had made its last contribution to the Indians, the Chippewas and Crees face actual starvation."[8]

Warmer seasons allowed them to travel the expanses between Montana cities and engage in gathering and selling of bones and horns and trading of bead work, ponies, and herbal medicine in exchange for money, horses, clothes, or food.[9] Winter did not allow such practices, and hence landless Natives then congregated sometimes where they could rely upon forests for game, but at least as often near city dumps, alleys, and streets for foraging. Again, Frank Linderman described it:

> Congregating in small bands on the outskirts of cities and towns they constructed flimsy camps, using scraps of canvas, gunny sacks, and old boxes. Firewood was scarce and far away, the winters bitterly cold. . . . Harried by police, jeered by white ruffians, the Chippewa and Cree women prowled each day through the alleys, searching garbage-cans for food. For years the cans, the cities' dumps, offal from slaughter-houses, with an occasional horse or cow found dead upon the plains, furnished a large portion of their food. To their great credit they did but little begging; and one must marvel that during all these years of suffering and exposure they somehow kept their health.[10]

The indigent state of Crees and Chippewas was insufficient to gain the sympathies of many Montanans. As expressed by the *Anaconda Standard*, Montanans were not oblivious to their grave condition but callous, using derisive terms to describe it. In 1897 the paper lamented:

> During the summer months they will be a standing menace to carelessly exposed property and if any high grade or blooded canines are missing henceforth the owners thereof may rest assured that the missing animal has been properly fricasseed and served as the main dish at a Cree banquet. The men [are] lazy, indolent thieves, without one redeeming trait, and the women are degraded filthy wenches who roam over the city soliciting attention and money for immoral purposes. Some means should be adopted to rid the community of the nauseating nuisance.[11]

Four years later, the *Standard* was no less cruel:

> Crees are irresistibly attracted to the garbage dumps of Montana . . . [the dumps] are rich in nutriment and infinite variety of material [and] are daily replenished from an inexhaustible source of supply. Compared with the bill of fare offered by the backyards of a Canadian Pacific way station, the Butte dump is a Waldorf-Astoria dining room, and the Anaconda dump a Delmonico banquet hall. . . . Here life is one long, long feast. Here is eating and drinking and rising up to play craps. Here is no taking thought of the morrow, what they shall eat, or what they shall drink. Without money and without price, they find the white men bringing them food by the cartload and spreading it before them in riotous profusion. To the Crees the garbage dumps of Montana are paradise regained, the real, unadulterated Garden of Eden, from which they refuse to be driven out by anything so little like the angel of the Lord as the United States government. They will resist to the last court, the last ditch, the last dump.

These views were also expressed in editorial cartoons (see figure 8.1). No longer was the Indian a "noble savage" or a military threat. Instead Indians were beggars and happily at home in Montana's urban garbage dumps. Such were many whites' views of Chippewa and Cree indigent subsistence.[12]

A report from Dupuyer, Montana, offered another white view of the Chippewa and Cree presence, identifying key elements of the predicament: Native desperation and non-Native annoyance:

> The nuisance is still fastened upon us, and the forest reserve is again assuming the appearance of an Indian reservation for the winter. If the three prisoners in the Dupuyer jail should be convicted of cattle stealing an example would be made, but the clamor of the hungry stomachs belonging to the rest of the tribe admits of no remedy but a plentiful supply of meat and well the Indian knows that a little care on his part will allay his hunger and render conviction practically impossible.[13]

Indeed, the "clamor of hungry stomachs" trumped Native desires to operate within legal boundaries. Although their plight was evident, complaints of their killing of cattle and antelope, deer, and other game either illegally or out of season persisted.[14] Stark disparity is evident. On the one hand, desperate Crees and Chippewas attempted to subsist on what game they could find,

The Modern Cree on the Warpath. *Be It Ever So Humble, There Is No Place Like Home.*

Figure 8.1. 1901 *Anaconda Standard* cartoons. Source: "Law, Lawyers and Litigants: And a Few Judges and Judgments," *Anaconda Standard*, May 12, 1901.

and on the other hand, Montanan resistance to this hardened. Entrenched with incompatible views and goals, repeating an annual winter standoff, the two parties would eventually take action to break the stalemate.

From the recollection of Chippewa and Cree elders, such conflict in the Butte area spurred Chief Rocky Boy to petition for lands. In particular, Rocky Boy was frustrated with the intermittent jailing of his people for, in his eyes, simply trying to provide for their starving families. "Rocky Boy did not like the way his people got in jail," and he was tired of being chased from place to place, explained Chippewa Cree Tribe member James Denny in the 1970s. Malcolm Mitchell recalled that Rocky Boy told his band that "he would try and get some land . . . he figured the US Government should let him have some of the land the whites took away without paying for."[15]

Chippewas from Billings faced similar problems, and they added to the efforts to receive lands of their own in Montana. Sometime during the early 1900s, Chief Day Child, a prominent Chippewa leader in the state, was arrested and sentenced to thirty days in jail for shooting and killing an antelope. After his release, he immediately contacted Rocky Boy and told him of his troubles and of the need for them to secure lands of their own. Chief Day Child's son Joe Day Child later explained that it was then that "they started to pull together."[16] A new attempt by Little Bear to secure lands for Crees began incorporating a broader coalition of landless Indian in Montana. It is unclear as to when Little Bear's Crees, largely based in the region around Havre, joined the efforts of Rocky Boy and Day Child. There may have been some animosity between Little Bear and Rocky Boy during these early years, but their joint efforts would increasingly meld their bands.[17] Even if leadership rivalries existed, their bands quickly became friends, sharing a "harsh existence" in Montana.[18]

As mentioned above, white Montanans' sense of Chippewas and Crees as annoyances evolved sometimes into fear. During the first years of the twentieth century, outbreaks of smallpox among Montana reservation tribes were regularly attributed to Crees. Given the Office of Indian Affairs self-imposed duty and goal to set order to the chaotic Native world, the "foreign" Crees served as a ready scapegoat. In the spring of 1901, the Flathead Reservation suffered a smallpox outbreak, reportedly from "a band of Canadian Crees."[19] Crees were quarantined on the reservation, and, as fears of an epidemic grew, the *Anaconda Standard* emphasized that the Crees were "Canadian Indians" and that Canadian authorities should be required to reimburse the United States for their care.[20] Crees were deemed unclean, uncontrolled, uncontrollable, and requiring removal. The secretary of the interior, however, said that the Department of Indian Affairs had no authority to move them.[21] Although deportation did not follow, these outbreaks reconfigured Cree (and Chippewa) landscapes in Montana, making them potentially more hostile than ever.[22]

The resurgence of Sun Dance exhibitions, however, helped Crees and Chippewas shift public rhetoric in a more positive direction, and for the first time the two began to be presented as a single culturally based polity. Coming after Governor Rickards banned the Sun Dance in 1894 and the subsequent deportation of 1896, this was a time of Cree resurgence. Beginning in 1899 and repeated in follow summers, Crees under Little Bear joined first with Assiniboines and then Chippewas in multiple days of dancing and ceremonies—all made available to the public for a small admission fee. Aside from serving religious and spiritual purposes, public dances served pragmatic ends, allowing Crees to assert a public cultural presence, collect sorely needed money, and forge more positive ties with neighboring whites. Joint and separate Sun Dances and Grass Dances were held several times a year by both groups for the next few years. Reports from Havre, where Little Bear's Crees held their dances, were largely positive, while those from Butte were derisive.[23]

These cultural spectacles, in which Montana townspeople took great interest, were an important platform from which landless Indians could make their presence and plight known. And to some degree they helped counterbalance the stereotypes of Indians as beggars and garbage dump residents. Uniting in these events, Crees and Chippewas also began to forge meaningful relationships with prominent white Montanans to help their cause. While still up against antagonistic whites entrenched in prejudices and resistant to Chippewa and Cree settlement, they may have had grounds for hope. The stage was set for a series of public debates and actions to solve the problem of landless, starving Indians in the borderlands.

Many Montanans mourned the failure of the 1896 deportation of Crees to Canada. After a short lull, proponents renewed the call for a deportation campaign during the first few years of the twentieth century. As Montanans had earlier influenced federal policy concerning foreign Natives, many sought to do so again. After state officials propagandized about the perceived smallpox threat, in 1901 the Indian Office gave the officials permission to remedy the problem themselves and contact Canadian authorities.[24]

It seems odd that international diplomacy of this sort was delegated to Montana. In essence, since refugee Crees were not under the jurisdiction of the Department of the Interior, the State of Montana was left to sort out its own transnational Native migration policy. This infuriated some concerned Montanans who saw continued federal disregard for state crises. Visiting North-West Mounted Police officials offered little help, claiming that Canadians were doing their best to prevent southward Cree border-crossings. Canadian officials proved well-informed about the transnational Crees and Chippewas but consistently avoided taking responsibility for controlling their movements.[25] Thus, a new round of public clamoring over the perceived "Cree problem" emerged, leading to general frustration by all parties. For the remainder of 1901 and extending into 1904, various groups voiced desires to eject Crees from the state.[26]

At the turn of the century, Crees themselves were overwhelmingly resistant to forced deportation. In 1901, a group that had been encamped on the Crow Reservation was forced to leave by reservation officials. "One day two Indian police came to the Cree camp and told us we had to move off the reservation, because we did not belong there," recalled Chippewa Cree Tribe member George Watson years later. The group sought respite in nearby Billings but was soon compelled northward. Elated, the press reported that the group had left with a vow to "move northward . . . until they reach Canada." Big Thunder Storm, a leader of the Billings group, was reported to have stated that "if the people of Montana did not want them they would go."[27] Whether they ever intended to cross into Canada or not (they may simply have been discouraged by hard winter travel), the group moved north, first to Glasgow and then to Havre, where they wintered.[28] Little Bear meanwhile expressed deep irritation over the deportation debate, professing "much love for Uncle Sam."[29] Though some would cross north into Canada to hunt in the Cypress Hills or visit relatives, few viewed such sojourns as permanent, and Crees persisted in their efforts to settle in Montana.

Rocky Boy's New Allies and Little Bear's Northward Gaze

Most of the resurgent pro-deportation rhetoric focused on Crees, leaving Chippewas apparently more secure. Appearances were deceiving, though. Chippewa cultural and familial networks were closely intertwined with Crees, and Chippewas like Rocky Boy increasingly sought to assert a unique identity in the state. Rocky Boy must have understood the extreme prejudice Montanans held against Little Bear's Crees, and he proved an astute politician in forging a path for himself and his people.[30] As a public and private figure, Rocky Boy "was liked by both white people and Indians, all who knew him," Chippewa Cree Tribe member Malcolm Mitchell would later say. Many were impressed "by the stately bearing of Rocky Boy, and by the sensible manner in which he spoke."[31] One newspaper account of the time stated that he had personal letters of recommendation from Idaho governor Frank W. Hunt and a district court judge, and free passes for BA&P (Butte, Anaconda & Pacific), Oregon Short Line, Rio Grande Western, and Southern Pacific railroads.[32] It is unclear how or when Rocky Boy met and forged favorable relationships with government and industry officials, but these speak to his adeptness at navigating white social networks.

Starting with his 1902 letter to President Theodore Roosevelt, Rocky Boy began to apply this talent to securing lands and a legal settlement for his people. By 1904, the federal government finally took action, and it was not in the direction that many Montanans had anticipated. Senate Bill 2705, "for the Relief of the Wandering American-Born Indians of Rocky Boy's Band, Montana," was introduced in Congress. Its object was to appropriate funds to settle and assist 110 "American-born Indian men, women and children of 40 acres each on the Flathead Reservation in Montana."[33] Though strongly supported by the Committee on Indian Affairs and Secretary of the Interior Ethan A. Hitchcock, the bill failed to pass. Its presentation to Congress did, however, stand as a promising sign for Chippewas hoping to find legal resolution to their plight. In order to push his cause further, and with more local support, Rocky Boy developed another useful strategy: friendship. Procurement of lands would require federal action on behalf of Rocky Boy's band. The failed 1904 bill underscored the lack of federal initiative to do so, and some Montanans had lobbied against Rocky Boy's cause in DC. With so much local press against the settling of foreign Indians, Chippewas needed to find prominent white Montanans to help them in their fight. Friendships Rocky Boy forged proved instrumental, and a few individuals merit specific mention.

By the time of their first appearance in public discourse, Rocky Boy's Chippewas had already apparently forged a friendship with Butte jailer Sol (Solomon) Levy. It was Levy who served as the Chippewa representative to Butte city officials in the planning of the first Sun Dance in 1901.[34]

As Chippewas had been regularly jailed for hunting out of season, it is possible that initial contact and friendship with Levy came during their confinement in the Butte jail. It was through him that the commissioner of Indian affairs had communicated with Rocky Boy during 1903 when federal officials were investigating the band's condition.[35] By 1904, Levy had become a confidant of both Chippewas and Crees in the Butte vicinity (sometimes called "Chief Solevy"), and he helped them shape a positive public image through various events. In Anaconda, Rocky Boy secured a similar friendship with a Métis man, W. A. Cameron, who would serve as interpreter and help him gain support in the community and gain occasionally neutral, if not positive, press.[36]

These local allies, however, did not have national influence. The first to help Rocky Boy in making federal connections was Butte attorney John W. James. By early 1902, he was recognized as the unofficial legal emissary for the Chippewa band encamped near Butte and had contacted the Department of the Interior concerning Rocky Boy's band. With the counsel of James, Rocky Boy presented his case to Butte locals and to President Roosevelt. Through James, Rocky Boy made allies of US congressional representatives Joseph M. Dixon and Paris Gibson, who introduced a bill in early 1904 in favor of Rocky Boy's Band. All proved important champions of Rocky Boy's cause and facilitators in gaining further allies in Montana and Washington.[37]

As Rocky Boy made significant strides in public relations, Little Bear's Crees suffered from the long-standing prejudices Montanans had forged against them. By late 1904 or early 1905, Little Bear had become so frustrated with conditions in Montana, that he reopened official communication with Canadian officials to negotiate a return north of the line. Little Bear recast his band's Montanan presence back into a borderlands context and returned to the Cree tradition of leveraging the line to their advantage. On February 10, 1905, Little Bear wrote to the secretary of the interior:

> I am anxious to return to Canada, and take with [me] my Cree Indians, who have wandered about Montana for a number of years. . . . You will find that we are peaceable and law abiding people, and anxious to do what is right and all we ask is to return to the land of our birth and be treated as the remainder of the tribe is. I trust you will give this matter your early attention, and hope that you will consider my proposition with favor.
>
> Very respectfully, Little Bear, Chief of the Cree Tribe of Indians[38]

Little Bear's cognizance of the particular prejudices laid against his people in Montana is evident in his petition to Canadian officials. The Department of the Interior in Canada took the matter up seriously, detailing in an internal memorandum the history of Little Bear from 1885–1896. The secretary of Canada's Department of Indian Affairs, J. D. McLean, wrote to Little Bear requesting details, and Little Bear responded, proclaiming his intent to bring only industrious Crees with him in the fall of 1905.[39]

A final agreement arrived from Canadian Indian commissioner David Laird in August 1905. Laird's message to Little Bear was threefold. First, Crees would be allowed to settle on the Onion Lake Reserve in Saskatchewan. Second, they would have to pay their way to the border but would thereafter be escorted and cared for on their journey to Onion Lake. Third, upon arrival they would be put on the "same footing as the present members of the various bands to which they wish to return." It was implied that they would need to obey the local Indian agent, just as longtime reserve residents were required to do.[40] The terms of the offer, in essence, were the same Little Bear had received in Ottawa in 1897. When word spread in Montana of Little Bear's intentions to leave the country by the end of October, various newspapers expressed elation.[41]

But problems soon arose in Little Bear's plans. Although the Canadian offer lined up exactly with Little Bear's original proposal, in early November he replied with an augmented set of requests. Perhaps his followers were unsatisfied with the terms Little Bear had secured and wanted to delay their migration. If the *Anaconda Standard*'s report was accurate in describing a Cree in Butte "quite indignant with the proposition," not all were prepared to submit to the Canadian government.[42] Little Bear's counterproposal rejected Onion Lake as a settlement site, claiming the land was poor for agriculture, hunting, and fishing. He stated his readiness to leave in the spring if granted three requests: first, that full bloods be given their own reservation on lands better than those at Onion Lake; second, that annuities owed them during their sojourn in the United States be paid retroactively; and third, that he, his family, and those with mixed Native and European heritage be made regular Canadian citizens, receiving scrip rather than treaty annuities.[43] It was a bold proposal, and one wonders if it was a bluff. Perhaps Little Bear had already decided to remain south. Canadian officials who conferred decided that it was "out of the question" that Little Bear's Crees be given superior lands or receive retroactive annuities. Eventually, Laird replied to Little Bear and said that the migrant Crees could choose from various existing reserves for settlement but would not be paid retroactive annuities, having forfeited those by being absent from the country for over five continuous years. Little Bear made no reply. By the following summer, Little Bear remained "firm in his determination" to reject Canada's counteroffer and deepened his resolve to remain in Montana.[44]

By early 1906, both Chippewas and Crees had fallen into familiar patterns of subsistence and survival, but their place in the United States remained uncertain. Ensconced around Butte, Havre, Great Falls, and other Montana cities, they had become fixtures in the urban social landscape.[45] But while many reports suggested a general familiarity and normalness about the Cree presence, whites took action in various communities to evict Crees from cities and even entire counties. Whites threatened that Indian dogs would be killed, ponies stampeded, and possessions confiscated if they would not leave, but these were met by defiant public statements by Rocky Boy.[46] Fergus County officials opened communications with the Department of Immigration in Washington, DC, and then publicized their findings that foreign Natives and Métis could not be naturalized citizens.[47] All such developments underscored the precariousness of Chippewas and Crees in the state.

Progress for Chippewas, Disappointment for Crees

Starting in 1908, the gulf between Cree and Chippewa experiences in Montana widened dramatically. For the following six to seven years, US government efforts to settle landless Indians in Montana focused almost exclusively upon Rocky Boy's Chippewa band, and it was not until the final stages of this process, in 1915–16 that Little Bear's group was joined with it. Therefore, much of the history of these interceding years oscillates between Rocky Boy's interaction with the US government and Little Bear's exclusion from those discussions.

In early 1908, Rocky Boy's developing friendship with US Senator Joseph Dixon bore fruit as Dixon determined to "make 1908 the year of decision," as Dixon biographer Jules Karlin terms it.[48] Dixon was spurred to action by inquiries from a farmer on the Flathead Reservation in late 1907 or early 1908.[49] Dixon responded by adding an amendment to the Indian appropriation bill authorizing the secretary of the interior to spend $30,000 to settle Rocky Boy's band.[50] By the time it passed committee and was put to vote on March 13, 1908, however, Dixon's amendment had been stricken and replaced by a call for further investigation.[51] Outraged,

Dixon violated protocol by speaking out of turn and demanding that his objections be fielded and asking why the funds had been excised from the bill after the secretary of the interior and commissioner of Indian affairs had submitted favorable reports.

> Here is $30,000 for the Wandering band of Chippewa Indians. I personally know their condition. The matter was investigated two or three years ago. I know they are starving and hungry, dying by the score every year. It is merely a matter of humanity to purchase land for these one hundred Indians. . . . I have on my desk a letter from, written within the last ten days, Chief Rocky Boy. . . . The old man thinks this bill has already passed Congress. . . . He said, "But for this, I and my children, some of them, would be dead before snow flies this fall."[52]

Thanks to Dixon's adamant objection, the bill was rejected by the Senate, taken up in the House committee of conference, and finally passed with Dixon's amendment on April 30, 1908.[53] The indispensability of Rocky Boy's personal relationships with Montanan allies was clear.

When Dixon returned to Montana during the summer of 1908, he and Rocky Boy exchanged a series of letters. Their friendship appeared to deepen, as titular salutations evolved from the formal "Dear Sir" to the more intimate "My Dear Friend." Rocky Boy expressed his gratitude and readiness to cooperate with government plans as Dixon explained possible sites for their settlement. The settlement process, however, was slow. "I want you to know how I suffer here for grub. It's hard to make my living. I am getting tired of making my living on the dump. I am like a chicken picking wheat, doesn't matter where I find it," Rocky Boy wrote to Dixon in June.[54] Dixon tried to accelerate the settlement process, but real progress did not begin until US Indian inspector Frank C. Churchill arrived in September to gather demographic data on the group.[55]

Churchill discovered that Rocky Boy's band was spread out, with fifty in Garrison (with Rocky Boy), ten near Billings, five near Havre, and six on the Flathead Reservation. However, he soon realized that Rocky Boy's claims of his band numbering between one hundred and two hundred likely meant that Little Bear's Crees were included in this total. With only $30,000, he determined it necessary to undertake the difficult task of separating the two and using the funds exclusively for Rocky Boy's Chippewas. Extensive intermarriage and bilingualism would make this difficult. As Churchill queried about the genealogies of his bands, Rocky Boy had to navigate delicately. Rocky Boy explained that while Little Bear himself was part Chippewa, the individuals in his current band were "all Chippewa Indians." Rocky Boy understood the Interior Department's unease with Little Bear's close association. When he presented his official census of one hundred Indians in his band, he asserted that there were others who ought to be added to the list. Churchill read this as a direct reference to Little Bear's Crees and pressed Rocky Boy: "Do you claim Little Bear and his people as a part of your band?" Rocky Boy said no, distancing himself from Little Bear's Crees and stating that he could not "take Little Bear's Band at all." Instead, he emphasized, there were US-born Chippewas "all over the world" who he needed to contact, gather, and enumerate.[56] For the time being, Rocky Boy, desperate to settle his people, focused his efforts on his Chippewas alone.

Churchill's initial visit also brought him to the Blackfeet Reservation, where he expressed doubts as to the land's suitability for the band's expressed desire for "plenty of timber [and] good hunting." His final assessment was not encouraging, stating that $30,000 would be "wholly inadequate . . . [to provide] suitable homes for these landless Indians." Finding Fort Belknap and Fort Peck equally problematic, he suggested that they be settled jointly with or near landless Turtle Mountain Chippewas newly arrived in Montana from North Dakota and occupying public lands northeast of Fort Peck. Noting that all necessary work would "come to a standstill during the very cold winter," the immediate relief of Rocky Boy's landless band proved illusive. With the group now clearly defined and comprising 129 individuals, Churchill forwarded final clarifications and recommendations concerning his suggested plan to settle them with the 1,066 Turtle Mountain Chippewas being allotted lands northeast of Fort Peck. The secretary of the interior concurred with Churchill's plans and directed him to move forward with an official census.[57]

Rocky Boy and Little Bear at Year's End

Though matters were not yet settled, 1908 had been momentous for Rocky Boy and his Chippewa band. The impact of Rocky Boy's success must have weighed heavily upon Little Bear, especially as it became clear that his people were not included in the April 30, 1908, appropriation bill. In the midst of Chippewa successes, however, new governor Edwin L. Norris said of the Crees: "They are literally starving, and we will have to send them to the penitentiary or poorhouses unless something is done. They cannot be tolerated to roam the state at will, as at present, and it is natural that they will steal, when forced by hunger, when opportunity offers."[58] Perhaps due to the combination of such statements, the disappointment of not being included in neighboring Chippewa success, and pressure from his Cree constituents, Little Bear reopened communications with Canadian officials early in the summer of 1908.[59] Governor Norris helped facilitate the communication.[60] Canadian officials said their 1905 offer still stood, but by September Canada had yet to receive any Crees at the border. It is unclear whether any chose to cross north at this time.

Little Bear's opposition to the move north infuriated Norris, who stated that "Montana will be absolved of all future responsibility as to the Crees. . . . If they refuse to take advantage of the opportunity offered, they are entitled to no more consideration from the people of Montana."[61] Norris seems to have failed to consider what followed Little Bear's returning to Canada in 1895 under the promise of amnesty. After having been seized and jailed, betrayed in his eyes, Little Bear may still have had suspicions about the move. Though the matter was resolved within a few months, it cannot be passed over as simply an interesting incident in the long Cree history in Montana. When considering this in the context of Rocky Boy's Chippewas and their progress toward settlement, one can imagine the disillusionment Crees felt. The federal government seemed to overlook them, the state government was impatient as ever to be rid of them, and all the while they had established meaningful roots in Montana that would be painful to sever. To stave off starvation during the following winter, they secured employment with the National Forest Service in Deer Lodge and Powell Counties, collecting lodgepole pinecones for nursery planting. The *Helena Independent* quipped sarcastically, "The stores of pine tree squirrels aided the Indians, who robbed them with impunity, and it is likely that many a squirrel family will go hungry this winter."[62] Though providing much-needed funds, the employment was little more than a stopgap.

Conclusion

At the end of 1908, Rocky Boy and Little Bear looked ahead to two divergent futures. Rocky Boy, having secured favor with the US government, looked ahead with warranted optimism that his wandering band of

Chippewas would soon till land of their own and have a stable place to build a community. For the band that for years had existed on the edge of Native and non-Native Montana society, this was momentous. Little Bear and his Crees faced a very different future. In the state for two decades, they seemed no closer to their similar goal of settlement and stability than they had at any time. If anything, Montanans' prejudice against them had worsened in breadth and depth. What Rocky Boy and Little Bear shared was a cadre of important white allies. It is unclear whether or not Little Bear realized it at the time, but his friendship with Frank Linderman and others would lead before long to a shared and positive fate.

Part 4

New Allies, New Efforts, and Final Resolutions

Potential solutions allowing "foreign" Indians to make a secure home in the United States while maintaining indigeneity were many but repeatedly denied to Crees, Chippewas, and Yaquis. The most logical solutions have been to integrate them into the "American" Indian system of tribal-federal relationships, reservations, and so forth. This could have been accomplished by having them join existing reservations or by creating new reservations for them. In the case of Montana, the first was attempted unsuccessfully. In Arizona, placing Yaquis in an existing reservation was never attempted. The ultimate solution for both would be federal tribal recognition and the establishment of new reservations. To attain this, all three groups succeeded in bringing allies from the surrounding white communities to their cause. They demonstrated great skill in politicking and networking. They forged friendships and alliances and kept their new advocates dedicated to their cause despite constant setbacks, disappointment, seeming futility, and resistance. This is not a story of white saviors but of Native success in enlisting privileged people to their cause.

As Cree, Chippewa, and Yaqui leaders and their allies began to engage more fully with local, state, and federal officials concerning their peoples' needs and desires, they met opposition at every turn. In this, Crees, Chippewas, and Yaquis shared common experiences. The most poignant examples come from the points in their histories when local outcry defeated otherwise successful arrangements for legal settlement. The 1908 appropriation to settle Rocky Boy's Chippewas was met with staunch opposition in all the places where attempts were made to purchase lands for them—on both the Blackfeet Reservation and in Valley County. Later, when US officials revealed plans to settle Chippewas and Crees at the Fort

Assiniboine Military Reserve, Hill County residents and boosters likewise cried foul, petitioning congressional representatives and vowing to derail the plans. When the Pascua Yaqui Association settled on the southwest edge of Tucson in 1963, surrounding landowners and real estate developers acted similarly. Expansions of the later Pascua Yaqui Reservation and Yaqui-owned lands in Guadalupe met stiff local opposition. This pattern of local opposition was nearly universal.

With their allies, Crees, Chippewas, and Yaquis pursued different tactics in arguing their cases. Crees and Chippewas sought recognition and settlement to finally establish a stable culture and community. In Arizona, Yaquis sought legal settlement in order to *preserve* their culture and community. Whereas the economic realities of the labor markets in Montana had denied Crees and Chippewas a space to grow their community, Yaqui's initial successful economic integration in Arizona had allowed them to establish community. By the mid-twentieth century, however, the booming mining, railroad, and irrigation markets that had aided Yaqui success were shifting, and the settler-colonial project of building Arizona had left many of their economic contributions in the past. This created crises of poverty that threatened to destroy the communities they had succeeded in building.

In this phase, the chronological difference between the Montanan and Arizonan stories is striking. All three groups crossed into the United States in roughly the same late-nineteenth-century time period. However, the Montanan Crees and Chippewas were recognized in 1916 and the Arizonan Yaquis not until 1978. These final chapters will examine the reasons behind this discrepancy.

By 1916 for Chippewas and Crees, and by 1978 for Yaquis, the groups had entered a new phase in their US experience. Though never shunning their transnational roots and still inhabiting the borderlands, they were for the first time, indisputably "American" Indians. This implied new relationships with local, state, and federal governments, new access to Indian programs, and new restrictions as well. For the joined Chippewas and Crees, this meant involvement in the Indian Reorganization Act, or Indian New Deal, during the Great Depression—accepting the act and being thus organized in 1935. This is a process Yaquis were not involved in, although some took part in other non-Indian New Deal programs. Entrance into these new relationships, the leaving behind of negative transnational legacies as "foreign" Indians, and full participation in their adopted homeland were events to be celebrated. For both, it was the fulfillment of years of struggle. However, it did not indicate the end of problems for either of the newly created tribes. Full studies could be (and have been) made of the post-recognition histories of these groups, and they are fraught with difficulties of poverty, loss of language, forced assimilation, and efforts to renew and rebuild Native cultures—problems that most Native American tribes share. Entrance into the US-Indian relationship, while providing valuable benefits for their struggling communities, brought with it new problems that subsequent generations would face and surmount. In years since recognition, both groups have used their traditions and strengths, forged in the fires of transnational and refugee pasts, to meet new challenges—always adapting, always dynamic.

Chapter 9

Cree and Chippewa Legislative Battles and Victories, 1908–1916

Nothing was done about this [Cree and Chippewa] state of affairs for a long time, although the Indians were considered a nuisance. Not that they broke laws—stole and the like, for I never heard of any such charges being brought against them, but people were tired of seeing this poverty at their door, and justly felt that some provision should be made for these exiles.

—MARGARET PLASSMANN[1]

If 1908 had encouraged Rocky Boy in his quest for legal settlement, 1909 started with even greater promise of success and resolution. By year's end his band would officially be allotted lands of its own, but the interceding months were turbulent, and the allotment would not lead immediately to permanent settlements. Throughout, the years from 1908 to 1916 revealed deep-seated resistance among some neighboring Montanans and required persistence and patience from Rocky Boy's Chippewas, Little Bear's Crees, and their white Montanan allies. The eventual 1916 recognition of the Chippewa Cree Tribe of Rocky Boy's Reservation was by no means a guaranteed eventuality. The process was slow and unsteady. While local and federal response was capricious and uncertain to the end, Cree and Chippewa persistence continued until they gained recognition in 1916.

Rocky Boy Allotment

The initial promise of 1908 was fueled in part by community fund-raising on behalf of Rocky Boy's Chippewas. After Rocky Boy went to Helena to petition a local judge for aid, the *Great Falls Tribune* took up his cause.[2] Backed by influential artist and cultural figure Charles (Charlie) Russell in Great Falls, he proclaimed, "It doesn't look very good for the people of Montana if they will sit and see a lot of women and children starve to death in this kind of weather."[3] In Helena, Judge William Hunt was quick to act, organizing food and clothing drives in the city. Within days, two delegations from the Montana State Bureau of Child and Animal Protection and the Helena Commercial Club braved a raging blizzard to deliver supplies collected in the community. "With tears streaming down his cheeks while resting in the snow on his knees, and with his hands lifted in supplication," the *Helena Daily Independent* reported, "Chief Rocky Boy of the Chippewas . . . offered thanks to the people of Helena who had donated clothing, food and blankets saying that God would bless them." Contacted by officials in Helena, Fred Morgan, superintendent of the Flathead Indian School in Jocko, Montana, opened communication with the Department of the Interior concerning his investigation into the destitution of Rocky Boy's band.[4]

As winter gave way to spring, the bureaucratic work of allotting lands for Rocky Boy's band began, but the momentum soon halted. After allotting agent Thralls W. Wheat conducted a rigorous and detailed census of Rocky Boy's people, being careful to exclude "Canadian Crees," sixty townships northeast of the Fort Peck Indian Reservation, in Valley County, were designated for Rocky Boy's band on June 30, 1909. With pressure from the Blackfeet Reservation, where Rocky Boy was then encamped, the commissioner of Indian affairs publicly announced the Valley County plan and forwarded detailed instructions for allotting agents to commence surveys and allotment.[5] But the backlash from nearby white communities was immediate and fierce.

Concerned citizens of Culbertson, Montana, wrote to their congressman, Thomas H. Carter, complaining of the "great injustice" being exacted upon them with neighboring public lands being set aside for Rocky Boy. Citizens of Scobey and Bainville, Montana, opposed the plan as well, claiming the Chippewas were the "lowest type . . . improvident, lazy, thriftless, and diseased, and wholly unfit to mingle with white people."[6] In response to letters he received, Congressman Charles N. Pray forwarded concerns to the Department of the Interior, saying that "Rocky Boy and his Indians will not meet with a very cordial reception by settlers."[7] Others complained of recently settled Turtle Mountain Chippewas, suspected that Rocky Boy's band were actually Crees, and worried that their presence would stymie white settlement and development of the region. While making no immediate moves against the allotment plans, government officials did their best to mollify unhappy citizens.[8]

Previously local white outcry had bent federal policy, but in mid-October 1908 special allotting agent John F. Armstrong was instructed to move forward in gathering Rocky Boy's people at Birdseye, Montana.[9] In the meantime, Montanan constituents continued to ventilate ire to Senator Carter, who wrote to Commissioner of Indian Affairs Robert G. Valentine and suggested that Rocky Boy's band be settled somewhere near the Blackfeet Reservation. Standing resolute for the moment, Valentine explained that lengthy investigations had deemed that region untenable for their settlement.[10] Simultaneously, however, the tides were turning. Fifty prominent Montanans and Louis W. Hill, president of the Great Northern Railroad—who had earlier demonstrated disregard for Rocky Boy's plight and made Rocky Boy's Chippewas the punch line of jokes—wrote a letter of protest to Moses E. Clapp, the chairman of the Senate Committee of Indian Affairs suggesting that the band be settled in some remote mountainous region rather than waste quality agricultural lands that could otherwise go to white homesteaders.[11] Valentine's office caved to the political pressure and requested the opinion of Fort Belknap Indian agent William R. Logan, who pointed to the mountain outlets of the Cut Bank, Milk River, and Two Medicine Creeks and the forest reserves on the Blackfeet Reservation.[12] Commissioner Valentine agreed and announced that the Indian Office would settle Rocky Boy's band on the Blackfeet Reservation for the winter—and in perpetuity.[13] Hill claimed victory, while Clapp lamented the "grievous error."[14] Rocky Boy's apparent triumph in gaining lands set aside for his band was short-lived.

The *Great Falls Tribune* expressed outrage at the unfair treatment of Rocky Boy's people, quickly earning it the nickname "Rocky Boy Defender."[15] "These Indians have suffered long and cruel injustice at the hand of Uncle Sam," the *Tribune* editorialized on November 3, 1909. "Reading the distinguished names appended to the petition on which Secretary Richard Ballinger acted," they explained, "we find men of large capital, large political power, of weight in the community in which they live," whose statements were "calculated to deceive and mislead the public on the whole."[16] The next issue, the newspaper continued its advocacy:

> Isn't it about time that Uncle Sam quit playing horse with these Chippewa Indians under Rocky Boy and redeem its pledge at par? . . . It

> took a dozen years of urgent pleading to get lands set aside for the Indians. In a dozen years Uncle Sam could not find time to make good his promises to the Indians. In seven days and on false representations concerning their status, Uncle Sam finds time to undo all that he had accomplished towards providing them with a home. . . . The Tribune appeals to the manhood and justice that lies in the surface always of Montana to come to the rescue of these Indians and see that they do get what is justly due them.[17]

John Armstrong offered his support to the *Tribune*, thanking them for exhibiting "the true elements of good citizenship to tell the whole truth about an unpopular subject."[18]

Settlement on the Blackfeet Reservation was consolation to some concerned parties, as the Chippewas would not be left utterly homeless in the winter months.[19] Some Chippewas would later hold that Blackfeet elders had been secretly lobbying for the Chippewas to be allotted surplus lands there for well over a year, rather than having that land go to white homesteaders.[20] Later tribal leaders recalled that Rocky Boy's people were content in their new home and initially got along well with their Blackfeet neighbors and found logging work nearby. For their part, the citizens of Valley County who had opposed the Rocky Boy plan were elated. The removal of lands from the public domain for Indians had been an affront to the white homesteading ethos, and their restoration was viewed as a matter of moral justice. A turbulent year, 1909 had ended on a tenuously positive note, with the permanent settlement of Rocky Boy's Chippewas all but complete.

After the spring thaws of 1910, the new special allotting agent, Charles Roblin, began the allotment process but expressed concern over which Indians were to be considered part of Rocky Boy's band. He cited discrepancies between previous censuses by Thralls Wheat and John Armstrong and the actual Natives present in Rocky Boy's camp—not a new quandary for US officials. By July, 101 individuals, about one-third of the band, including Rocky Boy, had selected allotments and expressed plans to build homes and occupy the lands as soon as they were able.[21] However, logistical problems followed in issuing of rations and supplies, and by December 1910, about 150 Chippewas under the leadership of Rocky Boy's brother Pennato, renounced their Blackfeet allotments, claiming that the people of Helena were more generous to them than the government.[22] Throughout the following year, various government agents struggled to locate and enumerate Rocky Boy's band, who circulated on and off the Blackfeet Reservation and allotments. The agents voiced concern about the band's ability to adapt to agriculture and complained of insufficient funds to supply them.[23] In essence, Rocky Boy's Chippewas had land, but it was not as much as promised, and they had insufficient means to subsist upon it.[24] Many wandered, and Montanan observers fretted over the failed resolution.[25]

While Rocky Boy's band spent time on (and off) the Blackfeet Reservation, Little Bear's Crees lodged with them on occasion (although they were banned from allotment), frequented familiar camp sites in northern Montana, and worked for allotted Indians on the Flathead and Crow Reservations.[26] After Little Bear told officials in Helena, "I need a reservation," Chippewa Cree Tribe member Malcolm Mitchell would later recall, they suggested he go to the Hobema Reserve in Canada, saying, "You'll never get . . . land here because you belong there." Mitchell would remember: "Little Bear hit the table with his fist, attempting to drive home the point he wanted a reservation and that was the single topic he was interested in pursuing."[27]

As he had in 1897, 1906, and 1908, Little Bear again explored the possibility of joining existent Cree reserves in Canada. In early 1911, he wrote to relations on the Onion Lake Reserve to see if his people could join it. As they had in 1908, the Office of Indian Affairs in Ottawa intimated that the initial 1905–6 offer was still valid. By July no move had been made, but letters suggest that Little Bear had expressed that his band would indeed come north across the line again. The Onion Lake Agency informed Little Bear that his people would be required to return to the bands to which they belonged, most of which were determined to be within the Onion Lake and Battleford Agencies.[28] However, as before, Little Bear suddenly ceased writing. Though he opted to remain in Montana in all three cases, a persistent desire to keep the Canadian settlement option alive is apparent. Successful settlement for his people in Montana was the preferred outcome.

Unsettled Matters for Settled Indians

During the winter of 1911–12, Pennato contacted Frank Linderman to aid in the Chippewa's cause.[29] A prominent Montanan and former state legislator, Linderman was an insurance man by 1911. To Crees, Chippewas, and other Natives in the state, he was a trusted ally. In 1885, when Linderman was a sixteen-year-old pioneer newly arrived from Ohio, he had befriended Cree refugees during their flight from the North-West Rebellion, and he had maintained ties with them throughout the years.[30] Little Bear once told him, "[Y]ou are the only white man I have ever known who does not lie."[31] Pennato mentioned to Linderman the possibility of settling on Fort Assiniboine Military Reserve, which was decommissioned in 1911.[32] Various interested parties were already debating what should be done with the land there.[33] It was a region with which Chippewas and Crees were familiar, and the prospect of settling in the Bear Paw Mountains held great appeal. For the time being, however, Linderman suggested that they return to the Blackfeet Reservation to be present when a delegation from Washington, DC, already en route, arrived to inspect the reportedly bad conditions.[34]

Pennato listened politely and then stated, "I will go wherever these soldiers take me, if you tell me that you wish me to go. But if I go to Browning [on Blackfeet Reservation] I shall die there within ten days." Linderman assured him that his band would be well treated. Many of Pennato's band left on trains, and Pennato himself rode to Browning on horseback. "This was the last time that I saw Full-of-Dew [Pennato]," Linderman recalled. "He died, as he had predicted, within ten days after reaching his destination." Before his death on May 15, 1912, Pennato directed his brother Rocky Boy to seek Linderman's aid. For Linderman, he left a dying wish that he "take [his] brother Rocky Boy into his heart, as he had [taken him]."[35] Though Pennato did not live to see his dream of Chippewa settlement in the Bear Paw Mountains, the seed of an idea had been planted. Feeling the weight of his dear friend's death, Linderman set forth to bring his dream to fruition.[36] Rocky Boy wrote to him on May 17 of Pennato's death, explained that he knew of Linderman's sincere desire to help, and pleaded, "I want you to work hard for me to try and get that land over at Fort Assiniboine."[37]

Conditions were grim during the months at Browning.[38] "An experienced farmer would not be able to make a living on the land allotted them," explained Arthur McFatridge to Commissioner Valentine. "The land . . . is practically worthless for farming purposes."[39] As he assessed the Chippewa plight, McFatridge also met with Little Bear. Little Bear requested that he and his fifteen lodges be allotted land with Rocky Boy, but McFatridge rebuffed him and said that no Canadian Indians could be given land. Instead McFatridge urged Little Bear to consult with Rocky

Boy about the sharing of rations.[40] Sensing the futility of the current situation, McFatridge and Flathead Reservation superintendent Fred Morgan separately concluded that it would be best if *all* landless Indians in the state, Chippewas and "Canadian" Crees, be gathered and settled on a single site of their own, apart from the Blackfeet Reservation.[41]

Frank Linderman wrote in February to colleague and friend George Bird Grinnell, then editor of *Forest and Stream* magazine, who agreed to raise the issue of Chippewa and Cree settlement with Commissioner Valentine later that month.[42] Whether a direct result of Grinnell's meeting with Valentine or not, in April the Office of Indian Affairs instructed Blackfeet Reservation officials to begin a new search for a contiguous tract of suitable lands for an "aggregate number between 400 and 500" non-reservation Indians. Rocky Boy's band had never boasted such high numbers, so the estimate implies that other landless Indians would be included. As the process moved forward, however, restrictions were put in place to define the members of Rocky Boy's band. In spite of local agents' suggestions that Crees, even those from Canada, be included in settlement, new instructions explicitly barred "full blood Cree Indians" from participation.[43] Fred A. Baker, an Indian schools supervisor from the Department of Indian Affairs, attempted to temper these restrictions, admitting that many were flocking "to the standard of Rocky Boy hearing the news that the question had been taken up anew by the Department." Baker wrote to Valentine that enrollment fraud could occur, but he did not single out "Canadian Crees." Rather he proposed an arduous and expensive interview process at the front end of the enrollment process that would save the government a considerable amount in the end.[44]

During these discussions, Pennato and Linderman's idea of a reservation at the Fort Assiniboine Military Reserve took root. Baker was part of the visiting government delegation at the Blackfeet Reservation for which Pennato had returned after meeting with Linderman. Baker reported that a large number of Rocky Boy's Chippewas were present, and Pennato, before dying, may have proposed the Fort Assiniboine site to him. Baker subsequently toured the state and made an enthusiastic recommendation of the newly available Fort Assiniboine. He offered four reasons, with extensive detailed support:

> First, the United States had "unquestioned title" to the Fort Assiniboine lands;

> Second, the tract provided fertile soil, timber, waterways, hunting and fishing—all essential to proper "Indian Country;"
>
> Third, two railroads already ran near the reservation;
>
> Fourth, buildings (although recently looted in some cases) were already available for agency headquarters.

He concluded, "Altogether a better place could not be found in the state of Montana. The only question which would arise is that the location is too good, instead of being too poor, or unsuited." Therefore Baker anticipated opposition from local non-Natives. Squatters and real estate speculators were already attempting to "gobble up" the lands, but they remained largely free for possible settlement.[45] Finally, Baker insisted that Fort Assiniboine was the final and only option to solve the "spectacle of having starving Indians living in wretchedness and unspeakable squalor."[46]

Baker reported to Valentine that the enrollment process was problematic, citing the great difficulty in distinguishing Crees from Chippewas since they both came from Algonquian stock, had intermarried, and had significant overlap in cultural traditions and history. With Rocky Boy and other elders serving on the "Identification Committee," Baker found that they were "inclined to be exceedingly liberal." Baker's preliminary roll excluded 145 persons. Final enrollment would take time, he reported, but the selection of lands should proceed with utmost speed.[47] This left Rocky Boy's band, both those with unusable Blackfeet Reservation allotments and those yet landless, without resolution and with winter approaching. Again resigned to seek shelter and aid on the outskirts of Billings, Helena, Butte, Great Falls, Havre, and other cities, their only respite was the knowledge that new efforts were being made and that allies such as Linderman continued to advocate for their cause and well-being in the state. Newly acquainted with their plight, Baker wrote to Linderman, imploring, "Use your influence and that of your friends," urging that a law be passed to settle the landless Chippewas and Crees.[48]

New Montana Allies and the Fight for Fort Assiniboine

Frank Linderman and, to an extent, his colleague and *Great Falls Tribune* editor, William Bole, dominate the subsequent history of political lobbying and struggle to secure the Fort Assiniboine lands for Rocky Boy's and Little Bear's people. Local Montanans lobbying for deportation and against various settlement plans had won previous battles. As Joseph Dixon's influence had before, the support of Linderman and Bole proved instrumental in combating resistant locals and forging federal policy for non-reservation Chippewas and foreign refugee Crees. Linderman's efforts exemplify the interplay between local and federal powers.

In late December 1912, Secretary of the Interior Walter L. Fisher wrote to Robert J. Gamble, chairman of the Senate Committee on Indian Affairs, forwarding the draft of a bill "designed to create a reservation for Rocky Boy's band of Chippewa Indians out of a part of the lands formerly embraced within the abandoned Fort Assiniboine Military Reservation, Montana." As had been the case with the 1909 proposal to settle Rocky Boy's band in Valley County, response to the Fort Assiniboine settlement plan was swift. In support, prominent Great Falls politician and former state senator Paris Gibson immediately wrote to Linderman, congratulating him and stating his plan to shield Senator Dixon and take "the sting out of the opposition" that would surely arise.[49] He was wise to do so, as the opposition came crashing in, with predictable diatribes against Rocky Boy's band as lazy, foreign, and generally undesirable neighbors.[50] State Senator D. S. MacKenzie opposed the plan—the "attempt to perpetuate such an outrage upon the people of this section"—and he soon presented a resolution to the Montana senate against the proposed settlement. When he introduced a bill in February to Montana's thirteenth Legislative Assembly to establish an industrial college on the Fort Assiniboine lands, Linderman rose to full stature as an advocate for landless Natives in the state. Linderman argued vehemently in support of the Fort Assiniboine settlement plan. Senator MacKenzie retorted that Linderman was deluded by "a too faithful reading of Leatherstocking Tales" and was fighting to have Rocky Boy "enthrone[ed]" at Fort Assiniboine with his "tribe of human scavengers."[51]

As politicking continued over the controversial Fort Assiniboine plan, Rocky Boy's and Little Bear's bands spread across the state, camping at Forts Harrison and Belknap, the Blackfeet and Crow Reservations, around Butte, Helena, Great Falls, and Havre, and in the Fort Assiniboine region. Some Crees, like Grant Chief Stick, were provided rations and tents at Fort Assiniboine, but food was scarce and temporary accommodations were "very cold." They even faced threats of eviction on various occasions.[52] US officials struggled to control the movements of the bands as they traveled to seek employment, resources, or better conditions. Valentine's successor, Commissioner of Indian Affairs Cato Sells, took action against supposed Chippewa allottees from the Blackfeet Reservation found at Fort Harrison, only to find that they were Crees from Little Bear's band. Sells attempted to find them employment on the Flathead Reservation, but the Crees instead left for Great Falls, to his consternation.[53]

Concurrently federal officials struggled to prevent Chippewas and Crees from returning to Fort Assiniboine in anticipation of the approaching winter.[54] Bole and Linderman requested permission for them to camp at the southern end of Fort Assiniboine, but this was denied by new secretary of the interior Franklin K. Lane.[55] Commissioner Sells told Bole not to encourage the Indians to move to Fort Assiniboine with the "expectancy of remaining there permanently" and, if they did go there, to not erect permanent structures. Some of Rocky Boy's band did proceed to make makeshift camps there throughout the fall. Sells confided to Secretary Lane that a solution was sorely needed and that they would suffer "considerable embarrassment until it [was] definitely settled in some permanent manner."[56] Also vying for the attention of federal officials, various individuals and groups continued to send letters, petitions, and delegations in opposition to the Fort Assiniboine plan.[57]

As protests continued, Secretary Lane and Commissioner Sells relied heavily upon the positive reports received from Linderman, Bole, and others. Through his passion and persistence, and no doubt his knowledge and eloquence, Linderman turned Sells from a skeptical bureaucrat to a strong advocate. After a visit to Montana, Sells wrote Linderman:

> I am delighted with them and their work. . . . They have been too often misrepresented and you men have told me the truth concerning them. I shall not abandon them but shall keep them in mind and if they continue to show themselves so worthy, I intend to further help them. . . . I know that these Indians are all right and I am their friend as you have been. Write to me and help me with your advice to the Indians for they believe in you and remember I shall always be glad to listen to what you have to say.[58]

Encouraged by Linderman, Lane and Sells strove to alleviate Chippewa and Cree suffering during the winter months and provide temporary shelter and provisions on the Blackfeet Reservation—but most opted to winter in Great Falls and Havre. Writing to Secretary Lane, Little Bear explained their plight, their refusal to return to another hard winter in Browning, and their determination to remain in Great Falls until spring. When plans were devised to forcibly remove the band from Great Falls, supporters such as Paris Gibson and Charlie Russell voiced their concern, "respectfully suggest[ing]" that Chippewas and Crees be allowed to remain "in their present comfortable camp." With their urging and financial support, Little Bear and Rocky Boy's bands were permitted to remain in Great Falls and Havre respectively, and rations were shipped to them at the encampments until spring.[59]

As always, the winter months were the most difficult for Rocky Boy's and Little Bear's people. The stress of their tenuous subsistence even caused division between the two groups. Perhaps frustrated by the government's repeated unwillingness to consider aiding his "foreign" Crees while expending considerable energies to settle the supposedly more American Chippewas, Little Bear lashed out in December 1913. Speaking publicly in Lewistown through his cousin Peter Kenawash as interpreter, Little Bear presented a case for his people that stressed their amenability to peaceful settlement—and Rocky Boy's continual troublemaking. "Rocky Boy is not a real chief," he declared.[60] This episode highlights Little Bear's understandable frustration and the fact that he and Rocky Boy's causes and people were not yet joined.

During the spring and summer of 1914, all parties renewed efforts to resolve the problem. Much to the dismay of Linderman and others, rations were cut off to those camped at Great Falls and Havre, with the explanation that the Indians should be able to support themselves during the spring and summer. "This causes me some embarrassment," Bole wrote to Commissioner Sells, since he and Linderman had conveyed to Rocky Boy and Little Bear the government's assurance that the two bands would be supported until lands were readied. They were now in an awkward position as federal officials reneged on their promise. "Fully 75% of the people in this camp are old men, women and children who cannot work even if given the opportunity," Linderman explained. Support was essential, but Lane feared that the people would become dependent.[61] Bole and Linderman urgently tried to redirect attention to the Fort Assiniboine plan, but this was to no avail. As the Indian Office hesitated, they soon realized that little could be done until the congressional sessions in December. Readying themselves for the renewed battle, they devised plans to sidestep Commissioner Sells, whose recent conduct they had found "disgusting," secure support in Congress, and focus efforts on Secretary Lane and President Woodrow Wilson.[62]

Linderman and Bole concurrently instructed Chippewas and Crees to prepare fall and winter camps at the south end of the Fort Assiniboine Reserve, despite lacking authority to do so. In October, Bole informed the Indian Office of what they had done and succeeded in convincing them to direct rations there instead of to Browning. Many Chippewas and Crees eagerly did encamp at Fort Assiniboine. Though based on tenuous legal grounds and with restrictions on activities there, the encampment of Little Bear's Crees and Rocky Boy's Chippewas at Fort Assiniboine was "good news," as Little Bear termed it.[63] News also circulated that Rocky Boy would preside over the joint group, with Little Bear to succeed him upon his death. While the tribe would eventually take Rocky Boy's name, not Little Bear's, it is unclear if this leadership arrangement ever materialized.[64]

The Final Push for Fort Assiniboine

As approval of the Fort Assiniboine settlement plan was pending in Congress, President Wilson placed a moratorium on the distribution or sale of Fort Assiniboine lands. The hold was to expire in March 1915, and by February 1915 both the House and Senate had approved white settlement of the former military reserve, without a clause granting lands for Rocky Boy's band. With Chippewas and Crees already camped there, their exclusion from the bill would have been the worst in a long succession of disappointments. Fortunately Linderman and Bole's lobbying of Secretary Lane bore fruit at this critical juncture. With the threat of a presidential veto on his side, Lane succeeded in having an additional bill submitted by Montana's US senator Henry Myers setting aside two townships for Rocky Boy's band.[65] This victory was significant but not conclusive. In the following months, Linderman and Bole divided their efforts between ensuring passage of Myers's bill and helping to care for the immediate needs of the indigent bands.

From the view of Chippewa and Cree leaders like Rocky Boy and Little Bear, the move to the Bear Paw Mountains fostered hope but was deceiving. It offered the prospect of a permanent home but was not supported by statutory authorization. The struggle to procure food, supplies, agricultural implements, and seed continued, and the attendant stresses caused tension and division between Rocky Boy's and Little Bear's constituents.[66] The transfer of stewardship over them from the Blackfeet Agency to the Fort Belknap Agency compounded these problems. Moreover, they were vexed by continued denial of their requests to cut timber to build shelter.[67] Their very presence on the land may have hinted at permanence, but their tents and inconsistent supply of meager rations belied this. Seeing the most desirable and arable tracts of land being surveyed for white settlement, Little Bear wrote to Sells:

> I and my people are anxious to have a home; to settle down and become self-supporting. Other tribes have their own land and a home. We are homeless wanderers. You have kindly given us permission to use a part of the Ft. Assiniboine Reservation to experiment in farming. It is like a child learning to take his first steps, and of course our attempts may be rather of a failure the first season. However, we are anxious to learn to farm and be given land that can be farmed, and which will be our own, we will soon be self-supporting.[68]

Their desired settlement was so close, but it appeared to be slipping away before their eyes.[69]

At the opening of the Sixty-Fourth Congress in December 1915, Secretary of the Interior Lane brought the concerns of Rocky Boy and Little Bear to John M. Stephens, chairman of the House Committee on Indian Affairs. Commissioner Sells had just received correspondence from Rocky Boy himself in which Rocky Boy pleaded for two additional townships just north of the two already surveyed for their settlement, due to the lack of arable lands on those two. Secretary Lane concluded that the additional two townships were essential, and Stephens's HR 6416, introduced on February 11, 1915, included Lane's recommendations.[70] Likely bowing to white constituent opposition, Senator Myers, and, in the House, Montana congressman Tom Stout introduced alternative bills, S 3646 and HR 9930—both granting less lands for the Chippewas and Crees.[71]

Linderman pressed Myers and undertook a campaign to lobby him, pushing for expanded lands as a "last whirl at this game" and even making veiled threats that he would use the might of his pen to attract national attention.[72] He rejected Myers's opinion that the Chippewas and Crees were "vagabonds and wanderers," pariahs, parasites on local and federal annuities, and properly wards of Canada, instead championing their virtue. Writing to Myers, he asserted their largely US-born pedigrees, and stated that out of all the Native peoples he knew, which were numerous—including Flatheads, Blackfeet, Kootenais, Crows—the Chippewas and Crees were "about the best of the lot." At this, Myers seems to have softened, writing back, "I regard very highly the noble emotions of humanity which you manifest. . . . I may have been largely misinformed about them. . . . Your correspondence has somewhat changed my opinion of these Indians and my ideas of what should be done for them." To underscore his new view, Myers vowed to add another township to his bill for Rocky Boy's band.[73] From this point forward, Rocky Boy could count Myers as a prospective ally, if not a certain one.

The question of the quantity of lands stood paramount among Linderman's concerns. He had replied positively to Myers's possible offer of another township, but he stressed to Commissioner Sells that they direly needed a fourth. Linderman again proposed that Rocky Boy's band could better make use of adjoining lands that had been set aside as a campground for local Havre residents, seeing these as fertile agriculture lands.[74] As members of Congress opposed adding land, Sells requested that Linderman come to Washington himself at once. Linderman was confident that they had secured three townships, and he conveyed his hopes to Rocky Boy and Little Bear in mid-March 2016. His optimism was well-founded, and Myers's final bill, SR 347, submitted on April 13, 1916, granted nearly four full townships to Rocky Boy's band.[75]

Passed in Senate on April 28, it came up for debate in the House in late July. The United States did "not owe these Indians anything," it was argued, and verbiage was added to make possible the later elimination of the reservation. Myers voiced immediate objection, and the bill was thus sent into conference. The amended bill was signed by the House on September 6 and by the Senate on September 7. President Wilson signed S 3646—providing for the opening of the Fort Assiniboine Reservation—into law on September 8, 1916.[76] After three decades Rocky Boy's Chippewas and Little Bear's Crees had a home in Montana.

The Creation of the Rocky Boy's Reservation and the Cost of Delay

As the congressional debate and approval process stretched through 1916, Chippewas and Crees camped on the southern edge of the Fort Assiniboine Military Reservation had continued to suffer, and Chief Rocky Boy had died on April 18.[77] He had not lived to see the signing of the documents creating the reservation that would eventually bear his name. According to Theodore Gibson, Paris Gibson's son:

> These are his last words on last breath. Never forget what I have tried to do for the homeless people in Montana, toward the government and . . . never forget Mr. William Bole and Theodore Gibson and his father [Paris Gibson] and Frank Linderman who [have] done and taken pains to get us a home from our government. And tell all his people to strive and labor hard so that the government may see that we are ambitious to get a home and land and also he told his people to be kind to one another and help one another.[78]

Rocky Boy left a mighty legacy. Linderman recalled that he was a kind soul, "without the least visible animosity towards the white race."[79] His people remembered him as a stalwart leader with a singular vision for their permanent settlement. The last ten to twenty years of his life had been dedicated to finding a home for his people. At this he succeeded.

For the Chippewas and Crees rejoicing over their new home, life was not without difficulty. The long years of wandering about Montana had fractured families. Though many gathered at Fort Assiniboine, kin remained scattered across the state.[80] Government distribution of rations and supplies was inconsistent, and in the winter months following the reservation's creation, many lived solely off what small game they could kill, mostly rabbits.[81] The task of building homes, roads, boundary fences, and other infrastructure was undertaken initially without pay and with what meager supplies they could muster.

Furthermore, the question of enrollment loomed menacingly. Officials had loosened some restrictions, including Little Bear's Crees on the reservation, but those with clear Canadian heritage stood on precarious ground.[82] In time, they would settle into their new home, but the process of establishing new relationships with the federal government as a recognized tribe entailed fits and starts. Over the decades they had established traditions that Indian Office agents would deem incompatible with settled reservation life, including nomadism, visits to relatives in Canada, hosting of visitors from Canada, and frequenting of Montana's cities. In the years following the recognition and reservation allotment, the struggles of securing food and clothing (especially in winter), establishing successful agriculture, and aiding or enrolling related non-reservation Crees, Chippewas, and Métis, made for many battles, and Native leaders continued to seek support from trusted allies.[83] Moreover, now integrated into the US Indian system, they now joined other Indian nations in the various struggles, movements, and victories associated with broader "American Indian" experiences. Although they had long been somewhat native to the place, the Montana Crees' and Chippewas' new legal status had real impact, providing foundations for stability and opening new paths for future prosperity.

Conclusion

A Chippewa ancestor had foretold that the Bear Paws would be a "rich place" where their people would live well. Now the Chippewas (along with Crees) were finally afforded a chance to fulfill that prophesy.[84] Crees and Chippewas had never been devoid of their own agency in crafting plans for their people. But they had lacked the tools or been denied the opportunity to navigate successfully the geopolitical landscape of federal policy entailing American Indians.[85] Not fully accepted as immigrants, denied naturalization and citizenship, inconsistently classified as "Indian" and "foreign Indian," Chippewas and Crees persisted on the periphery of a society, culture, and political system that denied them full participation. Now, with secure lands of their own, a homeland for their children, they might determine their own destiny and forge prosperity. Troubles would certainly arise, but they were wanderers no more. Little Bear's Crees and Rocky Boy's Chippewas were no longer landless. In some ways they had always been at home in Montana. Now, with legal status enacted, they were officially home.[86]

Chapter 10

Yaqui Struggle for Land and Federal Tribal Recognition, 1962–1980

As we are poor, it is our desire to live as a community in order to help each other in time of need. I realize that the United States Government has more important matters to consider in these trying times. However, with the Grace of God, I hope my people will be given some consideration in this matter. I am sure that the new community will be an asset to the city of Tucson, and am hoping that my people will be of value to the United States of America.

—ANSELMO VALENCIA to Congressman Morris K. Udall, December 21, 1962

Yaqui Indians never fought the United States, this country has never had to make a peace treaty with the Yaquis and—as a result—the Yaquis never have been eligible for federal aid under the Bureau of Indian Affairs.

—MARY JANE MARTINEZ in speech to Tucson Sunshine Kiwanis Club, June 1967[1]

Throughout the early to mid-twentieth century, Mexican-born and US-born Yaqui individuals, families, and communities strove to establish a stable existence in Arizona. They succeeded to varying degrees and through diverse means, consolidating unique settlements and forging a steady labor presence and cultural identity. Even after a generation had passed, however, and a greater percentage of Yaquis were US-born, most Americans viewed them as "Mexican" Indians, public rhetoric shows, and the US government did not recognize them as an American Indian tribe. As the Arizona Yaqui population became mostly US-born, more Yaquis desired to participate fully in state and US politics, and beginning in the 1960s they began to emerge as public "Indians." Nevertheless, they were still distinctly and proudly Yaquis.

Efforts to both define and strengthen Yaqui relationships with the US government marked this era. Whereas previous US-Yaqui dealings were almost entirely transnational in context, Yaquis now positioned themselves as American. Their physical presence north of the line was increasingly accepted, but their status in the United States as Natives remained undetermined. Three broad phases frame the evolution of Arizona Yaquis' public and national presence: first, the early-1960s creation of the Pascua Yaqui Association and securing of legal title to new lands for Yaqui settlement; second, a period of efforts to secure federal and private funding for Yaqui community development; and third, a time of struggle for federal tribal recognition and establishment of reservation lands in the mid-1970s. These efforts led to two congressional acts, one conveying public lands for Yaqui settlement (1964) and the other proclaiming federal recognition of the tribe (1978).

Predominantly based in and around Pascua and greater Tucson, these three phases feature Yaqui collaboration with influential white allies in a continual effort to move their people out of their legal limbo. Once termed Mexican Indians, Arizona Yaquis now sought to secure their rights as American Indians while retaining their identity. Their tenacious determination to remain uniquely Yaqui was based in a long history of contentious relationships with Spain and Mexico, if not the United States. Previous nineteenth-century Yaqui political organization, be it led by Juan Banderas, Cajeme, or Tetabiate, often had been highly structured and hierarchical in nature.[2] These Sonoran examples, however, did not apply directly to their Arizona refugee decedents. Displaced from their homelands and fearing possible deportation, Yaquis did not participate widely in politics. Public religious celebrations abounded, but political activism and organization did not. A few key exceptions deserve mention as relevant precursors to their 1960s and 1970s counterparts.

Some of the earliest Yaqui political activity in Arizona can be seen starting in 1912 in Guadalupe when Yaquis began negotiations with white allies to secure legal title to lands for their settlement and then 1918 in Tucson when Juan Pistola began his dealings as the first Yaqui "chief" recognized by the broader community.[3] Although self-appointed and controversial to some, he was later often remembered as one who dedicated himself to lifting up his community and did much good.[4] This was an important precedent: a Yaqui leader entering public spaces in Arizona, economic and political, to fight for Yaqui well-being. Various leaders and groups followed.

In 1923, Sociedad Guadalupe filed articles of incorporation with the stated aim of promoting "more thorough civilization of the Yaqui Indian Tribe."[5] This group pursued aid to improve the community in physical, social, cultural, and educational matters. In the 1930s, something of a power struggle emerged between Guadalupe Flores (who lived in the Scottsdale settlements and regularly conferred with Governors John C. Phillips and George Hunt), Cayetano Lopez in Pascua, and Jose Vatopiz in Guadalupe. In 1932 each sent delegations to Governor Hunt seeking recognition as the head chief and "undisputed authority" of all Arizona Yaquis. Hunt did not grant any title, but Lopez emerged as the predominant public voice.[6] These individuals' public actions helped affirm a sense of Yaqui organization, control, and planning. Coupled with religious hierarchies associated with Yaqui ceremonial dances and observances, the seemingly scattered and disorganized Arizona Yaquis were building a firm foundation upon which later political activism could be built. Moreover, they were stepping into the public sphere to advocate explicitly for Yaqui communities.

Securing Congressional Allies and New Lands

The first of the three primary phases of Yaqui political activism began in 1962. Late that summer, the freshman congressman from Arizona's Second District, Morris (Mo) Udall began corresponding with archivists at the Library of Congress to gather information on the "history and status" of Yaquis residing in Arizona. He had been prompted by Robert A. Roessel Jr., director of the Indian Education Center at Arizona State University and an advocate for Indian education and reform. Having tried and failed to get information from the Bureau of Indian Affairs and Library of Congress concerning Arizona's Yaquis, Roessell hoped to make inroads via Udall and to secure an ally in the process.[7]

The eventual reply from the Library of Congress offered a short bibliography of well-known studies concerning Yaquis, including works by Phoebe Bogan, Edward Spicer, W. C. Holden, and Muriel Thayer Painter. When Udall's office forwarded the information to Roessel, it expressed a sincere interest in Arizona Yaqui affairs. This marked the beginning of a decades-long dedication to their cause. "Certainly there is agreement that the Yaquis need assistance," the letter read. "[Congressman Udall] would appreciate having your ideas on such points as federal vs. state responsibility . . . and the utilization of a citizens group to assist in promoting progress."[8] Udall and his staff were apparently aware of the need for not only assistance but also development, and they seemed to understand the underlying problem of the Yaquis' ambiguous legal status. These two issues became the pillars in all subsequent reform efforts by Yaquis and their allies: assistance (and development) and resolution of their legal status. Were they refugees, Indians, regular immigrants, or something else?

The key public Yaqui leader collaborating in this effort was Pascua resident Anselmo Valencia. A World War II veteran, he emerged as community leader and spokesman for the Arizona Yaqui community throughout the 1950s—raising Yaquis' public image through the San Ignacio Club and public attendance of religious ceremonies and festivals. He collaborated with the Marshal Foundation (a charitable trust), Muriel Painter (a research associate at the Arizona State Museum), and Edward Spicer (at the University of Arizona) to help Yaquis pay delinquent taxes and purchase more of the land they lived on, and he and other Yaqui leaders forged ties with local and national politicians. By the early 1960s, however, the encroachment of surrounding Tucson neighborhoods and the often-bad influences they introduced into Pascua Village eroded their efforts.[9]

Valencia and others focused on a problem faced by most Arizona Yaquis: land ownership. Though many in Pascua Village had received deeds to their lands in 1950, the following years had brought challenges. In 1953, the Pima County Planning and Zoning Commission forwarded plans for a new surrounding industrial zone that would have rendered Pascua Village unlivable. Valencia and the Marshall Foundation (which had purchased much of Pascua Village, allowing Yaquis to remain after foreclosures) lobbied and succeeded in delaying these plans.[10] Despite the threat of worsening conditions, many in the community expressed reticence to move and clung to their land.[11] Tensions rose again in 1959 when Tucson annexed Pascua Village. Its residents had enjoyed relative autonomy from the growing sprawl of Tucson while still benefiting from employment and public services nearby, but annexation meant a possible decrease in Yaqui autonomy and community solidarity.[12] This drove Yaquis to act.

Valencia and others formed a coalition of concerned parties from the broader Tucson community. The resulting Committee for Pascua Community Housing (CPCH) in July 1962, chaired by Painter and co-chaired by Spicer, was the primary advocate for a Yaqui relocation and housing plan.[13] The committee included government, commercial, and civic leaders.[14] With nearly six hundred Tucson Yaquis crowded on the thirty-acre

Pascua site and conditions deteriorating, the committee planned to locate and purchase a site on public lands through a nonprofit corporation created for this purpose—or otherwise receive the land from the US government.[15] Those behind the new Yaqui campaign hoped local groups would help their cause.[16]

In October 1962, Valencia, the CPCH, Udall, and Bureau of Land Management officials toured a proposed two-hundred-acre resettlement site west of Tucson in the Avra Valley—just north of the San Xavier Papago (Tohono O'odham) Reservation.[17] Udall told Valencia that there was a "good chance" a bill could be passed in Congress to provide the land for Yaqui resettlement, and the CPCH sprang into action to capitalize on his apparent optimism.[18] In the following months the CPCH, Udall's offices in Washington, DC, and Arizona, and BLM offices in Phoenix discussed the proposed site.[19] Painter, Spicer, and the CPCH drafted a formal petition to present to Udall, printed a promotional brochure illustrating the Yaqui plight and stressing the solidarity of Yaqui community and culture, and gathered letters of support from an impressive group of prominent politicians and Tucson civic leaders.[20] The petition included a statement from Anselmo Valencia and signatures of 115 Pascua Village residents. Letters of recommendation extolled virtues of individual Yaquis, highlighted their cultural contribution to the region, and described in detail the problems faced in the overcrowded Barrio Pascua. The CPCH and its allies sought to strike a balance between portraying Yaquis as an Indian culture in need of preservation and stressing "Indianness," without overstepping the legal bounds of Yaquis' non-Indian status with the federal government.[21]

While awaiting the petition's arrival, Udall wrote to Francis J. Green, bishop of the Tucson Roman Catholic Diocese, to explain his plan to design a bill based on the CPCH proposal. If Congress failed to act, Udall worried, "the members of the Yaqui Tribe would ultimately be dispersed and their culture would die out."[22] After Udall received the petition, he quickly sent his legislative assistant Richard Olson to research the pros and cons of the proposal. Olson's subsequent memo to Udall detailed key issues. It cited two precedents of foreign Indians receiving land: the 1887 granting of land and reservation status to Canadian Tsimshians at Metlakatla, Alaska, and the 1916 creation of a reservation for Rocky Boy's band of Chippewas (and allied Crees) in Montana. It also discussed the need for a reversion clause (which would define how the land could be used), the cultural value Yaquis offered the Tucson region, and the BLM report approving the land for Yaqui settlement.

Perhaps most significant, however, was Olson's direct confrontation of the most significant potential obstacle: federal tribal recognition. "It's significant that the Yaquis are not seeking recognition by BIA," Olson stressed. In the light of the Bureau of Indian Affairs termination policy of the time—to "get out of the Indian business"—this was important. The Yaquis would do best to avoid a fight for federal tribal recognition. Furthermore, he continued:

> They are not asking anything for themselves. This request comes from the non-Indian community—a broad cross section of white leaders of Tucson. What is sought is a small tract of land—period." This statement contained both truth and fallacy. The impetus for the CPCH, though represented by a broad Anglo coalition, certainly had Yaqui roots and involvement. True, though, was the so-called "broad cross section of white leaders."[23]

Udall included Olson's report, in digest form, in his subsequent bill.

House Resolution 6233 and the Pascua Yaqui Association, Inc.

Congressman Udall introduced "A Bill to Provide for the Conveyance of Certain Land of the United States to the Pascua Yaqui Association, Inc." on May 9, 1963.[24] His press release stressed the careful study that had gone into the bill, explained that the land would be owned by the newly formed nonprofit Pascua Yaqui Association (PYA) and not deeded to individual Yaquis, and noted that fifteen acres were set aside to be conveyed to Pima County as a school site.[25] Moving the PYA forward was challenging. Formal Yaqui political organization had lain largely dormant since the 1930s, and the attempt to formalize who was to be included in the PYA and resettlement plan proved complicated. Answering questions of blood quantum and how to define membership would be challenging and was not something Valencia and his associates relished.[26] As the requisite processes progressed, the PYA and CPCH waited for Udall's bill to make its way through Congress.

As H.R. 6233 was a "simple grant of land" with no pretense of making Yaquis "a ward of the federal government," it met little opposition in Congress.[27] With some qualifying conditions amended, Udall and Arizona senator Carl Hayden made public statements to smooth the process, endured a backlog of bills from a Civil Rights Act filibuster, and eventually succeeded in moving the bill along until its passage on October 8, 1964.[28] Back in Tucson and Pima County, Udall's bill and the PYA's plan spurred some resistance. Within the Yaqui community, old leadership divisions reemerged over uncertainty of the plan—underscored by discomfort with Valencia terming himself a "chief."[29] Resistance from non-Yaqui communities came in two forms. First, landowners, real estate developers, and others cited perceived threats to their land values or business interests, anti-Yaqui prejudices based on sociocultural stereotypes of their foreign origins, and claims that they were not "real" Indians. Hiding behind a pseudonym, one objector exclaimed, "To place the Yaqui Indians out there would be even worse than having a Leprosy colony there."[30] Second, some religious and humanitarian groups expressed concern that the more remote location would worsen conditions.[31] Undeterred, Udall, Hayden, and the PYA soldiered on.

New Pascua Development

Long transient laborers, immigrants (legal and illegal), or refugees, Arizona Yaquis finally held indisputable title to land. However, Yaquis stood at the beginning of new struggles, and federal tribal recognition was yet to come. Beyond the immediate challenge of "engineering, planning, zoning, utilities, financing and the labor of building new dwellings for 80 families, with an average of six youngsters each," Pascua Yaquis faced a long and difficult road to reach prosperity and affirm and solidify their place in the United States.[32]

From the fall of 1964 into the spring of 1965, Yaquis made sunbaked adobe bricks and prepped other building materiel while waiting for roads and utilities surveys. Each home at New Pascua, explained Muriel Painter, would be "equipped with running water, showers, and bathroom facilities" and have typical Yaqui flat roofs and beamed ceilings.[33] Though modest, the homes would be a vast improvement for many Yaqui families. Yet they remained unbuilt, and an evident problem of funding loomed. In the spring of 1965, the PYA used funds from the Tucson Office of Economic Opportunity (OEO) to make a physical survey of the village, and it submitted a small craft training project proposal (378/2 Project 7–9) in June. The OEO rejected the project for being too small, so in October the PYA submitted a larger proposal that included provisions for adult education, vocational training, a multiservice center, an alcoholism rehabilitation and prevention program, relocation planning and assistance, and a small business training program.[34] This too was rejected. These setbacks frustrated the eager parties. In response, the PYA published a series of promotional brochures entitled "A Step Forward," "Yaqui Housing and Relocation," and "The Story of a Yaqui Indian Housing and Rehabilitation Effort," all of which emphasized community strength and need.[35] In short, they said, funds received would be put to worthy use.

In early 1966, the PYA and Edward Spicer included these brochures in their funding applications to various organizations. Along with another, more extensive $60,000 "Application for Community Action Program" sent to the OEO on May 27, 1966, Spicer sent applications to the Field Foundation, Phelps-Stokes Fund, William C. Whitney Foundation, and Ford Foundation in New York, Gamma Trust Fund in Virginia, and the Kaiser Family Foundation in California, among others, to secure a matching $60,000 from private interests.[36] Responses were disappointing, one even explaining that they could help only "American Indians." Thus, it was with great relief that, in September 1966, OEO announced approval of the Yaqui project and an appropriation of $99,000 for the construction of homes at New Pascua.[37]

With some funds secured, uphill battles to execute the plan encompassed much of the remainder of the decade. Again, familiar dissenting voices arose from educators and religious groups concerned that the remote location of New Pascua would harm Yaqui children or that certain denominations (e.g., Catholics) were being favored over others (e.g., Protestants). An anonymous source claimed that only six families wanted to move to the new site, and one concerned party said, "Most of the Yaqui families do not want to go to the new Pascua village but they are afraid to speak up."[38] Spicer refuted the claims, admitting that many Yaquis would regret leaving the old Pascua site and not denying the new challenges they would face, but he stressed short-term and long-term benefits to the voluntary move. Along with continued opposition from outside groups, internal divisions between Yaqui communities like Barrio Libre in South Tucson, or those too far away to benefit, like communities in Marana, Eloy or the Guadalupe-Scottsdale groups, added difficulty. Continued delays deepened frustrations. In 1970, the *Arizona Daily Star* concluded a four-part series on the Yaqui: "And the people of the old village sit and wait—for a new village home or for the newer promise of Tucson's Model Cities program that is not yet off the ground. 'Whichever comes first,' says a Yaqui woman with a shrug. 'We're used to waiting. And we're used to broken promises.'"[39] Be it economics, religion, or geography, the project faced obstacles.

The PYA attempted to surmount them, but funding problems continued. While the OEO's $99,000 was intended to fund a training program for Yaqui men to learn building and construction skills, it was later split to fund administrative and construction costs when the OEO's Multiple Service Center Project reneged on a promise for an additional $87,000. By the time of the PYA's July 1967 report on their first year's progress, seventeen houses were underway, with as many as fifty-seven families working on-site preparing adobe bricks. The consistent message of the PYA in its private correspondence, applications to local and federal agencies, and public rhetoric was one of optimism, though tempered by the dire need for funds. Luckily, the OEO grant funding training was renewed twice in the following two years, and PYA fund-raising efforts finally bore fruit, with an $80,000 grant from the Ford Foundation and a $60,000 grant from the Episcopal Church for construction of homes. By 1970, the PYA had received a total of $433,554 in federal funds and $218,000 in private contributions and in-kind services. This had facilitated the building of extensive infrastructure at New Pascua, including roads, a central plaza, water and electrical lines, eighteen completed houses, two community center buildings, five temporary homes for transient use, six more houses nearly completed, and twenty-three in various lesser stages of construction. Many lauded the progress, but dissident voices continually clamored.[40]

The passage of H.R. 6233 and slow development of New Pascua was a turning point in Arizona Yaqui history. Granted, the PYA and its New Pascua resettlement project did not represent all Arizona Yaquis. In terms of sheer demographics, it represented a minority. The divergent histories of Arizona's other Yaqui communities are important (and will be discussed below), but regardless of the PYA's inclusion or exclusion of them, the PYA forged inroads in local, state, and federal contexts for all Arizona Yaquis to follow, setting important precedents in working within US political structures. Through its efforts, a legally recognized Yaqui group secured *federal* lands, *federal* funds, and *federal* allies. The importance of this cannot be overstated.[41]

Non-Pascua Yaqui Developments prior to 1975

While Tucson-based Yaquis forged ahead with the establishment of New Pascua, thousands of Yaquis in other settlements faced a variety of struggles. Most notable were the efforts of Salt River Valley Yaqui communities to publicize their needs amid the encroaching sprawl of Phoenix, Tempe, and Scottsdale. In many ways, the challenges mirrored those of the Old Pascua Yaquis. In the light of Tucson Yaquis' struggle with land ownership, those in Guadalupe began asking questions of their own land holdings. The State of Arizona held their lands in trust, and the lack of individual deeds concerned many. They attempted to attain individual legal title to land, but the requisite property taxes made it impossible for many. It was not until the nonprofit Guadalupe Organization won court battles in 1975 that Yaquis received the trust lands and individual deeds.[42] The H.R. 6233 process and PYA heightened awareness of Guadalupe in the 1960s and 1970s. The Guadalupe Organization served as a political arm for advocacy, but not all Salt River Valley Yaquis accepted it. Eventually the organization did succeed in securing development funds and in 1975 incorporated Guadalupe as a town. By 1979, when Guadalupe Yaquis faced the decision of whether or not to enroll in the new Pascua Yaqui Tribe, they had surmounted various challenges and had a unique Guadalupe Yaqui character.[43]

To the north, Yaquis in Scottsdale's Turicate Village and Northside Salt River Valley Water Users Association (SRVWUA) camps faced turbulent decades as well. The SRVWUA Northside camp closed in 1957, and its associated Turicate settlement soon vanished, as many moved to the new Vista del Camino subdivision along McDowell Road and the Indian Bend Wash in Southeast Scottsdale. Also called Pénjamo, Vista del Camino flourished throughout the first half of the 1960s, with Yaquis establishing the Organization for Improvement of Vista del Camino to foster community growth and development. In 1966, a major flood severely damaged Pénjamo, but the Yaquis persisted, organizing politically and focusing on urban renewal programs. After more periodic flooding and then catastrophic flooding in 1972, Pénjamo received funds to relocate on new lands just above the wash and to the southeast, where there remains today a consolidated Yaqui neighborhood. Many would eventually enroll in the Pascua Yaqui Tribe, but their independent struggles, community development, and history left a cultural marker of pride for the Yaquis of the various Scottsdale settlements.[44]

Yaquis in other settlements across Arizona were similarly affected by the development of New Pascua. In general, the larger the Yaqui settlement, the closer it got to attaining critical mass to organize politically. For some, the successes at New Pascua were far out of reach. One Yaqui from Eloy made observations that may be representative of other more isolated Yaqui communities and individuals. Commenting on his inability to move to New Pascua and benefit from the new developments there, he stated, "We couldn't move down here into a new village. We're farmers. We'd be out of jobs. Why won't they use some of that money to help us get education? Man, if we could get a junior college or trade school we could handle our own problems."[45] Some eventually formed organizations like the San Ignacio Council, founded in Old Pascua in 1978, but for those living more distant from New Pascua, the focus was on surviving and on prosperity for individual families, not on pan-Yaqui political efforts. As these groups moved through their own problems and development, efforts at New Pascua would forge on, pushing ever closer to full integration into the US—and American Indian—body.

The Fight for Federal Recognition

After the first few years of New Pascua development, the PYA found it increasingly difficult to secure funds needed to improve conditions for its people. Efforts with the Department of Housing, Education and Welfare's new Native American Programs and the Model Cities Program provided some help during the lean years of the early 1970s but not enough.[46] By 1975, with the OEO and its funding gone, conditions had worsened considerably, and the PYA faced two solutions: either renegotiate its relationship with the federal government or somehow raise money through foundations and individual donors.[47] As Yaquis had in the early 1960s, they turned to friend and ally Congressman Udall. In 1970, Udall had scribbled a note to Edward Spicer on the margins of a letter he had received from the former. It read, in part, "You deserve much credit for things which have been accomplished. Let's keep in touch, let me know if I can help."[48] The PYA took this invitation to heart and approached Udall with a new campaign sometime in early 1975: federal tribal recognition. On July 8, 1975, Congressman Udall introduced H.R. 8411, "A Bill to Provide for the Extension of Certain Federal Benefits, Services, and Assistance to the Pascua Yaqui Indians of Arizona, and for Other Purposes."[49] The PYA moved down the final length of the road to full integration into the United States—as "American Indians."

This was not the first discussion of pursuing federal tribal recognition for Arizona's Yaquis. There were at least two earlier occasions when tribal recognition was considered. First, during the repatriation efforts of the late 1930s, a concerned Arizonan wrote to Senator Hayden that the Yaquis in Arizona should be "brought under the Indian service and given the benefits of protection of our government. . . . They are a freedom-loving, independent people who have always made their own way. But they do deserve a trifle better treatment at the hands of our own citizens. They deserve the right to education and an opportunity to make the most of their abilities. That has in some measure been denied them so far."[50]

In two subsequent letters, the same writer reiterated her view that rather than pursuing naturalization and citizenship processes for the Yaquis, the Indian Service should take responsibility to aid them. Hayden forwarded the views to the Bureau of Indian Affairs. Commissioner John Collier responded, explaining that specific legislation declaring naturalization or federal recognition were the only options. "The latter course would raise many questions and would require a careful study of the situation," he concluded.[51] Preliminary interdepartmental discussion of the matter was decisively negative. Sumner Wells, acting secretary of the interior, wrote to Secretary of State Charles West, "The Indian service with its limited appropriations is in no position to undertake such an investigation without encroaching upon funds needed to assist [the] Indians who are now its responsibility." Couching his reply as concern about offending the Mexican government, Hayden forwarded the disappointing report to Fitzgerald soon thereafter.[52] For the time being, the US government was not even willing to make inquiries into the idea of Yaqui tribal recognition.

Subsequently, the Yaquis in Guadalupe had made a bid for tribal recognition. Documentary evidence does not indicate if the later Tucson-based efforts were modeled on this one. In 1971, Antonio Coronado, chairman of the Guadalupe Yaqui Tribal Council, wrote to Arizona's US senator Barry Goldwater. Citing various socio-economic problems plaguing his community, Coronado declared, "Having our Indian Rights would greatly increase the chances of eliminating some of these problems." He continued:

> One thing that many people bring to our attention is that because we are not a Native tribe, we do not qualify for such rights. But we are Indians, not Mexicans. We are US Citizens and born in the United

> States and we cannot change from Indian to Mexican. The only thing that separates us from American Indian is the name. We feel our request is justified, though it is late in coming, and we would like to be informed of the possibilities and alternatives of our request.[53]

Goldwater inquired of the Bureau of Indian Affairs and was given a synopsis of the Yaquis' history in the state.[54] The BIA's reply linked the Guadalupe Yaquis to those at Pascua, disregarding their historic separation, unique backgrounds, and lack of access to the recent developments initiated by the PYA.

> The Guadalupe Yaqui are not, in the true sense, American Indians but are descendants of alien refugee Indians. It appears that they seek federal recognition as an Indian tribe, not from any pride in their Indian ancestry, but solely because they believe it would work to their economic advantage. The only manner in which they may acquire such recognition is by congressional action. Since the Pascua Yaqui were expressly denied the benefits accruing to a federally recognized Indian tribe in 1964, and both Yaqui groups possess the same history, it seems that there is little possibility that Congress would extend those benefits to the Guadalupe Yaqui.[55]

Arizona Yaquis were, in the eyes of the BIA, regular US citizens and should be directed to non-Indian service and relief programs. It seemed that the fate of Arizona Yaqui communities would rise and fall together when it came to tribal recognition.

Just a few years later, the political and economic landscape of Washington, DC, was changing. The building liberal momentum around the civil rights movement, American Indian Movement, and efforts to end the termination program and reinstate terminated tribes all set the stage for Yaqui recognition. Early in 1975, Pascua Yaquis began preparing to make an appeal to the federal government, and responses to their first inquiries were promising. At the request of the PYA, Congressman Udall, now wielding the weight of his chairmanship of the House Committee on Interior and Insular Affairs, queried the Department of Justice (DOJ). Could Yaquis qualify, he asked, for Crime Control Act funding under the associated "other aboriginal groups" clause in the act's language. A DOJ response concluded that "origin of the tribal group is immaterial since they are now presently located within the United States."[56] However promising this news was, Yaquis faced immediate resistance from other Arizona Native groups.

The Inter-Tribal Council of Arizona (ITCA) had already passed a resolution opposing federal recognition of new "tribes" on March 17, 1975, and approved an amended resolution on June 5, 1975, singling out opposition to Yaqui recognition. The Arizona Commission of Indian Affairs, which allowed Anselmo Valencia to speak on the Yaquis' behalf, concurred with the ITCA resolution, stating its dedication to securing state funding for already recognized Arizona Indians.[57] Officials from the Tucson Indian Center, San Carlos Apache Nation, Colorado River Indian Tribes, and Tucson MAYO organization (Mexican-Americans, Yaquis and Others), likewise expressed opposition.[58] Efforts to secure state recognition from Arizona governor Raul Castro were equally frustrated. The opinions of these groups had no official bearing on subsequent formation of federal policy, but most previous federal negotiations had been steered by local opinion. Failure to secure Arizona Indian support was a heavy blow to Valencia's efforts, but with the continued support of Udall, they forged ahead. On July 8, 1975, Congressman Udall submitted H.R. 8411, and public debate took fire, parsing the details of Yaqui tribal recognition and all the associated oversight, funds, and federal protections promised under the Bureau of Indian Affairs.

The bill sought to designate New Pascua as the Pascua Yaqui Indian Reservation and offer tribal membership to one thousand to two thousand of Arizona's six thousand Yaquis. "Our argument," explained Valencia, "is that those of us who were born here and served this country in various wars . . . deserve some recognition and BIA aid."[59] Few discounted the dire situation Arizona Yaquis faced. Even those opposing the bill admitted to the crises of housing, health services, education, employment, and sanitation with which Yaquis struggled. Others, including Arizona state senator Paul Fannin, expressed concern that if tribal recognition was not defined carefully, it might lead to a new influx of Mexican Yaqui immigration.[60] Arizona Yaquis still maintained ties with their Mexican kin and friends, but in large part the passing of generations distanced them from their Sonoran roots. Nevertheless, history inextricably drew them back to transnational borderlands contexts. For these and other reasons, outspoken opposition emerged among non-Yaquis.

A number of Yaquis voiced opposition as well. Old Pascua resident (and later tribal historian) Ernesto Quiroga opposed the bill due to a "misunderstanding about being called Indians, because there is a strong feeling that we are 'Yaquis' first and 'Indians' second." Another Old Pascua resident, Alcario Gastelum, countered this conclusion, stating, "If it takes calling us American Indians to get the money we need, then we'll have to be called American Indians." For Gastelum, the greater problem was that the bill was too focused on the minority of Arizona Yaquis who resided at New Pascua.[61] Gastelum feared the bill would be either too restrictive or too coercive. First, he wanted an inclusive "clause added that would include off-reservation Yaquis under the new government benefits." In response, PYA chairman Raymond Ybarra explained that PYA and tribal membership only required proof of one-quarter (later one-half) Yaqui ancestry. On the other hand, Gastelum cautioned, many off-reservation Yaquis felt that the bill might be a plot to force all Yaquis to move to the reservation. This, he explained was a highly unpopular idea.[62] Coupled with non-Yaqui opposition, the bill faced an uphill battle.

In Ybarra's estimation, H.R. 8411 stood a fifty-fifty chance of passing. As critics voiced dissent, the bill stalled in the House Subcommittee on Interior and Insular Affairs. Hoping to move it forward, bill supporters feverishly wrote letters to their legislators.[63] The efforts failed, and the PYA and Udall backed away from the issue during the following 1976 and early 1977 legislative sessions. In the interlude, Spicer and the PYA pushed the recognition campaign along different lines, testifying before the American Indian Policy Review Commission's hearing on unrecognized and terminated tribes. During this process, Spicer's extensive research honed and strengthened the cause's arguments for federal recognition.[64] While these efforts were underway, 1976 presented considerable difficulties for maintaining New Pascua Village, and battles with Pima County over building codes and related matters dominated PYA energies after H.R. 8411 failed. PYA leaders leveraged their fight with Pima County officials as further evidence of the need for federal protection for their people.[65]

The Final Push: S. 1633 and H.R. 6612

In 1977, two recognition bills were introduced in the House of Representatives and Senate. Congressman Udall submitted H.R. 6612 in April, and James Abourezk (D-SD) submitted S. 1633 in June.[66] The fact that members of both houses of Congress were pushing bills offered significant momentum. Previously, Udall's 1975 H.R. 8411 did not have a matching bill in the Senate, and that had hindered progress. The two 1977 bills differed in only one major way from the 1975 bill. Rather than restricting the legislation's coverage to PYA members, an additional clause offered inclusion for Yaquis "who hereafter" became PYA members. While internal divisions among Arizona's many Yaqui communities had stymied previous efforts, this terminology offered broad (and voluntary) inclusion.

The Senate Committee on Indian Affairs held hearings on S. 1633 in September 1977. Tribal Chairman David Ramirez, PYA executive director Anselmo Valencia, and Native American Rights Fund attorney Raymond Cross appeared in person to testify. Some debate arose as to whether or not the bill would "establish the Pascua Yaqui council as an Indian tribe." Clarifying the bill's purpose, Raymond explained that the bill simply extended federal benefits offered to other Indians, but the official organization of the PYA as a "recognized tribe" would require a vote by PYA members, in accordance with the Indian Reorganization Act. Cross explained that such a vote would likely come, but, for the time being, S. 1633 aimed to repeal section 4 of the act of October 8, 1964 (78 Stat. 1197) that specifically barred PYA members from receiving federal benefits as "Indians." At the invitation of Senator Abourezk, chairman of the Senate Committee on Indian Affairs, Spicer provided a written testimony to be included in the hearings.[67]

The first hearing revealed opposition from the BIA. In response, attorney Cross requested further testimony from Spicer. Spicer's testimony was also used in House subcommittee debates on H.R. 6612. Spicer stressed Arizona Yaquis' tenure in the "American" Southwest and cited the precedent of other transnational Natives being granted federal recognition. In both House and Senate hearings, the primary points of contention revolved around the date of Yaqui entrance into the United States and the duration of their residence. Could they be considered "American" Indians? Much to the elation of bill supporters, the House and Senate committees approved the bill by early March 1978.[68]

In the months to follow, the two bills passed through the lengthy processes of amendment and passage in the House and Senate, subsequent conference reports to reconcile the two bills and final signing into law by President Jimmy Carter on September 18, 1978.[69] The primary amendments to H.R. 6612 and S. 1633 were the inclusion of Yaqui eligibility for Indian Health Service aid and defining tribal members as current PYA members and any person of Yaqui blood who applied for membership in the year subsequent to the bill's enactment.[70] Throughout the process, bill supporters conferred with each other, worked behind the scenes to ensure its passage, and offered comments to interested media outlets. Even in the last moments, Edward Spicer was urged to write directly to President Carter as rumors of a veto circulated.[71] For too long, Yaquis had remained "in sort of limbo," commented Congressman Udall, but no more.[72]

Conclusion

Although Arizona Yaquis were not yet officially organized as a tribe, Public Law 95–375 was, in essence, federal recognition of them as American Indians. This was a historic moment. Nearly a full century after their forebears began their northward transnational move across the border from Mexico, Yaquis secured their place in the United States as official "Indians." For the Yaquis, however, the road to full tribal organization and anticipated prosperity was not immediately ahead. Yaquis already members of the PYA had until September 17, 1979, to enroll in the new tribe, and non-PYA Yaquis had until September 17, 1980. The process of organizing Yaquis to enroll by those dates required coordination—not only at New Pascua but also at Old Pascua, Marana, Guadalupe, and Scottsdale. While many flocked to the prospect of a united Yaqui tribe, many others in the non-Pascua communities chafed at being coerced into politically joining Yaquis with whom they had had very little intimate contact. By October 1979, only a fraction of the estimated seven thousand Yaquis in the United States had enrolled with the Pascua Yaqui Tribe. "To us," explained Guadalupe vice-mayor Gabriel Alvarez, "it has never been made clear what it really means to be recognized as an American Indian tribe."[73] Many, however, did end up joining, and today many of the Yaqui houses in Guadalupe and Scottsdale bear testament to their allegiance: newspaper boxes labeled "Pascua Yaqui Tribe" attached to many house fronts. Two years after Public Law 95–375 was signed, Barry Goldwater wrote to David G. Ramirez, the Pascua Yaqui Tribal council chairman, with some words of commendation and support:

> The Pascua Yaqui Indians should be very proud of their accomplishments which have been achieved in such a short time. Unemployment has been reduced by half; the annual family income has been increased by at least $1000 to $1500; and, economic development progress has been made. The tribe has built a sound economic foundation

> for its members and the health, housing, and education programs are steadily improving. All of you are to be congratulated for making the self-determination concept a reality, and I wish you continued success in the years ahead.[74]

Indeed, progress and improved conditions were encouraging, but the project of organizing and administering a new tribal nation—dispersed across Arizona—would take some time.

In the years to follow, the Pascua Yaqui Tribe made steady efforts to expand its control over land and assert political sovereignty. Almost immediately after President Carter signed its recognition into law, a campaign was started to expand the reservation to include an adjoining five hundred or more acres of BLM land (H.R. 4364).[75] Passed as Public Law 97–386 in 1982, the much-needed expansion for some six hundred new home sites was opposed by some in the Tucson region. A similar opposition emerged in 1998 when the Pascua Yaqui Tribe attempted to extend reservation trust status to twenty-three acres it owned in Guadalupe. While these efforts expanded the reservation's land base, Yaquis in Old Pascua and other outlying non-reservation Yaqui settlements faced considerable hardships. Tribal recognition and reservation lands had opened doors for future Yaqui well-being but had not assured prosperity.[76]

In the political sphere, the Pascua Yaqui Tribe made similar attempts to expand its control and assert tribal sovereignty. The first major hurdle, passing a tribal constitution, took ten years to come to fruition in 1988.[77] Fraught with difficulties dealing with BIA bureaucracy and oversight, this process prompted a subsequent effort by the Pascua Yaqui Tribe to break away from some BIA entanglements. In the early 1990s, it pushed for new legislation to be defined by the Bureau of Indian Affairs as a "historic" tribe rather than a "created" tribe. This designation, which was secured in 1994 (Public Law 103–357), gave Yaquis the ability to amend their tribal constitution without BIA interference and to levy taxes, condemn property, and regulate law and order on reservation lands.[78] With the ability to rewrite their constitution, Yaquis planned to reopen enrollment, increase tribal membership, and push for increased federal assistance.[79]

Just as H.R. 6233 and the PYA had been termed "a step forward" in the mid-1960s, Yaqui federal tribal recognition proved much the same—the end of one set of struggles and beginning of new ones.[80] It advanced Yaqui interests in the United States deeply and broadly, and it opened as many doors as it closed. Over the decades of transnational Yaqui migration and settlement in the United States, each step toward securing a stable and prosperous life had initiated new challenges. At each step, the resolution of previous problems never promised escape from challenges ahead with subsequent fuller integration into US society. Yaquis had entered the United States under duress, and for much of their twentieth-century history in Arizona failed to find the workers' paradise—free from danger or oppression—that some had imagined when fleeing across the border. Nevertheless, life in the United States offered possibilities for autonomous Yaqui organization and action. Those possibilities required significant energy, struggle, and toil, but over the course of the century the struggle paid rich dividends.

All the while, Yaquis worked to balance their unique cultural identity with the reality that being labeled transnational refugees or immigrants, borderlands wanderers, and even troublemakers—drove deep divisions between them and their neighbors in Arizona. It was a fine line to walk, and for much of the century, Yaquis seldom enjoyed steady success. As a borderlands narrative, Yaquis' Arizona history is complex and nuanced, full of contradiction and tension. In their economic, cultural, and political lives as valuable laborers, public icons, "Mexican" Indians, and foreign refugees, Yaquis consistently adjusted to new identities that allowed them to survive in the borderlands on their own terms. Given the immense obstacles—transnational passage, securing employment, establishing settlements, organizing politically, and facing discrimination and ambiguous legal status—their tenacity is striking. In their push for title to land and federal recognition, Yaquis demonstrated community solidarity and political acumen in successfully negotiating turbulent waters.

Epilogue

Borderlands Revelations

What do these stories reveal about the nature of borders, borderlands, and the edges of expanding empires, and about people bisected by borders and who combine in borderlands? Generations of Crees, Chippewas, and Yaquis negotiated successive configurations of British, French, Spanish, Mexican, and US borderlands. Their border crossings of the late nineteenth century continued the peoples' traditions of transnational negotiation. However, the increasingly policed nature of these international boundaries entailed new contexts and evolving identities for these peoples. Even when the Yaquis and the combined Crees and Chippewas succeeded in emerging from imposed transnational identities, the borderlands continued to inform their experience. And in both cases it was significant that peoples affect borders and borders affect peoples.

The purpose of the international borders is to define jurisdiction and authority and to regulate or restrict the movement of peoples into or out of a nation. But new or changing borders, porous and unpoliced, are fraught with opportunity and dangerous. It might be assumed that living near an international border would restrict opportunities for economic activity or social and political expression, by restricting free movement across the landscape. For many, this has been the case, but with Crees, Chippewas, and Yaquis, the borders created opportunity.

For one thing, living in the borderlands of Canada, Mexico, and the United States, gave Native peoples the opportunity to cross international borders "illegally" as a means of escaping pursuit, persecution, or otherwise poor conditions in their homelands. In some cases, borders bisected Native homelands, so some Native people were considered transnational in the eyes of Euro-American powers, simply due to what side of the line they were on. Definitions of transnationality aside, Crees and Yaquis both used the imposed Euro-American borders to their advantage. Various northern

Native groups referred to the US-Canadian border as the Medicine Line due to its apparent ability to keep pursuing US or Canadian troops from following them across. Though they may not have recognized the authority of the borders to restrict their movements, they readily co-opted its properties to their advantage when necessary. Imposed transnationality had its advantages.

On the other hand, borders created new opportunities for Euro-Americans. As the US government faced crises in American Indian policy, the forced removal of Native peoples was a long-standing tradition. In successive waves, the federal government and American settlement drove Natives westward, and the government eventually removed them to Indian Territory, reservations, and other bordered Native lands. The migration of "foreign" Indians into the United States created new opportunities for the US government in developing Indian policy. Forced "removal" of American Indians nevertheless left those Natives in the United States. But an international border offered US officials the opportunity to expel Natives out of the country and out of their jurisdiction. In this book's narratives, borders created specific unique opportunities that proved essential to those who crossed them.

The influence of peoples on the borders themselves and how Euro-Americans and Natives viewed or interacted with the borders also warrants comment. Indigenous violation of international boundaries had an immediate and lasting impact on how the United States dealt with the border. At the earliest signs of transnational Cree livestock thieving and the carrying of stolen goods across the border in the 1870s, the United States dedicated more resources and troops to police the line. Increased Native border crossing led to increased regulation by the United States. Similarly, Yaqui-Mexican violence and Yaqui arms trafficking across the border led to increased border policing.

It is important to keep in mind the kind of Natives crossing and the kinds of Native crossings. When defined as "friendly" Natives, such as the case of early 1860s Cree traders crossing south or Yaqui miners crossing north of the line, border crossings were of no concern. When transnational Natives were defined in negative terms, the border took on new meanings, and its security became a more pressing demand. Likewise, the nature of Native border-crossings led to divergent outcomes. When Yaqui refugees fled Sonora and entered the United States as valuable laborers, blending in with non-Yaqui Mexican migrant laborers, the United States acted much differently than when Cree refugees fled Canadian prosecution and crossed the line south. The latter were seen as troublemakers, with no immediate or long-term prospects for contributing to Montana development. These were as much questions of the Natives' identity, who they were, as it was the context of their transnationality. Both were refugees fleeing under duress, but in the eyes of Americans they clearly were not equal.

Comparison of Cree, Chippewa, and Yaqui narratives of transnational passage significantly implies that there is value in breaking out of familiar and comfortable molds. Broadly considering and comparing their experiences closes gaps in history and fosters more nuanced understanding of North American borderlands and US Indian policy. Examining labor history, borderlands and Indigenous history, federal-state relations, and international politics, this book has interrogated differences in border regimes and questioned assumptions of what indigeneity meant in the United States when not all Natives were federally recognized as such. These narratives have intrinsic value, and I hope that Chippewa, Cree, Yaqui, and other Native readers will gain new insights to add to their already rich understandings of their communities' histories.

Can the Chippewa Cree Tribe, Yaquis, and others use these narratives as a basis for inter-community dialogue concerning their shared and contrasting historical experiences? I hope that they can. Despite decades of setback, their immediate ancestors achieved great things through persistence and wise socio-political and economic negotiations. Once defined as refugees and immigrants, intermittently considered "illegal," these transnational Natives accomplished an astounding transmogrification from transnational and foreign to American—and they did this while asserting and maintaining their own unique indigeneity—native, but foreign no longer.

Notes

Prologue

1. Chief Stick's genealogy differs in conflicting reports. When interviewed in the mid-1970s, Chief Stick stated that he was "Cree, and part Blackfeet." His father was Sharp Nose, brother to Walking Child. His mother, whose name he did not know, was sister to Shorty Young Boy. The 1917 report made by Inspector James McLaughlin, however, says otherwise. Chief Stick was there listed as half Assiniboine and half Blackfeet, "with slight strain of French in his Blackfeet blood; he is Little Bear's stepson." James McLaughlin, "Tentative Role," Rocky Boy's Reservation Records, 1909–1917, SC 903, Montana State Historical Society, Helena (hereafter MSHS).

2. In the 1920 US census, Chief Stick's entry lists both of his parents as Cree speakers born in Canada. While offering a possible birthplace, their subsequent migrations remain unclear. See US Department of Commerce, Bureau of the Census, "Census of 1920," Series T625, Roll 197, p. 177.

3. The North-West Rebellion, or Riel Rebellion, was a collaborative attempt by Métis, Crees, and other Natives to wrest portions of the Canadian prairie from the control of Canada. Along with Métis leader Louis Riel, Crees such as Big Bear and Poundmaker also played prominent roles.

4. Interview with Grant Chief Stick, March 20, 1975, Rocky Boy School Archive, Box Elder, Montana (hereafter RBSA).

5. Interviews with Chief Stick, March 20, 1975, and undated, RBSA.

6. Interview with Grant Chief Stick, August 27, 1974, RBSA.

7. Ibid.

8. Chief Stick married Bad Looking Big Wind, daughter of Rocky Boy enrollees Big Wind and Head Woman, by tribal custom on January 12, 1916. According to early records, they bore the following children: daughter Springtime Chief Stick (born April 12, 1917), son Little Chief Stick (born 1919, died March 6, 1919), and son Ray Chief Stick (born April 17, 1920, died October 28, 1922). Later children included John, Mike, and Pat Chief Stick. Chief Stick remarried in 1966, wedding Emma Light Foot. A collection of early census reports and genealogical information is held at Stone Child College. See Diane Bynum, Rocky Boy Census 1900–1920, Stone Child College Library, Box Elder, Montana. Other information provided by Stone Child College foundations and research director Ed Stamper via personal communication, September 1–14, 2009.

9. His age at death must be viewed as an approximation since his exact birth date is uncertain. The most reliable sources place his birth between 1894 and 1895, making him 100–101 years old at the time of his passing.

10. Edward Spicer, *People of Pascua* (Tucson: University of Arizona Press, 1988), 110.

11. Yaquis mounted major resistance to Spanish and Mexican control in 1825, 1834, 1857–62, 1899, and again in the 1910s and 1920s. See Raphael Brewster Folsom, *The Yaquis and the Empire: Violence, Spanish Imperial Power, and Native Resilience in*

Colonial Mexico (New Haven: Yale University Press, 2014); Evelyn Hu-DeHart, *Yaqui Resistance and Survival: The Struggle for Land and Autonomy, 1821–1910* (Madison: University of Wisconsin Press, 1984); and Edward Spicer, *Cycles of Conquest: The Impact of Spain, Mexico and the United States on the Indians of the Southwest, 1533–1960* (Tucson: University of Arizona Press, 1962), 61–65, 79–81.

12. Quoted in Spicer, *People of Pascua*, 110.

13. Spicer, *People of Pascua*, 114.

14. Quoted in ibid., 116.

Introduction

1. After the disastrous federal termination policy mid-forties to mid-sixties, many unrecognized tribes were engaged in the bureaucrat requirements necessary for those hoping to regain tribal recognition. Additionally, there were—and still are—many who have never had federal recognition. See David R. M. Beck, *Seeking Recognition: The Termination and Restoration of the Coos, Lower Umpqua, and Siuslaw Indians, 1855–1984* (University of Nebraska Press, 2009); Amy E. Den Ouden and Jean M. O'Brien, eds., *Recognition, Sovereignty Struggles, and Indigenous Rights in the United States: A Sourcebook* (Chapel Hill: University of North Carolina Press, 2013); Donald L. Fixico, *Termination and Relocation: Federal Indian Policy, 1945–1960* (Albuquerque: University of New Mexico Press, 1990); Brian Klopotek, *Recognition Odysseys: Indigeneity, Race, and Federal Tribal Recognition Policy in Three Louisiana Indian Communities* (Durham: Duke University Press, 2011); Bruce Granville Miller, *Invisible Indigenes: The Politics of Nonrecognition* (Lincoln: University of Nebraska Press, 2003); Mark Edwin Miller, *Claiming Tribal Identity: The Five Tribes and the Politics of Federal Acknowledgment* (Norman: University of Oklahoma Press, 2013); and Mark Edwin Miller, *Forgotten Tribes: Unrecognized Indians and the Federal Acknowledgment Process* (Lincoln: University of Nebraska Press, 2006).

2. US Congress, Senate, Committee on Interior and Insular Affairs, Providing for the Conveyance of Certain Land of the United States to the Pascua Yaqui Association, Inc., 88th Cong., 2nd sess., September 8, 1964, S. Rep. 1530, serial 12617, 4.

3. At the time, a legislative assistant made explicit mention of the fact that Yaquis were *not* seeking federal recognition—understanding the lingering sentiment in favor of termination atmosphere. At the time of the report, the last termination—of the Ponca Tribe of Nebraska—was only one year past. See Richard Olson, "Memo RE Yaqui Bill," 1963, Morris K. Udall Papers, MS 325 (hereafter Udall Papers), University of Arizona Library Special Collections (hereafter UASC), subgroup 2, series 3, box 162, folder 14.

4. The US-Canadian border was formed westward to the Rockies along the Forty-Ninth Parallel by the Jay Treaty of 1794 and Convention of 1818, and the US-Mexican border was established via the 1848 Treaty of Guadalupe-Hidalgo and 1853 Gadsden Purchase.

5. Eric Meeks, *Border Citizens: The Making of Indians, Mexicans, and Anglos in Arizona* (Austin: University of Texas Press, 2007), 11.

6. See this book's companion website, www.nativebutforeign.org, for a full bibliography of borderlands scholarship with extensive Native content. Pay particular attention to works by the following scholars, many of which are cited elsewhere herein: James F. Brooks, Brian DeLay, Jerome A. Greene, Ryan Hall, Pekka Hämäläinen, Michel Hogue,

Katrina Jagodinsky, Andrae Marak, David G. McCrady, Sheila McManus, Eric Meeks, Cynthia Radding, Joshua Reid, Jeffrey Schulze, Jeffrey P. Shepherd, Taylor Spence, Samuel Truett, and Natale Zappia.

7. See Ryan Hall, *Blackfoot Country: The Indigenous Borderlands of the North American Fur Trade* (Chapel Hill: University of North Carolina Press, forthcoming); Shelley Bowen Hatfield, *Chasing Shadows: Apaches and Yaquis along the United States-Mexico Border, 1876–1911* (Albuquerque: University of New Mexico Press, 1998); David G. McCrady, *Living with Strangers: The Nineteenth-Century Sioux and the Canadian-American Borderlands* (Toronto: University of Toronto Press, 2010); Hana Samek, *The Blackfoot Confederacy 1880–1920: A Comparative Study of Canadian and US Indian Policy* (Albuqueque: University of New Mexico Press, 1987); and Jeffrey P. Shepherd, "Race, Blood, and Belonging: Transnational Blackfoot Bands and Families along the US-Canada Border, 1855–1915," in *Laying Down the Law: Critical Legal Histories of the North American West*, ed. Pablo Mitchell and Katrina Jagodinski (Lawrence: University of Kansas Press, forthcoming).

8. The Canadian Tsimshians who were settled at Metlakatla, Alaska, in 1887 are another example of foreign Indians being incorporated into the United States, but their transnational story was quite different in context. Act of March 3, 1891, 26 Stat. 1101, 48 USC. § 358. See this book's companion website, www.nativebutforeign.org, for secondary sources on Metlakatla.

9. In October 2016, National Public Radio featured a discussion in Montana about refugee settlement. The discussion bears remarkable similarity to the public debates featured in this book about Native refugee settlement. See "Refugee Resettlement Evokes Fear, Debate on Montana," *All Things Considered*, NPR, October 17, 2016, www.npr.org/2016/10/17/498292069/refugee-resettlement-evokes-fear-debate-in-montana.

10. This has resulted in a paucity of Arizona Yaqui and Montana Cree research and publications—in stark contrast to the robust literature on Yaquis in Mexico and Crees in Canada. Many works mention the Arizona and Montana groups, but few offer extensive detail or narrative. For the best existing treatments of those who crossed into the United States, see Larry Burt, "In a Crooked Piece of Time: The Dilemma of the Montana Cree and the Métis," *Journal of American Culture* 9 (Spring 1986): 45–52; Verne Dusenberry, *The Rocky Boy Indians: Montana's Displaced Persons* (Helena: Montana Historical Press, 1954); Verne Dusenberry, *The Montana Cree: A Study in Religious Persistence* (1962; repr., Norman: University of Oklahoma Press, 1998); Leah Glaser, "The Story of Guadalupe, Arizona: The Survival and Preservation of a Yaqui Community" (master's thesis, Arizona State University, 1996); Leah Glaser, "Working for Community: The Yaqui Indians of the Salt River Project." *Journal of Arizona History* 37 (Winter 1996): 337–56; Edward Spicer, *People of Pascua* (Tucson: University of Arizona Press, 1988); Edward Spicer, *The Yaquis: A Cultural History* (Tucson: University of Arizona Press, 1980); and Meeks, *Border Citizens*.

11. Sheila McManus, "Fraternal Twins or Distant Cousins? The Two Borders of the United States West," paper presented at the annual meeting of the Western Historical Association, Denver, October 8, 2009. Very few works consider both borders, but for an excellent source for beginning to think about comparative endeavors, see Benjamin H. Johnson and Andrew R. Graybill, eds., *Bridging National Borders in North America: Transnational and Comparative Histories* (Durham: Duke University Press, 2010).

12. After the 1846 Oregon Treaty, some conflict arose over the extension of the Forty-Ninth Parallel across the Puget Sound. Those disagreements were settled by 1872. The other US-Canadian border, between Alaska and Yukon, was finalized along the 114th

Meridian in 1903. In 1889, the United States and Mexico created the International Boundary and Water Commission to define water rights and boundaries along the border, but the boundary's cartography remained the same.

13. One Yaqui tribal historian notes: "We were first, Surem; then, Yo'emem and Yaquis or 'hiakim.' The latter terms we use interchangeably. Yaqui people today are multi-faceted and have had varying experiences . . . peoples in adaptive transition usually do." Ernesto Quiroga, e-mail correspondence, December 18, 2008.

14. *Encyclopaedia Britannica* online, for one, notes in this order: "'Ojibwa,' also spelled 'Ojibwe' or 'Ojibway,' also called 'Chippewa,' self-name 'Anishinaabe.'" "Ojibwa," *Encyclopaedia Britannica*.

15. See Herbert E. Bolton, *Spanish Borderlands* (Albuquerque: University of New Mexico Press, 1996); John Francis Bannon, *The Spanish Borderlands Frontier, 1513–1821* (University of New Mexico Press, 1974); and David J. Weber, *The Spanish Frontier in North America* (Yale University Press, 1994).

16. Richard White, *The Middle Ground: Indians, Empires, and Republics in the Great Lakes Region, 1650–1815* (Cambridge: Cambridge University Press, 1991), x.

17. See Jeremy Adelman and Stephen Aron, "From Borderlands to Borders: Empires, Nation-States, and the Peoples in between in North American History," *American Historical Review* 1043 (June 1999): 814–41.

18. Ibid., 816. See also John R. Wunder and Pekka Hämäläinen, "Of Lethal Places and Lethal Essays," *American Historical Review* 104 (October 1999): 1229–34.

19. David McCrady, *Living with Strangers: The Nineteenth-Century Sioux and the Canadian-American Borderlands* (Lincoln: University of Nebraska Press, 2006), 4.

20. Consider Mark Rifkin's dense but revelatory work on the construction of space and identity, *Manifesting America: The Imperial Construction of US National Space* (Oxford: Oxford University Press, 2009).

21. See, for example, Theodore Binnema, *Common and Contested Ground: A Human and Environmental History of the Northwestern Plains* (Norman: University of Oklahoma Press, 2001); Colin G. Calloway, *One Vast Winter Count: The Native American West before Lewis and Clark* (Lincoln: University of Nebraska Press, 2003); and James Brooks, *Captives and Cousins: Slavery, Kinship, and Community in the Southwest Borderlands* (Chapel Hill: University of North Carolina Press, 2002).

22. In 1978, Richard White made an early step in highlighting the expanding nature of Sioux empires during the seventeenth and eighteenth centuries. See Richard White, "The Winning of the West: The Expansion of the Western Sioux in the Eighteenth and Nineteenth Centuries," *Journal of American History* 65 (September 1978): 319–43. More recently, Pekka Hämäläinen's treatment of Comanche expansion drastically rewrites southwestern history in terms of Native empire building. See Pekka Hämäläinen, *The Comanche Empire* (New Haven: Yale University Press, 2008).

Chapter 1

1. "Sad Is the Story of the Crees," *Anaconda (MT) Standard*, March 30, 1913; Pedro Tamarón y Romeral, *Demostración del vastísimo obispado de la Nueva Vizcaya, 1765* (Mexico: Biblioteca Historia Mexicana de Obras Inéditas, 1937), 246–47.

2. See David Goodman Mandelbaum, *The Plains Cree: An Ethnographic, Historical, and Comparative Study* (Regina: Canadian Plains Research Center, University of Regina, 1979); John Sheridan Milloy, *The Plains Cree: Trade, Diplomacy, and War,*

1790 to 1870 (Winnipeg: University of Manitoba Press, 1988); and Floyd W. Sharrock, "History of the Cree Indian Territorial Expansion from the Hudson Bay Area to the Interior Saskatchewan and Missouri Plain," in John C. Ewers, *Ethnological Report on the Chippewa Cree Tribe of the Rocky Boy Reservation and the Little Shell Band of Indians*, Chippewa Indians, vol. 6. (New York: Garland, 1974), 183–407.

3. Dale Russell, *Eighteenth-Century Western Cree and Their Neighbors* (Hull, Quebec: Canadian Museum of Civilization, 1991), 36.

4. John C. Ewers, *Ethnological Report of the Chippewa Cree Tribe of the Rocky Boy Reservation, Montana and the Little Shell Band of Indians*, Chippewa Indians 6 (New York: Garland, 1974), 19.

5. David Thompson, *David Thompson's Narrative, 1784–1812* (Toronto: Champlain Society, 1962), 48–49, 72, 107, 240. Thompson placed "Cheepawyans" to the north and extending "westward by the Peace River to the Rocky Mountains." These Chipewyans are a Na-Dené people, not to be confused with Algonquian Chippewas.

6. Alexander Mackenzie, *Journals and Letters of Alexander Mackenzie* (Cambridge: Hakluyt Society, 1970), 174, 179, 271, 275, 281.

7. Russell, *Eighteenth-Century Western Cree and Their Neighbors*, 36.

8. Ewers, *Ethnological Report of the Chippewa Cree Tribe*, 22–23.

9. Floyd W. Sharrock and Susan R. Sharrock, *History of the Cree Indian Territorial Expansion from the Hudson Bay Area to the Interior Saskatchewan and Missouri Plains* (New York: Garland, 1974), 12; and David G. Mandlebaum, *The Plains Cree: An Ethnographic, Historical, and Comparative Study* (Regina: Canadian Plains Research Center, University of Regina, 1979), 31.

10. Donald B. Smith, "The Original Peoples of Alberta," in *Peoples of Alberta: Portraits of Cultural Diversity*, Howard and Tamara Palmer, eds. (Saskatoon: Western Producer Prairie Books, 1985), 55–57.

11. Walter Denny, *Stories from the Old Ones* (Missoula, MT: Rising Wolf, 1979), 29–33.

12. Walter Denny, "Story of the Bear Paws," undated manuscript, RBSA.

13. Interview with Four Souls, May 1975, in Catherine Isabel Littlejohn, "The Indian Oral Tradition: A Model for Teachers" (master's thesis, University of Saskatchewan, 1975), 91.

14. For more on Fidler, see Theodore Binnema, *Enlightened Zeal: The Hudson's Bay Company and Scientific Networks, 1670–1870* (Toronto: University of Toronto Press, 2014), 96–123.

15. J. G. Nelson, *The Last Refuge* (Montreal: Harvest House, 1973), 44.

16. Gary Moulton, ed., *The Journals of the Lewis and Clark Expedition August 25, 1804-April 6, 1805*, vol. 3 (Lincoln: University of Nebraska Press, 1987), 433.

17. Ewers, *Ethnological Report of the Chippewa Cree Tribe*, 26–27.

18. Alexander Henry and David Thompson, *New Light on the Early History of the Greater Northwest*, ed. Elliott Coues (New York, 1897), 1:53, 1:314, 1:408, 1:419, 2:540–87, 3:938.

19. Ewers, *Ethnological Report of the Chippewa Cree Tribe*, 32–34.

20. The term "Métis" is French and denotes individuals of mixed Native and non-Native heritage. Historically, this often refers specifically to the population that grew out of the Red River region of Manitoba and associated bison trade networks. French traders had made common practice of intermarriage with First Nations women, and their descendants were numerous and maintained distinct culture. Many contemporary documents referred to them as half-breeds, or simply "breeds," but most current

scholarship uses “Métis.” Cree and Chippewa were among the most common ancestries for plains Métis.

21. Michel Hogue, *Metis and the Medicine Line: Creating a Border and Dividing a People* (Chapel Hill: University of North Carolina Press, 2015). One Cree history explained, “The Cree considered the half-French, half-Scots mixed bloods, or halfbreeds, their relatives. For in essence they were all Indian.” “The Cree,” undated manuscript, RBSA, 1.

22. Nicholas Vrooman’s work on the Little Shell Tribe of Montana demonstrates the deep interconnectedness of Cree, Chippewa, Métis, and other Native peoples. See Nicholas C. P. Vrooman, *“The Whole Country Was . . . ‘One Robe’”: The Little Shell Tribe’s America* (Helena, MT: Drumlummon Institute, 2012).

23. See Gerhard J. Ens, *Homeland to Hinterland: The Changing Worlds of the Red River Metis in the Nineteenth Century* (Toronto: University of Toronto Press, 1996), 154.

24. See Martha Harroun Foster, *We Know Who We Are: Métis Identity in a Montana Community* (Norman: University of Oklahoma Press, 2006).

25. The 1900 US Census used various labels in a number of Montana counties to designate full- and mixed-blood Crees, Chippewas, and Chippewa-Crees. See the book’s companion website, www.nativebutforeign.org, for sources and discussion.

26. The terms “mixed-blood” and “full-blood” represent terminology used in the census reports. All Métis (whether or not labeled “Métis”) were mixed-bloods, but not all mixed-bloods (including Chippewas and Crees with mixed Anglo and French heritage) were Métis.

27. For more information on Montana Métis and their transnational movements, see Gerhard J. Ens, “The Border, the Buffalo, and the Métis of Montana,” in *The Borderlands of the American and Canadian Wests: Essays on Regional History of the Forty-Ninth Parallel*, ed. Sterling Evans (Lincoln: University of Nebraska Press, 2006), 139–54.

28. *Helena Independent*, June 26, 1896.

29. For the best and most comprehensive resource on Spanish-Yaqui relations, see Raphael Brewster Folsom, *The Yaquis and the Empire: Violence, Spanish Imperial Power, and Native Resilience in Colonial Mexico* (New Haven: Yale University Press, 2014).

30. Evelyn Hu-DeHart, *Missionaries, Miners and Indians: Spanish Contact with the Yaqui Nation of Northwestern New Spain, 1533–1820* (Tucson: University of Arizona Press, 1981), 10.

31. Edward Spicer, *The Yaquis: A Cultural History* (Tucson: University of Arizona Press, 1980), 13; Folsom, *Yaquis and Empire*, 71–73; José Francisco Velasco, *Noticias Estadísticas del Estado de Sonora* (Mexico: Imprenta de Ignacio Cumplido, 1850), 15–16; and Rodolofo F. Acuña, *Sonoran Strongman: Ignacio Pesqueira and His Times* (Tucson: University of Arizona Press, 1974), 5–6.

32. Claudio Dabdoub, *Historia de El Valle del Yaqui* (Mexico: Libreria Manuel Porrua, S.A., 1949), 64. Edward Spicer reports that by 1623, nearly all thirty thousand Yaquis had been baptized, and the Yaqui themselves had already built eight churches across their territories. See Spicer, *Yaquis*, 15.

33. Spicer, *Cycles of Conquest*, 52.

34. Dabdoub, *Historia de El Valle del Yaqui*, 50. All translations by author.

35. Folsom, *Yaquis and the Empire*, 181.

36. See this book's companion website, www.nativebutforeign.org, for sources and discussion of debates regarding potential earlier Yaqui sojourns in Arizona with Jesuit father Eusubio Kino.

37. See Jay J. Wagoner, *Early Arizona: Prehistory to Civil War* (Tucson: University of Arizona Press, 1975), 96.

38. See John L. Kessell, *Friars, Soldiers, and Reformers: Hispanic Arizona and the Sonora Mission Frontier, 1767–1856* (Tucson: University of Arizona Press, 1976), 71.

39. By 1801, these Yaqui laborers official serving the mission had been replaced by "gente de razón"—Spanish tradesmen and their families. Ibid., 190, 202. See this book's companion website, www.nativebutforeign.org, for sources and discussion of concurrent tensions between Yaquis and Spanish in the region.

40. See James E. Officer, *Hispanic Arizona, 1536–1856* (Tucson: University of Arizona Press, 1987), 31.

41. Kessell, *Friars, Soldiers, and Reformers*, 239. See this book's companion website, www.nativebutforeign.org, for discussion of Tumacácori Yaquis and their continued influence in southern Arizona.

42. Kieran McCarty, ed., *A Frontier Documentary: Sonora and Tucson, 1821–1848* (Tucson: University of Arizona Press, 1997), 10–13, 26–28, 71–73, 153–154; and Officer, *Hispanic Arizona*, 161.

Chapter 2

1. Gustavus Doane to Mary Hunter Doane, March 26, 1882, Gustavus Doane Letters, MSHS; "Threaten to Cross Border, Uprising of Yaquis Causing Uneasiness in Arizona," Special Report from Nogales, Arizona, to the *St. Louis Globe Democrat*, *Lincoln County Leader* (Toledo, OR), August 11, 1899.

2. James Chambers, "21 June 1855, Fort Sarpy Journal," in *Contributions to the Historical Society of Montana*, vol. 10 (1940; repr., Boston: J. S. Canner, 1966), 130.

3. Edwin A. C. Hatch diary, June 26, July 5, July 6, 1856, SC 810, MSHS.

4. It should be noted that Chippewa traders were viewed similarly in their negotiations to the east. See John C. Ewers, *Ethnological Report of the Chippewa Cree Tribe*, 19, 26–27, 32, 34, 42; and Henry and Thompson, *New Light on the Early History*, 1:53, 1:314, 1:408, 1:419; 2:540–87.

5. Ramón Corral, "Biographía de José María Leyva Cajeme," in *Obras Históricas*, (Hermosillo, Sonora, Mexico: Biblioteca Sonorense de Geografía e Historia, 1959), 150. See this book's companion website, www.nativebutforeign.org for sources on and discussion of Yaqui activities in the California gold rush.

6. "The Wrath of Santa Rita," *Mohave County Miner* (Mineral Park, AZ), August 24, 1912.

7. "Terrible News from Arizona," *Weekly Jeffersonian* (Jefferson, Wisconsin), June 30, 1859. Seeking to ease racial tensions, the *Weekly Arizonian* (Arizona's first newspaper) immediately published a resolution condemning the massacre in both English and Spanish. See *Weekly Arizonian* (Tubac), May 19, 1859. See also Thomas E. Sheridan, *Los Tucsonenses: The Mexican Community in Tucson, 1854–1941* (Tucson: University of Arizona Press, 1986), 36.

8. Samuel Truett, *Fugitive Landscapes: The Forgotten History of the US-Mexico Borderlands* (New Haven: Yale University Press, 2006), 42.

9. *Las Dos Repúblicas*, July 27, 1927, as cited in Sheridan, *Los Tucsonenses*, 85.

10. Thomas Edwin Farish, *History of Arizona* (Phoenix: Thomas Edwin Farish, 1916), 96; and Edmund Wells, *Argonaut Tales: Stories of the Gold Seekers and the Indian Scouts of Early Arizona* (New York: Grafton Press, 1927), 379–86.

11. H. B. Wharfield, *Apache Indian Scouts* (El Cajon, CA: H. B. Wharfield, 1964), 1–2.

12. "The Yaqui Indians," *Oakland Evening Tribune*, September 27, 1876, and September 30, 1876. With Yaquis already having performed "with success" at the Woodwards Gardens and the Mechanics Institute in San Francisco, Oakland celebrated their arrival. It was reported that "the entertainment is said to be worthy of a liberal patronage."

13. Edward Spicer originally claimed this was the first Yaqui presence in the state, but he clearly recanted in all subsequent publications. Edward Spicer, "The Yaqui Indians of Arizona," *Kiva* 5 (March 1940): 23.

14. Rodolfo F. Acuña, *Corridors of Migration: The Odyssey of Mexican Laborers, 1600–1933* (Tucson: University of Arizona Press, 2007), 79.

15. Spicer, *Yaquis*, 236.

16. *Nogales (AZ) Oasis*, August 22, 1896; and *El Paso Herald* September 11, 1896, as cited in Edward Spicer to Ray Ibarra, September 26, 1976, Edward H. and Rosamond B. Spicer Papers (hereafter Spicer Papers), Arizona State Museum, Tucson (hereafter ASM), subgroup 6, box 1, folder 8.

17. "Pearl Fisheries," *Salt Lake Herald*, August 9, 1889.

18. Yaqui and Mayo activity in the Sea of Cortes pearl fisheries was well known. See *Obras Historicas* (Hermosillo, Sonora, Mexico: Biblioteca Sonorense de Geografia e Historia, 1959), 201; Dean Harris, *By Path and Trail* (Chicago: Chicago Newspaper Union, 1908), 61, 93; Bert H. Leonard, "Again the Yaqui," *Independent* (New York City) 118 (February 26, 1927): 236; Spicer, *Yaquis*, 120, 126; Spicer, *People of Pascua*, 68; and "Revengeful Indian Tribe," *Sun* (New York City), July 7, 1907. An 1898 report makes similar mentions of Yaquis freely and regularly circulating across the border for employment. A Harvard professor ("Penrose") explained, "A number of them come up to Arizona ever now and then and get a job in one of the mines. They work well. After accumulating enough for the needs of the immediate future, they go home and have a pleasant time. Then after a while they get a new job and earn some more money. So it goes." See "About the Yaqui Indians," *Wichita (KS) Daily Eagle*, January 20, 1898.

19. See Spicer, *Yaquis*, 236; *Nogales Oasis*, August 22, 1896; and *El Paso Herald* September 11, 1896, as cited in Edward Spicer to Ray Ibarra, September 26, 1976, Spicer Papers, ASM, subgroup 6, box 1, folder 8.

20. See this book's companion website, www.nativebutforeign.org, for examples of evolving American views of transnational Crees in the 1840s and 1850s.

21. For an overview of the three John Marshall Supreme Court cases that shaped relationship between Natives and the federal government, see David Eugene Wilkins and K. Tsianina Lomawaima, *Uneven Ground: American Indian Sovereignty and Federal Law* (Norman: University of Oklahoma Press, 2001), 52–63.

22. "The Overland Trail," David Higler Papers, 1867–1935, SC 864, MSHS.

23. "Our Fort Walsh Letter," *New North-West* (Deer Lodge, MT), August 1, 1879. Father Leon Doucet, an Oblate missionary in Alberta, recorded on June 5, 1879, that he witnessed Big Bear proposing an alliance with Blackfeet and Sioux against the whites. See "Extract from Father Doucet's Memoir," June 5, 1879, M4343, Glenbow Archives, Calgary, Alberta. In 1881, the rhetorical linkage between Sitting Bull and Big Bear was intimated by one Montanan paper that called Big Bear "the northern

Sitting Bull" because he demonstrated similar recalcitrant disposition. See "Views on the Indian Question," *Benton (MT) Weekly Record*, September 1, 1881.

24. See "Our Threatened Border," *Benton (MT) Record*, December 21, 1877; "Sitting Bull: A Big Buffalo Hunt near the Cypress Hill," *Daily Independent* (Helena), July 10, 1877; "Indian News: Where the Hostiles Are Now Ranging," *Daily Independent* (Helena), April 17, 1878; "Border Affairs: Emissaries from Sitting Bull's Camp," *Daily Independent* (Helena), February 10, 1878; and "Where the Reds Are: Chasing Buffalo in British America," *Daily Independent* (Helena), April 10, 1878.

25. See this book's companion website, www.nativebutforeign.org, for sources on the evolving prejudice and US military reactions to Cree activities in Montana.

26. Samuel Breck to Fort Assiniboine, August 15, 1881, Fort Assiniboine Telegrams Received, 1881, Collection 2457 (hereafter Ft. Assiniboine Telegrams), Montana State University Archives (hereafter MSU), Bozeman; and Patrice Breland to Doctor [unknown], November 24, 1878, record group 10, Black Series, volume 3687, file 13,607, reel c-10120, National Archives of Canada, Ottawa, Ontario (hereafter NAC).

27. Samuel Breck to Fort Assiniboine, August 15, 1881; and Samuel Breck to Ft. Assiniboine, August 23, 1881, Ft. Assiniboine Telegrams, MSU.

28. "The Indian Conundrum: What a Soldier Has to Say of Its Probable Solution," *Washington Post*, April 26, 1880.

29. For a brief summary of the Medicine Line concept and associated Native border crossing during this era, see Beth LaDow, *The Medicine Line: Life and Death on a North American Borderland* (New York: Routledge, 2002); and Beth LaDow, "Sanctuary: Native Border Crossings and the North American West," *American Review of Canadian Studies* (Spring/Summer 2001): 25–42.

30. "British Indians over the Line," *Benton Weekly Record*, August 3, 1882.

31. Ibid.

32. Gustavus Doane to Mary Hunter Doane, March 26, 1882, Gustavus Doane Letters, MSHS.

33. "Big Bear and His Blanketed Band," *Daily Independent* (Helena) May 17, 1882. Emphasis added.

34. "Big Bear's Surrender," *Benton (MT) Weekly Record*, December 28, 1882.

35. "Captured Reds," *Benton (MT) Weekly Record*, May 26, 1883; Patrick Burke to Mrs. Burke (mother), November 4, 1883, Patrick Francis "Frank" Burke Papers, MSHS; and "Hostile Crees," *Daily Independent* (Helena), June 8, 1884.

36. For a detailed chronicle of the early 1880s, see Brenden W. Rensink, "Cree Contraband or Contraband Crees: Early Montanan Experiences with Transnational Natives and the Formation of Lasting Prejudice, 1880–1885," in *Smugglers, Brothels, and Twine: Historical Perspectives on Contraband and Vice in North America's Borderlands*, ed. Andrae Marak and Elaine Carey (Tucson: University of Arizona Press, 2011), 24–43. See this book's companion website, www.nativebutforeign.org, for further sources and discussion of these years.

37. The fertile Yaqui River Valley and surrounding environs stood as prime examples of underdeveloped regions seen by the federal government as being in dire need of modernization, reform, and greater control. The independent, resistant, and otherwise "anti-progressive" Yaqui (and Mayo) presence on these lands was incompatible with Porfirian plans. Numbering some thirty thousand, Yaquis defied state control, refused to pay taxes, and had enjoyed de facto independence since Mexican national independence from Spain. For the Díaz regime, Yaquis were the sole obstacle blocking regional development. See in Spicer, *Yaquis: A Cultural History*, chap. 3 ("Yaquis versus

Hacendados, 1768–1910"); Fortunato Hernández, *Las Razas Indegenas de Sonora y la Guerra del Yaqui* (Mexico City: Talleres de la Casa Editorial "J. de Elizalde," 1902), vii, 101; Evelyn Hu-DeHart, "Development and Rural Rebellion: Pacification of the Yaquis in the Late *Porfiriato*," *Hispanic American Historical Review* 54 (February 1974): 74; and Manuel Balbás, *Recuerdos del Yaqui: Principales Episodios Durante la Campaña de 1899 a 1901* (Mexico City: Sociedad de Edición y Librería Franco Americana, S.A., 1927), 92, 103–4.

38. See *Mohave County Miner* (Mineral Park, AZ). May 25, 1889; "Condensed Telegrams," *Arizona Republican* (Phoenix), May 22, 1890; "From Old Mexico," *Arizona Republican*, October 1, 1890; "Trade with Sonora," *Arizona Republican* (Phoenix), November 23, 1890; "Indian War: Yaqui Indians in Mexico on the War Path," *Arizona Republican* (Phoenix), July 24, 1891; "Mexican Troops Ambushed: Yaqui Indians Kill Twenty Men with Stones," *Arizona Republican* (Phoenix), August 4, 1891; *Mohave County Miner* (Mineral Park, AZ), October 10, 1891; "Hotile [sic] Yaqui Indians: Carrying Consternation among Prosperous Mexican Farmers," *Arizona Republican* (Phoenix), April 20, 1892; "The Yaqui Indians," *Arizona Silver Belt* (Globe City), September 17, 1896; "Yaqui Outbreak," *Graham Guardian* (Safford, AZ), November 27, 1896; "Two Americans Killed by Yaqui Indians," *Graham Guardian* (Safford, AZ), August 11, 1899; "It Is All Over: Mexican Military Forces Have Routed the Yaquis and They Are Scattered," *Graham Guardian* (Safford, AZ) August 18, 1899; *Mohave County Miner* (Mineral Park, AZ), August 26, 1899; "Dwyer Died Like a Coward," *Arizona Republican* (Phoenix), January 24, 1903; and "Yaquis Are Tamed: Seek Civilization," *Bisbee Daily Review*, May 13, 1908, 5. See this book's companion website, www.nativebutforeign.org, for additional sources.

39. For a sample of US diplomatic correspondence dealing with these concerns, see US Department of State, *Papers relating to the Foreign Relations of the United States, with the Annual Message of the President Transmitted to Congress December 5, 1905* (Washington DC: Government Printing Office, 1905), 639–48. See also Hu-DeHart, *Yaqui Resistance and Survival*, 124.

Chapter 3

1. Herbert Whitaker, "Slaveholding Americans: A Reply to Critic of 'The Planter,'" *Harpers Weekly* 53 (May 22, 1909): 27; and Janette Woodruff and Cecil Dryden, *Indian Oasis* (Caldwell, ID: Caxton Printers, 1939), 229.

2. "Life History Material: Molonko (Juan Flores)—Pascua," Spicer Papers, ASM, subgroup 8, box 8, folder 473. A Yaqui worker named Tomás Alvarez noted the great discrepancy between wages on either side of the border. Working for the railroads in Arizona during the early twentieth century, he was paid a dollar a day in the United States, compared to only one peso a day in Sonora. See Refugio Savala, "Stories about Yaqui History," unpublished manuscript, 62, Spicer Papers, ASM, subgroup 8, box 5, folder 335. For historic exchange rates, see Markus A. Denzel, *Handbook of World Exchange Rates, 1590–1914* (Burlington, VT: Ashgate, 2010), 487–92.

3. Kenneth M. Stewart, "The Southwest Indians," unpublished manuscript, 21–22, Kenneth Stewart Papers, 1946–1981, MSS-182, box 11, folder 12, Labriola Center, Arizona State University Libraries, Tempe.

4. Manuel Balbás, *Recuerdos del Yaqui: Principales Episodios Durante la Campaña de 1899 a 1901* (Mexico City: Sociedad de Edición y Librería Franco Americana, S.A., 1927), 92.

5. For a long treatment of this history, see Spicer, *Yaquis*, chap. 3 ("Yaquis versus Hacendados, 1768–1910").

6. Aleš Hrdlička, "Notes on the Indians of Sonora, Mexico," *American Anthropologist* 6 (January–March 1904): 61. Anthropologist Thomas Sheridan rightfully challenges Hrdlička's Eurocentric statement. Yaquis were indeed a people without traditional written history but not a people with no history not entailing whites. See Thomas Sheridan, "How to Tell the Story of a 'People without History': Narrative versus Ethnohistorical Approaches to the Study of the Yaqui Indians through Time," *Journal of the Southwest* 30 (Summer 1988): 168–89.

7. Fortunato Hernández, *Las Razas Indegenas de Sonora y la Guerra del Yaqui* (Mexico City: Talleres de la Casa Editorial "J. de Elizalde," 1902), vii.

8. Hu-DeHart, "Development and Rural Rebellion," 74.

9. Justo Sierra, *Evolución Política del Pueblo Mexicano, Edición Digital* (1940; repr., Alicante, Spain: Biblioteca Virtual Miguel de Cervantes, 2000).

10. Hernández, *Las Razas Indegenas de Sonora y la Guerra del Yaqui*, 101. For an excellent overview and historiography of the broad violence and trauma Yaquis suffered during this time period, see Nicole M. Guidotti-Hernández, *Unspeakable Violence: Remapping US and Mexican National Imaginaries* (Durham: Duke University Press, 2011), 173–288.

11. Balbás, *Recuerdos del Yaqui*, 103–4.

12. Cornelius C. Smith Jr., *Emilo Kosterlitzky: Eagle of Sonora and the Southwest Border* (Glendale, CA: Arthur H. Clark, 1970), 59; and José Toro Velasco, "La Rebelion Yaqui en Sonora Durante el Siglo XIX," *Revista Mexicana de Sociología* 48 (January–March 1986): 240.

13. Ramón Corral, "Biographía de José María Leyva Cajeme," in *Obras Históricas*, (Hermosillo, Sonora, Mexico: Bilbioteca Sonorense de Geografía e Historia, 1959), 155, 149.

14. Under Cajeme's leadership, complex socio-economic and political structure emerged among the eight Yaqui villages. See Hu-DeHart, *Yaqui Resistance and Survival*, 94–100; and Toro, "La Rebelion Yaqui en Sonora Durante el Siglo XIX," 240–43.

15. Francisco P. Troncoso, *Las Guerras con las Tribus Yaqui y Mayo del Estado de Sonora* (Mexico City: Tipografía del Departmento de Estado Mayor, 1905), 64–74; "Meaning of the Mormon Mission," *Mohave County Miner* (Mineral Park, AZ), January 18, 1885; and "Territorial Items," *Arizona Champion* (Peach Springs, AZ), January 31, 1885. Later coverage took a turn, speculating that the Yaqui rebellion had been instigated by Mormons. See *Arizona Champion*, March 7, 1885.

16. F. Acuña, *Sonoran Strongman: Ignacio Pesqueria and His Times* (Tucson: University of Arizona Press, 1974), 121–35; and Eduardo W. Villa, *Historia del Estado de Sonora* (1937; repr., Hermosillo, Sonora, Mexico: Gobierno del Estado de Sonora, 1984), 320–54.

17. "The Yaqui War," *Arizona Champion*, April 4, 1885; "Yaqui Fight," *Arizona Champion*, May 16, 1885; "Battle with the Yaquis," *Salt Lake Herald*, May 19, 1885; "Two Americans Executed," *Arizona Champion*, June 13, 1885; and *Arizona Champion*, August 1, 1885.

18. "News of the Week," *Mohave County Miner* (Mineral Park, AZ), May 31, 1885.

19. Some Yaqui traditions point to betrayal on Cajeme's part prior to his execution. After Cajeme was apprehended in San José by federal troops, Sonorans with considerable funds at their disposal paid the troops to leave Cajeme in Sonora and paid Cajeme to resist transport to Mexico City. They didn't want Cajeme telling federal officials of

"the evil things they had been doing," wagered Yaqui elder Guadalupe Balthazar in 1940. Cajeme's purported malfeasance, however, was accepting large sums of money in exchange for the Yaqui River Valley. Regardless, after Cajeme's execution in April 1887, whites quickly took control of Yaqui lands. See "Oration on Yaqui History since 1800" and interview with Guadalupe Balthazar, November 5, 1940, Spicer Papers, ASM, subgroup 5, box 7, folder 464.

20. For more detailed description, see Claudio Dabdoub, *Historia de El Valle del Yaqui* (Mexico City: Libreria Manuel Porrua, S.A., 1949), 130–38; Hu-DeHart, *Yaqui Resistance and Survival*, 103–13; Spicer, *Cycles of Conquest*, 70–73; and Villa, *Historia del Estado de Sonora*, 359–67.

21. Troncoso, *Las Guerras con las Tribus Yaqui y Mayo del Estado de Sonora*, 154–55.

22. Report from El Paso, June 27, 1887, in "Subjugation of the Yaquis," *Sacramento Daily Record-Union*, June 29, 1887.

23. "The Yaqui War," *Arizona Champion*, July 31, 1886.

24. Hu-DeHart, *Yaqui Resistance and Survival*, 119–21; Rosalio Moisés, Jane Holden Kelley, and William Curry Holden, *A Yaqui Life: A Personal Chronicle of a Yaqui Indian* (Lincoln: University of Nebraska Press, 1971), xvii.

25. "Oration on Yaqui History since 1800" and interview with Guadalupe Balthazar, November 5, 1940, Spicer Papers, ASM, subgroup 5, box 7, folder 464.

26. For a detailed overview of this period, see Hu-DeHart, *Yaqui Resistance and Survival*, 118–54.

27. Villa, *Historia del Estado de Sonora*, 387.

28. "Oration on Yaqui History since 1800" and interview with Guadalupe Balthazar, November 5, 1940, Spicer Papers, ASM, subgroup 5, box 7, folder 464.

29. Alfonso Fabila, *Las Tribus Yaqui de Sonora: su cultura y anhelada autodeterminación* (Mexico City: Departamento de Asuntos Indigenas, 1940), 99.

30. *Mohave County Miner* (Mineral Park, AZ), May 12, 1894, 3.

31. "Says Yaqui War Was Started by Schemers," *San Francisco Call*, August 13, 1899. See also Gustav Eisen, "Mexico to Blame for Yaqui War," *San Francisco Call*, August 9, 1899.

32. William Walter Wells, "The Yaqui Indians," *Bourbon News* (Paris, Kentucky), September 1899. See also "Spartan Courage of the Yaqui Indians," *Deseret News* (Salt Lake City), October 2, 1902.

33. John Kenneth Turner, *Barbarous Mexico* (Chicago: Charles H. Kerr, 1911), 38.

34. Hu-DeHart, *Yaqui Resistance and Survival*, 155.

35. The use of the term "extermination" has led some scholars to apply "genocidal" to their discussion of Yaqui deportation. See Glaser, "Story of Guadalupe," 67; Evelyn Hu-DeHart, "La solución final: la expulsión de los Yaquis de su Sonora natal," in *Seis expulsiones y un adios*: *Despojo y exclusión de la historia del estado político en Sonora*, ed. Aaron Grageda (Mexico City: Plaza y Valdes Editores, 2003), 133–67; Hu-DeHart, *Yaqui Resistance and Survival*, 155; Thomas E. Sheridan and Nancy J. Parezo, *Paths of Life: American Indians of the Southwest and Northern Mexico* (Tucson: University of Arizona Press, 1996), 44; Alejandro Figueroa, *Los Que Hablan Fuerte*, *Desarrollo de la Sociedad Yaqui* (Hermosillo, Sonora, Mexico: Instituto Nacional de Antropología e Historia, 1985), 91; Juan Silverio Jaime León, *Testimonios de una Mujer Yaqui* (Mexico City: Conaculta, 1988). 1; Thomas E. Sheridan, *Landscapes of Fraud: Mission Tumacácori, the Baca Float, and the Betrayal of the O'odham* (Tucson: University of

Arizona Press, 2006), 167; and Allen Wells and Gilbert Joseph, *Summer of Discontent, Seasons of Upheaval: Elite Politics and Rural Insurgency in Yucatan, 1876–1915* (Stanford: Stanford University Press, 1996), 45. See this book's companion website, www.nativebutforeign.org, for additional sources and discussion of the framing of Yaqui in history in terms of genocide, extermination, et cetera.

36. Paul Conrad, "Indians, Convicts, and Slaves: An Apache Diaspora to Cuba at the Turn of the Nineteenth-Century," in *Linking the Histories of Slavery in North America and its Borderlands*, ed. James F. Brooks and Bonnie Martin (Santa Fe: School for Advanced Research Press, 2015), 67–96; Hu-DeHart, *Yaqui Resistance and Survival*, 29; and Miguel Tinker Salas, *In the Shadow of the Eagles: Sonora and the Transformation of the Border during the Porfiriato* (Berkeley: University of California Press, 1997), 61.

37. Hu-DeHart, *Yaqui Resistance and Survival*, 113.

38. "Fooling the Indians: A Chief Assassinated and His People Deported," *Chicago Daily Tribune*, January 3, 1888. *El Democrata* may have already been known to Yaquis as a prominent troop transport and even as the vessel upon which Cajeme had been detained prior to his execution in 1887. See Dabdoub, *Historia de El Valle del Yaqui*, 138; Villa, *Historia del Estado de Sonora*, 364; Corral, "Biographía de José María Leyva Cajeme," 191; and "Two Thousand Reds Entrapped at Bicam," *San Francisco Call*, August 9, 1899.

39. Turner, *Barbarous Mexico*, 41–42. *El Democrata* was used later to transport reinforcement troops from San Blas to Guaymas in 1899.

40. Elisha Hollingsworth Talbot, "The Truth about Mexico: Government and the Yaqui Indians," *Moody's Magazine* 9 (January 1910): 24.

41. Fabila, *Las Tribus Yaqui de Sonora*, 85, 96–97. See this book's companion website, www.nativebutforeign.org, for sources and discussion of concurrent persecution of neighboring Mayos.

42. Others were sent to Campeche, Quintana Roo, and Valle Nacional in Oaxaca.

43. This report originated from the *El Paso News* but was reprinted by the *Graham Guardian*, somewhat out of step with its otherwise insensitive treatment of the Yaquis' situation. "Yaqui Indians Murdered," *Graham Guardian* (Safford, AZ), February 28, 1908.

44. "Sonora's Prodigal Yaquis," *Modern Mexico* 10 (July 1938): 18.

45. Turner, *Barbarous Mexico*, 52.

46. Quoted in Jane Holden Kelley, *Yaqui Women: Contemporary Life Histories* (Lincoln: University of Nebraska Press, 1978), 134.

47. Salas, *In the Shadow of the Eagles*, 61.

48. Kelley, *Yaqui Women*, 134.

49. "The Yaqui Situation," *Alexandria Gazette* (Washington, DC), March 6, 1905.

50. "Prefer Death to Deportation," *New-York Tribune*, February 13, 1908; "Yaquis Dislike Yucatan," *Washington (DC) Herald*, February 14, 1908.

51. Talbot, "The Truth about Mexico: Government and the American Indians," 24.

52. "Deported Indians Dumped into Sea," *Washington (DC) Herald*, March 2, 1908. See also "Yaqui Indians Murdered," *Graham Guardian* (Safford, AZ), February 28, 1908.

53. Turner, *Barbarous Mexico*, 48.

54. For more information on Yaqui slave trafficking, see Raquel Padilla Ramos, *Yucatán, el fin del sueño yaqui: el tráfico de los Yaquis y el otro triumvirate* (Hermosillo, Sonora, Mexico: Gobierno del Estado de Sonora, la Secretaría de Educación y cultura, 1995).

55. Turner, *Barbarous Mexico*, 49. Those taken to the more southerly ports on the Isthmus of Tehautepec, rather than San Blas, were taken by rail over the mountains to Veracruz. See "Yaqui Indians Murdered," *Graham Guardian* (Safford, AZ), February 28, 1908.

56. Kelley, *Yaqui Women*, 135.

57. The purchase of Yaqui slaves by *hacendados* was recounted by Chepa Moreno and Dominga Ramírez, both women interviewed by Jane Holden Kelley 1968–72. See Kelley, *Yaqui Women*, 136, 159.

58. Turner, *Barbarous Mexico*, 49–51.

59. "Oration on Yaqui History since 1800" and interview with Guadalupe Balthazar, November 5, 1940, Spicer Papers, ASM, subgroup 5, box 7, folder 464.

60. John Kenneth Turner, "Barbarous Mexico: The Tragic Story of the Yaqui Indians," *American Magazine* 69 (November 1909): 39–40, 46. Most of these details were repeated in Turner, *Barbarous Mexico*.

61. Jane Holden Kelley to Edward Spicer, May 12, 1969, Spicer Papers, ASM, subgroup 5, box 1.

62. For a full history of the links between North American agriculture and Mexican henequen production, see Sterling Evans, *Bound in Twine: The History and Ecology of the Henequen-Wheat Complex for Mexico and the American and Canadian Plains, 1880–1950* (College Station: Texas A&M University Press, 2007). For detailed account of the deportation process, see León, *Testimonios de una Mujer Yaqui*.

63. John Turner claimed that slavery in Valle Nacional was even worse than in Yucatán. According to his sources, only 5 percent of Yaqui and other Indigenous slaves lived more than seven to eight months in Valle Nacional. According to Turner, one of Valle Nacional's largest tobacco growers told him: "By the sixth or seventh month they begin to die off like flies at the first winter frost, and after that they're not worth keeping. The cheapest thing to do is to let them die; there are plenty more where they came from." Turner, *Barbarous Mexico*, 67.

64. "Indians to Fight Indians: Mexico Pits Yaquis against Mayas, Decreasing Both Tribes," *Valentine (NE) Democrat*, December 5, 1907.

65. Claudia B. Haake, *The State, Removal and Indigenous Peoples in the United States and Mexico, 1620–2000* (Routledge: New York, 2007), 141–42. For information on the Yucatán plantation system into which Yaqui labor was integrated, see Allen Wells, *Yucatan's Gilded Age: Haciendas, Henequen, and International Harvester, 1860–1915* (Albuquerque: University of New Mexico Press, 1985); and Evans, *Bound in Twine*.

66. "Mexico Will Deport Yaqui Indians from Sonora," *Deseret Evening News* (Salt Lake City,) February 5, 1907; and Walter Adolf Roberts, "Tragedy of the Yaqui," *Overland Monthly* 52 (July 1908): 119–21.

67. Andres Molina Enríquez, *La Revolución Agraria en Mexico* (Mexico City: Instituto Nacional de Estudios Históricos de la Revolucíon Mexicana, 1976), 359.

68. Kelley, *Yaqui Women*, 136–39, 160–65.

69. For more recent overviews of the deportation process and experience of Yaquis exiled to the Yucatán, see Haake, *The State, Removal and Indigenous Peoples*, 121–56; and Evans, *Bound in Twine*, 67–90. For narratives of the return to or visiting of Sonora, see Kirstin C. Erickson, *Yaqui Homeland and Homeplace: The Everyday Production of Ethnic Identity* (Tucson: University of Arizona Press, 2008), 49–54.

70. Sheridan and Parezo, *Paths of Life*, 45.

71. Hu-DeHart, "Development and Rural Rebellion," 79; and Kelley, *Yaqui Women*, 159.

72. José Toro Velasco, "Colonización, Agua y Control Social: El Caso de los Yaquis de Sonora," in *Indigenismo, Evolución de Una Práctica* (Mexico: Instituto Nacional Indigenista, 1979), 42.

73. See Haake, *The State, Removal and Indigenous Peoples*, 134; and Hu-DeHart, "Development and Rural Rebellion," 83.

74. Hu-DeHart, "Development and Rural Rebellion," 83; and Sheridan and Parezo, *Paths of Life*, 44.

75. Figueroa, *Los Que Hablan Fuerte, Desarrollo de la Sociedad Yaqui*, 91.

76. Phoebe Bogan, "The Yaqui with Us, 1909," unpublished manuscript, 4, Bogan Manuscripts, 1909–1926, MS 0081, ASHS; Dane Coolidge, "The Yaquis in Exile," *Sunset* 23 (September 1909): 300; and "Yaquis Leaving Sonora," *Graham Guardian* (Safford, AZ), August 8, 1902.

77. Arizona Yaqui leader Juan Pistola, quoted in "Indian Immigrants," *Los Angeles Times*, October 13, 1920.

78. "Yaqui Dancers at San Xavier," *Arizona Republican* (Phoenix), September 15, 1890; *Star Nogales*, October 13, 1892; *Tucson Star*, April 20, 1894; "Badly Frightened: Superstitious Yaquis Take to the Woods," *Graham Guardian* (Safford, AZ), June 25, 1897, 1; Glaser, "Story of Guadalupe," 21; "Oration on Yaqui History since 1800" and interview with Guadalupe Balthazar, November 5, 1940, Spicer Papers, ASM, subgroup 5, box 7, folder 464; and Felipe Molina to Edward Spicer, 1980, "Yaqui Historical Chart," Spicer Papers, ASM, subgroup 5, box 5, folder 278. See also *Arizona Republican* (Phoenix), August 27, 1890; *Arizona Republican* (Phoenix), January 9, 1892; and *Mohave County Miner* (Mineral Park, AZ), April 7, 1895.

79. Nicole M. Guidotti-Hernández, *Unspeakable Violence: Remapping US and Mexican National Imaginaries* (Durham: Duke University Press, 2011), 202–3.

80. See Turner, "Barbarous Mexico"; Turner, *Barbarous Mexico*; "Yaquis in Slavery, Mexico Accused of Grave Crimes, Indians Said to Be Killed or Sold by Order of the Government," *New-York Tribune*, October 31, 1909; "Slavery in Mexico," *Pensacola Journal*, November 21, 1909; "Says Slavery Tale Is Not Distorted, Mexican Mining Man Adds His Confirmation: Declares that Kidnapping of Yaquis for Slavish Tasks in Yucatan Still Goes on in Sonora," *Los Angeles Herald*, December 23, 1909; and "Yaquis Should Have Their Rights," *Bisbee Daily Review*, July 6, 1911.

81. Edward Spicer, Notes from Immigration Office, November 22, 1936, Spicer Papers, ASM, subgroup 8, box 7, folder 438.

82. See this book's companion website, www.nativebutforeign.org, for sample reports of Yaqui-Mexico warfare that circulated throughout the United States and Arizona. Various American businesses petitioned US officials about the loss of capital and property due to the fighting in Sonora. At one point, concerned companies even solicited for American ex-soldiers to work as private security forces in Sonora. See "Ex-American Soldiers Wanted," *Graham Guardian* (Safford, AZ,) June 22, 1906. For a long account of Sonoran issues written at the time, see Harris, *By Path and Trail*, 7–55.

83. Marc M. Reynolds, "The Scourge of the Yaquis: Why American Lives and Capital in Mexico Are Menaced by a Handful of Savages," *Harpers Weekly* 52 (May 2, 1908): 12.

84. Quotation: "From Old Mexico," *Ogden (UT) Standard*, December 20, 1909. For examples of more apathetic renderings, see "Greene's Camp Sage: Mining Magnate Protected by the Mexican Government," *Salt Lake Herald*, July 9, 1906; and "Revengeful Indian Tribe: Yaquis' Deadly Enmity to Mexican Government," *Sun* (New York City), July 7, 1907.

85. See Elisha H. Talbot, "The Truth about Mexico," *Moody's Magazine* 8 (December 1909): 427–34; Talbot, "The Truth about Mexico: Government and the Yaqui Indians," *Moody's Magazine* 9 (January 1910): 16–30; Talbot, "The Truth about Mexico: Peonage," *Moody's Magazine* 9 (February 1910): 105–17; and Talbot, "The Truth about Mexico: Conclusion," *Moody's Magazine* 9 (March 1019): 181–89.

86. Powell Clayton to John Hay, March 16, 1905, in US Department of State, *Papers relating to the Foreign Relations of the United States . . . 1905*, 640.

87. News clippings from *Daily Record*, November 29, 1905, and *Mexican Herald*, December 31, 1905, cited in Fenton McCreery to John Hay, December 2, 1905, in ibid., 648; and Fenton McCreery to John Hay, January 2, 1906, in US Department of State, *Papers relating to the Foreign Relations of the United States with the Annual Message of the President Transmitted to Congress December 3, 1906*, vol. 2 (Washington, DC: Government Printing Office, 1906), 1134.

88. Gustav Eisen, "Mexico to Blame for Yaqui War," *San Francisco Call*, August 9, 1899.

89. Turner, *Barbarous Mexico*, 38.

90. "Mexico Will Deport Yaqui Indians from Sonora," *Deseret Evening News* (Salt Lake City), February 5, 1907. Mine and railroad operators in Sonora, especially those owned by US companies, were particularly vocal in such protest. See Shelley Bowen Hatfield, *Chasing Shadows: Apaches and Yaquis along the United States-Mexico Border, 1876–1911* (Albuquerque: University of New Mexico Press, 1998), 8.

91. "Part of the Yaquis Have Been Removed," *Graham Guardian* (Safford, AZ), January 11, 1901.

92. An exception was the *San Francisco Call*, which published a series of reports in 1903 and 1904 that were decidedly pro-Mexican. See "Yaqui Indians to Be Deported," *San Francisco Call*, August 23, 1903; "Savages Threaten Outbreak: Troops in Sonora Arrest Conspiring Yaquis," *San Francisco Call*, April 17, 1904; "Indians Kill from Ambush," *San Francisco Call*, August 5, 1904; and "Yaqui Indians Spread Terror," *San Francisco Call*, August 16, 1904.

93. "Almost a Truth," *Graham Guardian* (Safford, AZ) July 11, 1902. The *Guardian*'s report responded to stories such as one printed in the *Mohave County Miner* (Mineral Park, AZ), June 26, 1902.

94. Frank Aley, "The Only Nacozari, and How I Got There," *Graham Guardian* (Safford, AZ), January 26, 1906.

95. "Mexico Will Wage a War of Extermination," *Pensacola Journal*, January 8, 1905; Stephan Bonsal, "The Last Chapter in the History of a Race that is Doomed," *Washington Post*, March 8, 1908. See also "All Yaquis to Be Deported: Peaceful Members of Tribe Carried 2,000 Miles from Homes," *Washington Herald*, November 12, 1907; "Extinguishing a Race," *Imperial Valley Press* (El Centro, CA), March 7, 1908; Marc M. Reynolds, "Scourge of the Yaquis," *Harpers Weekly* 52 (May 2, 1908): 10–12; Walter Adolf Roberts, "Tragedy of the Yaqui," *Overland Monthly* 52 (July 1908): 119–21; Andrew Milligan Hoyt, "A Plea for the Yaqui," *Overland Monthly* 52 (July 1908): 122–23; "More Yaquis Deported," *Washington Herald*, July 21, 1908; Baily Millard, "The Yaquis: Most Stubborn Fighters on Earth," *Los Angeles Herald*, January 31, 1909; "Yaquis in Slavery, Mexico Accused of Grave Crimes, Indians Said to Be Killed or Sold by Order of the Government," *New-York Tribune*, October 31, 1909; "Slavery in Mexico," *Pensacola Journal*, November 21, 1909; "Says Slavery Tale Is Not Distorted, Mexican Mining Man Add His Confirmation: Declares that Kidnapping

of Yaquis for Slavish Tasks in Yucatan Still Goes On in Sonora," *Los Angeles Herald*, December 23, 1909.

96. Whitaker, "Slaveholding Americans."

Chapter 4

1. "Cree," undated manuscript, RBSA, 1.

2. James Daschuk, *Clearing the Plains: Disease, Politics, and Loss of Aboriginal Life* (Regina: University of Regina Press, 2013), 100–101.

3. "Riel Rebellion," *Daily Miner* (Butte), March 31, 1885; and "The Situation at Battleford," *River Press* (Fort Benton, MT), April 8, 1885.

4. See this book's companion website, hwww.nativebutforeign.org, for an extensive list of regional and national newspaper articles detailing Big Bear's activities.

5. For some of the conflicting portrayals of the events, see Joseph F. Dion, *My Tribe, the Crees* (Calgary: Glenbow Museum, 1979); Isabelle Little Bear, "My Own Story," in *Reflections: A History of Elk Point and District*, ed. Mary Bennett (Winnipeg: Elk Point and District Historical Society, 1977); and William Bleasdell Cameron, *Blood Red the Sun* (Edmonton: Hurtig, 1977).

6. Hugh Aylmer Dempsey, *Big Bear: The End of Freedom* (Lincoln: University of Nebraska Press, 1984), 120.

7. Thomas Flanagan, *Louis "David" Riel: Prophet of the New World* (Toronto: University of Toronto Press, 1979), 123.

8. Interview with George Denny, August 25, 1960, Verne Dusenberry Papers, 1927–1966, Accession 85015 (hereafter Dusenberry Papers), MSU, box 6, folder 11.

9. Ibid. See also D.G. Mandlebaum, "Peace Hills or Hobema transcript," Provincial Archives of Alberta, tape IH-DM.188, transcript disc 145. Also available at Ourspace, University of Regina, http://hdl.handle.net/10294/1824.

10. "Massacreing Settlers," *Springfield (OH) Globe-Republic*, April 11, 1885; "Fort Pitt and Frog Lake," *New North-West* (Deer Lodge, MT), May 1, 1885; and "Big Bear's Cruelty to Prisoners and Settlers," *Devils Lake (ND) Inter-Ocean*, May 30, 1885.

11. Joseph Edmund Collins, *The Story of Louis Riel the Rebel Chief* (Toronto: Rose Publishing, 1885), 151–52. Charles Mulvaney's 1885 history of the rebellion painted Big Bear in equally menacing light. See Charles Pelham Mulvaney, *The History of the North-West Rebellion of 1885* (Toronto: A. H. Hovey, 1885), 88–93. Other distrusted figures, such as Little Poplar, added to Canadian concern that trouble loomed. See J. M. Rae to L. Vankoughnet, March 31, 1885, in *Telegrams of the North-West Campaign, 1885*, ed. Desmond Morton and Reginald H. Roy (Toronto: Champlain Society, 1972), 70.

12. Norman MacLeod to Bessie MacLeod, June 7, 1885, Norman Thomas MacLeod, Personal Correspondence, M 785, Glenbow Archives, Calgary.

13. Collins, *Story of Louis Riel*, 175.

14. Inspector Morris to Major General Fred Middleton, April 9, 1885, in Morton and Roy, eds., *Telegrams of the North-West Campaign*, 154.

15. Jill St. Germain, *Broken Treaties: United States and Canadian Relations with Lakotas and the Plains Cree, 1868–1885* (Lincoln: University of Nebraska Press, 2009), 325.

16. This was true in individual Cree bands as well as broader Cree coalitions. For details on individual plains Cree leaders and the diversity of personalities, loyalties, and

allegiances, see Fraser A. William, "Plains Cree, Assiniboine, and Saulteaux (Plains) Bands, 1874–84," 1963, M 4379, PAM 970.3cr F842p, Glenbow Archives, Calgary.

17. Isabelle Little Bear, "My Own Story," 199.

18. Peter Charlebois, *The Life of Louis Riel* (Toronto: New Canada Publications, 1975), 161; and William Bleasdell Cameron, *Blood Red the Sun* (Edmonton: Hurtig, 1977), 46.

19. Isabelle Little Bear, "My Own Story," 199.

20. Cameron, *Blood Red the Sun*, 51; and Isabelle Little Bear, "My Own Story," 200. Mary Dion's firsthand account is similar to that of Isabelle Little Bear. "When more shots rang out as he rode to meet the onslaught, he cried at the top of his great voice, 'At least spare the men of prayer!' But he might as well have appeared to a pack of wolves; in a very short time all the male residents that could be found were slain." Quoted in Dion, *My Tribe, the Crees*, 96.

21. Charlebois, *Life of Louis Riel*, 161; and interview with Four Souls, May 1975, in Littlejohn, "Indian Oral Tradition," 103.

22. Interview with Mary PeeMee, Summer 1975, in Littlejohn, "Indian Oral Tradition," 107.

23. Old Kenyan, as voiced in Edward Ahenakew, *Voice of the Plains Cree* (Toronto: McClelland & Stewart, 1973), 108–9.

24. Interview with Mary PeeMee and interview with Four Souls, in Littlejohn, "Indian Oral Tradition," 107, 98. See this book's companion website, www.nativebutforeign.org, for information on Big Bear's relationship with Louis Riel and Riel's connection to Frog Lake.

25. Collins, *Story of Louis Riel*, 175.

26. Desmond Morton, *The Last War Drum: The North West Campaign of 1885* (Toronto: Canadian War Museum, 1972), 161.

27. Quoted in Dion, *My Tribe, the Crees*, 90–91; and interview with Four Souls, in Littlejohn, "Indian Oral Tradition," 87–88.

28. Interview with Jimmy Chief, in Dempsey, *Big Bear*, 153–54.

29. Wilbur Franklin Bryant, *The Blood of Abel* (Hastings, NE: Gazette-Journal, 1887), 85.

30. See interview, Sam Pritchard Fonds, M 4138, Glenbow Archives, Calgary; Cameron, *Blood Red the Sun*, 4; interview with Four Souls, in Littlejohn, "Indian Oral Tradition," 102; and D. Bruce Sealey, *The Métis, Canada's Forgotten People* (Winnipeg: Manitoba Métis Federation Press, 1975), 123.

31. See this book's companion website, http://www.nativebutforeign.org, for sources and discussion of Canadian military correspondence concerning Wandering Spirit.

32. Blair Stonechild, *Loyal till Death: Indians and the North-West Rebellion* (Calgary: Fifth House, 1997), 222; and Douglas W Light, *Footprints in the Dust* (North Battleford, Saskatchewan: Turner-Warwick, 1987), 534.

33. Bob Smallboy related that during their subsequent trek south to Montana, Imasees had a vision while fasting. A spirit bear visited him and gave him a new name, Kakikaymawkwa, or Forever Bear. He would later modify this to Maskosis, "Little Bear." Gary Botting, *Chief Smallboy: In Pursuit of Freedom* (Calgary: Fifth House, 2005), 25.

34. Stonechild, *Loyal till Death*, 224.

35. Isabelle Little Bear, "My Own Story," 199.

36. Dempsey, *Big Bear*, 144–45.

37. Quoted in ibid., 148; and Dion, *My Tribe, the Crees*, 88.

38. Interview with Four Souls, in Littlejohn, "Indian Oral Tradition," 85–86.

39. Interview with Mary PeeMee, in Littlejohn, "Indian Oral Tradition," 106.

40. Interview with Grant Chief Stick, Havre, Montana, August 26, 1974, RBSA.

41. Interview with Francis Harper, in Littlejohn, "Indian Oral Tradition," 110.

42. This comes from the eyewitness account of Joseph Dion's mother, in Dion, *My Tribe, the Crees*, 95.

43. Isabelle Little Bear, "My Own Story," 199.

44. Dion, *My Tribe, the Crees*, 88.

45. Auguste Henri de Tremaudan, *Hold High Your Heads: History of the Métis Nation in Western Canada* (Winnipeg: Pemmican Publications, 1982), 187.

46. Quoted in Norma Sluman and Jean Goodwill, *John Tootoosis: Biography of a Cree Leader* (Ottawa: Golden Dog Press, 1982), 63.

47. Dempsey, *Big Bear*, 149.

48. Ahenakew, *Voice of the Plains Cree*, 108–9. Years after the fact, white Montanans remembered Cree involvement, certainly affecting Cree settlement in Montana. For a good example, see "Riel Tampers with Indians" and "The Frog Lake Massacre," *Evening Star* (Washington, DC), July 5, 1905.

49. Isabelle Little Bear, "My Own Story," 199.

50. Interview with Four Souls, in Littlejohn, "Indian Oral Tradition," 91.

51. Raymond Gray, "The Cree Indians," Works Progress Administration, Federal Writers' Project, 1942, 257.

52. Interview with Chief Stick, Havre, Montana, August 26, 1974, RBSA.

53. Northwest Mounted Police Superintendent J. H. McIllree was quickly notified of Little Bear's flight, and he sent scouts in pursuit and notified Fort Assiniboine in Montana. See Hogue, *Crossing the Line*, 74. See this book's companion website, www.nativebutforeign.org, for sources and discussion of the rumors surrounding Little Bear's flight and suspected malfeasance.

54. See map from Stonechild, *Loyal till Death*, 194.

55. "Story of Little Bear," *Kalispell Times*, June 30, 1932. Cree elder Grant Chief Stick later explained that Little Bear's original contingent was only twenty people but that "more and more people joined him during the evening. There came to be quite a few going with him. When they moved up here [Montana] there were quite a few camps. They were all his people." Interview with Grant Chief Stick, August 27, 1974, RBSA, 6.

56. Gray, "Cree Indians," 238. One traditional story, related by Gabriel Belgarde, tells of two Cree men who accompanied the fleeing band. Traveling in the rear of the group, the two—A-pi-chee-s and Man-too-a-tim—both "had a feeling that there was going to be trouble." Quoted in Gray, "Cree Indians," 25–26.

57. "Louis Riel's Quest for Justice" manuscript, RBSA; and Gray, "Cree Indians," 203.

58. *Great Falls Tribune*, July 23, 1885.

59. "Riel Rebellion," *Daily Miner* (Butte), March 31, 1885.

60. "The Fenians Suspected," *Daily Independent* (Helena), April 9, 1885; and "Murderous Redskins," *Daily Miner* (Butte), April 11, 1885.

61. "Northern News," *River Press* (Fort Benton, MT) April 29, 1885; and *River Press* (Fort Benton, MT), October 7, 1885. See also James Dempsey, "Little Bear's Band: Canadian or American Indians?" *Alberta History* 41 (Autumn 1993): 3.

62. Thomas Wessel, "A History of the Rocky Boy's Indian Reservation," undated manuscript, Stone Child College Library, call no. A1 970.49 W86.

63. Four Souls recounted that around two hundred individuals had fled south. Interview with Four Souls, in Littlejohn, "Indian Oral Tradition," 112. See also Stonechild, *Loyal till Death*, 227–28.

64. Interview with Four Souls, in Littlejohn, "Indian Oral Tradition," 91. Four Souls's telling does not name the officer, but C. S. Otis was the post commander at the time and can be inferred as the man with whom the conversation took place.

65. Interview with Chief Stick, Havre, Montana, August 26, 1974, RBSA.

66. Verne Dusenberry's *Montana Cree* mistakenly stated that the first notice of the Cree presence was a *River Press* story on December 20, 1885, and many works have repeated this error. The fact that Crees arrived and were noticed by local and federal US officials earlier than December 30, 1885, is significant. For nearly two and a half months before that *River Press* article, military officials engaged in a complex debate over how to attend to the inbound Natives. They were not a transient population haphazardly discovered in late December. They had been a significant concern and object of instant debate. See Dusenberry, *Montana Cree*, 32.

67. US Department of the Treasury, *An Estimate from the Acting Secretary of the Interior of an Appropriation for the Relief of Renegade British Cree Indians in Montana, and to Prevent Their Starvation*, 49th Cong., 1st sess., House Executive Document 231, 1886, 2; and Sergeant Paterson of the Northwest Mounted Police Reporting on His Visit to Montana, 1885, record group 10, Black Series, volume 3722, file 24,125, reel c-10126, NAC, 4.

68. US Department of the Treasury, *An Estimate from the Acting Secretary*, 2.

69. Inspector M.A. Thomas to the secretary of the interior, October 19, 1885, Edward E. Barry Jr. Collection, 1874–1977, Collection 2058, series 1, box 1, MSU.

70. Ibid.

71. Sergeant Paterson of the Northwest Mounted Police Reporting on His Visit to Montana.

72. John Peter Turner, *North-West Mounted Police, 1873–1893*, vol. 2 (Ottawa: King's Printer, 1950), 253–54.

73. The State Department explained, "If . . . there is satisfactory proof that a demand is coming in due form, they can be arrested to await such demand. If they are guilty of offenses within the jurisdiction of the United States, they can be proceeded against for such offences; but they cannot be prosecuted in courts or before our military tribunals for offenses committed in the Dominion of Canada." See US Department of the Treasury, *An Estimate from the Acting Secretary*, 2.

74. "Pity in a Hostile Camp," *Forest and Stream* 26 (January 13, 1887): 481; and *River Press* (Fort Benton, MT), November 3, 1885.

75. Frank Bird Linderman, *Montana Adventure: The Recollections of Frank B. Linderman* (Lincoln: University of Nebraska Press, 1968), 2, 67.

76. Linderman to Mrs. Albert J. Roberts, March 12, 1918, Frank B. Linderman Estate. These papers are privately held and managed by Linderman's granddaughter Sally Hatfield. Mrs. Hatfield has actively published much of her grandfather's previously unpublished work over the past few years. The family still owns and maintains Linderman's cabin and property on Goose Bay, Flathead Lake, and lives in nearby Kalispell.

77. Jack Holterman, *Chippewa-Cree in Glacier Country* (West Glacier, MT: Glacier Natural History Association, 1991), 5.

78. US Department of the Treasury, *An Estimate from the Acting Secretary*, 3.

79. Dusenberry, *Montana Cree*, 32; and Larry Burt, "Nowhere Left to Go: Montana's

Crees, Metis, and Chippewas and the Creation of Rocky Boy's Reservation," *Great Plains Quarterly* 7 (Summer 1987): 199.

80. There is some confusion over this crucial communiqué. In the 1960s, Verne Dusenberry indicated that President Grover Cleveland declared the amnesty. As author of one of the few monograph-length works published on Montana's Crees, his statement has been cited by most scholars since. Dusenberry, however, offers no source for this assertion, and scholars have yet to locate such a communiqué in government or military records. Other reports indicated that the Department of the Interior directed the Department of War to prevent Fort Assiniboine from deporting them. It may be that Dusenberry assumed that this meant Cleveland had been the source of the Interior Department's directive. See "The Captured Crees," *River Press* (Fort Benton, MT), December 30, 1886; and Dusenberry, *Montana Cree*, 33.

81. Interview with Four Souls, in Littlejohn, "Indian Oral Tradition," 91–92.

82. Interview with Chief Stick, Havre, Montana, August 26, 1974, RBSA.

83. US Department of the Treasury, *An Estimate from the Acting Secretary*, 3.

84. Ibid., 3–4.

85. Ibid., 1.

86. Gray, "Cree Indians," 100. This concern continued well into 1887. In April, Canadian and American Indian agents each claimed that the other side's wards had engaged in horse-thieving raids, and neither side owned up to such a thing. See "Depredations by Indians," *New York Times*, April 15, 1887. They finally concluded the debate when stolen horses were returned in the early summer. "Stolen Horses Returned," *New York Times*, June 10, 1887.

87. *River Press* (Fort Benton, MT), November 3, 1886.

88. Gray, "Cree Indians," 105.

89. *River Press* (Fort Benton, MT), January 19, 1887. See also Dusenberry, *Montana Cree*, 33.

90. Gray, "Cree Indians," 101, 106.

91. *Helena Independent*, January 9, 1887.

92. Gray, "Cree Indians," 110–11.

93. *Helena Independent*, January 27, 1887.

94. Gray, "Cree Indians," 111.

95. *River Press* (Fort Benton, MT), April 24, 1887.

96. "No Room for the Crees," *River Press* (Fort Benton, MT), August 17, 1887. See also *Great Falls Tribune*, August 20, 1887; and *Butte Miner*, August 20, 1887.

97. Officials at Fort Assiniboine complicated matters further by moving ahead with plans to deport certain Crees. In October 1887, officials at Fort Assiniboine collaborated directly with NWMP officials at Maple Creek, just northeast of the Cypress Hills. A group of over one hundred, reportedly including Lucky Man and Little Bear, were sent to the line, but Fort Assiniboine troops left them there unattended. Many dispersed before the NWMP arrived. In the ensuing months, the NWMP was unable to sort out who had been deported and who had not. Evidence suggests that many simply returned to Montana. See R. B. Deane to G. E. Sanders, October 11, 1887; G. E. Sanders to G. H. McIlree, October 22, 1887; G. H. McIlree to commissioner of Indians affairs, October 23, 1887; Commission of Indian Affairs to G. E. Sanders, October 24, 1887; G. E. Sanders to commissioner of Indian affairs, October 26, 1887; and G. E. Sanders to G. H. McIlree, October 30, 1887—all in Gilbert Edward Sanders Correspondence and Reports, M 1093, file 58, Glenbow Archives, Calgary.

98. Commissioner J. D. C. Atkins to Department of the Interior, November 1, 1887,

in Department of Indian Affairs, *Relief for the Cree Indians, Montana Territory: Letter from the Secretary of the Interior*, 50th Cong., 1st sess., House Executive Document 341, 1888, 6.

99. By the end of 1887, the War Department had spent a total of $3,374.25 to furnish supplies to the Montana Crees. Ibid., 2.

100. Years later the *Anaconda Standard* related the story. "The cowboys poisoned several hundred coyotes and threw the carcasses into the ravines where the Indians found them and devoured them and seemed to grow fat on the poisoned meat." "Those Dirty Crees: Silver Bow County Would Gladly Part with the Renegades," *Anaconda Standard*, January 19, 1896.

101. Commissioner J. D. C. Atkins to Department of the Interior, November 1, 1887, in Department of Indian Affairs, *Relief for the Cree Indians, Montana Territory*, 2.

102. Ibid., 3.

103. *Journal of the Senate*, June 4, 1888, 50th Cong., 1st sess., Serial 2503, 910; and "Starving Indians," *Benton Weekly Record* (Fort Benton, MT), July 14, 1888.

104. One 1889 account notes that the military was escorting groups north, even without appropriations to support the effort or any orders do so. Later deportation policy, therefore, simply built on existing practice. See *Rising Sun* (Sun River, MT), May 12, 1889.

Chapter 5

1. US Attorney Elbert Weed to US Secretary of War Stephen Benton Elkins, December 2, 1892, Thomas O. Miles Reminiscence (hereafter Miles Remin.), SC 475, MSHS.

2. Dusenberry, *Montana Cree*, 35.

3. "Oust the Crees," *Montanian* (Choteau), May 30, 1890.

4. "Well Rounded Complaint," *River Press* (Fort Benton, MT), June 9, 1890.

5. Ibid.; Gray, "Cree Indians," 130. Crees' threat to whites was a common thread in the *River Press*'s campaign against the Crees. Of whites near Dupuyer Creek and Choteau the paper wrote, "This may be unintentional on the part of the Indians but it's tough on the white women and children to be scared out of their wits every time the husband and father leaves home for a few hours." See *River Press* (Fort Benton, MT), July 2, 1890.

6. Ibid., 141. A monthly grand jury report from Fort Benton stressed that tax payers could not afford to support the foreign interlopers, another growing common complaint. "Grand Jury Report, May Term 1890," *Montanian* (Choteau), May 30, 1890.

7. Gray, "Cree Indians," 136, 138–39; and *River Press* (Fort Benton, MT), January 21, 1891.

8. Thomas O. Miles to Governor Toole, November 22, 1891, Montana Governors Papers, Joseph K. Toole Administration, MC 35a (hereafter Toole Papers), MSHS, box 2, folder 5.

9. James G. Blaine to Elbert D. Weed, January 26, 1892, Miles Remin., MSHS.

10. Gray, "Cree Indians," 143–47.

11. Julian Pauncefote to James G. Blaine, April 6, 1892, Miles Remin., MSHS.

12. Report of the Canadian Privy Council, March 29, 1892, Miles Remin., MSHS.

13. Gray, "Cree Indians," 143.

14. L. A. Grant to Joseph Toole, September 24, 1892, Toole Papers, MSHS.

15. Gray, "Cree Indians," 147–52.

16. *Daily Inter-Mountain* (Butte, MT), November 30, 1892.

17. Elbert D. Weed to Thomas O. Miles, December 2, 1892, Miles Remin., MSHS.
18. Elbert D. Weed to L. A. Grant, December 2, 1892, Miles Remin., MSHS.
19. Quoted in *Anaconda Standard*, February 12, 1893.
20. *River Press* (Fort Benton, MT) October 18, 1893.
21. Gray, "Cree Indians," 18–19.
22. *Great Falls Leader*, July 20, 1893.
23. Little Bear to President Cleveland, October 14, 1893, RBSA.
24. See Governor Rickards to secretary of the interior, October 12, 1893, MSHS, Little Bear Vertical File; *River Press* (Fort Benton, MT), October 18, 1893, and November 15, 1893.
25. Gray, "Cree Indians," 21.
26. Little Bear to Governor Rickards, August 31, 1893, Little Bear Vertical File, MSHS.
27. "The Cree Indians," *Salt Lake Herald*, November 25, 1893.
28. "Little Bear and Other Crees Chiefs Explain All about the Sun Dance," *Great Falls Weekly Tribune*, May 25, 1894.
29. "The Ministers Protest," *Great Falls Weekly Tribune*, May 25, 1894.
30. See *Great Falls Weekly Tribune*, May 27, 1894; and "Minister Talks to the Crees," *Great Falls Weekly Tribune*, May 28, 1894.
31. Quoted in *Great Falls Daily Tribune*, June 3, 1894.
32. Governor Rickards' Sun Dance Proclamation, June 5, 1894, RBSA.
33. Quoted in "In the Crees Big Camp," *Havre Advertiser*, June 7, 1894.
34. "Letter to Editor," *Great Falls Tribune*, June 8, 1894; *Great Falls Tribune*, June 10, 1894; *Havre Advertiser*, June 14, 1894, and *Havre Advertiser*, June 21, 1894. Legal action was even taken against the governor's proclamation, seeking an injunction against its enforcement. The injunction was not granted. See *Great Falls Tribune*, June 12, 1894; and "That Sun Dance," *Havre Advertiser*, June 14, 1894.
35. "They Danced," *Havre Advertiser*, June 21, 1894.
36. *Montanian* (Choteau), June 19, 1894, as reported in "Twenty Years Ago," *Choteau Montanian*, June 19, 1914.
37. "General Assembly: The House," *Helena Weekly Independent*, January 31, 1895.
38. "Deportation of 1896," undated anonymous manuscript, 1, RBSA.
39. "Governor J. E. Rickards to Richard Olney, January 21, 1896, in Senate Committee on Foreign Relations, *Report to Accompany Amendment of Mr. Carter to HR 8293*, 54th Cong., 1st sess., S. Rep. 821, 2.
40. "Those Dirty Crees: Silver Bow County Would Gladly Part with the Renegades," *Anaconda Standard*, January 19, 1896.
41. Sharrock and Sharrock, *History of the Cree Indian Territorial Expansion*, 190; and "Deportation of 1896, 1, RBSA.
42. Frank B. Linderman, "The Rocky Boy Renegades," *Indians at Work* 4 (January 1937): 23–28.
43. In two cases, he saw that they were allowed to return to Montana. See Richard Burton Deane to NWMP Commissioner, June 26, 1896, record group 10, Black Series, vol. 3863, file 84,138–1, reel C-10152, NAC.
44. Sharrock and Sharrock, *History of the Cree Indian Territorial Expansion*, 345.
45. "Deportation of 1896," 1, RBSA.
46. Richard Olney to J. E. Rickards, January 30, 1896, in Senate Committee on Foreign Relations, *Report to Accompany Amendment of Mr. Carter to HR 8293*, 1.

47. J. E. Rickards to Richard Olney, April 8, 1896, in Senate Committee on Foreign Relations, *Report to Accompany Amendment of Mr. Carter to HR 8293*, 2, “Cree Indians Must Go: Montana Demands that the Disease-Breeders Be Removed Instanter,” *Daily Inter Ocean* (Chicago), February 7, 1896; A. E. Forget to J. E. Rickards, April 1, 1896, in Senate Committee on Foreign Relations, *Report to Accompany Amendment of Mr. Carter to HR 8293*, 3; “The Cree Indians: Canada Will Take Charge of Them All Hereafter,” *Los Angeles Times*, April 9, 1896; and “Cree Indians to Be Deported: The Canadian Government Consents to Take Charge of Them,” *Washington Post*, April 10, 1896.

48. “Crees to Be Deported,” *Montanian* (Choteau), April 17, 1896; “Deportation of 1896,” 2–3, RBSA; and “The Cree Situation,” *Great Falls Tribune*, June 11, 1896.

49. “Our Friends, the Crees,” *Montanian* (Choteau), May 1, 1896. See also “Round up the Crees,” *Anaconda Standard*, May 14, 1896; and *Columbian* (Columbia Falls, MT), June 18, 1896.

50. US Department of the Treasury, *Appropriations, New Offices, Etc.,* 54th Cong., 1st sess., S. Doc. 316, Serial 3360, 414; *Journal of the Senate*, 54th Cong., 1st sess., Serial 3346-A, 293; *Journal of the House*, 54th Cong., 1st sess., Serial 3367-A, pp. 468, 474, 504.

51. “They Are Willing,” *Montanian* (Choteau), May 22, 1896.

52. “Council of Cree . . . Will Go Conditionally,” *Anaconda Standard*, June 17, 1896.

53. “Buffalo Coat Will Resist,” *Great Falls Tribune*, May 21, 1896. See also “Buffalo Coat Petition to Stay,” *Anaconda Standard*, June 20, 1896; and “A Proclamation,” January 21, 1887, in *Acts of the Parliament of the United Kingdom* (Ottawa: Brown Chamberlain, 1887), clvi.

54. *Montanian* (Choteau), June 5, 1896.

55. Gray, “Cree Indians,” 42.

56. “More Facts About the Crees,” *Great Falls Tribune*, June 6, 1896.

57. “The Cree Situation,” *Great Falls Tribune*, June 11, 1896.

58. “Deportation of 1896,” 3, RBSA.

59. “The Cree Situation,” *Great Falls Tribune*, June 11, 1896.

60. Gray, “Cree Indians,” 32, 201–2.

61. Later, when interviewed after his triumphs in World War I as the general in charge of the American Expeditionary Force, he recalled his experiences in Montana as formative. See “Pershing Gained Friendship of Miles, Which Helped Him Advance, in Montana,” *Flathead Courier* (Polson, MT), March 20, 1919.

62. “The Crees Are under Arrest,” *Great Falls Tribune*, June 19, 1896.

63. NWMP officer Richard Burton Deane’s report to his superiors offers a detailed look, from the Canadian side, of the complicated deportation process. See Richard Burton Deane to NWMP Commissioner, June 26, 1896, record group 10, Black Series, vol. 3863, file 84,138–1, reel c-10152, NAC.

64. *Great Falls Tribune*, June 26, 1896; and “Deporting Red Men,” *Anaconda Standard*, June 23, 1896.

65. *Helena Independent*, June 26, 1896; and *Montanian* (Choteau), June 26, 1896. Chippewa elder Jim Denny later told that his Chippewa parents had the option to stay or leave. Initially they opted to join their relations in the trek to Canada. They traveled from the Flathead Reservation to Missoula, Helena, Choteau, and Dupuyer, where they decided to stay in Montana. They then traveled to Timber Butte and Silver Bow, where Rocky Boy was then living. James Denny, “About the Beginning of Rocky Boy Reserve,” undated interview, 1–2, RBSA.

66. Gray, "Cree Indians," 8; and *Great Falls Tribune*, June 23, 1896.

67. See "Repatriation of Refugee Indians," unpublished manuscript, R.B. Deane Fonds, M313, Glenbow Archives, Calgary.

68. "Deportation of 1896," 3–5, RBSA.

69. *Edmonton Bulletin*, March 15, 1897.

70. "A Proclamation," January 21, 1887, in *Acts of the Parliament of the United Kingdom* (Ottawa: Brown Chamberlain, 1887), clvi. This was also reported in "More Facts about the Crees," *Great Falls Tribune*, June 6, 1896. Internal discussion previously among Canadian officials had considered the possibility of pressuring the United States to extradite Lucky Man, likening the situation to when Sitting Bull fled to Canada. See Letter to Superintendent General of Indian Affairs, January 10, 1887, and Letter dated January 22, 1887, record group 10, Black Series, volume 3774, file 36,563, reel c-10136, NAC.

71. Diary of Catholic Priest at Lethbridge, June 29, 1896, 3, RBSA; "Arrested for Murder," *Great Falls Leader*, July 3, 1896; *Montanian* (Choteau), July 3, 1896; *Great Falls Tribune*, July 4, 1896; "Deportation of 1896," 6, RBSA; and interview with Four Souls, in Littlejohn, "Indian Oral Tradition," 99.

72. "Some More Crees." *Anaconda Standard*, July 23, 1896; "Crees Must Walk," *Great Falls Leader*, July 9, 1896; "Record of Events," June–August, NARA, record group 94, Returns from US Military Posts, Fort Assiniboine, 1892–1903, M617, roll 42; Gray, "Cree Indians," 15; *Montanian* (Choteau), August 21, 1896; and *Helena Weekly Herald*, July 30, 1896.

73. Michel Hogue, "Crossing the Line: The Plains Cree in the Canada–United States Borderlands, 1870–1900" (master's thesis, University of Calgary, 2002), 101; interview with Four Souls, in Littlejohn, "Indian Oral Tradition," 93; and Grover Cleveland, Eighth State of the Union Address, December 6, 1896.

74. "Arrested for Murder," *Great Falls Leader*, July 3, 1896; Gray, "Cree Indians," 10; and *Moose Jaw Herald Times*, August 7, 1896.

75. Z. M. Hamilton to Anne McDonnell (Montana State Historical Society), quoted in Gray, "Cree Indians,"14.

76. *Edmonton Bulletin*, August 13, 1896; "Little Bear," *Edmonton Bulletin*, February 8, 1897; and "Little Bear in Ottawa," *Moose Jaw Herald Times*, February 12, 1897; *Edmonton Bulletin*, March 1, 1897, and March 15, 1897; and *Seattle Post-Intelligencer*, October 22, 1899.

77. "Return of the Cree," *Anaconda Standard*, May 5, 1897; and *Great Falls Weekly Tribune*, August 14, 1896. Exasperated and sarcastic, a dispatch from Fort Assiniboine opined that the state would likely not attempt further deportation. "Crees Are Safe," *Fergus County Argus* (Lewistown, MT), November 26, 1896. For discussion of Canadian efforts to restrict Cree mobility and Crees' return to the United States, see Hogue, *Crossing the Line*, 104–106.

78. Peterson, "Imasees and His Band: Canadian Refugees after the North-West Rebellion," 33.

79. *Butte Weekly Miner*, January 2, 1897; "Return of the Cree," *Anaconda Standard*, May 8, 1897; "Crees Back in Montana, Report from Butte, MT," *Jamestown (ND) Weekly Alert*, November 4, 1897; "Crees Are Coming Back," *Anaconda Standard*, Ocotber 16, 1897; *Great Falls Leader*, October 18, 1897; and "Little Bear Arrives at Great Falls," *Salt Lake City Herald*, October 18, 1897; *Montanian* (Choteau), November 5, 1897; *Salt Lake Herald*, October 18, 1897; *Seattle Post-Intelligencer*, October 22, 1899. "Going berry picking": John Buffalo interview, Ermineskin Reserve, Alberta,

April 18, 1975, Provincial Museum and Archives of Alberta, tape IH-169, transcript disc 25, http://hdl.handle.net/10294/2001.

80. "Crees Ask for Help," *Great Falls Tribune*, April 19, 1898.

81. "Crees to Meet Here," *Great Falls Tribune*, April 29, 1898.

82. Two Crees made national headlines in September 1898 when they appeared in district court requesting citizenship. Holy Altar and Sitting Horse and their Métis interpreter Harry Denny presented character witnesses and received papers to fill out. The final outcome of their case is unknown. See "Indians Seek Citizenship," *New York Times*, September 6, 1898.

83. "Smallpox among the Crees," *Milk River Eagle* (Havre, MT), July 8, 1899. See also "Rounding up of Filthy Disease-Infested Crees," *Seattle Post-Intelligencer*, October 22, 1899, 16.

84. "Big Time among the Crees," *Milk River Eagle* (Havre, MT), July 22, 1899.

85. Another group of Chippewas, under the leadership of Little Shell, were also prominent in Montana. For a tremendous telling of Little Shell's history, see Nicholas C.P. Vrooman, *"The Whole Country Was . . . 'One Robe'": The Little Shell Tribe's America* (Helena, MT: Drumlummon Institute, 2012).

86. See Frank B. Linderman, "Rocky Boy Renegades," *Indians at Work* 4 (January 1937): 23; and "Chippewa," undated manuscript, RBSA.

87. "Chippewa," undated manuscript; James Denny, "About the Beginning of Rocky Boy Reserve," undated manuscript, 1; and Denny, "Story of the Bear Paws," RBSA.

88. "Chippewa," undated manuscript, RBSA.

89. Denny, "Story of the Bear Paws," RBSA. Chippewa elder Fred Huntley specified stops in Wisconsin and Devils Lake, North Dakota, in the group's itinerary. See interview with Fred Huntley, May 8, 1975, RBSA. Duncan Standing Rock, Rocky Boy's grandnephew, offers a similar geography and chronology. Chippewas left the Great Lakes region in the 1830s, with some staying in Michigan and others staying in Wisconsin. Another group continued westward and lived with the Mandans. A group of twenty-five families continued westward, traveling near Minot, North Dakota. At that point, some left for Canada to live at the Rocky Mountain House, while others continued to Montana, settling in the Garrison, Dillon, Missoula, and Lincoln areas. See Duncan Standing Rock interview, May 2004, unpublished transcript held by Edward Stamper, foundations and research director, Stone Child College, Box Elder, MT.

90. When interviewed in 1907, Chippewa Chief Rocky Boy stated that the "burial grounds of his forefathers for years and years had been at the present site of the city of Deer Lodge." This contradicts somewhat the other dominant narratives about Chippewa migration to Montana. Though impossible to verify, it may be read as an astute political move by Rocky Boy, asserting his (and his people's) right to settle permanently in the state by claiming a traditional ancestral presence. His father was buried in Silver Bow County. See "Dancing Indian in Bad Scrape," *Anaconda Standard*, September 1, 1907; and Rocky Boy to Frank Churchill, October 24, 1908, record group 75, Records of the Bureau of Indian Affairs, Indian Office Files Relative to Lands for Rocky Boy's Band of Chippewa Indians, entry 121, Central Classified Files, 1907–1939, Blackfeet-#900–1908–307.4 (record group 75, RB files), part 1, National Archives and Records Administration, Washington, DC (hereafter NARA-DC).

91. See interview with Malcolm Mitchell, May 3, 1974, RBSA; Malcolm Mitchell, "My Grandfather Day Child's Father Story," undated manuscript, RBSA; and Gray, "Cree Indians," 235.

92. In a 1908 statement, Rocky Boy stated that his people had come to Montana around eighteen years earlier, and he asserted they had come from the US side of the border with Canada. See Samuel Bellow to James R. Garfield, February 29, 1908, record group 75, RB files, part 1. In 1902 Rocky Boy had told Butte police chief William Taylor that his people had been in Montana for twelve years. Both are in accord with the 1890 arrival date. See "Want to Settle Down," *Anaconda Standard*, February 11, 1902.

93. Interview with James Denny, "About the Beginning of Rocky Boy Reserve," undated interview, 1–2, RBSA. Soon thereafter, a white sheep rancher forced them off their Silver Bow lands, and they moved camp to Timber Butte, south of Dillon, Montana.

94. See Rocky Boy to Frank G. Churchill, October 24, 1908, and Frank G. Churchill to James R. Garfield, November 10, 1908, record group 75, entry 121, Central Classified Files, 1907–1939, Blackfeet-#900-1908-307.4 (hereafter RB Files), part 1; and "Census of the Rocky Boy's Band of Chippewa Indians," April 8–14, 1909, Rocky Boy Reservation Records, 1909–17, SC 903, MSHS.

95. Samuel Bellow to James R. Garfield, February 29, 1908, record group 75, RB Files, part 1; and Ewers, *Ethnological Report of the Chippewa Cree Tribe*, 143.

96. Linderman, "Rocky Boy Renegades," 23; and Ewers, *Ethnological Report of the Chippewa Cree Tribe*, 143–47. Legal scholar Gary Botting has asserted that Rocky Boy crossed into Montana with Little Bear. His evidence, the 1917 McLaughlin Census of Rocky Boy's band that he cites, only notes Rocky Boy's future wife and Chippewa Speaker, a woman Botting identified as Rocky Boy's mother, crossing with Little Bear. From the census, Botting infers Rocky Boy was "likely" in the group. While this is not impossible, the 1917 document does not make this explicit. See Gary Botting, *Chief Smallboy: In Pursuit of Freedom* (Calgary: Fifth House, 2005), 23–24, 213; "Tentative Roll of Rocky Boy Indians, May 30, 1917," Rocky Boy's Reservation Records, 1909–1917, SC 903, MSHS; and James McLaughlin, "Family History of So-called Rocky Boy Indians," May 7–30, 1917, Geneva Stump's Rocky Boy Collection, M 7937, Glenbow Archives, Calgary.

97. Cowan's account, originally written for the *Great Falls Tribune*, was later published by other papers as well. See "Rocky Boy Indians Once Scavengers of Montana Cities Now Successful Farmers," *Box Elder (MT) Valley Press*, May 9, 1924; and "Rocky Boy Indians, Long Poverty Stricken, Made Rapid Advance When Opportunity Came," *Rocky Mountain News* (Denver), July 23, 1942.

98. Interview with Fred Huntley, May 8, 1975, RBSA.

99. Told to Verne Dusenberry by Four Souls. See Verne Dusenberry, *The Montana Cree: A Study in Religious Persistence* (1962; repr.: Norman: University of Oklahoma Press, 1998), 40.

100. See Linderman, "Rocky Boy Renegades," 24.

Chapter 6

1. Joe D. Romero to Edward Spicer, January 12, 1942, Spicer Papers, ASM, MS 5, subgroup 8, box 1, folder 54.

2. Edward Spicer, *Yaquis*, 160–61.

3. Ibid., 161. Spicer explains further, "Urban Yaquis, aware of the [deportation] conditions and fearful that at any time they would find themselves also in the jails, suffered greatly. They were living in what steadily became a world of informers. Men

and women revealed the identities of Yaquis in order to save their own skins. One never knew whether there was an informer in the midst of a family or compadre circle. The term *torocoyori*—'like a Yori,' or 'gray-faced Yaqui'—became a common term referring to Yaquis who were ready to betray other Yaquis into the hands of the Yoris. 'Yori' is the Yaqui word designating whites, Mexicans or other non-Yaquis."

4. "Marana Yaqui Village: Some Stories from the Past—Ferminia's Life Story," Spicer Papers, ASM, subgroup 8, box 5, folder 278.

5. See Moisés, Kelley, and Holden, *Yaqui Life*, 34.

6. Spicer, *Yaquis*, 158.

7. Those maintaining the gendered divisions of labor were more likely to be accepted by other Yaquis in the community. See Meeks, *Border Citizens*, 91–93.

8. "Yaquis Leaving Sonora," *Graham Guardian* (Safford, AZ), August 8, 1902.

9. Moisés, Kelley, and Holden, *Yaqui Life*, 35–36; and "Yaqui Stories about Entrance into US," Spicer Papers, ASM, series 6, box 5, folder 1.

10. In the 1870s a group of Yaqui *broncos*—resisters from the mountains above the seven pueblos—fled to Texas. Comprising ten families, they actively hid their Yaqui identity in Texas. Their descendants are now a state-recognized tribe in Texas but have not secured federal recognition. See Texas Band of Yaqui Indians, www.yaquitribetexas.com.

11. This list moves roughly in a south-to-north direction and is compiled from the following sources: Felipe Molina, "Arizona Yaqui Communities," Spicer Papers, ASM, subgroup 8, box 5, folder 278; William Simpson, "An Ethnographic Account of Yaqui Guadalupe Compared with the Culture of Poverty" (master's thesis, Arizona State University, 1969); Edward Spicer, "Yaqui Villages Past and Present," *Kiva* 13 (November 1947): 2–12; Spicer, *People of Pascua*, 6, 78; and Edward Spicer, Field Notes from Yuma, June 7, 1940, Spicer Papers, ASM, subgroup 8, box 7, folder 438.

12. Felipe Molina to Edward Spicer, 1980, "Yaqui Historical Chart," Spicer Papers, ASM, subgroup 5, box 5, folder 278.

13. Spicer, *Yaquis*, 237.

14. "Notes from Talk with Kirk Moore," August 22, 1934, Spicer Papers, ASM. subgroup 8, box 7, folder 446.

15. Interview with Refugio Savala, December 1, 1936, Spicer Papers, ASM, subgroup 8, box 6, folder 356.

16. Spicer, *Yaquis*, 248.

17. "Notes from Talk with Kirk Moore."

18. Interview with Lucas Chavez, "Re the History of Pascua," January 28, 1937, Spicer Papers, ASM, subgroup 8, box 1, folder 58.

19. Spicer, *Yaquis*, 248.

20. "Notes from Talk with Kirk Moore."

21. "Chief of the Arizona Yaqui Tribe Is Dead," *Coconino Sun* (Flagstaff, AZ), May 12, 1922; and Spicer, *Yaquis*, 247.

22. "Matus Selected Yaqui Leader: Arizona Indians Will Try to Buy Land They Now Are Squatting On," *Los Angeles Times*, July 3, 1922.

23. "Notes from Talk with Kirk Moore"; and "First Bond Issue," *Tucson Daily Citizen*, September 9, 1946.

24. C. L. Sonnichsen, *Tucson: The Life and Times of an American City* (Norman: University of Oklahoma Press, 1982), 238; Spicer, "Yaqui Villages Past and Present," 11; and Spicer, *People of Pascua*, 44.

25. "Population of Pascua Village," 1947, Spicer Papers, ASM, subgroup 8, box

6, folder 370; and Spicer, *Yaquis*, 239. This population would drop to around four hundred after the move of some eleven hundred to the Pascua reservation created by the US Congress in 1978. See "Arizona Yaqui Communities," Spicer Papers, ASM, subgroup 8, box 5, folder 278.

26. Interview with Lucas Chavez.

27. "Yaquis Will Have Church near Tucson," *Tucson Daily Citizen*, August 29, 1930.

28. The Pascua school was built to serve only students through the first grade. In 1946 upper elementary classes were taught at the neighboring Santa Rosa church. During the interceding decades, Yaqui students were forced to walk to such neighboring Tucson schools as Davis and Roosevelt Elementary. See "School Obtains Use of Church," *Tucson Daily Citizen*, September 7, 1946; and Maria Urquides, "Up from the Barrio," in *Arizona Memories*, ed. Anne Hodges Morgan and Rennard Strickland (Tucson: University of Arizona Press, 1984), 326.

29. Works Progress Administration, *Arizona: A State Guide* (New York: Hastings House, 1940), 297–98. Much of the WPA guide was researched and prepared by M. Warren Krause. His notes on the Yaqui sections of the book can be found in M. Warren Krause Collection, MSS108, Arizona Historical Foundation, Arizona State University Archives (hereafter ASUA), box 2, folder 10.

30. "Yaqui Town Owner Seeks Lower Taxes," *Tucson Daily Citizen*, June 4, 1932.

31. Spicer, *Yaquis*, 239.

32. Ibid. Around one thousand Yaquis still resided in its immediate South Tucson vicinity in 1980. See "Arizona Yaqui Communities," Spicer Papers, ASM, subgroup 8, box 5, folder 278.

33. Spicer, "Yaqui Villages Past and Present," 11; Spicer, *Yaquis*, 239. The Marana Yaquis were a permanent fixture in the region until the 1970s establishment of a Yaqui reservation south of Tucson, and Felipe Molina enumerated 190 Yaquis still in Marana in 1980. See "Arizona Yaqui Communities," Spicer Papers, ASM, subgroup 8, box 5, folder 278.

34. "Yaqui Indians Finding Peace at Little Village: Barrio Pascua Families Happy Because Liquor Is Banned," *Arizona Daily Star* (Tucson), June 6, 1931.

35. Mitzi Zipf, "New Goals for Guadalupe, Yaqui Townsite on 56th St.," *Arizona Republic* (Phoenix), October 1, 1963.

36. M. J. Dougherty, Exhibit C, "Memorandum in re Guadalupe Townsite," *Diocese of Tucson v. Guadalupe Community Association*, case no. 104499, microfiche, Maricopa County Superior Court, Phoenix, Arizona; Warranty of Deed of T. Reverend Peter Bourgade from Sylvester Roche, February 1, 1898, Office of the Recorder, Maricopa County; Glaser, "Story of Guadalupe," vii–viii, 21, 36n; and Simpson, "Ethnographic Account of Yaqui Guadalupe," 25.

37. Meeks, *Border Citizens*, 79.

38. See "An Unknown Region Just Outside Phoenix," *Arizona Republican* (Phoenix), July 7, 1908. See this book's companion website, www.nativebutforeign.org, for sources and discussion of early negative reactions by Arizonans to Guadalupe.

39. Dane Coolidge, "The Yaquis in Exile," *Sunset* 23 (September 1909): 300.

40. Octaviana V. Trujillo, "The Yaqui of Guadalupe, Arizona: A Century of Cultural Survival through Trilingualism," *American Indian Culture and Research Journal* 22, no. 4 (1988): 75–76. See also "Notes of News," *Arizona Republican* (Phoenix), July 7, 1910.

41. This process lasted for years and involved many individuals. For more information, see Glaser, "Story of Guadalupe," 21–36.

42. Statement by Senator Hayden, June 1964, Carl Hayden Papers, MSS1 (hereafter Hayden Papers), ASUA, box 341, folder 6.

43. Patent no. 442696, November 14, 1914, Hayden Papers, ASUA, box 203, folder 15.

44. Glaser, "Story of Guadalupe," 31–32.

45. Pat McAlister, "Guadalupe, Arizona, 1968," 2, Spicer Papers, ASM, subgroup 8, box 7, folder 434.

46. Interview with Ruby Wood, August 7, 1968, transcript, Oral History Collection, Arizona Historical Foundation, FM MSS #141, ASUA, box 8, folder 4–5.

47. "The Remnants of the Yaqui Indians," *Christian Science Monitor*, December 31, 1919.

48. Raphael Carlos Estrada, Historical Account of the Yaqui Indian, 1932, Spicer Papers, ASM, subgroup 8, box 5, folder 275.

49. Works Progress Administration, *Arizona*, 352.

50. Glaser, "Story of Guadalupe," 45.

51. See Felipe Molina to Edward Spicer, 1980, "Yaqui Historical Chart," Spicer Papers, ASM, subgroup 5, box 5, folder 278.

52. Glaser, "Story of Guadalupe," 46.

53. The name Eskatel was also used by the broader Mexican community in the immediate area. For information on the South Scottsdale Mexican community, see José María Burruel, *Mexicans in Scottsdale* (Charleston, SC: Arcadia, 2007).

54. Edward Spicer, "Field Notes from Scottsdale Deer Dance," July 28, 1904, Spicer Papers, ASM, subgroup 8, box 7, folder 436. For a well-illustrated though brief history of Eskatel, see *The Yaquis of Scottsdale, Arizona: Family, Indomitable Spirit, Generosity* (Scottsdale: Concerned Citizens for Community Health, 2002), 17–42.

55. See Leah Glaser, "Working for Community: The Yaqui Indians of the Salt River Project," *Journal of Arizona History* 37 (Winter 1996): 347.

56. Glaser, "Story of Guadalupe," 56, 61. For more details on the Northside camp and Turicate Village, including photos, see *Yaquis of Scottsdale, Arizona*, 43–88.

57. Glaser, "Story of Guadalupe," 55.

58. At present, Hightown consists of the three or four blocks immediately southeast of the Chandler Boulevard and McClintock Drive intersection in Chandler, Arizona. Sonora Town lies on the streets immediately southwest of the Warner Road and Gilbert Road intersection in Gilbert, Arizona, bordered diagonally to the south by the Consolidated Canal.

59. Edward Shaughnessy to Senator Carl Hayden, May 1, 1937, Hayden Papers, ASUA, box 625, folder 24.

60. Spicer, *Yaquis*, 240; and Glaser, "Working for Community," 346.

61. Mitzi Zipf, "New Goals for Guadalupe, Yaqui Townsite on 56th St.," *Arizona Republic* (Phoenix), October 1, 1963.

62. Simpson, "Ethnographic Account of Yaqui Guadalupe," 13.

63. Felipe Molina to Edward Spicer, 1980, "Yaqui Historical Chart," Spicer Papers, ASM, subgroup 5, box 5, folder 278.

64. The 1936 figure for Yaquis in the Sibakobi-Somerton settlement comes from Edward Spicer, Notes from Immigration Office, November 22, 1936, Spicer Papers, ASM, subgroup 8, box 7, folder 438. All other figures come from Spicer, "Yaqui Villages Past and Present," 10–11. Spicer interviewed a Mr. Schupbach, who employed Yaquis near Yuma in 1940. Schupbach spoke highly of the Yaquis' work ethic and generally disagreed with how the Department of Immigration was dealing with them.

See Field Notes, Yuma, Somaton, June 6, 1940, Spicer Papers, ASM, subgroup 8, box 7, folder 438.

65. James E. Cook, "Yaquis of Pascua to Vacate Site Occupied for 40 Years," *Arizona Republic* (Phoenix), November 28, 1964.

66. Restrictions on Asian immigration translated to increased demand for Mexican —and by extension—Yaqui labor in agribusiness and other industries. See Francisco E. Balderrama and Raymond Rodríguez, *Decade of Betrayal: Mexican Repatriation in the 1930s* (Albuquerque: University of New Mexico Press, 2006), 16–21; Camille Guernin-Gonzales, *Mexican Workers and American Dreams: Immigration, Repatriation, and California Farm Labor, 1900–1939* (New Brunswick, NJ: Rutgers University Press, 1994), 16–24; and Kelly Lytle-Hernández, *Migra! A History of the US Border Patrol* (Berkley: University of California Press, 2010), 23–26.

67. "Arizona Yaquis Go Back Home," *Los Angeles Times*, July 23, 1921.

68. Edward Spicer, who appears to have taken much of his material on Alvarez from a Refugio Savala manuscript, where the names and dates are inconsistent with later published accounts. See Refugio Savala, "Stories about Yaqui History," unpublished manuscript, 62, Spicer Papers, ASM, subgroup 8, box 5, folder 335; and Spicer, *People of Pascua*, 146–51.

69. Refugio Savala, *The Autobiography of a Yaqui Poet* (Tucson: University of Arizona Press, 1980), 6–7.

70. "Marana Yaqui Village: Some Stories from the Past, Martina Cruz's Life Story," compiled by Edward Spicer from a May 12, 1975, interview, Edward H. and Spicer Papers, ASM, subgroup 8, box 5, folder 278. Savala's autobiography offers a good picture of his and other Yaquis' continued railroad employment throughout the mid-twentieth century. See Savala, *Autobiography of a Yaqui Poet*, 5–7, 16, 25, 33–34, 38, 44, 48, 51–55, 62–66, 81–88, 95, 102–4, 113, 148–49, 147, 164, 72–174, 180, 192–94, 205.

71. Spicer, *People of Pascua*, 34; and Edward Spicer, introduction to Muriel Thayer Painter, *With Good Heart: Yaqui Beliefs and Ceremonies in Pascua Village* (Tucson: University of Arizona Press, 1986), xx–xxi.

72. In the 1960s, many railroads switched to mechanized road maintenance, putting many Yaquis out of work. Arizona state senator Tom Moore explained to the deputy assistant secretary for environment, safety and consumer affairs that the tracks were better maintained when Yaquis did it by hand. See Tom Moore to Herbert H. Kaiser, Jr., April 12, 1976, Personal and Political Papers of Senator Barry M. Goldwater, ASUA, MS FM MSS1, Series III, Legislative Files, box 210, folder 33.

73. "Labor Surplus in Arizona Decreases," *Graham Guardian* (Safford, AZ), July 15, 1921.

74. Abota Valenzuela, a miner well known in Casa Grande from his years in the Vekol Mine, reported his switch to bean and lettuce farming during the Great Depression. See *Casa Grande Dispatch*, February 15, 1935.

75. H. B. Wharfield, "A Fight with the Yaquis at Bear Valley, 1918," *Arizoniana*, Fall 1963, 2. Wharfield made this statement to support the larger claim that by 1918 Arizona Yaquis were using wages "to purchase firearms and ammunition, which they smuggled back into Mexico for their tribesman."

76. "The Remnants of the Yaqui Indians," *Christian Science Monitor*, December 31, 1919.

77. See this book's companion website, www.nativebutforeign.org, for information on cotton pricing and demand.

78. Glaser, "Story of Guadalupe," 42–43; and Savala, *Autobiography of a Yaqui Poet*, 32.

79. See this book's companion website, www.nativebutforeign.org, for sources discussing the ubiquitous nature of Yaquis in Arizona labor markets.

80. Glaser, "Working for Community," 337–56. Yaquis already had experience building and maintaining canals in Tucson near Pascua Village. Maintaining and cleaning irrigation ditches and canals had been an important employment source leveraged by Juan Pistola during the late 1910s and early 1920s. See interview with Guadalupe Balthazar, April 28, 1937, Spicer Papers, ASM, subgroup 8, box 1, folder 58.

81. Spicer, introduction to Painter, *With Good Heart*, xxi.

Chapter 7

1. Edward Spicer, "The Promised Land," unpublished manuscript, 25–26, Spicer Papers, ASM, MS 5, unprocessed papers in Accession 2000–175, box 21.

2. Throughout the previous decades, Mexico had regularly requested the extradition of criminals. Local papers report examples of how Yaquis wanted for crimes in Mexico were subject to extradition. This was different from refugee Yaqui deportation, but it was likely disconcerting nonetheless. See "Yaqui Indians Ordered Deported," *Tombstone Epitaph*, April 5, 1908; *Oasis* (Arizola, AZ), December 21, 1907; "Yaqui Indians Reported in Arizona," *Tombstone Epitaph*, March 1, 1908.

3. "Yaquis' Part in Insurrection: Indian, Many Times Reported Exterminated, Is a First Class Fightin' Man," *McCook (NE) Tribune*, August 8, 1911.

4. "Church Festival Seals Yaqui Peace," *Bisbee Daily Review*, January 21, 1910; "Yaquis Invade Arizona: Unmolested by Officers," *Los Angeles Herald*, October 19, 1910; and "Indian War a Century Old: Yaquis Have Been Fighting Both Mexico and the United States for a Hundred Years," *Washington Post*, July 24, 1910.

5. See, for example, "Insurgents Renew Attack," *Graham Guardian* (Safford, Arizona), August 1, 1913; and "Yaqui Indians Threaten Revolt," *Graham Guardian*, September 5, 1913.

6. "Yaqui Chiefs Pass through Arizona," *Tombstone Prospector*, July 26, 1911. See also "Yaquis Returning Home Stop in Arizona after Conference with Madero in Mexico," *Tombstone Epitaph*, January 7, 1912.

7. Spicer, *Yaquis*, 226–29.

8. "Marines to Land to Save Americans," *Atlanta Constitution*, May 16, 1915.

9. "Yaquis Kill Americans," *Washington Post*, May 14, 1915; "Wholesale Murders by Yaquis Reported," *Washington Post*, May 28, 1922. For general reporting concern over Yaqui threats to American lives and business in Sonora, see "The Yaqui Indians of the Southwest," *Bisbee Daily Review*, July 1, 1908; "American Killed by Yaqui Troops," *El Paso Herald*, June 19, 1912; "Yaquis Raid American Colony," *Tombstone Epitaph*, May 16, 1915; "Mexico, Again," *Oakland Tribune*, May 16, 1915; and "Why the Yaquis are Waging War," *University Missourian* (Columbia), June 21, 1915.

10. "American Troops Fire on Mexicans . . . Shells Damage Naco, Ariz," *New York Times*, October 12, 1914; and "Naco Is Evacuated by Carranza Force," *Nevada State Journal* (Reno), October 22, 1915.

11. "Many Yaqui Indians There," *San Antonio Light*, November 1, 1915; and "Bullets Rained on Town," *Denton (TX) Record-Chronicle*, November 2, 1915.

12. "The Bronco Yaquis of Sonora," *Tucson Citizen*, June 5, 1915.

13. "Yaqui Indians Are Leaving Arizona," *Courtland Arizonan*, May 26, 1917. On

the other hand, Edward Spicer's interviews with Yaqui leaders revealed US employers active in recruiting Yaquis to move in the opposite direction—into the United States. According to Lucas Chavez, a Mr. McDowell attempted to entice an interested group of twenty-five Yaquis to cross into Arizona in 1915. See Edward Spicer, Pascua Diary, March 25, 1937, Spicer Papers, ASM, subgroup 8, box 1, folder 54.

14. "Yaquis across Line, Some Consternation at Border City," *Tombstone Epitaph*, August 11, 1912. See this book's companion website, www.nativebutforeign.org, for sources and discussion of how Arizonans had long viewed *all* Yaquis as arms traffickers.

15. David K. Work, "Enforcing Neutrality: The Tenth US Cavalry on the Mexican Order, 1913–1919," *Western Historical Quarterly* 40 (Summer 2009): 179–200.

16. "Hunt for Indians," *Tucson Citizen*, June 25, 1914.

17. US Department of State, *Papers relating to the Foreign Relations of the United States*, *1918* (Washington DC: Government Printing Office, 1918), 552–55. A detailed report telling of US Army border patrols and of 1918 skirmishes with Yaqui arms smugglers in 1918 was published some years later by retired army colonel H. B. Wharfield. See H. B. Wharfield, "A Fight with the Yaquis at Bear Valley, 1918," *Arizoniana* 4 (Fall 1963): 1–8.

18. Spicer, *Yaquis*, 235. See this book's companion website, www.nativebutforeign.org, for sources and discussion of US reports on the new conflict.

19. US Department of State, *Papers relating to the Foreign Relations of the United States*, *1927*, vol. 3 (Washington, DC: Government Printing Office, 1927), 246–47.

20. Sonnichsen, *Tucson*, 238.

21. Frank M. Seibold, *Tales from the Sonoita* (San Antonio: Naylor, 1977), 42.

22. "All Quiet on Border Again: May Be Mere Lull in Storm," *Arizona Daily Star* (Tucson), May 21, 1927. Note that the US Border Patrol was simultaneously stretched thin in resources and funding due to ongoing tensions over Chinese immigration and deportations moving in both directions across the US-Mexican border. See Lytle-Hernández, *Migra!*, 79–80.

23. "Border Patrolmen 'Worn to Frazzle' by Yaqui Pursuit," *Tucson Citizen*, May 16, 1927.

24. There is one report from 1908 of Arizona Yaquis sending "an envoy" to Washington, DC, in the midst of Mexican Yaqui peace talks, but no further information of their reception is available. See "Yaquis Claim Arizona Lands," S.W. Press Association Report, *Fairmont West Virginian*, June 15, 1908.

25. "US Officials Confer with Yaqui Chiefs," *Ogden (UT) Standard*, June 10, 1919; and "Ask Arizona Yaquis to Put Stop to Rains in State of Sonora," *Bisbee Daily Review*, June 10, 1919.

26. "Officers Fear Trouble for Border Patrolmen in Hands of 33 Indians," *Arizona Daily Star* (Tucson), May 7, 1927.

27. "Yaqui Indians Now Wait Action of United States," *Arizona Daily Star* (Tucson), May 9, 1927; and "Officers Fear Trouble for Border Patrolmen in Hands of 33 Indians," *Arizona Daily Star* (Tucson), May 7, 1927.

28. "The Yaqui on American Soil," *Arizona Daily Star* (Tucson), May 10, 1927.

29. "More Yaquis Surrender to US Officials," *Arizona Daily Star* (Tucson), May 14, 1927.

30. "Thirty Yaquis Interned Here," *Arizona Daily Star* (Tucson), May 16, 1927; and "Mexico Invites Yaquis' Return to Home Valley," *Arizona Daily Star* (Tucson), May 26, 1927.

31. Rosamond Spicer to *Arizona Daily Star* editor, April 17, 1944, Spicer Papers, ASM, subgroup 5, box 1.

32. Interview with Refugio Savala, December 1, 1936, Spicer Papers, ASM, subgroup 8, box 6, folder 356.

33. "Indians Seek Citizenship," *Los Angeles Herald*, October 11, 1920; and "Indian Immigrants," *Los Angeles Times*, October 13, 1920.

34. In Arizona, this meshed with ongoing efforts to rid the state of alien populations viewed as drains on local resources. See "Jones Bill Is Not Arousing Wild Applause," *Weekly Journal-Miner* (Prescott, AZ), March 1908, 1922.

35. Julian Lim, *Porous Borders: Multiracial Migrations and the Law in the US-Mexico Borderlands* (Chapel Hill: University of North Carolina Press, 2017), 240.

36. Spicer, interview with Immigration Border Patrol Office, August 27, 1940, Spicer Papers, ASM, subgroup 8, box 7, folder 446.

37. Edward Spicer, Notes from Immigration Office, November 22, 1936, Spicer Papers, ASM, subgroup 8, box 7, folder 438.

38. Ibid.

39. Sonnichsen, *Tucson*, 238.

40. William Simpson, "Ethnographic Account of Yaqui Guadalupe," 53. Stories collected by Refugio Savala told of Yaqui informers who collaborated with federal officials. They came to Yaqui camps looking for specific individuals and were selective in their efforts. See Refugio Savala, "Stories about Yaqui History," 62.

41. "US Deports Pascua 'Chief'," *Arizona Daily Star* (Tucson), August 1, 1936.

42. Over eighteen thousand Mexican repatriates left Arizona between 1930 and 1932. Abraham Hoffman, *Unwanted Mexican Americans in the Great Depression: Repatriation Pressures, 1929–1939* (Tucson: University of Arizona Press, 1974), 122–23.

43. "Political Refugees," *Casa Grande (AZ) Dispatch*, March 13, 1936.

44. "US Deports Pascua 'Chief'," *Arizona Daily Star* (Tucson), August 1, 1936.

45. See "Arizona Yaquis Go Back Home," *Los Angeles Times*, July 23, 1921.

46. "Mexico Asked to Aid Yaquis," *Arizona Daily Star* (Tucson), May 24, 1931. Those joining Flores were Antonio Vasquez, Tomas Alvarez, Ramon Duarte, Ignacio Alvárez, Angel Acuña, Franck Acuña, Lauro Martinez, and Basilio Matus.

47. Edward Spicer, "The Promised Land," unpublished manuscript, 11, Spicer Papers, ASM, unprocessed papers in Accession Nr. 2000–175, box 21.

48. Ibid., 25–26. A slightly different version of this letter was printed in "Hunt Assures Yaqui Safety," *Arizona Daily Star*, September 23, 1931.

49. "Hunt Assures Yaqui Safety," *Arizona Daily Star*, September 23, 1931.

50. Deputy Commissioner of Immigration and Naturalization Shaughnessy informed Arizona's US senator Carl Hayden of this in 1937. See Edward Shaughnessy to Senator Carl Hayden, March 25, 1937, Hayden Papers, ASUA, box 625, folder 24.

51. "Aid for Yaqui, Yocupicio Plea," *Tucson Daily Star*, February 26, 1937; *Arizona Republic* (Phoenix), February 26, 1937; and Edward Spicer, *People of Pascua* (Tucson: University of Arizona Press, 1988), 45.

52. "Sonora's Prodigal Yaquis," *Modern Mexico* 10 (July 1938): 17–18, 22.

53. Alfonso Fabila, *Las Tribus Yaqui de Sonora: Su Cultura y Anhelada Autodeterminación* (Mexico City: Departamento de Asuntos Indigenas, 1940), 192. For correspondence between Sonoran Yaqui leaders and President Lázaro Cárdenas, including the eventual 1938 and 1939 presidential decrees officially restituting lands to Yaquis, see ibid., 295–313.

54. "Contra Regreso de Los Yaqui de Tucson a Sonora," *El Tucsonense*, April 6, 1937.

55. "Many Hatred Split Arizona Indian Clan," *Arizona Daily Star* (Tucson), June 30, 1932.

56. "Aged Yaquis Do Not Want to Go South," *Tucson Citizen*, February 27, 1937.

57. Interview with Rosario Escalante, Pascua Diary and Field Notes, May 18, 1937, Spicer Papers, subgroup 8, box 1, folder 58.

58. "US Deports Pascua 'Chief'," *Arizona Daily Star* (Tucson), August 1, 1936. This report suggests that Lopez was among the Yaquis who entered the United States during the 1926 uprising in Sonora. His late entry surely influenced his deportation ahead of more longtime residents, but it must have been a dire loss to Yaquis who looked to him for leadership.

59. Cordell Hull (State Department) to Senator Carl Haydn, March 16, 1937; and Senator Carl Hayden to Edward Shaughnessy, March 22, 1937, Hayden Papers, ASUA, box 625, folder 24.

60. Edward Shaughnessy to Senator Carl Hayden, March 25, 1937; and Edward Shaughnessy to Senator Carl Hayden, May 1, 1937, Hayden Papers, ASUA, box 625, folder 24.

61. See "Alien Registry Started Here," *Arizona Daily Star* (Tucson), August 29, 1940.

62. Edward Spicer, "A Report on Six Months Field Work in an Arizona Yaqui Village," 1937, Spicer Papers, ASM, subgroup 8, box 1, folder 61.

63. Registration data for alien registration, August 27, 1940, Spicer Papers, ASM, subgroup 8, box 7, folder 446. At the registration, postmaster Harold Collins pulled Spicer aside and said, "This is great stuff. Some of these Yaqui have jail records (just for being drunk, of course) that are so darned long there isn't room for them on the blanks." Thankfully, such minor offenses did not threaten Yaqui registration. See Alien Registration Notes, August 30, 1940, Spicer Papers, ASM, subgroup 8, box 7, folder 446.

64. Yaquis were well aware that criminal behavior jeopardized their standing in the United States. One tragic example became known in 1941 when a Yaqui named Vicente Gonzalez was arrested for the murder of a seven-year-old boy in 1918. Gonzalez fully confessed to the crime, telling of how he had lived out that subsequent twenty-three years wandering about the West. During the 1940 alien registration campaign, he had hid himself in the desert, terrified that registration would expose him. Gonzalez's crime is on one extreme of the criminal continuum, but other Yaquis likely echoed his sentiment, "I've always been afraid." Any criminal behavior brought unwanted focus on Yaquis already uncertain about their legal standing in the United States. See "Desert Murder of 23 Years Ago Is Solved by Yaqui Fugitive's Capture at Marana," *Arizona Republic* (Phoenix), August 20, 1941.

65. Interview with Immigration Border Patrol Office, August 27, 1940, Spicer Papers, ASM, subgroup 8, box 7, folder 446.

66. Spicer, *People of Pascua*, 43–45.

67. Rogers M. Smith, *Civic Ideals: Conflicting Visions of Citizenship in US History* (New Haven: Yale University Press, 1997), 131–32. See also Katherine Benton-Cohen, *Borderline Americans: Racial Division and Labor Wars in the Arizona Borderlands* (Cambridge: Harvard University Press, 2009), 30–32; and Matthew Frye Jacobson, *Whiteness of a Different Color: European Immigrants and the Alchemy of Race* (Cambridge: Harvard University Press, 1998), 7.

68. I-Mien Tsiang, *The Question of Expatriation in American prior to 1907* (Baltimore: Johns Hopkins Press, 1942), 81.

69. Previous policies, like those for Natives who accepted allotments under the 1887 Dawes Act and broke tribal ties or who served in the armed forces, had opened limited paths to citizenship. See Daniel McCool, Susan M. Olson, and Jennifer L. Robinson, *Native Vote: American Indians, the Voting Rights Act, and the Right to Vote* (Cambridge: Cambridge University Press, 2007), 7; Paul C. Rosier, *Serving Their Country: American Indian Politics and Patriotism in the Twentieth Century* (Cambridge: Harvard University Press, 2009), 352. For a broad overview of naturalization and citizenship, see James H. Kettner, *The Development of American Citizenship, 1608–1870* (Chapel Hill: University of North Carolina Press, 1978), 288–300. For discussion of how the Constitution and Bill of Rights have been applied to Native peoples and an in-depth case study in the fight for full citizenship, see Vine Deloria Jr., and David E. Wilkins, *Tribes, Treaties, and Constitutional Tribulations* (Austin: University of Texas Press, 1999); Frederick E. Hoxie, "The Good Citizenship Gun: Thomas Sloan, Omaha," chap. 6 in *This Indian Country: American Indian Political Activists and the Place They Made* (New York: Penguin Press, 2012); and John R. Wunder, *"Retained by The People": A History of American Indians and the Bill of Rights* (New York: Oxford University Press, 1994).

70. Spicer told of one Felipe Gastelo whose 1937 application was denied because he identified himself as "real Yaqui Indian." Had he identified himself as Mexican, his application apparently would have been approved. See Registration Data for Alien Registration, August 27, 1940, Spicer Papers, ASM, subgroup 8, box 7, folder 446; and Spicer, *People of Pascua*, 45.

71. Spicer, *People of Pascua*, 45, 310n9.

72. Alien Registration Notes, August 30, 1940, Spicer Papers, ASM, subgroup 8, box 7, folder 446.

73. Nicholas Perschl, "History Repeats Itself," *Indian Sentinel*, March 1941, 36.

74. See "Watchful Eye Kept on Mexican Yaquis," *Arizona Daily Star* (Tucson), October 21, 1933; and "Indians in Mexico Fight with Army," *Arizona Daily Star* (Tucson), January 6, 1940.

75. "The Yaqui Festivities," *Arizona Republican* (Phoenix), April 22, 1908. See this book's companion website, www.nativebutforeign.org, for sources and discussion of subsequent reports of Yaqui celebrations in Guadalupe as well as earlier Salt River Valley–based Yaqui dancers.

76. Edward Spicer and Refugio Savala placed the earliest Yaqui religious ceremonies at Guadalupe village, in 1906 or 1908, and at Tierra Floja Ranch near Tucson in 1909. Edward Spicer, introduction to Savala, *Autobiography of a Yaqui Poet*, xv; interview with Lucas Chavez, April 13, 1937, and interview with Guadalupe Balthazar, April 28, 1937, Edward Spicer Pascua Diary and Field Notes, Spicer Papers, ASM, subgroup 8, box 1, folder 58; and Rosamond Spicer to editor of the *Arizona Daily Star*, April 17, 1944, Spicer Papers, ASM, subgroup 5, box 2.

77. S. C. Warman, "Yaquis to Suspend Photo Ban for Special Fiesta," *Tucson Daily Citizen*, July 30, 1958; and Don Schellie, "Yaquis Set Out Food for Dead," *Tucson Daily Citizen*, November 3, 1958.

78. See Emily Brown, "The Passion at Pascua," pamphlet published by Tucson Chamber of Commerce, M. Warren Krause Collection, MSS108, Arizona Historical Foundation, ASUA box 2, folder 10; and Painter, *With Good Heart*, xviii. See this book's companion website, www.nativebutforeign.org, for sources and discussion of the monetization of Yaqui culture in Phoenix in 1916.

79. See this book's companion website, www.nativebutforeign.org, for sources and discussion of the 1930s national coverage and continued regional coverage of Yaqui festivals.

80. Occasional pieces in the Arizona press described museum exhibits on Yaqui history and ethnology, Yaqui participation in the armed services, and random personal interest stories concerning Yaqui individuals. All reinforced the conception of Yaquis as an explicitly foreign presence in the United States. See this book's companion website, www.nativebutforeign.org, for sources and discussion.

Chapter 8

1. From a speech Little Bear made in Helena, Montana, to the Lewis and Clark County commissioners. *Havre Plaindealer*, July 19, 1913.

2. Quoted in "To Deport the Crees," *Milk River Eagle* (Havre, MT), October 14, 1899.

3. *Salt Lake Herald*, October 18, 1897.

4. *Montanian* (Choteau), June 15, 1900.

5. See Frank B. Linderman, "Rocky Boy Renegades," *Indians at Work* 4 (January 1937): 24; and Frank B. Linderman, "Life on Rocky Boy's Indian Reservation: 1930–1938," report to the commissioner of Indian affairs, 2–3, record group 75, Still Pictures (75.29), RA-2, NARA.

6. "Crees Back in Montana," *Jamestown (ND) Weekly Alert*, November 4, 1897; *Kalispell Bee*, May 8, 1901; and Linderman, "Rocky Boy Renegades," 24.

7. James Denny, "About the Beginning of Rocky Boy Reserve," 2, undated manuscript, RBSA.

8. Linderman, "Rocky Boy Renegades," 24.

9. See interview with Malcolm Mitchell, "Mr. Mitchell's Words of Old Rocky Boy," undated interview, RBSA.

10. Linderman, "Rocky Boy Renegades," 24.

11. "Return of the Cree," *Anaconda Standard*, May 8, 1897.

12. "Law, Lawyers and Litigants, and a Few Judges and Judgments," *Anaconda Standard*, May 12, 1901.

13. "The Cree Indian Nuisance," *Anaconda Standard*, December 7, 1900.

14. "Game Law a Dead Letter," *Anaconda Standard*, October, 28, 1900; "Crees Are a Nuisance," *Anaconda Standard*, December 15, 1900; "Game Warden's Report," *Anaconda Standard*, December, 6, 1901; and "Indians Slaughter Game," *Anaconda Standard*, January 9, 1902.

15. James Denny, "About the Beginning of Rocky Boy Reserve," 2, RBSA; and interview with Malcolm Mitchell, "Mr. Mitchell's Words of Old Rocky Boy," RBSA.

16. Interview with Joe Day Child, September 17, 1924, RBSA.

17. Speaking of early dances the two groups held jointly, one account explained, "Rocky Boy was the leader of the Chippewas and Chief Little Bear was leader of the Crees and when Rocky Boy started to look and search for a place to live Little Bear wanted to be a chief and was very jealous of Chief Rocky Boy." There is little other evidence of significant interpersonal problems, but such feelings would have been understandable. Little Bear stood with a long history of struggle in Montana to attain land holdings for his people, and Little Bear may have viewed Rocky Boy's new efforts to do the same for his Chippewas as an affront. See Malcolm Mitchell, "My Grandfather Day Child's Father Story," undated manuscript, RBSA.

18. "The Chippewa," undated manuscript, RBSA.

19. "Danger of Epidemic," *Anaconda Standard*, March 18, 1901.

20. "Crees in Quarantine," *Anaconda Standard*, June 12, 1901; "The Ishmaelites of the Prairie," *Anaconda Standard*, June 16, 1901; *Kalispell Bee*, May 8, 1901; *Anaconda Standard*, June 23, 1901; *Montana Daily Record* (Helena), August 1, 1901; "Fighting Smallpox on the Reservation," *Anaconda Standard*, November 11, 1901; "To Chase Them Back," *Havre Plaindealer*, October 18, 1902; and "Smallpox on the Reservation," *Dupuyer Acantha*, October 23, 1902. See also "Many Crees Quarantined," *Havre Plaindealer*, October 25, 1902; "Small Pox Infected," *Kalispell Bee*, October 28, 1902, 3; "Goes to Other Shore," *Havre Plaindealer*, November 29, 1902; *Montanian and Chronicle* (Choteau), December 19, 1902; and *Dupuyer Acantha*, January 22, 1903.

21. *Great Falls Daily Tribune*, August 1, 1901; "Refuses to Interfere," *Kalispell Bee*, August 1, 1901; and *Butte Inter Mountain*, September 14, 1901a.

22. "Who Will Pay Claims against Crees," *Milk River Eagle*, October 19, 1901; "Want Crees Removed," *Havre Plaindealer*, November 11, 1902; "Is Costing Money," *Havre Plaindealer*, November 15, 1902; "Get Rid of Crees," *Butte Inter Mountain*, February 22, 1902; "Crees Must Move On," *Montanian and Chronicle*, May 9, 1902; "Tom Miles Wants to Deport Cree Indians," *Butte Inter Mountain*, July 19, 1902; and "No Right Here," *Butte Inter Mountain*, November 8, 1902.

23. See this book's companion website, www.nativebutforeign.org, for sources and discussion of positive and negative press coverage in Montana.

24. "Smallpox Spreaders," *Topeka State Journal*, April 9, 1896; Commissioner of Indian Affairs William A. Jones to Secretary of the Interior Ethan Hitchcock, July 15, 1901, RSBA; Acting Secretary of the Interior Thomas Ryan to Governor Joseph K. Toole, July 22, 1901, Montana Governors Papers, MC 35a, MSHS, box 9, folder 1; and "Crees Have Right to Remain," *Anaconda Standard*, August 1, 1901. See also *Great Falls Tribune*, August 1, 1901.

25. "The Best It Can Do," *Anaconda Standard*, August 1, 1901; and "It Is a Hopeless Task," *Anaconda Standard*, November 15, 1901. Records from 1902 and 1903 show Canadian officials well aware of border-crossing Natives, the spread of smallpox, et cetera. See "Northwest Territories: Correspondence regarding Vagrant American Sioux and an Outbreak of Smallpox among Straggling Chippewa and Cree Indians from the United States," record group 10, Black Series, volume 3797, file 47,554–2, reel C-10139, NAC.

26. See this book's companion website, www.nativebutforeign.org, for sources and discussion of the public groups campaigning for Cree deportation. See also "Want the Crees Deported," *Havre Plaindealer*, February 15, 1902.

27. "To this day," he continued, "I don't know what reason we had to move from the Crow reservation." Interview with George Watson, "Watson's Story," undated, RSBA; "Crees Are Moving North," *Anaconda Standard*, January 31, 1902.

28. George Watson recalled that there were two feet of snow on the ground when they left the Crow Reservation. At Billings, they had to shovel snow off the ground where they pitched their camp. The trip to Glasgow and Havre was difficult, with winter storms bringing new snowfall and winds blowing the fallen snow viciously. See interview with George Watson, "Watson's Story," undated, RSBA.

29. *Havre Eagle*, January 26, 1902.

30. The *Havre Plaindealer* commented in late 1902 that Crees made a regular habit of claiming to be Chippewa in order to secure "succor from the government." If true, Crees likewise understood the uphill struggle that they, as *Crees*, faced in attaining

their goals in Montana and the possible advantage that Chippewas held. See "Up to Uncle Sam," *Havre Plaindealer*, November 1, 1902.

31. Interview with Malcolm Mitchell, "Mr. Mitchell's Words of Old Rocky Boy," RSBA; and "Want to Settle Down," *Anaconda Standard*, February 11, 1902. Rocky Boy also had to navigate divisions within his band and challenges to his leadership and perceived outlook toward sedentary settlement. See "Indian at War," *Butte Inter Mountain*, March 11, 1902.

32. "Talk with the Travelers," *Anaconda Standard*, January 17, 1902; and "Indians before Judge," *Kalispell Bee*, July 11, 1901. See this book's companion website, www.nativebutforeign.org, for discussion of these sources and reports.

33. Senate Committee on Indian Affairs, Wandering American-Born Indians of Rocky Boy's Band, Montana, 58th cong., 2nd sess., S.R. 1020, Serial 4773, 1. The bill had its origin when a correspondent from a Washington, DC, paper wrote a humorous skit featuring Rocky Boy. The skit circulated around Capitol Hill until it caught the eye of Indiana senator Albert J. Beveridge. He was intrigued by the story, touched by their plight, and introduced the legislation. See Edward B. Clark, "Joke Starts Legislative Wheels," *Charlevoix County Herald* (East Jordan, MI), July 1, 1911.

34. See "Sun Dance Is Proposed," *Anaconda Standard*, June 20, 1901; and "Twas a Tame Sun Dance," *Anaconda Standard*, June 27, 1901.

35. See Samuel Bellow to Commissioner of Indian Affairs, February 29, 1906, RBSA. James Denny commented that Levy had helped Rocky Boy write letters in his initial efforts to forge official relationships with local and national officials. See James Denny, "About the Beginning of Rocky Boy Reserve," 2, RBSA.

36. "Butte News," *Anaconda Standard,* June 16, 1904. See this book's companion website, www.nativebutforeign.org for sources and discussion of Levy's and Cameron's efforts in publicly promoting the Cree and Chippewa cause.

37. See "Chippewa Indians Start War Dances in the Valley," *Anaconda Standard*, February 16, 1902; "Poor Chippewas without a Home," *Butte Inter Mountain*, September 17, 1903; "Looking Up Testimony of Rocky Boy Tribe," *Butte Inter Mountain*, September 25, 1903; "Rocky Boy Tribe," *Kalispell Bee*, December 22, 1903; "Homes for Rocky Boy's Band," *River Press* (Fort Benton, MT), January 6, 1904; "Chief Rocky Boy Pays a Visit to Mr. Dixon," *Anaconda Standard*, August 3, 1904. See also "Rocky Boy Visits Mr. Dixon," *Billings Gazette*, August 5, 1904; Frank G. Churchill to Secretary of the Interior James Garfield, October 14, 1908, record group 75, Records of the Bureau of Indian Affairs, Indian Office Files Relative to Lands for Rocky Boy's Band of Chippewa Indians, entry 121, Central Classified Files, 1907–1939, Blackfeet-#900–1908–307.4 (hereafter record group 75, RB Files), part 1, NARA-DC.

38. Little Bear to Secretary of the Interior Ethan Hitchcock, February 10, 1905, record group 10, Black Series, vol. 3863, file 84,138-1, reel C-10152, NAC.

39. "Memorandum on Cree Indians in the United States," February 20, 1905; J. D. McLean to Little Bear, February 21, 1905; and Little Bear to J. D. McLean, March 30, 1905, all in record group 10, Black Series, vol. 3863, file 84,138-1, reel C-10152, NAC.

40. David Laird to Little Bear, August 8, 1905, record group 10, Black Series, vol. 3863, file 84,138–1, reel C-10152, NAC.

41. "Little Bear Calls All His People to Their Native Land," *Great Falls Tribune*, October 12, 1905; "The Cree Indians Will Leave Montana," *Choteau Acantha*, October 5, 1905; "Back to Canada the Crees Will Go," *Anaconda Standard*, October 2, 1905; "Crees Will Hit the Trail," *Havre Plaindealer*, September 30, 1905; and "After

Twenty Years Indians Will Give Up," *San Francisco Call*, October 3, 1905. The *Havre Plaindealer* included the text of what they claimed to be the letter Little Bear sent out to his followers, but the language was so derogatory to Montana Crees that one has to wonder if the editors took liberties in what they printed. See this book's companion website, www.nativebutforeign.org, for discussion of these sources and reactions.

42. *Anaconda Standard*, October 31, 1905.

43. Little Bear to Frank Oliver, November 7, 1905, record group 10, Black Series, vol. 3863, file 84,138–1, reel C-10152, NAC; and "Little Bear Is Poor but He Is Also Proud," *Anaconda Standard*, November 19, 1905.

44. J. D. McLean to David Laird, November 15, 1905; David Laird to secretary of the interior, January 10, 1906; J. D. McLean to David Laird, January 16, 1906; and David Laird to Little Bear, January 24, 1906—all in record group 10, Black Series, vol. 3863, file 84,138–1, reel C-10152, NAC; and "G. Dupont Ally of Little Bear Dead," *Havre Plaindealer*, June 23, 1906.

45. Four Souls would later explain that Havre stood as the dividing line between distinct groups of Crees: eastern (downstream) Crees, spreading out along the Milk River Valley from Havre, and western (upstream) Crees, going (south)westward between Havre, Great Falls, and Helena. Rocky Boy's Chippewas remained largely to the west of Helena, migrating between Garrison, Deer Lodge, Anaconda, Butte, and Helena. Four Souls interview, May 3, 1983, Montanans at Work Oral History Project, OH 541, tape 2, MSHS.

46. See "Queer Spots in and about Butte: No. 11—The Cree Village," *Anaconda Standard*, May 27, 1906; "Queer Spots in and about Butte: No. 24—The Crematory," *Anaconda Standard*, August 26, 1906; "Undesirable Citizens Are Ordered to Move," *Anaconda Standard*, June 22, 1907; "Dirtier Than the Crees," *Anaconda Standard*, June 28, 1907; and "Dancing Indian in Bad Scrape," *Anaconda Standard*, September 1, 1907.

47. The Department of the Interior indicated that citizenship could only be conferred upon "free white persons, Africans or persons of African descent." See *Choteau Acantha*, April 4, 1907. This may have been in response to the success of Chippewa Métis securing land holdings and the influx of Turtle Mountain Chippewas (of possible Canadian descent) entering the region during the previous year. See "Allotment of land to Family of Breeds," *Anaconda Standard*, January 12, 1906; "Dakotas Reds May Crowd out Whites," *Havre Plaindealer*, March 10, 1906; "Transplanting of Indians," *Havre Plaindealer*, March 10, 1906; and "Flocking into Northern Montana," *Havre Plaindealer*, March 24, 1906.

48. Jules A. Karlin, *Senator Joseph M. Dixon and Rocky Boy: A Documentary Postscript, 1908* (Helena: Montana Historical Society Press, 1954), 1.

49. The farmer in question was D. D. Hull, and Acting Commissioner of Indian Affairs Charles F. Larrabee wrote to the Flathead Indian agent, Samuel Bellows, frustrated that the matter had been brought to Dixon rather than handled locally. See Charles F. Larrabee to Samuel Bellow, January 13, 1908, Dusenberry Fonds, Glenbow Archives, Calgary.

50. Cong. Rec., 60th cong., 1st sess., 1325. Compensation to the Flathead Indian agent for support of the Chippewas was simultaneously increased from $1,500 to $1,800 per year. See *Choteau Acantha*, April 2, 1908.

51. The committee process involved debate over the Chippewas' foreign status and whether they would be settled on an existing or new reservation. See Frank Pierce to Moses Clapp, February 15, 1908, in US Congress, Senate, Indian Appropriation Bill,

60th cong., 1st sess., S.R. 278; Samuel Bellow to Francis E. Leupp, February 29, 1908, record group 75, RB Files, NARA-DC, part 1; Charles F. Larrabee to Joseph Dixon, March 7, 1908, record group 75, RB Files, NARA-DC, Part 1; and Cong. Rec., 60th Cong., 1st sess., 1908, 3253.

52. Cong. Rec., 60th Cong., 1st sess., 1908, 3381.

53. The House rescinded its objections on April 9, 1908. Cong. Rec., 60th Cong., 1st sess., 1908, 4561.

54. See Karlin, *Senator Joseph M. Dixon and Rocky Boy*, 2–4. Rocky Boy and Little Bear also lobbied Montana's other US senator, Thomas H. Carter. In the summer of 1908, after a joint Sun Dance led by Little Bear and Rocky Boy, they held council with the senator at his house in Helena. John Calen Carter diary, July 5–7, 1908, SC 1978, MSHS.

55. Joseph Dixon to Francis Leupp, July 11, 1908, record group 75, RB Files, NARA-DC, part 1; and "Rocky Boy's Tribe to Receive Land," *Anaconda Standard*, September 26, 1908.

56. Rocky Boy to Frank C. Churchill, October 24, 1908, record group 75, RB Files, NARA-DC, part 3; Frank C. Churchill to James R. Garfield, November 11, 1908, record group 75, RB Files, NARA-DC, part 1; and Frank C. Churchill to Rocky Boy, November 10, 1908, record group 75, RB Files, NARA-DC, part 1. See also Rocky Boy to Frank C. Churchill, November 13, 1908; and Rocky Boy to Frank C. Churchill, November 22, 1908, record group 75, RB Files, NARA-DC, part 3.

57. Frank C. Churchill to Francis Leupp, October 14, 1908, record group 75, RB Files, NARA-DC, part 1; Frank C. Churchill to James R. Garfield, November 11, 1908, record group 75, RB Files, NARA-DC, part 1; Frank C. Churchill to James R. Garfield, November 28, 1908, record group 75, RB Files, NARA-DC, part 1; and James R. Garfield to Frank C. Churchill, December 15, 1908, record group 75, RB Files, NARA-DC, part 1.

58. "May Deport Cree Indians," *River Press* (Fort Benton, MT), July 15, 1908.

59. See David Laird to J. D. McLean, July 16, 1908; J. D. McLean to David Laird, July 23, 1908; David Laird to J. D. McLean, July 27, 1908; superintendent general of Indian affairs to governor general in council, August 1, 1908; J. D. McLean to David Laird, September 5, 1908; and Edwin L. Norris to David Laird, July 8, 1908—all in record group 10, Black Series, vol. 3863, file 84,138–1, reel C-10152, NAC; and *River Press* (Fort Benton, MT) September 23, 1908.

60. "Governor Makes Move to Rid State of Crees," *Anaconda Standard*, July 9, 1908. Seeking alternative avenues to relieve their suffering, Little Bear even attempted to enlist his people in the US Army, a move Rocky Boy later tried. See *Little Rockies Miner* (Zortman, MT), June 11, 1908; "Roy Boys Will Not Go to War," *Tacoma Times*, September 26, 1914; "Rocky Boy Passes to Happy Hunting Ground," *Enterprise* (Harlem, MT), April 27, 1916.

61. "Home Is Offered to Cree Indians," *Anaconda Standard*, September 16, 1908. See also "Crees Have a Home," *Little Rockies Miner* (Zortman, MT), October 3, 1908.

62. See "Rob Squirrels of Pine Cones," *Helena Daily Independent*, November 14, 1908.

Chapter 9

1. Martha Edgerton Plassmann Papers, MC 78, box 5, folder 6, MSHS.

2. "Charity at Home," *Great Falls Tribune*, January 8, 1909.

3. Those named first on a list of contributors included Charles Russell, William Bole, Sid Willis, William McKee, Oscar Frederickson, William Rance, and *Tribune*

employees. See "C. M. Russell Starts Fund," *Great Falls Tribune*, January 10, 1909. Within two days, the *Tribune* reported money "rolling in." "The Fund for Rocky Boy," *Great Falls Tribune*, January 12, 1909.

4. "Indians Appeal to the Court," *Evening Star* (Washington, DC), January 8, 1909; *River Press* (Fort Benton, MT), January 13, 1909; "Wards of Government Starve and Freeze," *Labor World* (Duluth, MN), January 23, 1909; "Offer Thanks to the People," *Helena Daily Independent*, January 10, 1909; Office of Indian Affairs to Fred C. Morgan, January 29, 1909; Office of Indian Affairs to Fred C. Morgan, February 19, 1909; and Office of Indian Affairs to Fred C. Morgan, March 2, 1909, all in Dusenberry Fonds, Glenbow Archives, Calgary.

5. See Superintendent Churchill to Robert G. Valentine, July 6, 1909, record group 75, entry 4, Copies of Official Letters Sent, box 11, National Archives and Records Administration, Rocky Mountain Region (hereafter NARA-RMR), Denver. See also "Good Riddance to Them," *Anaconda Standard*, July 25, 1909; "Lands Withdrawn for Rocky Boy's Band," *Great Falls Daily Tribune*, July 26, 1909; and "Preparing to Move Rocky Boy's Tribe," *Anaconda Standard*, August 10, 1909.

6. See *Searchlight* (Culbertson, MT), July 30, 1909; "Valley County's Protest," *River Press* (Fort Benton, MT), August 4, 1909; "Rocky Boys," *Searchlight* (Culbertson, MT), August 6, 1909; "Indians Locate in Valley County" and "Round up of Rocky Boy's Band," *River Press* (Fort Benton, MT), August 11, 1909; W. Lewis and C. S. Stafford to Thomas H. Carter, July 20, 1909, Thomas H. Carter Papers, MF 180 (hereafter Carter Papers), MSHS; and William Powers to Robert G. Valentine, July 22, record group 75, Records of the Bureau of Indian Affairs, Indian Office Files relative to Lands for Rocky Boy's Band of Chippewa Indians, entry 121, Central Classified Files, 1907–1939, Blackfeet-#900–1908–307.4 (record group 75, RB Files), part 1, NARA-DC.

7. Charles N. Pray to Frank Pierce, July 25, 1909, record group 75, RB Files, NARA-DC, part 1.

8. W. Matthews to Thomas H. Carter, July 31, 1909, Carter Papers, MSHS; F. S. Reed to Richard G. Ballinger and Thomas H. Carter, August 10, 1909, Carter Papers, MSHS; and Effa Goss to the Department of the Interior, July 17, 1909, Paul B. Babcock to Richard G. Ballinger, August 11, 1909, Albert R. Chapman to Frank Pierce, October 2, 1909, Frank Pierce to Effa Goss, July 23, 1909, John Francis Jr. to William Powers, August 14, 1909, and C. F. Hauke to Albert R. Chapman, October 16, 1909, all in record group 75, RB Files, NARA-DC, part 1.

9. John F. Armstrong to Robert G. Valentine, September 27, 1909; C. F. Hauke to John F. Armstrong, October 8, 1909; John F. Armstrong to Robert G. Valentine, October 13, 1909; John F. Armstrong to Robert G. Valentine, October 14, 1909; and John F. Armstrong to Robert G. Valentine, October 18, 1909, record group 75, RB Files, NARA-DC, part 2. See this book's companion website, www.nativebutforeign.org, for additional sources and discussion of local opposition to the Valley County plan.

10. Thomas H. Carter to Robert G. Valentine, October 16, 1909, record group 75, RB Files, NARA-DC, part 2; and C. F. Hauke to Thomas H. Carter, October 22, 1909, record group 75, RB Files, NARA-DC, part 2. Continued opposition mounted. On October 25, 1909, a large group of Culbertson citizens wrote a letter of protest to Commissioner Valentine, and, on the following day, news of such protests were reported in the national press. See Citizens of Culbertson to Robert G. Valentine, October 25, 1909, record group 75, RB Files, NARA-DC, part 2; "Strong Protest Sent," *Great Falls Leader*, October 26, 1909; and "Citizens Protest a Land Reserve," *Christian Science Monitor*, October 26, 1909.

11. See "To Remove Rocky Boys," *Searchlight* (Culbertson, MT), October 29, 1909; "Louis Hill Remembers His Northern Montana Friends," *Enterprise* (Harlem, MT), January 5, 1910; "Booster Bound for Helena," *Enterprise* (Harlem, MT), September 29, 1910; "Boosters at State Fair," *River Press* (Fort Benton, MT), October 5, 1910; and "Montana Boosters Trip" and "The Hill Special," *Searchlight* (Culbertson, MT), October 7, 1910.

12. *Great Falls Leader*, October 28, 1908; C. F. Hauke to William R. Logan, October 26, 1909; and William R. Logan to Robert G. Valentine, October 26, 1909, record group 75, RB Files, NARA-DC, part 2.

13. Robert G. Valentine to Richard A. Ballinger, October 27, 1909, record group 75, RB Files, NARA-DC, part 2. Upon receipt of Valentine's recommendation, Secretary of the Interior Ballinger notified a number of concerned parties. See Richard A. Ballinger to Moses Clapp, October 29, 1909; and Richard A. Ballinger to W.W. Heffelfinger, October 29, 1909, record group 75, RB Files, NARA-DC, part 2. Commissioner Valentine thus informed John Armstrong of his decision, wrote to Agent Logan to select a suitable tract on the Blackfeet Reservation, and informed Agent Churchill of the Blackfeet Reservation of their impending arrival. See Robert G. Valentine to William R. Logan, November 1, 1909; Robert G. Valentine to John F. Armstrong, November 1, 1909; and Robert G. Valentine to Clarence A. Churchill, November 1, 1909, record group 75, RB Files, NARA-DC, part 2. These developments worried those overseeing Turtle Mountain Chippewa allotment in Valley County. The Office of Indian Affairs wrote to the secretary of the interior requesting express protection of the Turtle Mountain Chippewas against similar encroachment and trouble from surrounding white settlers. See F. H. Abbott to Richard A. Ballinger, November 22, 1909, record group 75, RB Files, NARA-DC, part 2. Though not necessarily under duress, by 1911 some Turtle Mountain Chippewas had indeed been settled elsewhere than Valley County: 250 were in Miles City to the south, 100 were in Harlem to the northwest, and another 150 were south of Hingham, Montana. See "Fertile Lands Have Been Selected by Maj. Armstrong for Red Brother," *Havre Plaindealer*, June 10, 1911.

14. *Havre Promoter*, November 12, 1909; "Senator Clapp," *Searchlight* (Culbertson), October 29, 1909.

15. "Rocky Boy Defender," *Great Falls Daily Leader*, November 4, 1909.

16. "Rocky Boy and His Band," *Great Falls Tribune*, November 3, 1909.

17. "A Plea for Justice," *Great Falls Tribune*, November 6, 1909.

18. Ibid. See also "It Is Time to Rectify a Wrong," *Great Falls Tribune*, November 6, 1909. For his part, Rocky apparently attempted to compel his band to stay near Helena for a time. See "The Chippewa Tribe Is in Sore Straits near Helena," *Lake Shore Sentinel* (Polson, MT), October 15, 1909.

19. "For the Indians," *Great Falls Tribune*, November 12, 1909; "Rocky Boy Will Be Removed in Two Weeks," *Lake Shore Sentinel* (Polson, MT) November 12, 1901; *Dillon (MT) Tribune*, November 12, 1909; "Northern Montana Is Grateful," *Havre Plaindealer*, November 13, 1909; "A Home for the Chippewas," *Great Falls Tribune*, November 14, 1909; and "Rocky Boy on Road Home," *Great Falls Tribune*, November 15, 1909.

20. See James Denny, "About the Beginning of Rocky Boy Reserve," 3, and interview with Windy Boy, undated, RBSA. See this book's companion website, www.nativebutforeign.org, for sources and discussion of the reactions to Chippewa settlement on the Blackfeet Reservation, both for and against the plan.

21. Charles E. Roblin to Robert G. Valentine, April 11, 1910, Thralls Wheat to Robert

G. Valentine, July 21, 1910, and "Indians of Rocky Boy's Band Who Have Been Allotted on the Blackfeet Reservation," August 28, 1911, all in record group 75, RB Files, NARA-DC, part 3.

22. "Chippewas Abandon Reservation Again," *Anaconda Standard*, December 14, 1910.

23. Arthur McFatridge to Robert G. Valentine, January 27, 1911; F. H. Abbott to Arthur McFatridge, January 27, 1911; Arthur McFatridge to Robert G. Valentine, February 1, 1911; F. H. Abbott to Arthur McFatridge, February 24, 1911; Robert G. Valentine to Joseph M. Dixon, March 4, 1911; and Robert G. Valentine to Charles N. Pray, August 1, 1911—all in record group 75, RB Files, NARA-DC, part 3.

24. See John W. Coburn to Robert G. Valentine, July 31, 1911, record group 75, RB Files, NARA-DC, part 3.

25. See this book's companion website, www.nativebutforeign.org, for sources and discussion of Montanan concerns about the failing allotment process.

26. Interview with Malcolm Mitchell, March 31, 1975, RBSA; Flathead Agency to Robert G. Valentine, March 8, 1912, Dusenberry Papers, box 10, folder 9, MSU; and interview with Jim Gopher, May 25, 1975, RBSA.

27. Interview with Malcolm Mitchell, May 3, 1974, RBSA.

28. William Sibbald to David McLean, February 1, 1911; David McLean to William Sibbald, February 10, 1911; William Sibbald to David McLean, July 22, 1911; Peter Thunder to Little Bear, July 25, 1911; and David McLean to William Sibbald, August 2, 1911—all record group 10, Black Series, vol. 3863, file 84,138, pt. 2, reel C-10152, NAC.

29. Documents also spell Pennato's name with the following variations: Pennetou, Pun-ah-too, Panetoo.

30. In 1905, the *Missoulian* joked about Linderman's association with the Flathead tribe, asking why he had not enrolled as a member in order to secure allotment. The *Missoulian*'s answer: "Perhaps he is a Cree." This speaks to Linderman's intimacy with both groups and underscores the level to which Crees' landless plight had sunk into Montanan public rhetoric. See "Voice of the State Press," *Havre Plaindealer*, January 28, 1905, quoting the *Missoulian*.

31. Linderman, *Montana Adventure,* 143.

32. Pennato's translator, Fred Huntley, recalled, "Linderman was the head push, what I mean he carried Pennato through business deals, corresponding to Washington one thing after another. So Linderman is really the guy they ought to give credit to." See interview with Fred Huntley, May 8, 1975, RBSA.

33. See "What to Do with Fort Assiniboine," *Great Falls Tribune*, January 2, 1912.

34. See interview with Fred Huntley, May 8, 1975, RBSA. Four Souls also indicated that Pennato was the first to push for settlement in the Bear Paw Mountains. See Four Souls interview, Montanans at Work Oral History Project, tape 2, MSHS.

35. Linderman, *Montana Adventure*, 152.

36. See interview with Fred Huntley, May 8, 1975, 16, and interview with James Denny, undated, 4, RBSA.

37. See Rocky Boy to Frank B. Linderman, May 17, 1912, and Rocky Boy to Frank B. Linderman, May 24, 1912, Frank Bird Linderman Papers, MF 382 (hereafter Linderman Papers), MSHS. Interestingly, Little Bear wrote to Linderman on the same day, stating his desire to go to Washington as well and asserting that all of the Chippewas wanted him to go. See Little Bear to Frank B. Linderman, May 24, 1912, Linderman Papers, MSHS.

38. See this book's companion website, www.nativebutforeign.org, for sources and discussion of Rocky Boy's band during early 1912.

39. Arthur McFatridge to Robert G. Valentine, February 28, 1912, record group 75, RB Files, NARA-DC, part 4.

40. Interview with Malcolm Mitchell, March 31, 1975, RBSA. Apparently unwilling to ask that Rocky Boy share his meager rations, Little Bear made no mention of McFatridge's suggestion. Suggesting his deep concern for Little Bear and his Crees, Rocky Boy immediately approached McFatridge and told him to give rations to Little Bear and his followers. This act of goodwill garnered two full months of rations and clothing for Little Bear's Crees.

41. Arthur McFatridge to Robert G. Valentine, February 28, 1912, record group 75, RB Files, NARA-DC, part 4; and Fred Morgan to Robert G. Valentine, March 2, 1912, Dusenberry Fonds, Glenbow Archives, Calgary. Simultaneously, $185,000 was appropriated, with the reimbursement of Blackfeet Indians for Rocky Boy allotments as one of the reasons. See US Department of the Treasury, *Blackfeet Indians: Letter from The Secretary of the Treasury*, 62nd Cong., 2nd sess., HR doc. 553, February 20, 1912, Serial 6326.

42. George Bird Grinnell to Frank B. Linderman, February 20, 1912, Linderman Papers, MSHS.

43. C. F. Hauke to Fred A. Baker, April 29, 1912, record group 75, Records of the Blackfeet Agency, Allotting Agents Correspondence, box 1, NARA-RMR.

44. Fred A. Baker to Robert G. Valentine, August 20, 1912, record group 75, RB Files, NARA-DC, part 4. At the same time, pressure mounted for Crees. Having had a Sun Dance canceled in Great Falls in June, talk of deportation arose again. See *Choteau Montanian*, June 19, 1914.

45. Fred A. Baker to C. F. Hauke, August 23, 1912, record group 75, RB Files, NARA-DC, part 4.

46. Fred A. Baker to Robert G. Valentine, August 20, 1912, and Fred A. Baker to C. F. Hauke, August 23, 1912, record group 75, RB Files, NARA-DC, part 4.

47. Fred A. Baker to Robert G. Valentine, October 11, 1912, record group 75, RB Files, NARA-DC, part 4.

48. Fred A. Baker to Frank B. Linderman, December 6, 1912, Linderman Papers, MSHS. See this book's companion website, www.nativebutforegin.org, for sources and discussion of Chippewa and Cree conditions during late 1912 and early 1913.

49. Walter L. Fisher to Robert J. Gamble, December 19, 1912, record group 75, Records of the Blackfeet Agency, Allotting Agents Correspondence, box 1, NARA-RMR; and Paris Gibson to Frank B. Linderman, January 11, 1913, Linderman Papers, MSHS.

50. "Objection to Rocky Boy," *Havre Plaindealer*, January 11, 1913. See also "Plan Giving Assiniboine to Rocky Boy and Braves," *Havre Plaindealer* January 11, 1913; "Rocky Boy Causes Another Big Howl," *Anaconda Standard*, January 14, 1913; "Against Rocky Boy," *Great Falls Tribune*, January 18, 1913; "Rocky Boy and his People," *Great Falls Tribune*, January 19, 1913; "Don't Want Rocky Boy," *River Press* (Fort Benton, MT), January 22, 1913; and "Protests Against Placing Indians at Assiniboine," *Havre Plaindealer*, January 25, 1913.

51. "Will Resist Foisting Rocky Boy on Havre," *Havre Plaindealer*, January 18, 1913; *Havre Plaindealer*, February 22, 1913; "At Fort Assiniboine," *Great Falls Tribune*, March 1, 1913; *Havre Plaindealer*, March 15, 1913; and Henry L. Myers to Frank B. Linderman, January 9, 1913, Linderman Papers, MSHS.

52. See this book's companion website, www.nativebutforeign.org, for sources and discussion of the political maneuvering of various officials and conditions of Crees and Chippewas across the state during early 1913.

53. See Cato Sells to Fred C. Morgan, August 14, 1913, Fred C. Morgan to Cato Sells, August 18, 1913, Lewis Main to Fred C. Morgan, August 24, 1913, Fred C. Morgan to Cato Sells, August 25, 1913, Fred C. Morgan to Cato Sells, August 26, 1913, Fred C. Morgan to Cato Sells, August 28, 1913, and Fred C. Morgan to E. F. Tabor, September 2, 1913—all in Dusenberry Fonds, Glenbow Archives, Calgary; Fred C. Morgan to Cato Sells, August 21, 1913, Dusenberry Papers, box 10, folder 9, MSU; and "Rocky Boy's Band Helped Again by Morgan," *Daily Missoulian*, August 16, 1913.

54. Grant Chief Stick indicated that they had been allowed to winter there previously, given rations, and allowed to plant crops. See interview with Chief Stick, August 27, 1974, RBSA. See this book's companion website, www.nativebutforeign.org, for further sources and discussion of Chippewa and Cree conditions in late 1913.

55. See this book's companion website, www.nativebutforeign.org, for further sources and discussion of numerous parties writing in support of Chippewa and Cree settlement during these months.

56. Cato Sells to William Bole, November 26, 1913; and Cato Sells to Franklin K. Lane, November 26, 1913, record group 75, RB Files, NARA-DC, part 4.

57. The delegation from Havre and Kalispell consisted of state senator and Havre mayor D. S. MacKenzie, along with L. K. Devlin and C. F. Morris. See "Protest in Hands of Secretary Lane," *Havre Plaindealer*, November 29, 1913; *River Press* (Fort Benton, MT), December 10, 1913. See also David J. Goss to Franklin K. Lane, November 13, 1913; Resolution Adopted by the City Council of Havre, Montana, November 17, 1913, record group 75, RB Files, NARA-DC, part 4; "Boles Argument for Chippewas," *Havre Plaindealer*, November 22, 1913; "Protest in Hands of Secretary Lane," *Havre Plaindealer*, November 29, 1913; E. B. Meritt to Arthur McFatridge, November 20, 1913; and Arthur McFatridge to Cato Sells, November 28, 1913, record group 75, RB Files, NARA-DC, part 4.

58. Frank B. Linderman, "A Square Deal for Rocky Boy's Braves," *Ekalaka (MT) Eagle*, November 24, 1916.

59. Little Bear and Peter Kennewash to Franklin K. Lane, December 26, 1913, Geneva Stump's Rocky Boy collection, M 7937, Glenbow Archives, Calgary. See this book's companion website, www.nativebutforeign.org, for sources and discussion of Chippewa and Cree reluctance to return to the Blackfeet Reservation for the winter, officials' communication on their wintering in Great Falls, and public comment on the plan.

60. "Gossip of the Town," *Fergus County Democrat* (Lewistown, MT), December 30, 1913.

61. William Bole to Cato Sells, May 25, 1914, Frank B. Linderman to Cato Sells, May 23, 1914, Franklin K. Lane to William Bole, June 2, 1914, Arthur McFatridge to Office of Indian Affairs, July 15, 1914—all in record group 75, RB Files, NARA-DC, part 5.

62. William Bole to Frank B. Linderman, June 9, 1914, Linderman Papers, MSHS.

63. William Bole to Frank B. Linderman, October 13, 1914, Frank B. Linderman to Franklin K. Lane, November 23, 1914, and Franklin K. Lane to Frank B. Linderman, December 7, 1914—all in Linderman Papers, MSHS.

64. See this book's companion website, www.nativebutforeign.org, for sources and discussion of the debated leadership roles of Rocky Boy and Little Bear in the joint group.

65. William Bole to Cato Sells, February 3, 1916, and Department of the Interior to E. B. Meritt, February 10, 1915—both in record group 75, RB Files, NARA-DC, Part 5; "Congress Authorizes the Opening of Assiniboine," *Havre Plaindealer*, February 6, 1915; "Asks Allotment of Land to Red Men Rather than Endanger Ratification of Measure," *Havre Plaindealer*, February 13, 1915; and Henry Myers to Frank B. Linderman, February 1, 1915, Linderman Papers, MSHS.

66. See Charles Ellis to William Bole, April 6, 1915, Charles Ellis to Rocky Boy, April 8, 1915, Rocky Boy to Charles Ellis, April 10, 1915, Charles Ellis to Rocky Boy, April 17, 1915, Rocky Boy to Charles Ellis, April 24, 1915, Rocky Boy to Charles Ellis, April 30, 1915, and Roger St. Pierre to Charles Ellis, June 25, 1915—all in record group 75, Records of the Blackfeet Agency, entry 5, Superintendents Subject Files, box 19, folder 229, NARA-RMR.

67. See this book's companion website, www.nativebutforeign.org, for extensive sources on the struggles faced during these tenuous months of encampment.

68. Little Bear to Cato Sells, June 14, 1915, record group 75, RB Files, NARA-DC, part 5.

69. See this book's companion website, www.nativebutforeign.org, for sources and discussion of the debates over which lands were to be reserved for white and which for Native settlement.

70. Rocky Boy to Cato Sells, November 29, 1915, record group 75, Belknap Agency Letters, NARA-RMR; and Franklin K. Lane to John M. Stephens, December 16, 1915, Linderman Papers, MSHS. Both Rocky Boy's letter and a letter from Little Bear were included in the final S.R. 347 report on the necessity for the lands therein set aside for their bands. See Senate Committee on Public Lands, *Fort Assiniboine Military Reservation, Mont.*, 64th Cong., 1st sess., April 12, 1916, S. Rep. 347, Serial 6898, 3. See also Cong. Rec., 64th cong., 1st sess., 435.

71. Cong. Rec., 64th cong., 1st sess., 1186, 1481; and William Bole to Frank B. Linderman, February 8, 1916, Linderman Papers, MSHS.

72. Celeste Rivers, "A Mountain in His Memory: Frank Bird Linderman, His Role in Acquiring the Rocky Boy Indian Reservation for the Montana Chippewa and Cree, and the Importance of That Experience in the Development of his Literary Career" (master's thesis, University of Montana, 1990); Frank B. Linderman to Henry Myers, January 25, 1916, Frank B. Linderman to Little Bear, January 26, 1916, Frank B. Linderman to Rocky Boy, January 26, 1916, Frank B. Linderman to Henry Myers, February 1, 1916, and Frank B. Linderman to Henry Myers, February 9, 1916—all in Linderman Papers, MSHS.

73. Frank B. Linderman to Henry Myers, February 8, 1916, Linderman Papers, MSHS; and Henry Myers to Frank B. Linderman, February 12, 1916, Linderman Papers, MSHS. See also *Enterprise* (Harlem, MT), January 13, 1916; and "Myers New Bill for Reservation," *Enterprise* (Harlem, MT), January 27, 1916. Myers's overall opinion of the Chippewas and Crees may not have changed significantly as his bill seemed to have also been motivated by a desire to be rid of the Rocky Boy "nuisance," as he later termed them. "Part of What Senator Myers Has Accomplished for the Homesteaders of Montana," *Big Timber (MT) Pioneer*, October 19, 1916.

74. Linderman expressed to Myers that a third township would "satisfy" more people than he probably realized. To Commissioner Sells, however, he clarified that this statement should have been interpreted less as approval and more as "we will take what we can get." See Frank B. Linderman to Henry Myers, February 19, 1916, and Frank B. Linderman to Cato Sell, February 21, 1916—both in Linderman Papers, MSHS.

75. Frank B. Linderman to Henry Myers, March 13, 1916, Frank B. Linderman to George Bird Grinnell, March 24, 1916, Frank B. Linderman to Little Bear and Rocky Boy, March 13, 1916—all in Linderman Papers, MSHS; and Cong. Rec., 64th cong., 1st sess., April 13, 1916, 6002.

76. Cong. Rec., 64th cong., 1st sess., April 24, May 2 and 4, July 27, August 1, September 2, 5, 6, 7, and 8, 6726, 7247, 7369, 11703–4, 11912, 13731–32, 13844, 13873–74, 13953, 13961, 14135. See this book's companion website, www.nativebutforeign.org, for sources and discussion of Montana press coverage of the congressional process.

77. See this book's companion website, www.nativebutforeign.org, for sources and discussion of Rocky Boy's health and death.

78. "Rocky Boy Has Passed," *Havre Promoter*, April 24, 1916.

79. Linderman, *Montana Adventure*, 161.

80. Big Rock, a Chippewa residing on the Blackfeet Reservation, provides a good example. Accustomed to his Blackfeet allotment, he was reticent to move to Fort Assiniboine, and he corresponded with Frank Linderman concerning this. This likely represents other individuals who remained off-reservation. See Big Rock to Frank B. Linderman, June 6, 1916, July 16, 1916, December 1, 1916, and Frank B. Linderman to Big Rock, December 11, 1916—both in Linderman Papers, MSHS.

81. Interview with Malcolm Mitchell, undated, RBSA.

82. In May 1917, Inspector James McLaughlin and Blackfeet superintendent Charles L. Ellis made an official enrollment list. See "Tentative Roll of Rocky Boy Indians, May 30, 1917," Rocky Boy's Reservation Records, 1909–1917, SC 903, MSHS; and James McLaughlin, "Family History of So-called Rocky Boy Indians," May 7–30, 1917, Geneva Stump's Rocky Boy collection, M 7937, Glenbow Archives, Calgary.

83. See this book's companion website, www.nativebutforeign.org, for sources and discussion on the ongoing struggles of difficult conditions in establishing the reservation.

84. Walter Denny, "Story of the Bear Paws," undated manuscript, RBSA.

85. Vine Deloria Jr. and Clifford M. Lytle, *American Indians, American Justice* (Austin: University of Texas Press, 1983), 24.

86. The Chippewa Cree Tribe was organized, with resultant tribal constitution, bylaws, and council, under the aegis of the New Deal Indian Reorganization Act in 1935. See Chippewa Cree Indians of the Rocky Boy's Reservation, Montana, *Constitution and Bylaws of the Chippewa Cree Indians of the Rocky Boy's Reservation, Montana Law and Order Code of the Chippewa Cree Tribe of the Rocky Boy's Reservation, Montana* (Box Elder, MT: The Tribe, 1935).

Chapter 10

1. Anselmo Valencia to Morris K. Udall, December 21, 1962, in Petition for Land for the Relocation of Residents of Pascua Village of Tucson, Arizona," Spicer Papers, ASM, subgroup 6, box 1, folder 9; and Udall Papers, UASC, subgroup 2, series 3, box 162, folder 14; "Pascua Project Outlined: Yaquis Weren't 'Enemy' so US Aid Is Limited," *Arizona Daily Star* (Tucson), June 29, 1967.

2. For Juan Banderas, Cajeme, and Tetabiate (Juan Maldonado), see Hu-Dehart, *Yaqui Resistance and Survival*.

3. For a more detailed explanation, see Spicer, *People of Pascua*, 46–47.

4. Interview with Guadalupe Balthazar, April 28, 1937, Spicer Papers, ASM, subgroup 8, box 1, folder 58; interview with Cayetano Lopez on the "History of Chief-

tainship," August 2, 1940, Spicer Papers, ASM, subgroup 8, box 8, folder 472; and "Yaquis Seek Education," *Christian Science Monitor*, November 5, 1920.

5. "Civilization of Yaqui Indians Is Aim of Association," *Morning Sun* (Yuma, AZ), October 2, 1923. Sociedad Guadalupe was followed in 1948 by the Yaqui- and Mexican-run Guadalupe Home Convenience Cooperative Association, which succeeded in improving town infrastructure and access to utilities, and in 1960 by the Guadalupe Health Council. The latter incorporated itself in 1964 as the Guadalupe Organization and in the following years served as the first true political voice for Guadalupe residents, leading to social organizations, health services, and training programs. See Glaser, "Story of Guadalupe," 33–34, 71, 79.

6. "Yaquis Battle in Arizona for Tribe Control," *Ogden (UT) Daily Standard*, February 19, 1932. See also "Many Hatreds Split Arizona Indian Clan," *Arizona Daily Star*, June 30, 1932. Some of the other influential leaders from the 1910s to the 1950s included Guadalupe Flores, Jose Maria Aumada, Angel Matus, and Juan Martinez in Scottsdale; Felipe Valenzuela, Francisco Tavena, and Francisco Valencia in Guadalupe; and Juan Pistola, Lucas Chavez, Francisco Matus, Cayetano Lopez, Enrique Sabala, and Francisco Valencia in Tucson.

7. Richard Olsen to Drs. Gilbert and Langone, September 6, 1962, Richard Olsen to Robert. A. Roessel Jr., September 6, 1962, and Robert A. Roessel Jr. to Roger Lewis, October 22, 1962—all in Udall Papers, UASC, subgroup 2, series 3, box 165, folder 13.

8. Roger Lewis to Robert A. Roessel Jr., October 18, 1962, Udall Papers, UASC, subgroup 2, series 3, box 165, folder 13.

9. See Anselmo Valencia to Stewart Udall, December 4, 1961, and Stewart Udall to Anselmo Valencia, January 18, 1962—both in Spicer Papers, ASM, subgroup 8, box 1, folder 53; and Miller, *Forgotten Tribes*, 86–89.

10. Miller, *Forgotten Tribes*, 88.

11. Jim Hart, "Yaqui Indians May Lose Village Here," *Tucson Daily Citizen*, September 26, 1953; "Yaqui Indians to Stay Put and As Is," *Arizona Daily Star*, November 21, 1953; and "'Progress' and Pascua Village," *Tucson Daily Citizen*, November 26, 1953.

12. See Blake Brophy, "Tucson's Pascua Village—A Community in Two Worlds," *Tucson Daily Citizen*, May 3, 1959, 7–8, 10–11.

13. For a short biography and description of Painter's long dedication to the Arizona Yaqui community, see Spicer, introduction to Painter, *With Good Heart*, xi–xxi.

14. The rest of the committee included University of Arizona anthropologist and executive director of the Arizona Children's Home Association Carleton S. Wilder (serving as secretary), University of Arizona anthropology professor Edward Dozier, Tucson Chamber of Commerce manager Robertson M. Fort, Tucson Community Council executive director Thomas Jordan, Holy Family Church's Reverend Maurice McCarthy, Tucson superintendent of schools Robert D. Murrow, F. Ronstadt Hardware Company owner Gilbert Ronstadt, Tucson attorney S. Leonard Scheff, Tucson city councilman G. Freeman Woods, and Tucson attorney Charles McPhee Wright.

15. For information on a 1934 effort by outside groups to purchase lands on behalf of Tucson Yaquis, see George Pierre Castile, "Yaquis, Edward H. Spicer, and Federal Indian Policy: From Immigrant to Native Americans," *Journal of the Southwest* 44 (Winter 2002): 393–95.

16. See this book's companion website, www.nativebutforeign.org, for sources and discussion of the importance of humanitarian work in directing the form and content Yaqui-Arizonan relations in the early to mid-twentieth century.

17. The proposed site consisted of a portion of Sections 13 and 24 of Township 15S, Range 12E, GSR Meridian.

18. "Tucson's Yaquis Seek Land for New Village," *Arizona Daily Star*, October 30, 1962. See this book's companion website, www.nativebutforeign.org, for sources and discussion of the divided response from Tucsonans concerning the plan.

19. Roy T. Helmandollar to Morris K. Udall, November 27, 1962, Roy T. Helmandollar to Muriel Thayer Painter, November 27, 1962, Muriel Thayer Painter to Theodore Heyl (District Assistant to Morris K. Udall in Tucson), November 28, 1962, Theodore Heyl to Anselmo Valencia, December 1962, and Theodore Heyl to Anselmo Valencia, December 4, 1962—all in Udall Papers, UASC, subgroup 2, series 3, box 165, folder 13; Andre M. Faure to Morris K. Udall, December 13, 1962, Udall Papers, UASC, subgroup 2, series 3, box 162, folder 14; Painter Diary, Muriel Thayer Painter Papers, MS 13, ASM, subgroup 4, folder 8; and miscellaneous correspondence, Muriel Thayer Painter Papers, ASM, subgroup 4, folder 7.

20. Muriel Thayer Painter to CPCH members, January 1963, Spicer Papers, ASM, subgroup 6, box 1, folder 1. The letters addressed to Congressman Morris K. Udall were from Florence O. Albaugh, Pima County director, Arizona State Department of Public Welfare; Lee Davis, mayor, Tucson; Andre M. Faure, director, Pima County Planning Department; Robertson Fore, manager, Tucson Chamber of Commerce; Francis J. Green, bishop, Roman Catholic Diocese of Tucson; Don Hummel, former mayor, Tucson; Mundey Johnston, vice-chairman of the board, Bank of Tucson; Frederick H. Lowry, executive director, Tucson Festival Society; William A Mitchell, president, Tucson Community Council; Robert D. Murrow, superintendent, Tucson Public Schools; Robert L. Nugent, executive vice president, University of Arizona; Gilbert Ronstadt, F. Ronstadt Hardware Co.; Bernie Roth, manager, Tucson Sunshine Climate Club; Pete Rubi, Board of Supervisors member, Pima County, Arizona; William A. Small, publisher, *Tucson Daily Citizen*; Harold M. Solorio, publisher, *La Prensa* (Tucson's "Mexican-American Newspaper"); and Harold Steinfeld, president, Steinfeld's Department Store.

21. The petition is available in its entirety in Spicer Papers, ASM, subgroup 6, box 1, folder 9; and Udall Papers, UASC, subgroup 2, series 3, box 162, folder 14. For a good explanation of the aims and goals of the petition and the delicate balance it had to strike, see Miller, *Forgotten Tribes*, 92–94.

22. Morris K. Udall to Rev. Francis J. Green, January 8, 1963, Udall Papers, UASC, subgroup 2, series 3, box 165, folder 13.

23. Richard Olson, "Memo RE Yaqui Bill," 1963, Udall Papers, UASC, subgroup 2, series 3, box 162, folder 14.

24. US Congress, House, A Bill to Provide for the Conveyance of Certain Land of the United States to the Pascua Yaqui Association, Inc., HR 6233, 88th Cong., 1st sess., May 9, 1963.

25. Press release from Morris K. Udall, May 9, 1963, Udall Papers, UASC, subgroup 2, series 3, box 165, folder 13. Anselmo Valencia and Geronimo Estrella were listed as the primary PYA incorporators. "Article of Incorporation of Pascua Yaqui Association," May 13, 1963, Udall Papers, UASC, subgroup 2, series 3, box 165, folder 13. The elected PYA board included Anselmo Valencia, Ygnacio Alvares, Filipa Suarez, Eusebia Salvador, Raul Silvas, Antonio Valencia, Juan Alvarez, Virginia Valenzuela, and Geronimo Estrella—all Pascua Village residents.

26. See Painter Diary, February 18, 1964, Muriel Thayer Painter Papers, ASM, subgroup 4, folder 8.

27. Morris K. Udall to Wayne Aspinall, May 14, 1963, Udall Papers, UASC, subgroup 2, series 3, box 165, folder 13.

28. See "Rep. Udall Seeks 200-Acre Land Grant for the Yaquis," *Arizona Daily Star* (Tucson), May 15, 1964; statement by Senator Hayden, June 1964, Hayden Papers, ASUA, box 341, folder 6; US Congress, House, Committee on Interior and Insular Affairs, *Providing for the Conveyance of Certain Land of the United States to the Pascua Yaqui Association, Inc.*, 88th cong., 2nd sess., August 14, 1964, H. Rep. 1805, serial 12620; US Senate, Committee on Interior and Insular Affairs, *Providing for the Conveyance of Certain Land of the United States to the Pascua Yaqui Association, Inc.*, 88th cong., 2nd sess., September 8, 1964, S. Rep. 1530, serial 12617; and Cong. Rec., 88th Cong., 2nd sess., 1964, 19726, 20096–97, 20561, 21656, 22841, 23099, 23208, 23209, 23861 and 24062. See this book's companion website, www.nativebutforeign.org, for sources and more detailed discussion of the legislative process and public discourse surrounding the bill's passage.

29. Painter Diary, March 26, 1963, Muriel Thayer Painter Papers, ASM, subgroup 4, folder 8.

30. "Even worse than having a Leprosy colony": A. Turney Smith to Morris K. Udall, August 11, 1964. See also Morris K. Udall to A. Turney Smith, August 13, 1964, Monte Seymour to Morris K. Udall, August 10, 1964, Morris K. Udall to Monte Seymour, August 13, 1964, Vivian Arnold to Morris K. Udall, August 17, 1964, and Morris K. Udall to Vivian Arnold, August 25—all in Udall Papers, UASC, subgroup 2, series 3, box 165, folders 13–14; A. Turney Smith to Carl Hayden, September 21, 1964, Carl Hayden to A. Turney Smith, September 21, 1964, Monte Seymour to Carl Hayden, August 10, 1964, Carl Hayden to Monte Seymour, August 20 and September 21, 1964, and Monte Seymour to Carl Hayden, October 16, 1964—all in Hayden Papers, ASUA, box 341, folder 6.

31. Morgan Maxwell to unknown newspaper editor, July 1964, Joseph R. Cesare to Morris K. Udall, August 17, 1964, and Morris K. Udall to Joseph R. Cesare, August 25, 1964—all in Udall Papers, UASC, subgroup 2, series 3, box 165, folder 13; Joseph R. Cesare to Senator Henry M. Jackson, September 12, 1964, Udall Papers, UASC, subgroup 2, series 3, box 162, folder 14; and Dennis Deconcini, Joseph R. Cesare, Vivian Arnold, and Howard Misner to Carl Hayden, September 16, 1964, Hayden Papers, ASUA, box 341, folder 6. See this book's companion website, www.nativebutforeign.org, for excerpts and discussion of these sources expressing opposition to Udall's bill.

32. James E. Cook, "Yaquis of Pascua to Vacate Site Occupied for 40 Years," *Arizona Republic* (Phoenix), November 28, 1964.

33. Margaret Kuehlthau, "Dust and Dreams," *Tucson Daily Citizen*, March 13, 1965.

34. Pascua Yaqui Advisory Committee to Melvin Mogulof, October 6, 1965, Spicer Papers, ASM, subgroup 6, box 1, folder 1.

35. Spicer Papers, ASM, subgroup 6, box 1, folder 9, and box 4, folder 7.

36. Edward Spicer and Anselmo Valencia to Office of Manpower Programs Evaluation and Review, April 5, 1966, Spicer Papers, ASM, subgroup 6, box 1, folder 1; and "Office of Economic Opportunity Application for Community Action Program, Grant No: ARIZ CAP 66–378, Component Project No: 7–33A," Spicer Papers, ASM, subgroup 6, box 2, folder 1.

37. Spicer's letters date August–September 1966. Spicer Papers, ASM, subgroup 6, box 1, folder 1; F. D. Patterson, president, Phelps-Stokes Fund, to Edward Spicer,

September 14, 1966, Spicer Papers, ASM, subgroup 6, box 1, folder 1. See also Margaret Kuehlthau, "Work Due Soon: Yaquis Receive Federal Grant to Build Village," *Tucson Daily Citizen*, September 15, 1966.

38. Margaret Kuehlthau, "Federally Financed Segregation: Resettlement of Yaqui Indians Branded Discrimination," *Tucson Daily Citizen*, September 20, 1966.

39. Tom Turner, "Yaquis Weary of Unfulfilled Vows by 'Do-Gooders,'" *Arizona Daily Star*, March 11, 1970.

40. See this book's companion website, www.nativebutforeign.org, for sources on these figures as well as extensive sources on the funding challenges, fund-raising campaigns and successes, opposition challenges, and related issues.

41. For an in-depth firsthand account and analysis of the New Pascua project, see William Willard, "The Community Development Worker in an Arizona Yaqui Project" (PhD diss., University of Arizona, 1990).

42. A woman named Ruby Wood corresponded with Carl Hayden concerning land deeds on behalf of Guadalupe Yaquis in 1955. Hayden said that the lands could only be deeded by the State of Arizona and that the federal government had no say in the matter. See Ruby Wood to Carl Hayden, October 4, 1955, Paul Eaton (administrative assistant to Senator Hayden) to Ruby Wood, October 10, 1955, Ruby Wood to Paul Eaton, October 14, 1955, Paul Eaton to Roger Laveen (Maricopa County recorder), November 18, 1955, Edward Woozley to Carl Hayden, December 22, 1955, and Paul Eaton to Ruby Wood, December 29, 1955—all in Hayden Papers, ASUA, box 203, folder 15. See also "County to Iron out Guadalupe Tangles," *Arizona Republic*, January 4, 1961. The process of attaining land titles extended to 1975, when Maria Valdez, a forty-year Guadalupe resident, received the first title. Pat Sabo, "Widow Gets First Deed to Guadalupe Trust Land," *Phoenix Gazette*, June 28, 1975.

43. See this book's companion website, www.nativebutforeign.org, for extensive sources on public perceptions of Guadalupe, internal debates over political actions, the processes of community organizing and incorporation, and community identity.

44. For an insightful and well-illustrated, though brief, examination of this Scottsdale history, see *The Yaquis of Scottsdale, Arizona: Family, Indomitable Spirit, Generosity* (Scottsdale: Concerned Citizens for Community Health, 2002). See also José María Burruel, *Mexicans in Scottsdale* (Charleston, SC: Arcadia, 2007).

45. Tom Turner, "Yaquis Weary of Unfulfilled Vows by 'Do-Gooders,'" *Arizona Daily Star*, March 11, 1970.

46. In addition, some Yaquis outside of New Pascua were succeeding in creating their own economic opportunities. Successes in Marana, Rillito, Tumacácori, Continental, and Sahuarita were promising but not representative of broader trends. See "Co-Ops Successful: Yaquis Making Progress with Minimum of Help," *Tucson Daily Star*, April 3, 1970.

47. New Pascuans faced another crisis in the mid-1970s as Pima County officials attempted to impose new building codes on New Pascua. As it was federal land, there was debate over whether local ordinances applied, and the debate highlighted deteriorating conditions at the settlement. For a more in-depth discussion of the early 1970s problems, see Miller, *Forgotten Tribes*, 104–9.

48. Morris K. Udall notation on Spicer report and letter, August 3, 1970, Udall Papers, UASC, subgroup 3, series 1, box 557, folder 25.

49. US Congress, A Bill to Provide for the Extension of Certain Federal Benefits, Services, and Assistance to the Pascua Yaqui Indians of Arizona, and for Other Purposes, HR 8411, 94th Cong., 1st sess., July 8, 1975.

50. J. R. Fitzgerald to Carl Hayden, November 7, 1937, Hayden Papers, ASUA, box 625, folder 24. See also J. R. Fitzgerald to Carl Hayden, November 19, 1937 and November 20, 1937, Hayden Papers, ASUA, box 625, folder 24.

51. John Collier to Carl Hayden, December 6, 1937, Hayden Papers, ASUA, box 625, folder 24. During this era, Yaquis at Guadalupe succeeded in having New Deal programs from the Federal Emergency Relief Act and Works Progress Administration instituted in their community, but this was very different from true federal investment in Yaqui tribal recognition.

52. Sumner Wells to Charles West, December 31, 1937, Hayden Papers, ASUA, box 625, folder 24; and Carl Hayden to J. R. Fitzgerald, January 10, 1938, Hayden Papers, ASUA, box 625, folder 24.

53. Antonio Coronado to Barry Goldwater, June 10, 1971, Personal and Political Papers of Senator Barry Goldwater, FM MSS1, Arizona Historical Foundation, ASUA, series 3, box 196, folder 24.

54. Barry Goldwater to Nick Laird (Bureau of Indian Affairs), June 29, 1971, Personal and Political Papers of Senator Barry Goldwater, FM MSS1, Arizona Historical Foundation, ASUA, series 3, box 196, folder 24.

55. Harrison Loesch (assistant secretary of the interior) to Barry Goldwater, October 1, 1971, Personal and Political Papers of Senator Barry Goldwater, FM MSS1, Arizona Historical Foundation, ASUA, series 3, box 196, folder 24.

56. Thomas J. Madden (assistant administrator, Office of General Council, Law Enforcement Assistance Program) to Dale Wing (Office of Regional Operations, Indian Program Section, Law Enforcement Assistance Program), April 17, 1975, Udall Papers, UASC, subgroup 3, series 1, box 581 folder 19.

57. Resolution 5–75, March 17, 1975, and Resolution 22–75, June 5, 1975, Intertribal Council of Arizona, Spicer Papers, ASM, subgroup 6, box 1, folder 10; and Arizona Commission of Indian Affairs business meeting minutes, June 27, 1975, Udall Papers, UASC, subgroup 2, series 3, box 203, folder 3.

58. "Yaquis Seek Federal Recognition from Congress," *Qua'Toqti* (Oraibi, AZ), September 18, 1975; Richard La Course, American Indian Press Association Reports, Udall Papers, 1975, Udall Papers, UASC, subgroup 2, series 3, box 203, folder 3; Morris K. Udall to Anselmo Valencia, November 13, 1975, Udall Papers, UASC, subgroup 3, series 1, box 581, folder 19; Anthony Drennan Sr. (chairman, Colorado River Indian Tribes) to Barry Goldwater, June 23, 1975, Buck Kitcheyan (tribal chairman, San Carlos Apache Nation) to Barry Goldwater, July 31, 1975, and Tucson Indian Center to Sandy McNabb (US Department of Labor), September 31, 1975—all in Personal and Political Papers of Senator Barry Goldwater, FM MSS1, Arizona Historical Foundation, ASUA, series 3, box 210, folder 33. See this book's companion website, www.nativebutforeign.org, for excerpts from these sources on Arizona Native opposition.

59. "Yaquis Want Government Aid," *Daily Dispatch* (Douglas, AZ), October 20, 1975.

60. "Editorials: American Yaqui Indians Facing Dilemma," *Arizona Daily Star* (Tucson), September 26, 1975; and Bryan Michener (legislative assistant to Paul Fannin) to Edward Spicer, August 1, 1975, Spicer Papers, ASM, subgroup 8, box 5, folder 317. See also "New Pascua Yaquis Get Better Housing but Still No Bus," *Arizona Daily Star* (Tucson), August 24, 1975; and "Udall Bill Would Recognize Yaquis," *Arizona Daily Star* (Tucson), September 19, 1975. For more information on Fannin's involvement with Yaqui recognition, see Fannin Papers, box 94/9, folders 6–7.

61. "Yaqui Elders Rebel at Becoming Wards," *Tucson Daily Citizen*, November 19, 1975.

62. Judy Donovan, "New Pasqua [*sic*] Yaquis Hope Village Will Become Reservation," *Arizona Daily Star* (Tucson), November 23, 1975. For related comments, see "Yaqui Elders Rebel at Becoming Wards," *Tucson Daily Citizen*, November 19, 1975.

63. Richard La Course, American Indian Press Association Reports, Udall Papers, 1975, Udall Papers, UASC, subgroup 2, series 3, box 203, folder 3; Roger C. Wolf to Senators Paul J. Fannin and Barry Goldwater, January 9, 1976, and Edward Spicer to Paul J. Fannin, January 9, 1975, Spicer Papers, ASM, subgroup 6, box 1, folder 8; and Udall Papers, UASC, subgroup 2, series 3, box 203, folder 3.

64. See this book's companion website, www.nativebutforeign.org, for information and sources on Spicer's testimony.

65. For information on the conflict between the PYA and Pima County concerning building codes, the sewer system, and other issues, see Elaine Nathanson, "Federal Grants Sought: Yaquis Request Status as Tribe," *Arizona Daily Star* (Tucson), May 23, 1976; Dan M. Huff, "Battling County Code," *Tucson Daily Citizen*, August 7, 1976; "Yaquis Have Earned Legal Recognition," *Arizona Daily Star* (Tucson), November 27, 1976; and Karen Fowler, "No Special Privileges [editorial]," *Arizona Daily Star* (Tucson), December 9, 1976.

66. A Bill to Provide for the Extension of Certain Federal Benefits, Services and Assistance to the Pascua Yaqui Indians of Arizona, and for Other Purposes, HR 6612, 95th Cong., 1st sess., April 25, 1977; and A Bill to Provide for the Extension of Certain Federal Benefits, Services and Assistance to the Pascua Yaqui Indians of Arizona, and for Other Purposes, S 1633, 95th Cong., 1st sess., June 7, 1977.

67. Edward Spicer to James Abourezk, September 21, 1977, Spicer Papers, ASM, subgroup 6, box 1, folder 8; and US Congress, Senate, Select Committee on Indian Affairs, *Trust Status for Pascua Indians of Arizona: Hearings on S 1633*, 95th Cong., 1st sess., September 27, 1977.

68. Raymond Cross to Edward Spicer, October 19, 1977, and Edward Spicer to Raymond Cross, October 27, 1977, Spicer Papers, ASM, subgroup 6, box 1, folder 8; Ben Cole, "House Panel Favors Bill Giving Yaquis Equal Treatment," *Arizona Republic* (Phoenix), February 17, 1978, Edward Spicer to Morris K. Udall, March 1, 1978, and Edward Spicer to Congressman Teno Roncalio, March 1, 1978—all in Spicer Papers, ASM, subgroup 6, box 1, folder 8; Doug Underwood, "Would Allow Reservation: Panel OKs Bill Giving Yaquis Tribal Status," *Tucson Daily Citizen*, March 10, 1978; and Judy Donovan, "2 Bills May Ease Yaqui Problems," *Arizona Daily Star* (Tucson), March 20, 1978.

69. HR 6612 was reported with amendment (H. Report 1021) on April 3, amended and passed by the House, and laid on the table awaiting passage of the Senate bill on April 17. Cong. Rec., 95th Cong., 2nd sess., 1978, 8499, 10204 and 10215–6. S 1633 was reported with amendment (S. Report 719) on March 22, amended and passed on April 5, and tabled for reconciliation with the House bill on April 17. On May 2, the Senate disagreed with certain House amendments and called for a conference. Conference members included Morris K. Udall, Teno Roncalio, Theodore Risenhoover, James Johnson, James Abourezk, Howard Metzenbaum, John Melcher, Dewey Bartlett, Mark Hatfield, and Dennis DeConcini. They submitted their report (H. Report 1339) on July 11. The House agreed to the report on August 16 and submitted it to the Senate, where it was agreed to on August 25. The bill was subsequently examined and signed in the Senate and presented to President Carter on September 6, and it was signed by President Carter as Public Law 95–375 on September 18, 1978. Cong. Rec., 95th Cong., 2nd

sess., 1978, 8058, 8766, 10215, 12167, 12168, 14696, 15205, 20032, 26497, 27770, 28032, 28184, 28032, 29790.

70. For full details, see US Congress, Senate, Select Committee on Indian Affairs, Extension of Benefits and Services to the Pascua Yaqui Indians of Arizona, 95th Cong., 2nd sess., March 22, 1978, S. Rep. 719, serial 13197–2; US Congress, House, Committee on Interior and Insular Affairs, Providing for the Extension of Certain Federal Benefits, Services and Assistance to the Pascua Yaqui Indians of Arizona, and for Other Purposes, 95th Cong., 2nd sess., March 30, 1978, H. Rep. 1021, serial 13201–3; and US Congress, House, Providing for the Extension of Benefits and Services to the Pascua Yaqui Indians of Arizona: House Conference Report, 95th Cong., 2nd sess., June 11, 1978, H. Rep. 1339, serial 13201–9.

71. See Raymond Cross to Edward Spicer, May 3, 1978, Spicer Papers, ASM, subgroup 8, box 5, folder 317; Anselmo Valencia to Edward Spicer, August 22, 1978, and Edward Spicer to Jimmy Carter, August 26, 1978—both in Spicer Papers, ASM, subgroup 6, box 1, folder 8; Mike Quinn, "Yaquis Surrounded by Anglo society," *Tucson View*, May 8, 1978; and "Conferees Approve Yaqui Tribal Status," *Tucson Daily Citizen*, June 24, 1978.

72. "It's Official: Yaquis Win Tribal Status," *Tucson Daily Citizen*, September 18, 1978. For other reports on the recognition, see "New Law Makes Yaquis an Official Tribe," *Arizona Daily Star*, September 19, 1978; "Status for needy Yaquis," *Arizona Daily Star* (Tucson), September 21, 1978; Rick Lanning, "Once-Fierce Yaquis Taken into US Fold," *Phoenix Gazette*, November 2, 1978; and Bill Shaw, "Tribal Status Promises a Better Life for Yaquis," *Arizona Daily Star* (Tucson), December 27, 1978.

73. Ron Rich, "The Troubles of Being Arizona's Newest Indian Tribe," *Arizona Republic* (Phoenix), October 2, 1979. See also Kevin O'Brien, "Yaquis Fear Many Will Miss Sept. Deadline for Official Tribal Signup," *Arizona Daily Star* (Tucson), June 3, 1979.

74. Barry Goldwater to David G. Ramirez, October 18, 1980, Personal and Political Papers of Senator Barry Goldwater, FM MSS1, Arizona Historical Foundation, ASUA, series 3, box 222, folder 2.

75. See US Congress, House, Committee on Interior and Insular Affairs, Declaring that the United States Holds in Trust for the Pascua Yaqui Tribe of Arizona Certain Lands in Pima County, Arizona, 97th Cong., 1st sess., November 20, 1981, H. Rep. 347, serial 13435; and US Congress, Senate, Select Committee on Indian Affairs, To Declare that the United States Holds in Trust for the Pascua Yaqui Tribe of Arizona Certain Lands in Pima County, Arizona, 97th Cong., 2nd sess., October 1, 1982, S. Rep. 657, serial 13455.

76. See this book's companion website, www.nativebutforeign.org, for sources and discussion on these legal battles.

77. For extensive discussion of this, see William Willard, "Self-Government for Native Americans: The Case of the Pascua Yaqui Tribe," in *American Indian Policy: Self-Governance and Economic Development*, ed. Lyman Letgers and Fremont Lyden (Westport, CT: Greenwood Press, 1994).

78. US Congress, House, A Bill to Amend the Act Entitled "An Act to Provide for the Extension of Certain Federal Benefits, Services, and Assistance to the Pascua Yaqui Indians of Arizona, and for Other Purposes," HR 734, 103rd Cong., 2nd sess., October 14, 1993.

79. Mary Benanti, "Yaquis Closer to Recognition as Tribe," *Tucson Citizen*, May 1, 1993; Ellen Gamerman, "Pascua Yaquis Seek Status of Sovereign Tribe," *Arizona Daily Star* (Tucson), May 3, 1993. For a more detailed discussion of this process, see Castile, "Yaquis, Edward H. Spicer, and Federal Indian Policy," 412.

80. "Pascua Pueblo—A Step Forward," undated brochure, circa 1966, Spicer Papers, ASM, subgroup 6, box 1, folder 9, and box 4, folder 7.

Bibliography

This comprehensive bibliography includes sources cited in the text as well as those featured in supplementary materials at this book's companion website, www.nativebutforeign.org, with the exception of some newspaper titles.

Archival Collections

Arizona State Historical Society (ASHS), Tucson

Bogan Manuscripts, 1909–1926, MS 0081
Felipe Molina, Oral History Interview, 1977–1981, AV 0360 20
Pearce Reminiscences, 1903–1907, MS 0651
Tucson Ephemera Files (under "Indians of North America-Yaqui")

Arizona State Museum (ASM), Tucson

Edward H. and Rosamond B. Spicer Papers, MS 5 (Spicer Papers)
Edward H. and Rosamond B. Spicer Papers, Unprocessed Papers in Accession 2000-175
Felipe Molina Interview, ca. 1977–1981, AV 0360 20
Muriel Thayer Painter Papers, MS 13 (Painter Papers)

Arizona Historical Foundation, Arizona State University, Tempe

M. Warren Krause Collection, MSS 108
Oral History Collection, FM MSS 141
Personal and Political Papers of Senator Barry Goldwater, FM MSS 1
Political Papers of Paul Fannin, MS FM MSS 2

Arizona State University Archives (ASUA), Tempe

Carl Hayden Papers, MSS1 (Hayden Papers)
Chicano Research Collections, Cecilia Teyechea Denogean de Esquer Papers, MSS 132 (Esquer Papers)

Arizona State University Libraries, Labriola Center, Tempe

Kenneth Stewart Papers, 1946–1981, MSS-182

Frank B. Linderman Estate, Kalispell, Montana

Glenbow Archives, Calgary, Alberta

Dusenberry Fonds, Microfilm (Dusenberry Fonds)
"Extract from Father Doucet's Memoir," June 5, 1879, M4343

Fraser A. William, "Plains Cree, Assiniboine, and Saulteaux (Plains) Bands, 1874–84," 1963, M 4379, PAM 970.3cr F842p, GA
Geneva Stump's Rocky Boy Collection, M 7937
Gilbert Edward Sanders, Correspondence and Reports, 1887–1908, M 1093
Norman Thomas MacLeod, 1882–1885, Personal Correspondence, M 785
Richard Burton Deane Fonds, M 313
Sam Pritchard Fonds, M 4138
William H. Metzler Fonds, Diary of William H. Metzler, NWMP, 1880–85, M836

Montana State Historical Society (MSHS), Helena

David Higler Papers, 1867–1935, SC 864
Edwin A. C. Hatch Diary, 1856, SC 810
Eli Guardipee Reminiscence, 1940, SC 772
Fort Assiniboine Records, MC 46
Frank Bird Linderman Papers, MF 382 (Linderman Papers)
Gustavus Doane Letters, SC 28
John Calen Carter Diary, SC 1978
Martha Edgerton Plassmann Papers, MC 78
Montanans at Work Oral History Project
  OH 541, Four Souls Interviews
  OH 542, James Gopher Interview
  OH 543, William Denny Sr. Interview
Montana Governors Papers, Joseph K. Toole Administration, MC 35a (Toole Papers)
Patrick Francis "Frank" Burke Papers, SC 304
Rocky Boy's Reservation Records, 1909–1917, SC 903.
Thomas H. Carter Papers (Carter Papers), MF 180
Thomas O. Miles Reminiscence (Miles Remin.), SC 475
Vertical Files
  Cree Indians
  Little Bear
  Rocky Boy
  Rocky Boy Indian Reservation
  Royal Canadian Mounted Police

Montana State University Archives (MSU), Bozeman

Cowan Family Papers, 1893–1966, Collection 643
Edward E. Barry, Jr. Collection, 1874–1977, Collection 2058
Fort Assiniboine Telegrams Received, 1881, Collection 2457 (Ft. Assiniboine Telegrams)
J. W. "Duke" Wellington Papers, 1876–1974, Collection 2029
Lloyd C. Pickett Papers, 1934–1975, Collection 2053
Merrill G. Burlingame Papers, 1880–1990, Collection 2245
Verne Dusenberry Papers, 1927–1966, Accession 85015 (Dusenberry Papers)

Rocky Boy School Archive (RBSA), Box Elder, Montana

National Archives of Canada (NAC), Ottawa, Ontario

Department of Indian Affairs, record group 10, Black Series
Volume 3687, File 13,607, Reel c-10120
Volume 3770, File 33,725, Reel c-10135
Volume 3722, File 24,125, Reel c-10126
Volume 3740, File 28,748–1, Reel c-10130
Volume 3740, File 27,748–2, Reel c-10130
Volume 3774, File 36,563, Reel c-10136
Volume 3797, File 47,554–2, Reel c-10139
Volume 3863, File 84,138–1, Reel c-10152

National Archives and Records Administration, Rocky Mountain Region (NARA-RMR), Denver, Colorado

Records of the Bureau of Indian Affairs
Fort Belknap Agency, Letters Received from the Commissioner of Indian Affairs, 1827–1927
Fort Belknap Agency, Letters Sent to the Commissioner of Indian Affairs, 1880–1924
Records of the Blackfeet Agency, Allotting Agents Correspondence
Records of the Blackfeet Agency, Entry 4, Copies of Official Letters Sent
Records of the Blackfeet Agency, Entry 5, Superintendent's Subject Files

National Archives and Records Administration (NARA-DC), Washington, DC

Records of the Bureau of Indian Affairs, RG 75
Indian Office Files Relative to Lands for Rocky Boy's Band of Chippewa Indians, Entry 121 Central Classified Files, 1907–1939, Blackfeet-#900–1908–307.4, Parts 1–5
Still Pictures (75.29), RA-2

Stone Child College Library, Box Elder, Montana

University of Arizona Special Collection (UASC), Tucson

Morris K. Udall Papers, MS 325 (Udall Papers)
Papers of Tom Miller, 1852–2003, MS 377

University of Montana, Maureen and Mike Mansfield Library, Missoula

Rocky Roy Reservation Records, RG 75, Microfilm

Government Documents

Chippewa-Cree Indians of the Rocky Boy's Reservation, Montana. *Constitution and Bylaws of the Chippewa Cree Indians of the Rocky Boy's Reservation, Montana Law and Order Code of the Chippewa Cree Tribe of the Rocky Boy's Reservation, Montana*. Box Elder, Montana: The Tribe, 1935.

US Bureau of the Census. *US Census, 1900*. Series T623. Rolls 909, 910, 912–915.

———. *US Census, 1920*. Series T625, Roll 197.

US Congress. House. A Bill to Provide for the Conveyance of Certain Land of the United States to the Pascua Yaqui Association, Inc. HR 6233, 88th Cong., 1st sess., May 9, 1963.

———. A Bill to Amend the Act Entitled "An Act to Provide for the Extension of Certain Federal Benefits, Services, and Assistance to the Pascua Yaqui Indians of Arizona, and for Other Purposes." HR 734. 103rd Cong., 2nd sess., October 14, 1993.

———. A Bill to Provide for the Extension of Certain Federal Benefits, Services, and Assistance to the Pascua Yaqui Indians of Arizona, and for Other Purposes. HR 8411. 94th Cong., 1st sess., July 8, 1975.

———. A Bill to Provide for the Extension of Certain Federal Benefits, Services, and Assistance to the Pascua Yaqui Indians of Arizona, and for Other Purposes. HR 6612. 95th Cong., 1st sess., April 25, 1977.

———. *Blackfeet Indians: Letter from the Secretary of the Treasury*. 62nd Cong., 2nd sess., 1912. H. Doc. 553. Serial 6326.

———. An Estimate from the Acting Secretary of the Interior of an Appropriation for the Relief of Renegade British Cree Indians in Montana, and to Prevent Their Starvation: Report from the US Department of Treasury. 49th Cong., 1st sess., 1886. House Executive Document 231.

———. *Hearings on the Indian Appropriation Bill, 1918*. 64th Cong., 2nd sess., 1917.

———. *Hearings on the Indian Appropriation Bill, 1922*. 1921.

———. Providing for the Extension of Benefits and Services to the Pascua Yaqui Indians of Arizona: House Conference Report. 95th Cong., 2nd sess., June 11, 1978. H. Rep. 1339. Serial 13201–9.

———. Relief for the Cree Indians, Montana Territory: Letter from the Secretary of the Interior. 50th Cong., 1st sess., 1888. House Executive Document 341.

US Congress. House. Committee on Interior and Insular Affairs. Declaring that the United States Holds in Trust for the Pascua Yaqui Tribe of Arizona Certain Lands in Pima County, Arizona. 97th Cong., 1st sess., November 20, 1981. H. Rep. 347. Serial 13435.

———. Providing for the Conveyance of Certain Land of the United States to the Pascua Yaqui Association, Inc. 88th Cong., 2nd sess., August 14, 1964. H. Rep. 1805. Serial 12620.

———. Providing for the Extension of Certain Federal Benefits, Services and Assistance to the Pascua Yaqui Indians of Arizona, and for Other Purposes. 95th Cong., 2nd sess., March 30, 1978. H. Rep. 1021. Serial 13201–3.

US Congress. Senate. A Bill to Provide for the Extension of Certain Federal Benefits, Services and Assistance to the Pascua Yaqui Indians of Arizona, and for Other Purposes. S. 1633. 95th Cong., 1st sess., June 7, 1977.

———. Appropriations, New Offices, Etc., Report from the US Department of the Treasury. 54th Cong., 1st sess., 1896. S. Doc. 316. Serial 3360.

US Congress. Senate. Committee on Foreign Relations. Report to Accompany Amendment of Mr. Carter to HR 8293. 54th Cong., 1st sess., 1896. S. Rep. 821.

US Congress. Senate. Committee on Indian Affairs. Wandering American-Born Indians of Rocky Boy's Band, Montana. 58th Cong., 2nd sess., 1904. S.R. 1020, Serial 4773.

US Congress. Senate. Committee on Interior and Insular Affairs. Providing for the Conveyance of Certain Land of the United States to the Pascua Yaqui Association, Inc. 88th Cong., 2nd sess., September 8, 1964. S. Rep. 1530. Serial 12617.

US Congress. Senate. Committee on Public Lands. Fort Assiniboine Military Reservation, Mont. 64th Cong., 1st sess., April 12, 1916. S. Rep. 347. Serial 6898.

US Congress. Senate. Select Committee on Indian Affairs. Extension of Benefits and Services to the Pascua Yaqui Indians of Arizona. 95th Cong., 2nd sess., March 22, 1978. S. Rep. 719. Serial 13197–2.

———. To Declare that the United States Holds in Trust for the Pascua Yaqui Tribe of Arizona Certain Lands in Pima County, Arizona. 97th Cong., 2nd sess., October 1, 1982. S. Rep. 657. Serial 13455.

———. Trust Status for Pascua Indians of Arizona: Hearings on S. 1633. 95th Cong., 1st sess., September 27, 1977.

US Department of State. *Papers Relating to the Foreign Relations of the United States with the Annual Message of the President Transmitted to Congress December 3, 1906*. Washington, DC: Government Printing Office, 1906. 2 volumes.

———. *Papers Relating to the Foreign Relations of the United States, 1905*. Washington, DC: Government Printing Office, 1905.

———. *Papers Relating to the Foreign Relations of the United States, 1907*. Washington, DC: Government Printing Office, 1907.

———. *Papers Relating to the Foreign Relations of the United States, 1918*. Washington, DC: Government Printing Office, 1918.

———. *Papers Relating to the Foreign Relations of the United States 1927*. Washington, DC: Government Printing Office, 1927. 3 volumes.

US Office of Indian Affairs. *1844 Annual Report of the Commissioner of Indian Affairs*. Washington, DC: T. Barnard, 1846.

Articles and Book Chapters

Adelman, Jeremy, and Stephen Aron. "From Borderlands to Borders: Empires, Nation-States, and the Peoples in between in North American History." *American Historical Review* 1043 (June 1999): 814–41.

Bogan, Phoebe M. "The Yaqui Indian Dances." *Progressive Arizona* 2, no. 5 (May 1926): 21–23, 35.

Burt, Larry. "In a Crooked Piece of Time: The Dilemma of the Montana Cree and the Métis." *Journal of American Culture* 9 (Spring 1986): 45–52.

———. "Nowhere Left to Go: Montana's Crees, Métis, and Chippewas and the Creation of Rocky Boy's Reservation." *Great Plains Quarterly* 7 (Summer 1987): 195–209.

Castile, George Pierre. "Yaquis, Edward H. Spicer, and Federal Indian Policy: From Immigrant to Native Americans." *Journal of the Southwest* 44 (Winter 2002): 383–435.

Conrad, Paul. "Indians, Convicts, and Slaves: An Apache Diaspora to Cuba at the Turn of the Nineteenth-Century," in *Linking the Histories of Slavery in North America and its Borderlands*, ed. James F. Brooks and Bonnie Martin, 67–96. Santa Fe, NM: School for Advanced Research Press, 2015.

Coolidge, Dane. "The Yaquis in Exile" *Sunset* 23 (September 1909): 299–302.

Cosulich, Bernice. "A Yaqui Passion Play in Arizona." *Travel* 56 (March 1931): 35–38, 54–55.

Dempsey, James, "Little Bear's Band: Canadian or American Indians?" *Alberta History* 41 (Autumn 1993), 2–9.

Glaser, Leah. "Working for Community: The Yaqui Indians of the Salt River Project." *Journal of Arizona History* 37 (Winter 1996): 337–56.

Harrington, Janette T. "New Hope for a Desert Town," *Presbyterian Life*, August 15, 1965, 1–9.

Holterman, Jack. *Chippewa-Cree in Glacier Country*. West Glacier, MT: Glacier Natural History Association, 1991.

Hoyt, Andrew Milligan. "A Plea for the Yaqui." *Overland Monthly* 52 (July 1908): 122–23.

Hrdlička, Aleš. "Notes on the Indians of Sonora, Mexico." *American Anthropologist* 6 (January–March 1904): 51–89.

Hu-DeHart, Evelyn. "Development and Rural Rebellion: Pacification of the Yaquis in the Late *Porfiriato*." *Hispanic American Historical Review* 54 (February 1974): 72–93.

———. "La solución final: la expulsión de los Yaquis de su Sonora natal." In *Seis expulsiones y un Adios. Despojo y Exclusión de la Historia del Estado Político en Sonora*, edited by Aaron Grageda, 133–67. Mexico City: Plaza y Valdes Editores, 2003.

"Incidents of the Rebellion as Related by Fine Day." In *The Cree Rebellion of '84, or, Sidelights on Indian Conditions subsequent to 1876*, edited by Campbell Inness, 11–18. Battleford, Saskatchewan: Battleford Historical Society Publications, 1926.

LaDow, Beth. "Sanctuary: Native Border Crossings and the North American West." *American Review of Canadian Studies* (Spring/Summer 2001): 25–42.

Leonard, Bert H. "Again the Yaqui." *Independent* (New York City) 118 (February 26, 1927): 235–36.

Linderman, Frank B. "Rocky Boy Renegades." *Indians at Work* 4 (January 1937): 23–28.

Little Bear, Isabelle. "My Own Story." In *Reflections: A History of Elk Point and District*, edited by Mary Bennet, 197–202. Winnipeg: Elk Point and District Historical Society, 1977.

McKay, W. Henry. "Lucky Man's Flight." *Canadian Cattlemen* (December 1948), 132–33, 136–37, 152.

Perschl, Nicholas. "History Repeats Itself." *Indian Sentinel*, March 1941, 35–36, 45.

Peterson, Hans. "Imasees and His Band: Canadian Refugees after the North-West Rebellion." *Western Canadian Journal of Anthropology* 8 (1978): 21–37.

"Pity in a Hostile Camp." *Forest and Stream* 26 (January 13, 1887): 481.

Rensink, Brenden W. "Cree Contraband or Contraband Crees: Early Montanan Experiences with Transnational Natives and the Formation of Lasting Prejudice, 1880–1885." In *Smugglers, Brothels, and Twine: Historical Perspectives on Contraband and Vice in North America's Borderlands*, edited by Andrae Marak and Elaine Carey, 24–43. Tucson: University of Arizona Press, 2011.

Reynolds, Marc M. "The Scourge of the Yaquis: Why American Lives and Capital in Mexico Are Menaced by a Handful of Savages." *Harpers Weekly* 52 (May 2, 1908): 10–12.

Roberts, Walter Adolf. "Tragedy of the Yaqui." *Overland Monthly* 52 (July 1908): 119–21.

Sharrock, Floyd W., and Susan R. Sharrock. "History of the Cree Indian Territorial Expansion from the Hudson Bay Area to the Interior Saskatchewan and Missouri Plains." In John C. Ewers, *Ethnological Report of the Chippewa Cree Tribe of the*

Rocky Boy Reservation, Montana and the Little Shell Band of Indians, Chippewa Indians vol. 6, 183–407. New York: Garland, 1974.

Shepherd, Jeffrey P. "Race, Blood, and Belonging: Transnational Blackfoot Bands and Families along the US-Canada Border, 1855–1915." In *Laying Down the Law: Critical Legal Histories of the North American West*, edited by Pablo Mitchell and Katrina Jagodinski, eds. Lawrence: University of Kansas Press, forthcoming.

Sheridan, Thomas. "How to Tell the Story of a 'People without History': Narrative versus Ethnohistorical Approaches to the Study of the Yaqui Indians through Time." *Journal of the Southwest* 30 (Summer 1988): 168–89.

"Sonora's Prodigal Yaquis." *Modern Mexico* 10 (July 1938): 17–18, 22.

Sperry, Elizabeth. "The Politics of Performance: Montana's Landless Indians and Beveridge's Montana Wildest West Show." *Montana: The Magazine of Western History* 62 (Spring 2012): 48–64.

Spicer, Edward. Introduction to *The Autobiography of a Yaqui Poet*, by Refugio Savala. Tucson: University of Arizona Press, 1980.

———. Introduction to *With Good Heart: Yaqui Beliefs and Ceremonies in Pascua Village*, by Muriel Thayer Painter. Tucson: University of Arizona Press, 1986.

———. "The Yaqui Indians of Arizona." *Kiva* 5 (March 1940): 21–24.

———. "Yaqui Villages Past and Present." *Kiva* 13 (November 1947): 2–12.

Stewart, M. K. "Dances of the Yaqui Indians at Easter Time." *Progressive Arizona* 6, no. 3 (March 1928): 13, 33–34.

Talbot, Elisha Hollingsworth. "The Truth about Mexico." *Moody's Magazine* 8 (December 1909): 427–34.

———"The Truth about Mexico: Conclusion." *Moody's Magazine* 9 (March 1019): 181–89.

———. "The Truth about Mexico: Government and the Yaqui Indians." *Moody's Magazine* 9 (January 1910): 16–30.

———. "The Truth about Mexico: Peonage." *Moody's Magazine* 9 (February 1910): 105–17.

Trujillo, Octaviana V. "The Yaqui of Guadalupe, Arizona: A Century of Cultural Survival through Trilingualism." *American Indian Culture and Research Journal* 22, no. 4 (1988): 67–88.

Turner, John Kenneth. "Barbarous Mexico: The Tragic Story of the Yaqui Indians." *American Magazine* 69 (November 1909): 39–40, 46.

Urquides, Maria. "Up from the Barrio." In *Arizona Memories*, edited by Anne Hodges Morgan and Rennard Strickland, 319–30. Tucson: University of Arizona Press, 1984.

Velasco, José Toro. "Colonización, Agua y Control Social: El Case de los Yaquis de Sonora." In *Indigenismo, Evolución de Una Práctica*. Mexico City: Instituto Nacional Indigenista, 1979.

———. "La Rebelion Yaqui en Sonora Durante el Siglo XIX." *Revista Mexicana de Sociología* 48 (January–March 1986): 237–56.

Wharfield, H. B. "A Fight with the Yaquis at Bear Valley, 1918." *Arizoniana*, Fall 1963, 1–9.

Whitaker, Herbert. "Slaveholding Americans: A Reply to Critic of 'The Planter." *Harpers Weekly* 53 (May 22, 1909): 27.

White, Richard. "The Winning of the West: The Expansion of the Western Sioux in the Eighteenth and Nineteenth Centuries." *Journal of American History* 65 (September 1978): 319–43.

Willard, William. "Self-Government for Native Americans: The Case of the Pascua Yaqui Tribe." In *American Indian Policy: Self-Governance and Economic Development*, edited by Lyman Letgers and Fremont Lyden. Westport, CT: Greenwood Press, 1994.

Winners of the West 8, no. 10 (September 30, 1931).

Work, David K. "Enforcing Neutrality: The Tenth US Cavalry on the Mexican Border, 1913–1919." *Western Historical Quarterly* 40 (Summer 2009): 179–200.

Wunder John R., and Pekka Hämäläinen. "Of Lethal Places and Lethal Essays." *American Historical Review* 104 (October 1999): 1229–34.

Books and Pamphlets

Acuña, Rodolfo F. *Corridors of Migration: The Odyssey of Mexican Laborers, 1600–1933*. Tucson: University of Arizona Press, 2007.

———. *Sonoran Strongman: Ignacio Pesqueira and His Times*. Tucson: University of Arizona Press, 1974.

Ahenakew, Edward. *Voice of the Plains Cree*. Toronto: McClelland & Stewart, 1973.

Balbás, Manuel. *Recuerdos del Yaqui: Principales Episodios Durante la Campaña de 1899 a 1901*. Mexico City: Sociedad de Edición y Librería Franco Americana, S.A., 1927.

Balderrama, Francisco E., and Raymond Rodríguez, *Decade of Betrayal: Mexican Repatriation in the 1930s*. Albuquerque: University of New Mexico Press, 2006.

Bannon, John Francis. *The Spanish Borderlands Frontier, 1513–1821*. Albuquerque: University of New Mexico Press, 1974.

Beck, David R. M. *Seeking Recognition: The Termination and Restoration of the Coos, Lower Umpqua, and Siuslaw Indians, 1855–1984*. Lincoln: University of Nebraska Press, 2009.

Bennett, Mary, ed. *Reflections: A History of Elk Point and District*. Winnipeg: Elk Point and District Historical Society, 1977.

Benton-Cohen, Katherine. *Borderline Americans: Racial Division and Labor Wars in the Arizona Borderlands*. Cambridge: Harvard University Press, 2009.

Binnema, Theodore. *Common and Contested Ground: A Human and Environmental History of the Northwestern Plains*. Norman: University of Oklahoma Press, 2001.

———. *Enlightened Zeal: The Hudson's Bay Company and Scientific Networks, 1670–1870*. Toronto: University of Toronto Press, 2014.

Binnema, Theodore, and Susan Neylan, eds. *New Histories from Old: Changing Perspectives on Canada's Native Pasts*. Vancouver: University of British Columbia Press, 2007.

Bolton, Herbert E. *Spanish Borderlands*. Albuquerque: University of New Mexico Press, 1996.

Botting, Gary. *Chief Smallboy: In Pursuit of Freedom*. Calgary: Fifth House, 2005.

Brooks, James. *Captives and Cousins: Slavery, Kinship, and Community in the Southwest Borderlands*. Chapel Hill: University of North Carolina Press, 2002.

Bryant, Wilbur Franklin. *The Blood of Abel*. Hastings, NE: Gazette-Journal, 1887.

Burruel, José María. *Mexicans in Scottsdale*. Charleston, SC: Arcadia, 2007.

Calloway, Colin G. *One Vast Winter Count: The Native American West before Lewis and Clark*. Lincoln: University of Nebraska Press, 2003.

Cameron, William Bleasdell. *Blood Red the Sun*. Edmonton, Alberta: Hurtig, 1977.

Charlebois, Peter. *The Life of Louis Riel*. Toronto: New Canada, 1975.

Collins, Joseph Edmund. *The Story of Louis Riel, the Rebel Chief*. Toronto: Rose, 1885.

Contributions to the Historical Society of Montana. 1940; repr., Boston: J. S. Canner, 1966.

Corral, Ramón. *Obras Históricas*. Hermosillo, Sonora, Mexico: Biblioteca Sonorense de Geografía e Historia.

Cummings, Laura L. *Pachucas and Pachucos in Tucson: Situated Border Lives*. Tucson: University of Arizona Press, 2009.

Dabdoub, Claudio. *Historia de El Valle del Yaqui*. Mexico City: Libreria Manuel Porrua, S.A., 1949.

Daschuk, James. *Clearing the Plains: Disease, Politics, and Loss of Aboriginal Life*. Regina, Saskatachewan: University of Regina Press, 2013.

Deloria, Vine, Jr., and Clifford M. Lytle, *American Indians, American Justice*. Austin: University of Texas Press, 1983.

Deloria, Vine, Jr., and David E. Wilkins, *Tribes, Treaties, and Constitutional Tribulations*. Austin: University of Texas Press, 1999.

Dempsey, Hugh Aylmer. *Big Bear: The End of Freedom*. Lincoln: University of Nebraska Press, 1984.

Denny, Walter. *Stories from the Old Ones: As Told to Walter A. Denny*. Missoula: Rising Wolf, 1979.

Den Ouden, Amy E., and Jean M. O'Brien, eds. *Recognition, Sovereignty Struggles, and Indigenous Rights in the United States: A Sourcebook*. Chapel Hill: University of North Carolina Press, 2013.

Denzel, Markus A. *Handbook of World Exchange Rates, 1590–1914*. Burlington, VT: Ashgate, 2010.

Dion, Joseph F. *My Tribes, the Crees*. Calgary: Glenbow Museum, 1979.

Dusenberry, Verne. *The Montana Cree: A Study in Religious Persistence*. 1962; repr., Norman: University of Oklahoma Press, 1998.

———. *The Rocky Boy Indians: Montana's Displaced Persons*. Helena: Montana Historical Press, 1954.

Enríquez, Andres Molina. *La Revolución Agraria en Mexico*. Mexico City: Instituto Nacional de Estudios Históricos de la Revolucíon Mexicana, 1976.

Ens, Gerhard J. *Homeland to Hinterland: The Changing Worlds of the Red River Métis in the Nineteenth Century*. Toronto: University of Toronto Press, 1996.

Erickson, Kirstin C. *Yaqui Homeland and Homeplace: The Everyday Production of Ethnic Identity*. Tucson: University of Arizona Press, 2008.

Evans, Sterling. *Bound in Twine: The History and Ecology of the Henequen-Wheat Complex for Mexico and the American and Canadian Plains, 1880–1950*. College Station: Texas A&M University Press, 2007.

Ewers, John C. *Ethnological Report on the Chippewa Cree Tribe of the Rocky Boy Reservation and the Little Shell Band of Indians*. Chippewa Indians, vol. 6. New York: Garland, 1974.

Fabila, Alfonso. *Las Tribus Yaqui de Sonora: su cultura y anhelada autodeterminación*. Mexico City: Departamento de Asuntos Indigenas, 1940.

Farish, Thomas Edwin. *History of Arizona*. Phoenix: Thomas Edwin Farish, 1916.

Figueroa, Alejandro. *Los Que Hablan Fuerte, Desarrollo de la Sociedad Yaqui*. Hermosillo, Sonora, Mexico: Instituto Nacional de Antropología e Historia, 1985.

Fixico, Donald L. *Termination and Relocation: Federal Indian Policy, 1945–1960*. Albuquerque: University of New Mexico Press, 1990.

Flanagan, Thomas, ed. *The Diaries of Louis Riel*. Edmonton: Hurtig, 1976.

———. *Louis "David" Riel: Prophet of the New World*. Toronto: University of Toronto Press, 1979.

Folsom, Raphael Brewster. *The Yaquis and the Empire: Violence, Spanish Imperial Power, and Native Resilience in Colonial Mexico*. New Haven: Yale University Press, 2014.

Foster, Martha Harroun. *We Know Who We Are: Métis Identity in a Montana Community*. Norman: University of Oklahoma Press, 2006.

García, Navarro. *La Sublevación Yaqui de 1740*. Seville, Spain: Escuela de Estudios Hispano-Americanos, 1966.

Guernin-Gonzales, Camille. *Mexican Workers and American Dreams: Immigration, Repatriation, and California Farm Labor, 1900–1939*. New Brunswick, NJ: Rutgers University Press, 1994.

Guidotti-Hernández, Nicole M. *Unspeakable Violence: Remapping US and Mexican National Imaginaries*. Durham, NC: Duke University Press, 2011.

Haake, Claudia B. *The State, Removal and Indigenous Peoples in the United States and Mexico, 1620–2000*. Routledge: New York, 2007.

Hall, Ryan. *Blackfoot Country: The Indigenous Borderlands of the North American Fur Trade*. Chapel Hill: University of North Carolina Press, forthcoming.

Hämäläinen, Pekka. *The Comanche Empire*. New Haven: Yale University Press, 2008.

Harris, Dean. *By Path and Trail*. Chicago: Chicago Newspaper Union, 1908.

Hatfield, Shelley Bowen. *Chasing Shadows: Apaches and Yaquis along the United States-Mexico Border, 1876–1911*. Albuquerque: University of New Mexico Press, 1998.

Henry, Alexander, and David Thompson. *New Light on the Early History of the Greater Northwest*. Edited by Elliott Coues. New York, 1897.

Hernández, Fortunato. *Las Razas Indegenas de Sonora y la Guerra del Yaqui*. Mexico City: Talleres de la Casa Editorial "J. de Elizalde," 1902.

Hoffman, Abraham. *Unwanted Mexican Americans in the Great Depression: Repatriation Pressures, 1929–1939*. Tucson: University of Arizona Press, 1974.

Hogue, Michel. *Métis and the Medicine Line: Creating a Border and Dividing a People*. Chapel Hill: University of North Carolina Press, 2015.

Howard, Joseph. *Strange Empire*. New York: William Morrow, 1952.

Hoxie, Frederick E. *This Indian Country: American Indian Political Activists and the Place They Made*. New York: Penguin Press, 2012.

Hu-DeHart, Evelyn. *Missionaries, Miners and Indians: Spanish Contact with the Yaqui Nation of Northwestern New Spain, 1533–1820*. Tucson: University of Arizona Press, 1981.

———. *Yaqui Resistance and Survival: The Struggle for Land and Autonomy, 1821–1910*. Madison: University of Wisconsin Press, 1984.

Indigenismo, Evolución de Una Práctica. Mexico City: Instituto Nacional Indigenista, 1979.

Jacobson, Matthew Frye. *Whiteness of a Different Color: European Immigrants and the Alchemy of Race*. Cambridge: Harvard University Press, 1998.

Johnson, Benjamin H., and Andrew R. Graybill, eds. *Bridging National Borders in North America: Transnational and Comparative Histories*. Durham, NC: Duke University Press, 2010.

Karlin, Jules A. *Senator Joseph M. Dixon and Rocky Boy: A Documentary Postscript, 1908*. Helena: Montana Historical Society Press, 1954.

Kelley, Jane Holden. *Yaqui Women: Contemporary Life Histories*. Lincoln: University of Nebraska Press, 1978.

Kessell, John L. *Friars, Soldiers, and Reformers: Hispanic Arizona and the Sonora Mission Frontier, 1767–1856*. Tucson: University of Arizona Press, 1976.

———. *Mission of Sorrows: Jesuit Guevavi and the Pimas, 1691–1767*. Tucson: University of Arizona Press, 1970.

Kettner, James H. *The Development of American Citizenship, 1608–1870*. Chapel Hill: University of North Carolina Press, 1978.

Klopotek, Brian. *Recognition Odysseys: Indigeneity, Race, and Federal Tribal Recognition Policy in Three Louisiana Indian Communities*. Durham: Duke University Press, 2011.

LaDow, Beth. *The Medicine Line: Life and Death on a North American Borderland*. New York: Routledge, 2002.

León, Juan Silverio Jaime. *Testimonios de una Mujer Yaqui*. Mexico City: Conaculta, 1988.

Letgers, Lyman, and Fremont Lyden, eds. *American Indian Policy: Self-Governance and Economic Development*. Westport, CT: Greenwood Press, 1994.

Light, Douglas W. *Footprints in the Dust*. North Battleford, Saskatchewan: Turner-Warwick, 1987.

Lim, Julian. *Porous Border: Multiracial Migrations and the Law in the US-Mexico Borderlands*. Chapel Hill: University of North Carolina Press, 2017.

Linderman, Frank Bird. *Montana Adventure: The Recollections of Frank B. Linderman*. Lincoln, University of Nebraska Press, 1968.

Lopach, James J., Margery Hunter Brown, and Richmond L. Crow. *Tribal Government Today: Politics on Montana Indian Reservations*. Boulder: University of Colorado Press, 1998.

Lytle-Hernández, Kelly. *Migra! A History of the US Border Patrol*. Berkley: University of California Press, 2010.

Mackenzie, Alexander. *Journals and Letters of Alexander Mackenzie*. Cambridge: Hakluyt Society, 1970.

Macleod, Bob, and Rod Beal. *Prairie Fire: The 1885 North-West Rebellion*. Edmonton: Hurting, 1984.

Mandelbaum, David Goodman. *The Plains Cree: An Ethnographic, Historical, and Comparative Study*. Regina, Saskatchewan: Canadian Plains Research Center, University of Regina, 1979.

McCarty, Kieran, ed. *A Frontier Documentary: Sonora and Tucson, 1821–1848*. Tucson: University of Arizona Press, 1997.

McCool, Daniel, Susan M. Olson, and Jennifer L. Robinson. *Native Vote: American Indians, the Voting Rights Act, and the Right to Vote*. Cambridge: Cambridge University Press, 2007.

McCrady, David. *Living with Strangers: The Nineteenth-Century Sioux and the Canadian-American Borderlands*. Lincoln: University of Nebraska Press, 2006.

Meeks, Eric. *Border Citizens: The Making of Indians, Mexicans, and Anglos in Arizona*. Austin: University of Texas Press, 2007.

Miller, Bruce Granville. *Invisible Indigenes: The Politics of Nonrecognition*. Lincoln: University of Nebraska Press, 2003.

Miller, Mark Edwin. *Claiming Tribal Identity: The Five Tribes and the Politics of Federal Acknowledgment*. Norman: University of Oklahoma Press, 2013.

———. *Forgotten Tribes: Unrecognized Indians and the Federal Acknowledgment Process*. Lincoln: University of Nebraska Press, 2004.

Milloy, John Sheridan. *The Plains Cree: Trade, Diplomacy, and War, 1790 to 1870*. Winnipeg: University of Manitoba Press, 1988.

Moisés, Rosalio, Jane Holden Kelley, and William Curry Holden. *A Yaqui Life: A Personal Chronicle of a Yaqui Indian*. Lincoln: University of Nebraska Press, 1971.

Morgan, Anne Hodges, and Rennard Strickland, eds. *Arizona Memories*. Tucson: University of Arizona Press, 1984.

Morton, Desmond. *The Last War Drum: The North West Campaign of 1885*. Toronto: Canadian War Museum, 1972.

Morton, Desmond, and Reginald H. Roy, eds. *Telegrams of the North-West Campaign, 1885*. Toronto: Champlain Society, 1972.

Moulton, Gary, ed. *The Journals of the Lewis and Clark Expedition August 25, 1804–April 6, 1805*, vol. 3. Lincoln: University of Nebraska Press, 1987.

Mulvany, Charles Pelham. *The History of the North-West Rebellion of 1885*. 1885. Reprint, Toronto: Coles, 1971.

Nelson, J. G. *The Last Refuge*. Montreal: Harvest House, 1973.

Officer, James E. *Hispanic Arizona, 1536–1856*. Tucson: University of Arizona Press, 1987.

Padilla Ramos, Raquel. *Yucatán, el fin del sueño yaqui: el tráfico de los Yaquis y el otro triumvirate*. Hermosillo, Sonora, Mexico: Gobierno del Estado de Sonora, la Secretaría de Educación y Cultura, 1995.

Painter, Muriel Thayer. *With Good Heart: Yaqui Beliefs and Ceremonies in Pascua Village*. Tucson: University of Arizona Press, 1986.

Palmer, Howard, and Tamara Palmer, eds. *Peoples of Alberta: Portraits of Cultural Diversity*. Saskatoon, Saskatchewan: Western Producer Prairie Books, 1985.

Reid, Jennifer. *Louis Riel and the Creation of Modern Canada: Mythic Discourse and the Postcolonial State*. Albuquerque: University of New Mexico Press, 2008.

Rifkin, Mark. *Manifesting America: The Imperial Construction of US National Space*. Oxford: Oxford University Press, 2009.

Rosier, Paul C. *Serving Their Country: American Indian Politics and Patriotism in the Twentieth Century*. Cambridge: Harvard University Press, 2009.

Russell, Dale. *Eighteenth-Century Western Cree and their Neighbors*. Hull, Quebec: Canadian Museum of Civilization, 1991.

St. Germain, Jill. *Broken Treaties: United States and Canadian Relations with the Lakota and Plains Cree, 1868–1885*. Lincoln: University of Nebraska Press, 2009.

Salas, Miguel Tinker. *In the Shadow of the Eagles: Sonora and the Transformation of the Border during the Porfiriato*. Berkeley: University of California Press, 1997.

Samek, Hana. *The Blackfoot Confederacy 1880–1920: A Comparative Study of Canadian and US Indian Policy*. Albuquerque: University of New Mexico Press, 1987.

Savala, Refugio. *The Autobiography of a Yaqui Poet*. Tucson: University of Arizona Press, 1980.

Sealey, D. Bruce *The Métis, Canada's Forgotten People*. Winnipeg: Manitoba Métis Federation Press, 1975.

Seibold, Frank M. *Tales from the Sonoita*. San Antonio: Naylor, 1977.

Sheridan, Thomas E. *Arizona: A History*. Tucson: University of Arizona Press, 1995.

———. *Landscapes of Fraud: Mission Tumacácori, the Baca Float, and the Betrayal of the O'Odham*. Tucson: University of Arizona Press, 2006.

———. *Los Tucsonenses: The Mexican Community in Tucson, 1854–1941*. Tucson: University of Arizona Press, 1986.

Sheridan, Thomas E., and Nancy J. Parezo. *Paths of Life: American Indians of the Southwest and Northern Mexico*. Tucson: University of Arizona Press, 1996.

Sierra, Justo. *Evolución Política del Pueblo Mexicano*, digital ed. 1940. Reprint, Alicante, Spain: Biblioteca Virtual Miguel de Cervantes, 2000.

Sluman, Norma, and Jean Goodwill. *John Tootoosis: Biography of a Cree Leader*. Ottawa: Golden Dog Press, 1982.

Smith, Cornelius C., Jr. *Emilo Kosterlitzky: Eagle of Sonora and the Southwest Border*. Glendale, CA: Arthur H. Clark Company, 1970.

Smith, Rogers M. *Civic Ideals: Conflicting Visions of Citizenship in US History*. New Haven: Yale University Press, 1997.

Sonnichsen, C. L. *Tucson: The Life and Times of an American City*. Norman: University of Oklahoma Press, 1982.

Spicer, Edward. *Cycles of Conquest: The Impact of Spain, Mexico and the United States on the Indians of the Southwest, 1533–1960*. Tucson: University of Arizona Press, 1962.

———. *People of Pascua*. Tucson: University of Arizona Press, 1988.

———. *The Yaquis: A Cultural History*. Tucson: University of Arizona Press, 1980.

Stamper, Ed, Helen Windy Boy, and Ken Morsette, eds. *The History of the Chippewa Cree of Rocky Boy's Indian Reservation*. Box Elder, MT: Stone Child College, 2008.

Stanley, George Francis Gilman. *The Birth of Western Canada: A History of the Riel Rebellions*. University of Toronto Press, 1995.

Stonechild, Blair. *Loyal till Death: Indians and the North-West Rebellion*. Calgary: Fifth House, 1997.

Suttles, Wayne, ed. *Handbook of North American Indians*, vol. 7. Washington, DC: Smithsonian Institute, 1990.

Tamarón y Romeral, Pedro. *Demostración del vastísimo obispado de la Nueva Vizcaya, 1765*. Mexico City: Biblioteca Historia Mexicana de Obras Inéditas, 1937.

Thompson, David. *David Thompson's Narrative, 1784–1812*. Toronto: Champlain Society, 1962.

Tremaudan, Auguste Henri de. *Hold High Your Heads: History of the Métis Nation in Western Canada*. Winnipeg: Pemmican Publications, 1982.

Troncoso, Francisco P. *Campaña de 1910 a 1911, estudio en general de las operaciones que han tenido lugar del 18 de doviembre de 1910 al 25 de mayo de 1911, en la parte que corresponde a aa 2.a zona militar*. Mexico City: Secretaría de Guerra y Marina, 1913.

———. *Las Guerras con las Tribus Yaqui y Mayo del Estado de Sonora*. Mexico City: Tipografía del Departmento de Estado Mayor, 1905.

Truett, Samuel. *Fugitive Landscapes: The Forgotten History of the US-Mexico Borderlands*. New Haven: Yale University Press, 2006.

Tsiang, I-Mien. *The Question of Expatriation in America Prior to 1907*. Baltimore: Johns Hopkins Press, 1942.

Turner, John Kenneth. *Barbarous Mexico*. Chicago: Charles H. Kerr, 1911.

Turner, John Peter. *The North-West Mounted Police, 1873–1893*. Ottawa: King's Printer, 1950.

Velasco, José Francisco. *Noticias Estadísticas del Estado de Sonora*. Mexico City: Imprenta de Ignacio Cumplido, 1850.

Villa, Eduardo W. *Historia del Estado de Sonora*. 1937. Reprint, Hermosillo, Sonora, Mexico: Gobierno del Estado de Sonora, 1984.

Vrooman, Nicholas C.P. *"The Whole Country Was . . . 'One Robe'": The Little Shell Tribe's America*. Helena, MT: Drumlummon Institute: 2012.

Wagoner, Jay J. *Early Arizona: Prehistory to Civil War*. Tucson: University of Arizona Press, 1975.

Weber, David J. *The Spanish Frontier in North America*. New Haven: Yale University Press, 1994.

Wells, Allen. *Yucatan's Gilded Age: Haciendas, Henequen, and International Harvester, 1860–1915*. Albuquerque: University of New Mexico Press, 1985.

Wells, Allen, and Gilbert Joseph. *Summer of Discontent, Seasons of Upheaval: Elite Politics and Rural Insurgency in Yucatan, 1876–1915*. Stanford: Stanford University Press, 1996.

Wells, Edmund. *Argonaut Tales: Stories of the Gold Seekers and the Indian Scouts of Early Arizona*. New York: Grafton Press, 1927.

Wharfield, H. B. *Apache Indian Scouts*. El Cajon, CA: H. B. Wharfield, 1964.

White, Richard. *The Middle Ground: Indians, Empires, and Republics in the Great Lakes Region, 1650–1815*. Cambridge: Cambridge University Press, 1991.

Wilkins, David Eugene, and K. Tsianina Lomawaima. *Uneven Ground: American Indian Sovereignty and Federal Law*. Norman: University of Oklahoma Press, 2001.

Woodruff, Janette, and Cecil Dryden, *Indian Oasis*. Caldwell, ID: Caxton Printers, 1939.

Works Progress Administration. *Arizona: A State Guide*. New York: Hastings House, 1940.

Wunder, John R. *"Retained by the People": A History of American Indians and the Bill of Rights*. New York: Oxford University Press, 1994.

The Yaquis of Scottsdale, Arizona: Family Indomitable Spirit, Generosity. Scottsdale: Concerned Citizens for Community Health, 2002.

Dissertations, Theses, and Other Unpublished Monographs

Glaser, Leah. "The Story of Guadalupe, Arizona: The Survival and Preservation of a Yaqui Community." Master's thesis, Arizona State University, 1996.

Gray, Raymond. "The Cree Indians." Works Progress Administration, Federal Writers Project, 1942. Available at the University of Montana Mansfield Library, Missoula, and the Montana State Historical Society, Helena.

Hogue, Michel. "Crossing the Line: The Plains Cree in the Canada-United States Borderlands, 1870–1900." Master's thesis, University of Calgary, 2002.

Littlejohn, Catherine Isabel. "The Indian Oral Tradition: A Model for Teachers." Master's thesis, University of Saskatchewan, 1975.

McManus, Sheila. "Fraternal Twins or Distant Cousins? The Two Borders of the United States West." Paper presented at the annual meeting of the Western Historical Association, Denver, October 8, 2009.

River, Celeste. "A Mountain in His Memory: Frank Bird Linderman, His Role in Acquiring the Rocky Boy Indian Reservation for the Montana Chippewa and Cree, and the Importance of That Experience in the Development of His Literary Career." Master's thesis, University of Montana, 1990.

Simpson, William. "An Ethnographic Account of Yaqui Guadalupe Compared with the Culture of Poverty." Master's thesis, Arizona State University, 1969.

Well-off-Man, John Phillip. "The History of Chief Rocky Boy and His Band and the Founding of Rocky Boy Reservation." Master's thesis, University of Montana, 2007.

Willard, William. "The Community Development Worker in an Arizona Yaqui Project." PhD diss., University of Arizona, 1990.

Index